Oracle Application Express 4.0 with Ext JS

Deliver rich, desktop-styled Oracle APEX applications using the powerful Ext JS JavaScript library

Mark Lancaster

[PACKT] enterprise 🏵
PUBLISHING
professional expertise distilled

BIRMINGHAM - MUMBAI

Oracle Application Express 4.0 with Ext JS

First published: March 2011

Production Reference: 1180311

Published by Packt Publishing Ltd.
32 Lincoln Road
Olton
Birmingham, B27 6PA, UK.

ISBN 978-1-849681-06-3

www.packtpub.com

Cover Image by David Guettirrez (bilbaorocker@yahoo.co.uk)

Credits

Author
Mark Lancaster

Reviewer
Vincent Stanislaus

Acquisition Editor
Amey Kanse

Development Editors
Reshma Sundaresan
Roger D'souza

Technical Editors
Gaurav Datar
Azharuddin Sheikh

Indexer
Monica Ajmera Mehta

Editorial Team Leader
Vinodhan Nair

Project Team Leader
Lata Basantani

Project Coordinator
Leena Purkait

Proofreader
Clyde Jenkins

Graphics
Geetanjali Sawant

Production Coordinator
Arvindkumar Gupta

Cover Work
Arvindkumar Gupta

About the Author

Mark Lancaster has been delivering business solutions using Oracle tools and technology since 1995. He switched to using Oracle APEX in 2007 after using MOD_PLSQL for years - "APEX is much better".

He has had the good fortune of consulting for a wide variety of organizations in industries, including commercial fishery management, mineral resources, superannuation regulation, property asset management, distance education, casinos, and debt collection.

Mark is an Oracle ACE, having been actively involved in the Oracle community for many years on national and state committees, as well as writing articles and presenting at conferences.

He is the AUSOUG QLD Branch President, and maintains a blog at `http://oracleinsights.blogspot.com`.

One of the really nice things about working with Oracle APEX is the sense of community you gain through the forums with people scattered all over the globe.

I've had the good fortune to have met face to face with several members of the APEX development team and APEX enthusiasts after communicating with them via forums and e-mails. It's really surprising how much personality comes through in the written word.

One of the strengths of APEX is how accessible the APEX development team is to the development community. They really are interested in your feedback and making the APEX better. It's a real buzz when one of your suggestions is incorporated into the product.

Finally, I'd like to thank my beautiful wife Jackie for giving me the time and support to write this book. Oh, and for continuing to put up with me for over twenty years now. You rock my world.

About the Reviewer

Vincent Stanislaus has been working in the IT industry for over 12 years, with half of this time spent in the Finance Industry (especially around the Global Wealth Management area) as Technical Team Leader/Senior Application Development Analyst involved in several high-profile projects.

In the last couple of years, he has been focusing on enforcing standards within the development team and is involved extensively in reviewing code to ensure that they conform to technology standards.

Early on in his career, he focused on various projects involving government organizations and universities, focusing on developing/enhancing their management systems.

He currently resides in Melbourne, Australia with his wife Robina and his two children, Jonathan and Marilyn.

www.PacktPub.com

Support files, eBooks, discount offers and more

You might want to visit www.PacktPub.com for support files and downloads related to your book.

Did you know that Packt offers eBook versions of every book published, with PDF and ePub files available? You can upgrade to the eBook version at www.PacktPub.com and as a print book customer, you are entitled to a discount on the eBook copy. Get in touch with us at service@packtpub.com for more details.

At www.PacktPub.com, you can also read a collection of free technical articles, sign up for a range of free newsletters and receive exclusive discounts and offers on Packt books and eBooks.

![PACKTLIB logo]

http://PacktLib.PacktPub.com

Do you need instant solutions to your IT questions? PacktLib is Packt's online digital book library. Here, you can access, read and search across Packt's entire library of books.

Why Subscribe?

- Fully searchable across every book published by Packt
- Copy and paste, print and bookmark content
- On demand and accessible via web browser

Free Access for Packt account holders

If you have an account with Packt at www.PacktPub.com, you can use this to access PacktLib today and view nine entirely free books. Simply use your login credentials for immediate access.

Instant Updates on New Packt Books

Get notified! Find out when new books are published by following @PacktEnterprise on Twitter, or the *Packt Enterprise* Facebook page.

Table of Contents

Preface

Oracle Application Express (APEX) is a rapid web application development tool integrated directly into the Oracle database. APEX is a completely web-based application featuring many ready to use components, allowing developers to build and deploy professional web applications rapidly. Using SQL and PL/SQL as the development language it provides a number of advanced features out of the box, including several authentication mechanisms such as Lightweight Directory Access Protocol (LDAP), Data Access Descriptors (DAD), Single Sign-On (SSO), authorization services, built-in session state management, and logging functionality.

Modern websites are moving towards Rich Internet Applications (RIA), where web applications have many characteristics of desktop applications. This has led to the growing popularity in JavaScript libraries to provide that rich interactivity and ease the burden of providing support for multiple web browsers.

There are several excellent JavaScript libraries which provide functionality to retrieve, traverse, and manipulate the Document Object Model (DOM) using cross-browser compatible code. They also provide cross-browser event handling and Asynchronous JavaScript and XML (AJAX) functionality, for request and response objects to exchange data between the browser and server, avoiding full page reloads.

The story is very different when you examine the User Interface (UI) and User Experience (UX) enhancements currently offered by JavaScript libraries. Major libraries such as jQuery, Prototype, and MooTools choose to limit the UI and UX functionality offered. Developers are forced to integrate officially sanctioned UI extension libraries with limited sets of UI components, such as jQuery UI, Prototypes Scripty2, and MooTools.More.js extension, or integrate third-party unsupported widgets.

The notable exceptions here are the Yahoo! User Interface library (YUI) and Ext JS.

YUI provides a large collection of UI widgets in version 2, including buttons, tabs, trees, menus, sliders, charting, dialogs, rich text editors, and more. YUI released YUI 3 in September 2009, completely rebuilding the library from the ground up. In 2011, some of the major widgets have been migrated to YUI 3, with many more still to be migrated. YUI widgets have basic CSS styling only, requiring you to modify the CSS to achieve a professional finish. While YUI is a mature library, its UI components and documentation feel unfinished.

Ext JS also provides the UI widgets including tabs, charts, windows, trees, desktop styled toolbars, menus, rich text editors, calendars, layout managers, ComboBoxes, and many more. All the Ext JS widgets are styled to a very high standard, giving a professional interface out of the box. They are designed to be customizable, and at the same time, allow you to re-theme them to suit your own requirements.

The Ext JS widgets are built using an advanced JavaScript application development framework, with components constructed using object-oriented design principles. This allows you to modify the existing components easily, or combine and extend them to develop custom components.

Documentation of the Ext JS API is well organized, with clear descriptions of configuration options, properties, methods, and events for each of the components and classes making up the library. Support services include an extensive library of examples, showing individual and combined samples, very active public forums, and premium support forums.

Combining APEX with the very professional Ext JS UI components allows developers to build amazing web applications rapidly using the latest Rich Internet Application functionality.

What this book covers

Chapter 1, Setting up an Oracle APEX and Ext JS Environment, takes you through the process of setting up a productive development environment for both Oracle Application Express (APEX) and Ext JS options for setting up a local installation, where you have direct access to the database. Web servers are covered, including the Oracle HTTP Server, the Embedded PL/SQL Gateway, and the Oracle APEX Listener. Setting up on a hosted environment, where you only have web browser access, is also covered.

Automating your build processes is a great way to improve productivity. We set up a source code repository, integrating an automated backup and commit process as the first step to aid your development. A number of other automation opportunities are also discussed. By the end of the chapter, you will be fully set up and ready to code.

Chapter 2, Getting Acquainted with Ext, introduces the Ext JS API, spending time familiarizing you with some of the functionality Ext JS provides for manipulating the Document Object Model (DOM). Topics covered include how to build a standalone testing page, cross-browser element manipulation using the Ext.Element class, DOM traversal using the Ext.DomQuery class, and defining event handlers to add interactivity to your web pages.

Many of the examples are run using the Mozilla Firefox browser with the Firebug Plug-in. Firebug provides fantastic debugging tools for inspecting and editing the HTML, DOM, JavaScript, and CSS components that make up a web page. It also includes a JavaScript console, allowing you to inspect JavaScript errors and execute JavaScript code. This chapter shows you how to make use of the Firebug command-line console for quick prototyping and testing.

Chapter 3, Building a Ext JS Theme into APEX, provides a background on APEX themes and how to create a theme from scratch. A page template is developed based on the Ext.Viewport component, starting with a standalone prototype, before integrating it into an APEX page template.

Applying JavaScript DOM manipulation to page elements can result in input items appearing outside the form element, with some very nasty side effects. This chapter demonstrates the issue and shows the consequences, before providing a solution to ensure that this never happens to you.

Chapter 4, Ext Themed Regions, Labels, and Lists, develops templates for regions, labels, and lists using Ext JS components. Static region templates based on Ext.Panel are created, and then collapsible versions are added with a few lines of JavaScript to the templates. Inline error messages for labels can cause issues with page layout, so you are shown how Ext.QuickTips can be used to neatly solve the problem. Simple list templates are developed before a more complex example implementing a TreePanel is developed, showing how templates can also be used to produce JavaScript code and JSON objects, and not just HTML.

Chapter 5, Ext Themed Buttons, Popups, Calendars, and Reports, develops templates for the remaining template types: Buttons, popup list of values, breadcrumbs, calendars, and reports. The Ext JS Grid component is one of the most advanced and widely used components in the library. For the report template, you will learn how to "fake it", using the built-in functionality of an APEX Classic report and combining it with some CSS, so it looks like a read-only Ext JS Grid with AJAX paging.

Once the template types are completed, you are shown how to remove unused templates quickly using the APEXExportSplitter Java class, before publishing the theme.

Chapter 6, Adding Ext Layout Elements, offers a number of "low-hanging fruit" solutions, providing you with functionality that can significantly and broadly improve parts of your application with minimal implementation effort.

Some of the solutions improve existing HTML components, such as automatically replacing the APEX Classic DatePicker with the advanced `Ext.DatePicker` component, a solution to make all text areas resizable, or better still, auto-sizing so that text areas automatically grow as you type. Select lists are automatically transformed to combo boxes allowing lists to filter data progressively as more keys are typed. Completely new functionality using Ext JS components includes a `tab panel` template using APEX 4.0 nested sub regions, along with a toolbar and menu template.

Chapter 7, Working with Plug-ins and Dynamic Actions, introduces Plug-ins and Dynamic Actions, two of the most exciting new features in APEX 4.0 for developers. For the first time, you have the ability to add custom "widgets" easily and directly into APEX that can be used declaratively in the same way as native APEX components. Plug-ins and Dynamic Actions are supported with back-end integration, allowing developers to make use of APEX provided PL/SQL APIs to simplify component development.

APEX 4.0 introduced the Number Field as a new item type, allowing you to configure number range checks by optionally specifying minimum and maximum value attributes. This chapter provides a gentle introduction to the Plug-ins and Dynamic Actions, building a better Number Field than the native APEX item type.

Chapter 8, Data Stores, AJAX-enabled Plug-ins, and Dynamic Actions, continues working with Plug-ins, creating a complex ComboBox Plug-in, dealing with more advanced Plug-in concepts, including AJAX processing and interacting with Dynamic Actions.

ComboBoxes use data stores, providing the Ext JS framework with the ability to store data on the client browser, acting much as an in-memory database. This makes the process of integrating AJAX functionality into Plug-ins far simpler, because AJAX processes are focused on just passing data between the client browser and the database. The Ext components already contain the client-side functionality to update the display.

For the ComboBox, you are taken through the process of modifying the Ext JS components to work within the Dynamic Actions framework.

Chapter 9, Getting Interactive with GridPanels, integrates the `Ext JS GridPanel`, one of the most powerful and widely used components in Ext JS, into APEX. Taking the approach of extending existing functionality in APEX, the GridPanel is integrated as a Plug-in for classic reports.

The GridPanel Plug-in includes column management features including sorting, resizing, drag-and-drop column reordering, and show/hide columns. APEX functionality is combined to make the GridPanel stateful, saving user settings back into APEX preferences.

Chapter 10, IFrame Tabs, Panels, and Popup Windows, shows you how iFrames can completely transform the way your APEX applications work. This chapter looks at using iFrames in three different ways: Embedding other pages within a page using iFramed Panels, making modal popup windows, and creating a tabbed document interface, allowing users to easily switch backward and forward between pages without opening multiple browser tabs.

Chapter 11, Performance Tuning your JavaScript, rounds out the book by looking at performance tuning your JavaScript. Topics look at ways of keeping JavaScript lightweight, using recommendations from Yahoo! and Google add-ons for Firebug.

Reducing file size at the source is also covered, learning how to use **JSBuilder2** to build a customized lighter version of the Ext Library with unused components removed. JSBuilder2 is also used to combine and minify custom application JavaScript.

What you need for this book

At the absolute minimum, this book requires basic skills in Oracle Application Express, access to an Oracle Application Express development environment through a web browser, and the Ext JS library.

Oracle Application Express and Ext JS library are both directly accessible on the Internet:

- Oracle provides an online Application Express evaluation instance, where you can request a workspace
- Sencha provides free CDN hosting (cache delivery network) for the Ext JS framework

Productivity wise, a better approach is to set yourself up properly with a local environment. Typically this will be a development database and web server, set up by your company's database administrators, but could just as easily be Oracle Database Express Edition (XE), a free edition of the database running on your computer.

Running a local web server on your computer will greatly assist with JavaScript development, saving time by editing the file directly on the web server, rather than the save-deploy-test cycle. It also reduces friction in a team environment, when that little change you make breaks every page in the application. You can happily work in isolation until you are ready to deploy to a wider audience.

Having good editing and debugging tools makes any developer more productive. Long gone are the days where Oracle database development was done using SQL*Plus and Notepad (or vi). Most developers will already have their favorite editor, either one of the excellent free tools SQL Developer or JDeveloper provided by Oracle, or an equivalent commercial product.

Similarly, you can do web development using any plain text editor to edit your HTML, CSS, and JavaScript. A more powerful open source environment is Aptana Studio.

Aptana Studio is a complete web development environment that combines powerful authoring tools for HTML, CSS, and JavaScript. It provides JavaScript code completion for all the popular JavaScript libraries including Ext JS, and even provides code completion for your own JavaScript libraries.

Mozilla Firefox and Firebug are an absolute must have for working on your live application. Firebug allows you to edit, debug, and monitor CSS, HTML, and JavaScript live in any web page.

Many of the examples in this book depend entirely on Firebug, either issuing commands from the console, inspecting HTML, and CSS, or inspecting and debugging AJAX requests from the browser to the server.

You'll also need other tools such as image editors, version control, and FTP tools, but they are less essential at the beginning.

Who this book is for

This book is intended for application developers who are building web applications using the Oracle Application Express development environment.

In combination with Ext JS, a cross-browser JavaScript library for building rich internet applications, you will learn how to create an innovative, visually appealing web user interface with most of the characteristics of the desktop applications.

The majority of Oracle Application Express developers come from a database development background, so they already have the necessary database skills, but are less familiar with web development HTML, CSS, and JavaScript syntax.

You may already be an experienced Application Express developer, looking to take your applications to the next level, to go beyond the "out of the box" functionality.

If so, this book is for you.

Conventions

In this book, you will find a number of styles of text that distinguish between different kinds of information. Here are some examples of these styles, and an explanation of their meaning.

Code words in text are shown as follows: "In the earlier custom build I've kept the `pkg-grid-editor.js` package for editable grids"

A block of code is set as follows:

```
function createMyPanel(config) {
    return new Ext.Panel(Ext.apply({
        // Pre-configured config options go here
        width: 300,
        height: 300,
        plugins: [ new Ext.ux.MyPluginClass() ]
    }, config));
};
```

When we wish to draw your attention to a particular part of a code block, the relevant lines or items are set in bold:

```
listeners: {
    render: function(p){
        new Ext.Resizable(p.getEl(), {
            handles: 'all',
            pinned: true,
            transparent: true,
            resizeElement: function(){
                var box = this.proxy.getBox();
                p.updateBox(box);
                if (p.layout) {
                    p.doLayout();
                }
                if (Ext.isIE) {
                    this.syncHandleHeight();
                }
                return box;
            }
        });
    }
}
```

New terms and **important words** are shown in bold. Words that you see on the screen, in menus or dialog boxes for example, appear in the text like this: "It also includes a **Create** button which opens the same DML form page to insert new records."

> Warnings or important notes appear in a box like this.

"A good reference discussing creating custom components by extending, overriding or using factory patterns can be found at: http://www.sencha.com/learn/Tutorial:Creating_new_UI_controls"

Reader feedback

Feedback from our readers is always welcome. Let us know what you think about this book—what you liked or may have disliked. Reader feedback is important for us to develop titles that you really get the most out of.

To send us general feedback, simply send an e-mail to feedback@packtpub.com, and mention the book title via the subject of your message.

If there is a book that you need and would like to see us publish, please send us a note in the **SUGGEST A TITLE** form on www.packtpub.com or e-mail suggest@packtpub.com.

If there is a topic that you have expertise in and you are interested in either writing or contributing to a book, see our author guide on www.packtpub.com/authors.

Customer support

Now that you are the proud owner of a Packt book, we have a number of things to help you to get the most from your purchase.

Downloading the example code

You can download the example code files for all Packt books you have purchased from your account at http://www.PacktPub.com. If you purchased this book elsewhere, you can visit http://www.PacktPub.com/support and register to have the files e-mailed directly to you.

Errata

Although we have taken every care to ensure the accuracy of our content, mistakes do happen. If you find a mistake in one of our books—maybe a mistake in the text or the code—we would be grateful if you would report this to us. By doing so, you can save other readers from frustration and help us improve subsequent versions of this book. If you find any errata, please report them by visiting http://www.packtpub.com/support, selecting your book, clicking on the errata submission form link, and entering the details of your errata. Once your errata are verified, your submission will be accepted and the errata will be uploaded on our website, or added to any list of existing errata, under the Errata section of that title. Any existing errata can be viewed by selecting your title from http://www.packtpub.com/support.

Piracy

Piracy of copyright material on the Internet is an ongoing problem across all media. At Packt, we take the protection of our copyright and licenses very seriously. If you come across any illegal copies of our works, in any form, on the Internet, please provide us with the location address or website name immediately so that we can pursue a remedy.

Please contact us at copyright@packtpub.com with a link to the suspected pirated material.

We appreciate your help in protecting our authors, and our ability to bring you valuable content.

Questions

You can contact us at questions@packtpub.com if you are having a problem with any aspect of the book, and we will do our best to address it.

1
Setting up an Oracle APEX and Ext JS Environment

In this chapter, we will go through the process of setting up a productive development environment for both Oracle Application Express (APEX) and Ext JS.

APEX applications are accessed by a web browser via an HTTP Server, which may use the Oracle APEX Listener, Oracle HTTP Server with the mod_plsql plug-in, or the Embedded PL/SQL Gateway to act as the web server.

Each of the web server options has advantages and disadvantages. We will examine the relevant merits of each option separately, before showing how to configure them to support development with Ext JS.

Setting up a development environment is more than just installing the relevant software. It's also about managing versioning and dependencies of your code, and configuration files and other project assets. Automating your backup and build processes ensures that you are able to deliver your software in a repeatable and consistent manner. Regular software releases should be a straightforward activity and not a major issue.

Making good choices setting up your development environment at the beginning of a project can be enormously beneficial for the entire lifecycle of the project. Getting it wrong can be equally as bad!

This chapter covers:

- APEX installation considerations
- Brief overview of the Ext JS SDK
- Merits of each of the web tier options: Oracle APEX Listener, Oracle HTTP Server with the mod_plsql plug-in, and the Embedded PL/SQL Gateway

- Loading the Ext JS SDK on each of the web tier options, and also onto hosted environments where you don't have direct access to the web server
- Setting up a Subversion source code repository for project assets
- Automating backup and build processes to simplify application deployments and reduce errors

By the end of the chapter, you will be fully set up and ready to code.

Setting up for success

One of the reasons for the outstanding success of Oracle APEX is that you can build applications really quickly. Within a couple of hours, you can have a development database set up, and using the built-in themes, you've started building an application.

This can be really dangerous for us as developers. At the beginning of a project, particularly when you're using a new or unfamiliar technology, there is a pressure to prove yourself—either as an individual starting a new role or as a team proving a technology to management.

Experienced programmers recognize this; the challenge is convincing everyone involved on what the ultimate goals of the project are, and not just take a short-term, short-sighted approach.

While not a dedicated practitioner of the methodology, some of the principles behind the Agile Manifesto (`http://agilemanifesto.org/principles.html`) are a great reminder of on what we should be focusing.

The ultimate goal of any project is to write *valuable* software, and by valuable I mean software that is going to be used and is useful. There is no point writing software unless it delivers real business outcomes—either tangibly in increasing business revenue, streamlining business processes, or less directly by reducing time spent on non-productive activities.

Working software is the primary measure of progress. The more time that we, as developers, can spend on regularly delivering valuable software in short time periods, the more successful our project is.

Regularly deploying working software implies that we need an efficient build process. This is the art of maximizing the amount of work not done! By taking a little extra time at the beginning to set up our development environment properly, it should be largely self sustaining and require almost no ongoing maintenance.

Installing Oracle APEX

Oracle APEX 4.0 requires a minimum database edition of 10.2.0.3, or Oracle XE, which, despite reporting as being 10.2.0.1, includes additional features that didn't make it into the supported versions of the database.

> This book won't be going into the details on how to install Oracle APEX into the database, as that is very well covered by the documentation provided with the product and available online at `http://download.oracle.com/docs/cd/E17556_01/doc/install.40/e15513/toc.htm`.

Oracle APEX now comes pre-installed on all editions of Oracle database 11.1 upwards, and is also pre-installed in Oracle XE — the free edition of the database. In both cases, you will need to upgrade your Oracle APEX installation to Oracle APEX 4.0 — the version covered in this book. Go to Oracle Application Express on the **Oracle Technology Network (OTN)** at `http://www.oracle.com/technetwork/developer-tools/apex/index.html`, and download the latest production version of Oracle APEX.

Regardless of whether you're installing or upgrading Oracle APEX, there is one important decision you need to consider before you proceed. By default, Oracle APEX is installed into the **SYSAUX** tablespace.

> You have the option when installing or upgrading to specify an alternative tablespace.

The **SYSAUX** tablespace is installed as an auxiliary tablespace to the **SYSTEM** tablespace when the database is created. It holds a number of database components that you may or may not use, depending on the nature of your applications, such as Oracle Text, Oracle Spatial, and Oracle interMedia.

It also contains components such as Enterprise Manager and Automatic Workload Repository which, depending on several factors, such as number of active sessions, data retention period, and snapshot intervals, can require significant storage volumes and contain highly volatile data, leading to disk I/O contention.

By installing Oracle APEX into its own tablespace, database administrators (DBAs) are able to manage it in isolation from other database components, allowing more flexibility in performing database operations. For example, you can reduce I/O contention by storing the underlying data files of the APEX tablespace on different disk drives to the **SYSAUX** tablespace.

Similarly, taking the individual Oracle APEX tablespace offline to perform a data recovery operation allows other applications to remain online, providing better overall availability. Or in another scenario, take advantage of transportable tablespaces to copy your Oracle APEX environment to another database quickly.

Downloading Ext JS

The Ext JS SDK (software development toolkit) can be downloaded as a single zipped file from the Sencha website at `http://www.sencha.com/products/extjs/ download`. This book is based on version 3.3.1, the latest release at the time of writing. As the Ext framework is now quite mature, you should be safe to use later releases of version 3 with this book, should they be available.

Ext JS is released under both open source and commercial licenses to suit both implementations and provides support to developers through community support forums, as well as subscription-based support and maintenance.

The download of the Ext JS SDK is nearly 15MB, and once extracted, is roughly 105MB. The reason for the large size becomes apparent once we start examining the extracted files.

Name	Size
adapter	349 976
docs	29 658 584
examples	9 988 887
pkgs	3 576 651
resources	2 040 486
src	3 547 250
test	237 885
welcome	108 395
ext-all-debug-w-comments.js	2 855 033
ext-all-debug.js	1 367 826
ext-all.js	715 483
ext.jsb2	48 947
gpl-3.0.txt	35 147
INCLUDE_ORDER.txt	860
index.html	8 193
license.txt	1 564
release-notes.html	4 691

The screenshot shows the contents of the top directory within the Ext JS SDK zip file. It comprises everything you need to work with Ext JS, including documentation, resources, and examples.

Let's briefly go through the directories shown in the screenshot.

File/folder	Description
adapter	Contains the ext-base.js file used to provide browser-independent base-level DOM and AJAX functions for use by the main Ext JS library. It also contains adapter files that allow you to work with other JavaScript libraries, including jQuery, Dojo, and YUI.
docs	Documentation for the library.
examples	Individual component and combination examples. This is a veritable treasure trove of information and working solutions to be integrated into Oracle APEX.
pkgs	Assembled subsets of the JavaScript library, designed to assist building customized versions of Ext JS.
resources	Images, CSS files, and Flash objects used by Ext JS.
src	JavaScript source code for Ext JS.
test	Test cases used by Sencha for automated testing harness.
ext.jsb2	Control file used to merge JavaScript files from src into pkgs files, and also ext-all.js and ext-all-debug.js. Merged files have the comments stripped and code minified. Merged files with the -debug suffix are a non-compressed version, preferred during development so that debugging is easier.
ext-all.js	Full Ext JS library, excluding the adapter, compressed and minified. The uncompressed version without comments, ext-all-debug.js, is useful for debugging during development. The uncompressed with comments version is ext-all-debug-w-comments.js.
*other	Other files not described: index.html, gpl-3.0.txt, INCLUDE_ ORDER.txt, license.txt, and so on.

As you can see from the relative sizes of the folders, the Ext JS SDK has placed an emphasis on documentation and examples. This greatly assists in learning to use the library and is a real credit to the Ext JS developers.

The ext-all.js file and the adapter and resources folders are the only files you need to deploy to your production web server. While saying this, my preference is to deploy the entire SDK. That way all the documentation and examples are on hand.

> Many of the examples need to be run from a web server and cannot be run directly from your computer. This is also true of the documentation. So if you're wondering why you just see a spinning image when you open the documentation file locally, now you know.

Which web server to use?

Oracle APEX is accessed through a browser via a HTTP server, which may be the **Oracle HTTP Server (OHS)** with the mod_plsql plug-in, the **Embedded PL/SQL gateway (EPG)**, or most recently the **Oracle APEX Listener** certified against Oracle WebLogic Server, OC4J, and Oracle Glassfish Server. The APEX Listener can be installed on any modern J2EE Server, such as Tomcat.

> The APEX 4.0 Installation Guide covering each of the web server options is available at http://download.oracle.com/docs/cd/E17556_01/doc/install.40/e15513/toc.htm.

Here, I'm assuming you're working in a team environment, and we're setting up a dedicated development web server, only accessible within the intranet.

I'll go through the relevant merits of each option separately, before showing how to configure them to support development with Ext JS. Once again, rather than repeat the standard installation documentation provided by Oracle, I will simply assume that you have made your choice and installed your preferred web server into your development environment together with Oracle APEX.

Storing your web assets

The virtual path the web server uses to point to the `images` directory distributed with the Application Builder in Oracle APEX defaults to the alias `/i/`.

Regardless of which web server you use, it's a good idea to keep your web assets in a different location from where Oracle stores them. Later sections in this chapter for each of the web server options will cover storing assets in a different location and configuring the web server to reference your assets with the alias `/ux/`, which stands for user extensions.

Storing your web assets in a different location makes life a whole lot easier when it comes to upgrading Oracle APEX again. All you have to do is follow the upgrade notes, secure in the knowledge that you are not going to delete any of your application files accidentally.

It allows your server administrator to secure the Oracle APEX directories, preventing anyone from making changes to the standard Application Builder configuration. Similarly, your application directory can be accessed only by the necessary people.

Customizing application builder files

If you ever have the need to modify some of the CSS rules or JavaScript provided by Oracle, here is one way to do it. By copying the Oracle APEX directories from the /i/ location to your /ux/ location, you can customize the standard Application Builder files without impacting anyone else.

To use your customized version, you need to update the application preferences image prefix to point to your alias, as shown in the following screenshot. To edit application properties, log into **Oracle Application Express**, and then select the appropriate application from the **Application Builder**. Click the **Edit Application Properties** button, top right on the **Application Definition** page.

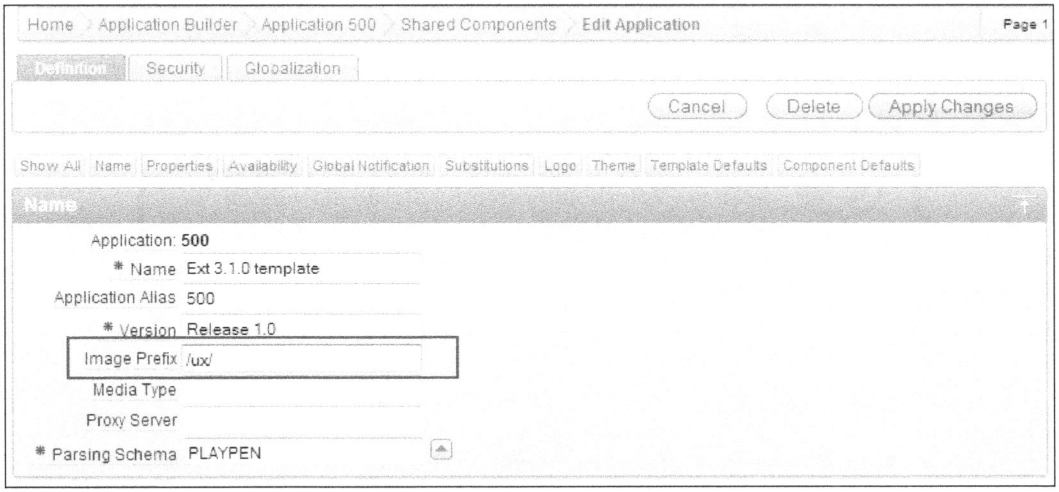

Oracle HTTP Server

The **Oracle HTTP Server (OHS)** is the most mature of the three web server options available, and is the typical choice for Oracle APEX production and development environments today. OHS is based on the proven Apache web server, with the Apache code base dependant on which version of the database you are using. Oracle HTTP Server, distributed with Oracle Database 11g, uses the Apache 2.2 code base; on the other hand, Oracle Application Server 10g is based on Apache 1.3 or Apache 2.0 for the standalone version.

Apart from the proven reliability and broad support available for the Apache web server software, the other main advantage cited for using OHS is the ability to separate the application server tier from the database tier, allowing the web server to be installed on a different server from the database.

> For production environments, where factors such as security, performance, and load balancing have a much higher priority, the ability to separate the application server tier from the database tier is an important consideration.

However, as we are looking at a development environment, the restricted-use license for OHS will probably be a deciding factor. Included with the Oracle Database 10g and 11g releases is a restricted use licence for OHS for all editions except Oracle XE, which allows OHS to be used, provided it is on the same server as the database. Running OHS on another server requires the other server to be licensed to use OHS either through a database licence or an Oracle Application Server licence.

One of the most confusing aspects of OHS is which version to install, as Oracle has released over 10 different versions of OHS, (see My Oracle Support Note 260449.1 for the complete list).

> Do not blindly install the version supplied with the database. You should carefully decide the version you'd like to install.

My Oracle Support Note 400010.1 - Steps to Maintain Oracle Database 10.2 Companion CD Home (for Oracle HTTP Server) states:

> *Something to think about...*
>
> *The Oracle HTTP Server delivered with the Oracle Database 10.2 Companion CD is provided to initially get HTMLDB installed and running. However, it's an older version with limited functionality and support. Both the Oracle HTTP Server and HTMLDB from this CD would need to be upgraded at this time. The Companion CD also installs a mix of 10.2 and 10.1 products which is more difficult to maintain. Consider using a newer installation of the Oracle HTTP Server, and then configure APEX (formerly HTML-DB) accordingly.*

The message here is Oracle doesn't recommend you to install the version that comes with the database. If you're going to install the standalone version of OHS, take the extra step of downloading the version that comes packaged with the Application Server. This is because the main versions of OHS are built for the Application Server releases. OHS can be downloaded from `http://www.oracle.com/technetwork/middleware/ias/index-091236.html`.

Loading Ext JS onto the Oracle HTTP Server

Depending on the version of the Oracle HTTP Server you are running, the location for the Application Builder `images` directory is held in either the `httpd.conf`, `marvel.conf` or `dads.conf` files. Search for the text alias `/i/`.

For example:

```
Alias /i/  "ORACLE_HTTPSERVER_HOME/Apache/images/"
Alias /ux/ "ORACLE_HTTPSERVER_HOME/Apache/ux/"
```

Here, `ORACLE_HTTPSERVER_HOME` is the location where the HTTP Server is installed.

Edit the file, adding another `Alias /ux/` as shown in the preceding snippet, pointing to the location where you will upload the Ext JS files. Having done this, upload the Ext JS files onto the web server at the location you specified. Remember, you can either deploy all the files in the Ext SDK, or just the minimal set comprising the `ext-all.js` file and the `adapter` and `resources` folders.

You will need to stop and restart the Oracle HTTP Server before your changes are detected, which is done using the `opmnctl` executable.

For Unix and Linux, execute the following:

```
ORACLE_HTTPSERVER_HOME/opmn/bin/opmnctl stopproc ias-component=HTTP_
Server
ORACLE_HTTPSERVER_HOME/opmn/bin/opmnctl startproc ias-component=HTTP_
Server
```

For Windows, execute the following:

```
ORACLE_HTTPSERVER_HOME\opmn\bin\opmnctl stopproc ias-component=HTTP_
Server
ORACLE_HTTPSERVER_HOME\opmn\bin\opmnctl startproc ias-component=HTTP_
Server
```

To verify that the Ext JS library is now accessible on the web server, just check that you can successfully fetch one of the files. Substituting the appropriate host and port values, use your browser to verify you can now see the Ext JS asset:

`http://host:port/ux/ext-3.3.1/resources/images/default/tree/drop-yes.gif` should show a tick, as seen in the following screenshot:

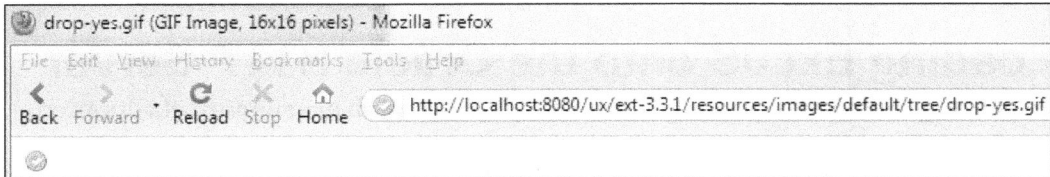

If you decide to do the full Ext JS SDK install, now is a good time to bookmark the documentation and samples:

- `http://host:port/ux/ext-3.3.1/docs/index.html`
- `http://host:port/ux/ext-3.3.1/examples/index.html`

Embedded PL/SQL Gateway

The **Embedded PL/SQL Gateway** (**EPG**) runs within the database as part of the XML DB HTTP Protocol listener and provides equivalent core features to the Oracle HTTP Server (OHS). The EPG works only in Oracle XE, and Oracle Database 11g and greater. If you are going to use Oracle APEX on 10g editions of the database, you will need to use the OHS or APEX Listener, as the EPG is not supported for any version below 11g.

Because the EPG runs entirely within the 11g database, and it comes pre-installed (but not pre-configured), it is simple to maintain. As it is not possible to separate the XML DB HTTP listener from the database, Oracle recommends not using it for internet-based applications, due to the potential security risk when exposing the database server directly to the Internet.

A number of other limitations exist for EPG when compared with Oracle HTTP Server, including features such as dynamic HTML caching, system monitoring, and logging in the Common Log Format.

The EPG is an appropriate solution for setting up APEX quickly for a proof of concept approach, development environments, or for low-volume intranet-based applications. EPG is an easy and convenient setup, but this comes at the price of flexibility and performance. It should not be considered for serious production environments.

Loading Ext JS onto the Embedded PL/SQL Gateway

Before loading Ext JS, the EPG needs to be configured and enabled. To check this step has been done, attempt to log into APEX as the admin user from a browser using `http://machine.domain:port/apex` and substituting the appropriate values for machine, domain, and port (default is 8080). If this is unsuccessful, review the database installation documentation on Application Express post-install configuration steps before proceeding.

When using the EPG, the Application Builder images referenced by the alias `/i/` are stored in the database within the Oracle XML DB repository. You can access these images using either WebDAV or FTP. I've found FTP to be more reliable, especially when doing bulk file transfers, hence the instructions will be for FTP.

> If you're interested in accessing the XML DB repository using WebDAV, Dietmar Aust provides instructions in his blog at `http://daust.blogspot.com/2006/03/where-are-images-of-application.html`.

The first thing to do is check whether FTP has been enabled, which is done using the following SQL code:

```
SQL> select dbms_xdb.getftpport from dual;

GETFTPPORT
----------
         0
```

If the FTP port is set to `0`, FTP is currently disabled.

To enable it, connect to SQL*PLUS as XDB or SYSTEM, or any account with DBA or XDBADMIN privileges, and issue the following commands:

```
SQL> exec dbms_xdb.setftpport('2100');        -- 1

PL/SQL procedure successfully completed.

SQL> alter system register;                   -- 2

System altered.

SQL> select dbms_xdb.getftpport from dual;    -- 3

GETFTPPORT
----------
      2100
```

- Statement 1 sets the FTP port to 2100.
- Statement 2 forces the database to reregister with the listener immediately.
- Statement 3 verifies the port has been changed successfully.

You should now be able to log in via FTP. For the time being, it's easier to log in as SYSTEM. There are many FTP tools available, so it's just a matter of choosing one based on personal preference. In my case, I'm using the free FileZilla client, available from http://filezilla-project.org/, in both Windows and Linux versions.

If you're using XE, you should see something similar to what's shown in the following screenshot:

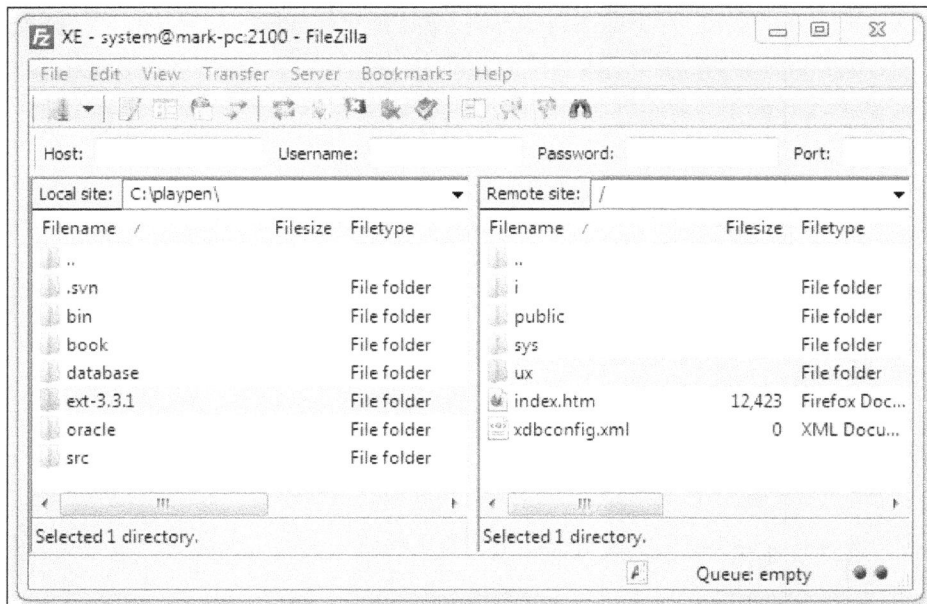

Create a new folder named /ux/ in the XML DB repository, and then upload the Ext JS files into this folder. Remember, you can either deploy all the files in the Ext SDK, or just the minimal set comprising the ext-all.js file and adapter and resources folders.

To verify the Ext JS library is now accessible on the web server, check whether you can successfully fetch one of the files. Substituting the appropriate host and port values, use your browser to verify you can now see the Ext JS assets:

`http://host:port/ux/ext-3.3.1/resources/images/default/tree/drop-yes.gif` should show a tick, as seen in the following screenshot:

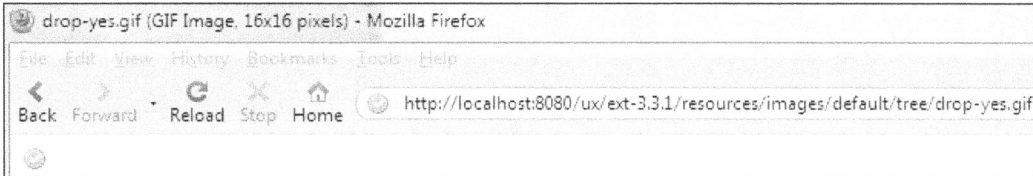

If you decided to do the full Ext SDK install, now is a good time to bookmark the documentation and samples:

- `http://host:port/ux/ext-3.3.1/docs/index.html`
- `http://host:port/ux/ext-3.3.1/examples/index.html`

Oracle APEX listener

The Oracle APEX listener is a Java-based replacement for the OHS **mod_plsql** plugin for all Oracle APEX releases. It provides a number of advantages over **mod_plsql**, including file system caching, native Excel uploads, generating PDF documents using Apache FOP (Formatting Objects Processor), and improved file uploading to support multiple file uploads for the first time. The APEX listener has been designed to be extensible, allowing developers to customize pre-and post-processing of form submissions, file uploads, among other things. The APEX listener is another key feature certain to increase adoption of the technology.

The APEX Listener is a Java servlet, capable of running on just about any application server that follows the **Java Enterprise Edition** (**JEE**) standard. Oracle provides instructions for deployment to Oracle WebLogic, OC4J, and Oracle Glassfish.

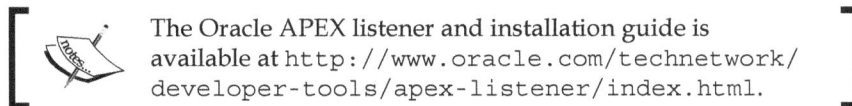

> The Oracle APEX listener and installation guide is available at `http://www.oracle.com/technetwork/developer-tools/apex-listener/index.html`.

Opening up the choice to a variety of web servers allows us to take advantage of features such as HTTP compression, which is not installed on the Oracle HTTP Server. (It can be configured, but is not supported by Oracle.)

HTTP compression makes better use of network bandwidth by compressing data on the server before sending it to the client. This allows content to be sent over the network in a more compact form and can result in a dramatic reduction in download time, reducing latency in your application and an improved user experience.

Given the enhanced functionality it offers over **mod_plsql**, the Oracle APEX listener will eventually become the preferred listener for Oracle APEX. However, in the short term, most production systems will continue to use Oracle HTTP Server with **mod_ plsql,** until the new listener has been proven by early adopter sites.

Loading Ext JS for the Oracle APEX listener

Once you have installed your choice of web server, the Oracle APEX Listener, and uploaded the APEX images using the Oracle Installation Guide, you can load Ext JS.

The process for loading Ext JS is similar for each of the referenced web server options (Oracle WebLogic, and OC4J, and Oracle Glassfish). The instructions here are for Oracle Glassfish.

You can deploy directly to a physical directory on the web server:

1. Create a folder named `ux` in `GLASSFISH_DIRECTORY/domains/DOMAIN_NAME/docroot`.

2. Copy the Ext JS files to `GLASSFISH_DIRECTORY/domains/DOMAIN_NAME/docroot/ux`.

Or to a virtual directory on the web server:

1. Copy the Ext JS files to the web server, for example `C:\playpen\web\ux`.

2. In the GlassFish Admin Console, expand **Configuration | Virtual Servers**. Select **server**, then scroll to the bottom of the page and click the **Add Property** button. Enter `alternatedocroot_1` in the **Name** field, and `from=/ux/* dir=C:/playpen/web/` in the **Value** field, as shown in the next screenshot. This will map the URL `http://hostname:port/ux/` to the physical directory `C:/playpen/web/ux/`.

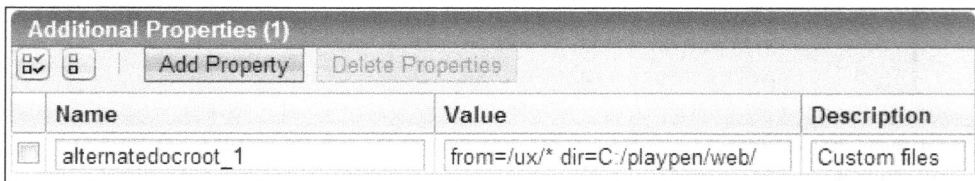

Additional Properties (1)		
Add Property Delete Properties		
Name	**Value**	**Description**
alternatedocroot_1	from=/ux/* dir=C:/playpen/web/	Custom files

Remember that you can either deploy all the files in the Ext SDK, or just the minimal set comprising the `ext-all.js` file and the `adapter` and `resources` folders. When adding a virtual directory alias, you may need to restart the web server before the alias is recognized.

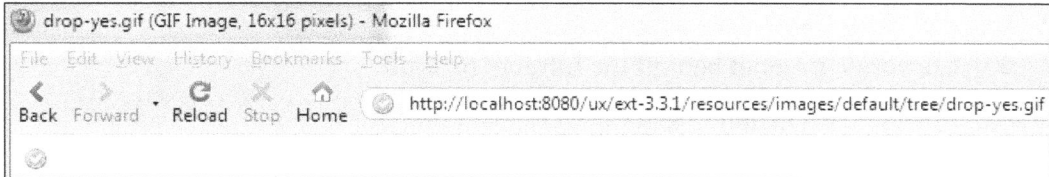

To verify that the Ext JS library is now accessible on the web server, just check that you can successfully fetch one of the files. Substituting the appropriate host and port values, use your browser to verify you can now see the Ext JS assets:

`http://host:port/ux/ext-3.3.1/resources/images/default/tree/drop-yes.gif` should show a tick, as seen in the preceding screenshot.

Overviewing the production setup

Consider the architecture diagram in the next screenshot:

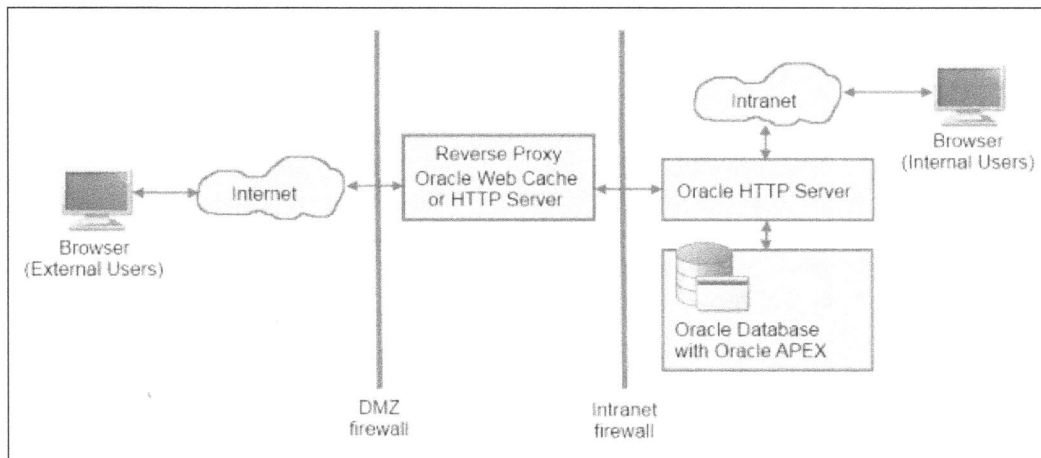

The diagram is a well-known and generally accepted Internet-Firewall-DMZ-Firewall-Intranet architecture and shows the following zones:

- External internet, outside the DMZ firewall
- External web server tier acting as a reverse proxy between the DMZ firewall and the Intranet firewall
- Corporate intranet behind the Intranet firewall

If your Oracle APEX instance is going to be used only for Intranet applications, we need to consider only the corporate intranet component on the right-hand side of the diagram. This is the basic configuration documented earlier for the Oracle HTTP server.

For Internet-accessible applications, security becomes a much more important factor. Various high-profile hacking attacks have proven that web security is one of the most critical issues facing any business that conducts its operations online. Compared to intranet-only applications, internet-accessible applications have far larger numbers of potential hackers.

Firewalls are configured to allow only specific types of access (HTTP/HTTPS). In DMZ architectures, firewalls are used to restrict the flow of network data so that all inbound traffic from the internet and outbound traffic from the intranet must be processed by web servers acting as proxy servers in the DMZ zone. By using a reverse proxy server, such as Oracle Web Cache or HTTP Server in tandem with internal and external firewalls, you can greatly reduce the risk of exposing your backend data resources.

So what exactly does a reverse proxy do? When a client sends a request to your website, the request goes to the proxy server. The proxy forwards the client's request through a specific path in the intranet firewall to the content web server. The content web server processes the request, passing the result back through the path to the proxy. The proxy server sends the information to the client, rewriting any URLs as though it was the actual content server.

Reverse proxies can be additionally configured to perform extra tasks such as compressing files to optimize network traffic, or facilitating secure transmission of information utilizing **Secure Socket Layers** (**SSL**), to provide an encrypted connection between the proxy server and the client.

Using Ext JS in a hosted APEX environment

Oracle APEX is designed to support hosted development, where the only access you have to your workspace is via a browser. The Application Builder and SQL Workshop contain all the necessary functionality to build an application from scratch without any other tools.

Typically in a hosted environment such as `http://apex.oracle.com`, you don't have access to the web server to upload the Ext JS files. In this situation, you can take advantage of Ext partnering with CacheFly, a global content network, to provide free CDN hosting for the Ext JS framework.

A **Content Delivery Network (CDN)** is a collection of web servers distributed across multiple locations to deliver content more efficiently to users. The server selected for delivering content to a specific user is typically based on a measure of network proximity.

For example, the server with the fewest network hops or the server with the quickest response time is chosen; that is, using a CDN to deliver static content, such as Ext JavaScript, CSS, and images will result in your pages getting downloaded significantly faster.

In the hosted environment, you don't load the Ext files onto the server, instead simply reference the Ext content in your Oracle APEX page templates from the CacheFly site. The following code will be added to Oracle APEX page templates:

```
<link rel="stylesheet" type="text/css" href="http://extjs.cachefly.
net/ext-3.3.1/resources/css/ext-all.css" />
<script type="text/javascript" src="http://extjs.cachefly.net/ext-
3.3.1/adapter/ext/ext-base.js"></script>
    <script type="text/javascript" src="http://extjs.cachefly.net/ext-
    3.3.1/ext-all.js"></script>
```

We will look at page templates and how to integrate Ext JS content in greater detail in *Chapter 3, Building an Ext Theme into APEX*.

Installing a source code repository

One of the very first tasks you should do in any software project, even before you write a single line of code, is to install a source code repository. This is where the development team keeps all of its code in a centralized location, using version control software to track and manage changes to files over time.

Version control systems are appealing to developers because they back up source code and keep track of changes. So when a new code version introduces a bug, it's easy to compare with earlier versions using text differencing tools to highlight what's changed and identify the problem.

Managers like version control systems because it helps prevent loss of data, and provides tagging capabilities for releases making it very easy to check a production version for error correction without disrupting the current development version.

I'll be discussing Subversion (`http://subversion.apache.org/`) in this book, so if you're already using another version control system, the same principles apply, although the solution might be a little different.

Subversion (SVN) has rapidly become the de facto standard free/open source version control system today. Binary versions of SVN are available for all major operation systems. Installation of the SVN server is very much dependent on the operating system, so refer to the installation instructions for your operating system.

VisualSVN Server (`http://visualsvn.com/server/`) is an excellent free solution for the Windows systems, and with a one-click installation, you really can't get an any simpler setup. There are a number of third-party clients available; TortoiseSVN is a popular choice on Windows, as it is integrated directly into Windows Explorer.

For batch programming, you will need to use a SVN command-line client, such as CollabNets' version (`http://www.open.collab.net/downloads/subversion/`). Subversion's integrations into various IDEs are also common, including JDeveloper, SQL Developer, TOAD, and Apanta.

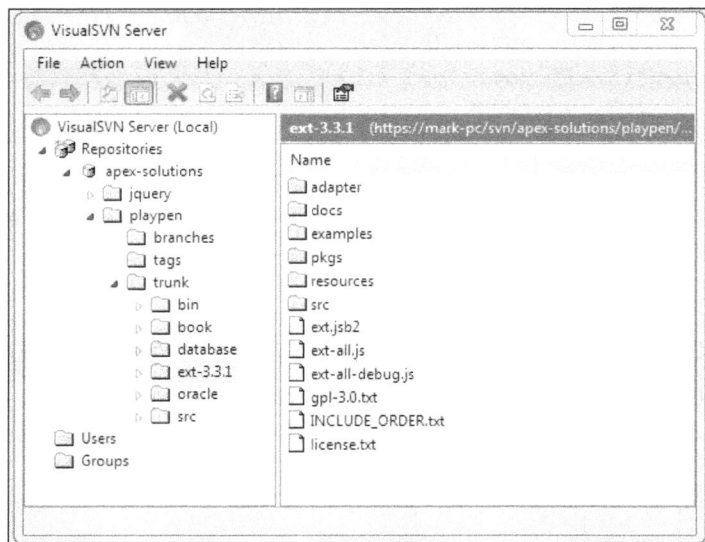

The previous screenshot shows the VisualSVN Server, containing a single repository named apex-solutions, with two projects named jquery and playpen respectively. The playpen project is used for this book, and contains a standard recommended layout: the trunk directory to hold the "main line" of development, a branches directory to contain branch copies, and a tags directory to contain tag copies.

The question of what to store in SVN is also partly answered in the screenshot we just saw. The short and simple answer is "everything to do with the project". You can use the example of a new developer starting on the project as a litmus test. Given a virgin machine, they should be able to do a single checkout, and be able to do a full build of the system. You may make exceptions for things that are large, or complicated to install and stable, for example, the database and IDE tools, such as JDeveloper or SQL Developer.

Here is a basic list of some of the types of files you would typically want to store in your code repository for an Oracle APEX application:

- **Database object scripts**: Everything you use to define your application in the database. This includes a current Oracle Initialization Parameter (init.ora) file, scripts to create your users, tables, views, packages, procedures, functions, and so on. If your application isn't too large, you could also include database schema exports to ensure you include absolutely everything.

- **APEX application and related files**: You can export and import your application definitions, including workspace users, application, CSS, images, files, themes, and user interface defaults stored in Oracle APEX. These exports provide a complete snapshot of your APEX application, allowing you to deploy it to another environment, or restore your application to an earlier state. The export files also allow you to recover individual components.

- **Web server assets**: Your Ext JS files, application JavaScript, CSS, images, and so on, and all configuration files for your web server.

- **Documentation**: Project management documentation, as well as the user help and administration documentation.

- **Utilities and command scripts**: This is a catch-all for scripts that don't fit into any of the previous categories. Examples include scripts used to export and import the application, to stop and start processes, FTP files to web servers, deploying the application to other environments, and so on.

Automating the build process

Version control systems commonly provide command line interfaces, providing you the opportunity to automate source control tasks you regularly perform using batch files.

One of the tasks you'll want to do on a regular basis is to back up and check in your APEX application into Subversion.

Oracle has provided a Java utility named **APEXExport** that allows you to export Oracle APEX applications from the command line, without requiring a manual export via the web interface. We'll go through how to set up your Subversion repository to support a fully automated backup process.

Once again, I will provide instructions for a Windows environment, but because APEXExport is a Java utility, minor adaptations to the instructions will allow you to run it in a Linux/Unix environment.

Configuring and using APEXExport

In the root of the Oracle APEX installation files, you will find a utilities folder containing a readme.txt file. The file provides detailed instructions on how to set up and use the APEXExport utility.

Pre-requites for the utility include installation of the **Java Development Kit (JDK)** of version 1.5 or greater, and the inclusion of classes12.jar in the CLASSPATH.

I wrote earlier that we should store "everything to do with the project" in our SVN repository, so that with a single checkout we could do a full build of the system. Also raised was the possibility of exceptions to this rule for things that are large, or complicated to install and stable, for example, the database and IDE tools such as JDeveloper.

Let's make an exception by assuming the JDK is already installed on your computer — either as a standalone installation, or as part of an IDE for example in SQL Developer or JDeveloper. If you didn't want to make this exception, add SQL Developer (which includes the JDK) into your SVN repository.

The classes12.jar file is the Oracle JDBC library for Oracle database 10g, found in the %ORACLE_HOME%\jdbc\lib directory. For Oracle database 11g, the equivalent file is ojdbc5.jar for Java 5 or ojdbc6.jar for Java 6. Generally for Oracle database 11g, you should use ojdbc6.jar.

Because developers may have very different setups on their computers, even within a small team, the easiest way to manage the location of the JDBC library is by using the **Oracle Instant Client**. The Instant Client allows you to run your applications without the standard Oracle client, and includes additional libraries for **SQL*Plus**.

Instant Client comes in two versions—Basic and Basic Lite. Both versions are suitable for Oracle APEX: Basic Lite is a smaller version of the Basic, with only English error messages and supporting only specific character sets, including AL32UTF8, used by Oracle APEX. Installation is simply extracting the Instant Client files into a directory. Download a copy of Instant Client for your database version and operating system from `http://www.oracle.com/technology/tech/oci/instantclient/index.html`.

Also download the **SQL*Plus Instant Client**, which is installed by extracting it into the same directory as the Instant Client.

Before we go any further, let's take a look at the intended layout of the SVN repository.

```
VisualSVN Server (Local)
  Repositories
    apex-solutions
      playpen
        branches
        tags
        trunk
          bin
            backup_apex.bat
            split.bat
          database
          ext-3.3.1
          oracle
            instantclient_10_2
            instantclient_11_1
            utilities
              oracle
                apex
                  APEXExport.class
                  APEXExportSplitter.class
              readme.txt
          src
```

The preceding screenshot shows the layout of my SVN repository. You can see that within the trunk folder of the apex-solutions/playpen project, I've created a series of folders to partition my application logically. The bin folder holds my batch scripts, including the backup_apex.bat script, detailed shortly. Also, note the oracle folder, which contains Oracle Instant Client software for database releases 10.2 and 11.1. And finally, the utilities folder to which I've copied the APEXExport. class and APEXExportSplitter.class from the Oracle APEX installation.

Let's look at the code for backup_apex.bat:

```
@echo off

setlocal

REM Set BASE to parent directory of this scripts location.
set HOME=%CD%
cd /d %~dp0
cd ..
set BASE=%CD%
cd /d %HOME%
```

The setlocal command ensures any environment changes are localized to the batch script. Setting the HOME variable allows the script to return to the execution start directory.

Next, navigate to the script location using the convoluted expression cd /d %~dp0, and in turn to its parent directory to set our BASE variable to be the "root" folder of our repository. For example, my repository path to the backup_apex.bat script is C:\playpen\bin\backup_apex.bat, so my BASE variable becomes C:\playpen. Your repository path could be a completely different, but provided your script finishes with \bin\backup_apex.bat, the BASE variable will be set correctly.

> Knowing the path to our BASE folder is an important step, as we now have our bearings to reference our java libraries and navigate to other folders.

```
REM ----------------------------------------------------------
REM Database 11g specific
REM ----------------------------------------------------------
set CLASSPATH=%CLASSPATH%;%BASE%\oracle\instantclient_11_1\ojdbc6.jar
set CLASSPATH=%CLASSPATH%;%BASE%\oracle\utilities

REM ----------------------------------------------------------
REM Database 10g specific
REM ----------------------------------------------------------
REM set CLASSPATH=%CLASSPATH%;%BASE%\oracle\instantclient_10_2\
classes12.jar
REM set CLASSPATH=%CLASSPATH%;%BASE%\oracle\utilities
```

Next, we set the CLASS_PATH to our JDBC drivers and export utilities. I'm using the Oracle JDBC library for Oracle database 11g, with the equivalent Oracle 10g version commented out.

```
cd /d %BASE%\database\apex

REM Make sure our local copy is up to date
if not ("%SVN_HOME%") == () "%SVN_HOME%"\svn update
```

We change folders, as the **APEXExport** utility exports files into the current working directory.

Before running the export, we update our repository, refreshing the current directory and subdirectories using the command-line version of SVN. In this case, I'm referencing an externally defined environment variable SVN_HOME to identify the home directory of the SVN command line client. SVN_HOME is usually defined as a Windows environment variable when the SVN command line client is installed.

Using conditional logic, allows this step to be skipped if the variable has not been set for your computer.

```
java oracle.apex.APEXExport -db mark-pc:1521:XE -user playpen
-password playpen -workspaceid 1038420889063720 -skipExportDate
```

APEXExport allows you to either export an individual application, a workspace, or the entire Oracle APEX instance. The utility is run through Java using a JDBC connection to the database; for complete syntax details refer to the readme.txt file included in the utilities folder.

In this batch script here, I am exporting a workspace. To find out the workspace ID for your environment, you can run the following query in SQL Workshop within Oracle APEX:

```
select v('WORKSPACE_ID') from dual
```

Exporting a workspace will create a separate script for each application in your workspace. So for application 150, a file named f150.sql will be created.

```
REM Check if SVN_HOME has been set
if ("%SVN_HOME%") == () goto :no_svn_home

"%SVN_HOME%"\svn add *.sql --force
"%SVN_HOME%"\svn commit -m "Automated backup and check in."

goto exit

:no_svn_home
```

```
echo ERROR
echo ERROR: SVN_HOME environment variable is not set, no automated SVN
check in.
echo ERROR

goto exit

:exit
endlocal
```

Once the APEX application exports have completed, we check the export files into SVN. We start by seeing if the SVN_HOME environment variable is set; if not, skipping the check-in and raising an error message. If set, the svn add command is used to ensure that when any new applications are added to the repository, then the svn commit command is executed, with a required check-in message.

SVN detects whether or not files have been modified as part of the check-in process, so if no changes have been made to an application, it won't be checked in. The following screenshot shows the output of the batch script, where five applications are exported from the database, but only one had been modified, so only that application was transmitted to the SVN repository.

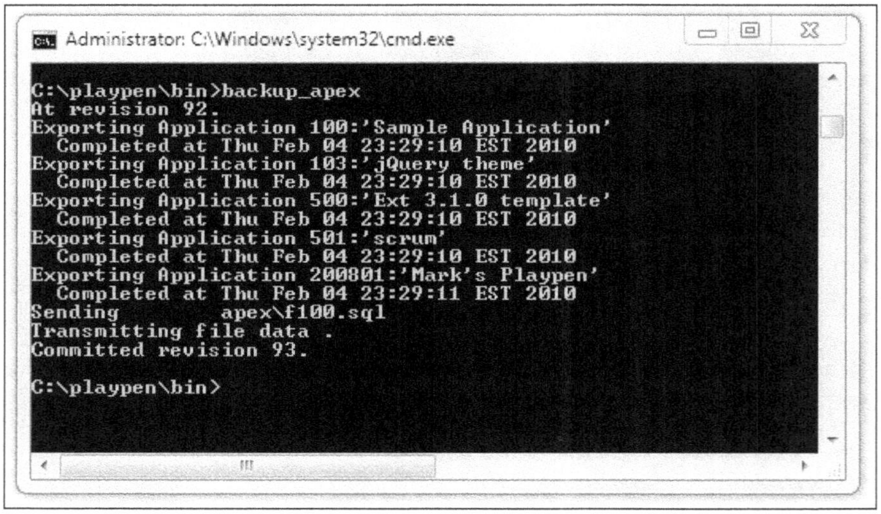

Now that we have our batch script set up, the last step is to schedule the script to be run automatically every day. Ideally, this would be configured to run on the SVN server; however, you could run the script from team members' computers, because as we've just seen in the previous screenshot, only modified applications are committed to the SVN repository.

Scheduling the batch file to run automatically each day is simply a matter of calling the batch script, using the Windows built-in scheduler to define when and how often you want the batch file to run, as shown in the following screenshot:

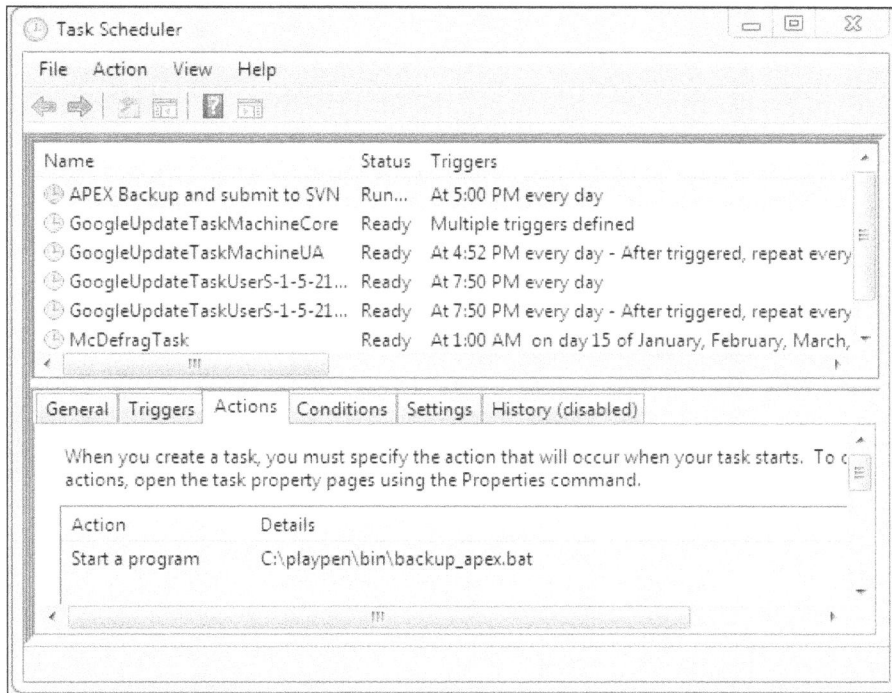

For additional security, it would be preferable to pass the password to the batch file using the scheduled task, rather than having it directly in the batch file.

More ideas for automating the build process

As developers, we work to automate processes for end-users; yet, many of us overlook opportunities to automate our own development processes. Using a single source repository for all your application assets and using simple scripts as we have here to schedule repetitive tasks are the first steps in a journey towards continuous integration.

Version control systems, including Subversion, include hooks, so that the act of checking a file into the repository triggers an event to execute your hook program or batch file. So in an APEX application context, you could automatically FTP your web assets to your web-server. Or checking in a JavaScript file may trigger a process to minify and combine your JavaScript files into a single application JavaScript file, something we will cover in *Chapter 11, Performance tuning your JavaScript*.

Oracle SQL Developer 2.1 now includes a unit testing framework that allows you to build a set of sequential steps to create test cases for testing your PL/SQL code. Along with providing a GUI interface within SQL Developer to run unit tests and suites, a command line interface is provided for both Windows and Linux. Here, you could schedule a process to run your unit tests overnight, and the next morning check a unit testing report to verify the results.

Other opportunities for automation include generating documentation, website pages, statistics, and distribution files.

Automating your build process can use sophisticated Continuous Integration tools, which may require significant initial setup, or grow organically starting with small and humble beginnings using command scripts as we've done here.

[Either way, the most important point is to keep looking for opportunities to improve your software quality and streamline development and deployment processes.]

Setting up a local web server

It's very worthwhile having a local web server on your computer, in addition to the team's web server. This allows you to modify and test "application" JavaScript in isolation from the rest of the development team. For some reason, people get upset when you're making a change to a core JavaScript function and suddenly every page stops working!

Setting up a local web server is much the same as we've outlined previously for the Oracle HTTP Server or APEX Listener. The only real change is to set your /ux/ alias to point to your SVN repository for your JavaScript, CSS, and other web assets.

By doing this you can work directly on the JavaScript files locally and not need to copy them onto the web server every time you need to test a change.

Summary

In this chapter we've discussed the merits of the different web server options available for Oracle APEX, covering the Oracle HTTP Server, the Embedded PL/SQL gateway, and the Oracle APEX Listener. Installation of the Ext JS library into each of these environments, including using Ext JS in a hosted APEX environment where you don't have access to the web server, has also been covered.

In setting up for success, we discussed the importance of taking a little extra time at the beginning of a project to set up a productive development environment. To aid the development process, we set up a SVN source code repository and included some tools to allow the automated backup and commit of an Oracle APEX workspace to the repository. A number of other automation opportunities were also discussed.

Let's now start to get acquainted with the Ext JS library, looking at some of the functionality it provides for manipulating the Document Object Model (DOM).

2
Getting Acquainted with Ext

In this chapter we will be familiarizing ourselves with some of the functionality the Ext JS library provides for manipulating the Document Object Model.

The **Document Object Model (DOM)** is an API that provides a structural representation of a HTML document. This allows developers to manipulate web pages using the properties, methods, and events exposed by the DOM. Manipulation of DOM elements is one of the basic staple tasks that almost every JavaScript code will do.

Ext JS provides a library of methods that allow you to do cross-browser DOM manipulation, allowing you to focus on adding business functionality, rather than having to build separate solutions for different browsers.

This chapter explores some of the functionality Ext JS provides, with topics including:

- Building a sandbox for standalone testing
- Cross-browser DOM manipulation and traversal
- Sizing and positioning elements
- CSS classes and styling
- Defining event handlers
- Parameter passing using object notation
- Using namespacing to avoid collisions

Building a sandbox

Before attempting to integrate Ext JS and APEX, it's good practice to develop your interface design using a prototyping approach. This allows for the exploration of features and functions in isolation, to explore a design approach without the temptation of building the final solution at the first try.

To do this, we are going to use a **sandbox** to isolate our code and experiments from the main development code until we are ready to merge the functionality into our APEX application. Sandboxes contain just enough functionality to accurately test the code under development.

Using a sandbox allows you to rapidly build and test new functionality, identify potential problems at an earlier stage, and solve those problems before incorporating the new functionality in the full design.

Our sandbox comprises the Mozilla **Firefox** browser with the **Firebug** plugin, along with a series of standalone HTML pages containing static HTML markup and file includes to the Ext JS library and CSS stylesheets.

Using Firefox with the Firebug plugin is a very common development platform for web developers, as Firebug provides fantastic debugging tools for inspecting and editing the HTML, DOM, JavaScript, and CSS components that make up a web page. It also includes a JavaScript console, allowing you to inspect JavaScript errors and execute JavaScript code.

Other browsers also have debugging tools such as Internet Explorer Developer Toolbar, Google Chromes' Inspector, and Opera Dragonfly. While these tools all provide many similar functions, Firebug remains the most popular and powerful web development tool and will be used throughout this book.

> Mozilla Firefox can be downloaded from `http://www.mozilla.com/en-US/firefox/`. You can learn more about Firebug and download it from `http://getfirebug.com/`.

Once you install Firebug, the first step to using Ext JS is to reference the JavaScript libraries and CSS stylesheet in your page templates.

```html
<html>
<head>
  <title>Example 2.1</title>
  <!-- Ext stylesheet -->
  <link rel="stylesheet" type="text/css"
      href="../../extjs/resources/css/ext-all.css" />

  <!-- Application stylesheet goes here -->

  <!-- Ext adapter and library -->
  <script type="text/javascript"
      src="../../extjs/adapter/ext/ext-base.js">
  </script>
  <script type="text/javascript" src="../../extjs/ext-all.js">
```

```
    </script>

    <!-- Application javascript library goes here -->

</head>
<body>
    <!-- body content -->
</body>
</html>
```

This code contains the minimum requirements for a page to use Ext JS, the source located in `chapter02\Example 2.1.html` of the example code for the book. To use Ext JS, we need to include references to the following files, and the files *must be in the include order listed*:

- `ext-all.css`: This is the main Ext CSS file that controls the look and feel for the Ext framework and widgets. Rather than making modifications to this file to customize or make adjustments to the CSS, you should include a separate "application" CSS file. When using an application CSS file, it should be included after the `ext-all.css` file and before any JavaScript files. When determining which CSS rule is applied by the browser, two factors are considered—CSS specificity and order. When two CSS rules have the same specificity, the last rule is applied.

- `ext-base.js`: This provides an adapter layer of base-level functionality for DOM manipulation, event handling animation, and so on. Prior to version 1.1, Ext required the use of one of the following base libraries: YUI, jQuery, or Prototype. By creating adapters for each of the external libraries, Ext maintained a separation of concerns, allowing developers to choose which external library to use. Beginning with Ext version 1.1, Ext included its own native Ext adapter, so external libraries are no longer required.

- `ext-all.js`: This contains the entire JavaScript for all of the Ext components and widgets. When developing, it's easiest to include `ext-all.js` or `ext-all-debug.js`, which is an uncompressed, unminified version better for debugging. Not all sites require the full Ext library, so cut-down versions can be assembled by including just the components being used. This is discussed further under performance considerations in *Chapter 11, Performance Tuning your JavaScript*.

Similarly to include application CSS files after the `ext-all.css`, you should include your application JavaScript files. When two JavaScript functions have the same specification signature, the last version of the function is the one called.

So, if you haven't already done so, open the `chapter02\Example 2.1.html` in Firefox, start Firebug, and type the following command into the console:

```
Ext.Msg.alert('Hello World', 'Ext JS is very cool!');
```

Provided your include paths are correct, you should see a modal alert that prevents you from interacting with the rest of the page until the alert is closed, similar to that shown in the following screenshot. If not, you probably have an error message **Ext is not defined**; adjust your include path to reference the Ext JS library files correctly.

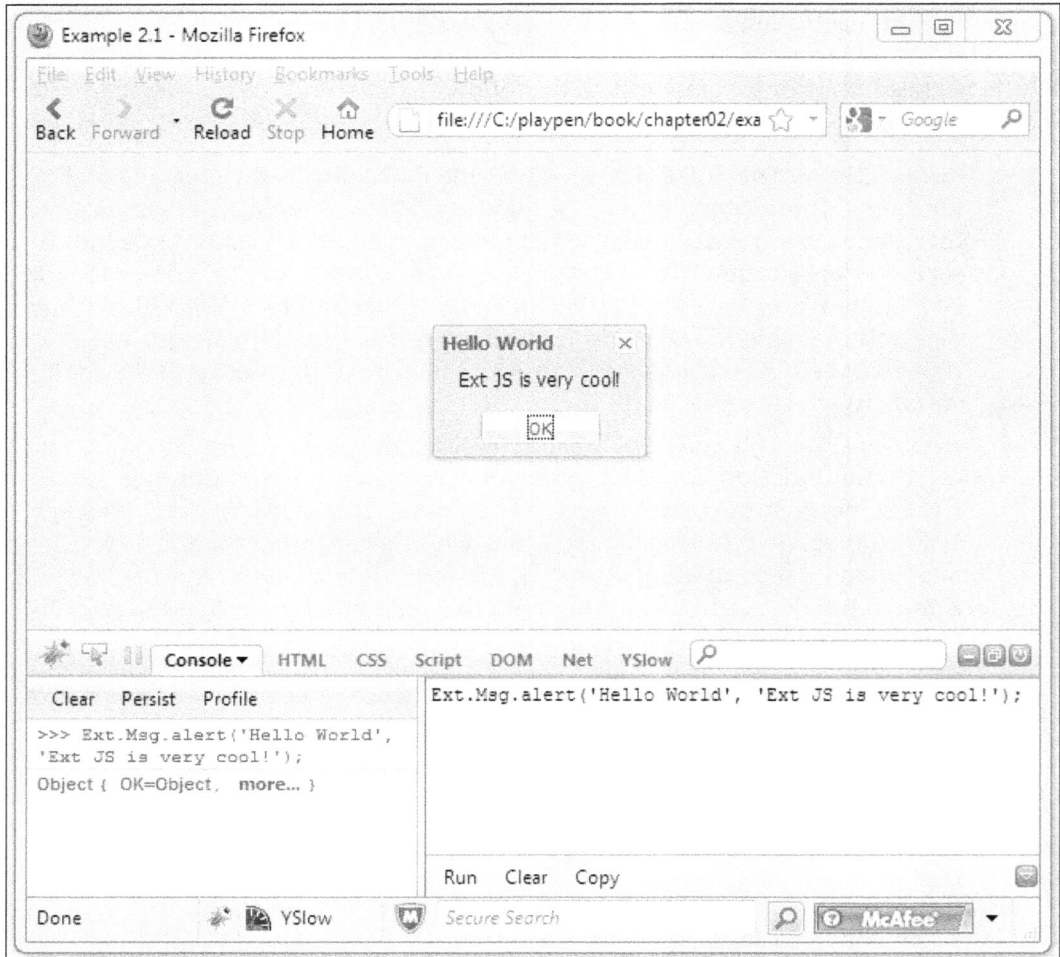

In fact, you're not really looking at a modal alert, despite your being able to move it around within the browser window, and it behaving like one. It's really just a bunch of HTML tags combined with CSS and some JavaScript events. If you switch to the HTML tab in Firebug, you will see something similar to the following screenshot:

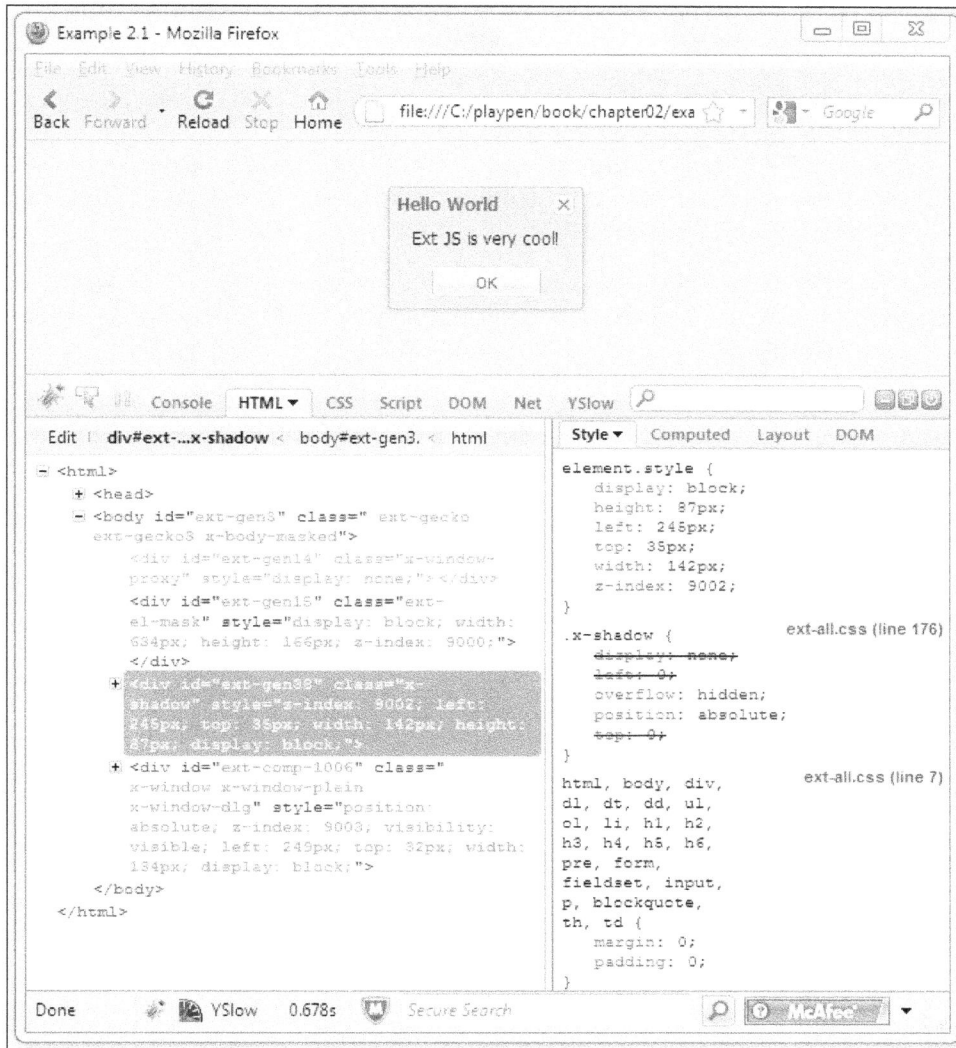

Remember, our page originally had no HTML within the body. Everything you see in the previous screenshot has been created dynamically using JavaScript and our call to Ext.Msg.alert. Imagine coming up with the CSS and JavaScript to do this yourself! This is a small glimpse at why **Ext JS is very cool!**

Cross-browser DOM manipulation with Ext.Element

One of the great challenges facing web developers when writing JavaScript is the lack of consistency in how the Document Object Model (DOM) has been implemented by the different software vendors.

The **World Wide Web Consortium (W3C)** was founded in 1994 to promote open standards for the Internet, publishing standards for browser scripting languages (ECMAScript) in 1997, and a standardized DOM in 1998. Today, browsers have varying levels of conformance to the current DOM Level 3 specification published by the World Wide Web Consortium (W3C) in 2004.

To allow for many differences between different browser implementations, Ext provides the `Ext.Element` class, which encapsulates a DOM element and provides cross-browser simple DOM manipulation methods.

Open `chapter02\Example 2.2.html` in Firefox, which includes all of the content of the earlier `Example 2.1.html`, along with the following styles and body content:

```html
<html>
    <head>
        ...
        <style type="text/css">
        ...
            .box {
                border: 1px solid #c0c0c0;
                padding: 5px;
            }

            .ux-selected {
                background-color: #dfe8f6;
                border-color: #a3bae9;
            }
        </style>
        ...
    </head>
    <body>
        <!-- body content -->
        <div id="test" class="box">
            <div id="el-1">one</div>
            <div id="el-2">two</div>
            <div id="el-3">three</div>
            <div id="el-4">four</div>
```

```
            <div id="el-5">five</div>
            <div id="el-6">six</div>
            <div id="el-7">seven</div>
            <div id="el-8">eight</div>
        </div>
    </body>
</html>
```

Ext provides the `Ext.get` method (shorthand for `Ext.Element.get`) to retrieve any element as an Ext.Element. Let's see it in action, running the following commands in the Firebug Console:

```
var el = Ext.get('test');
console.dir(el);
```

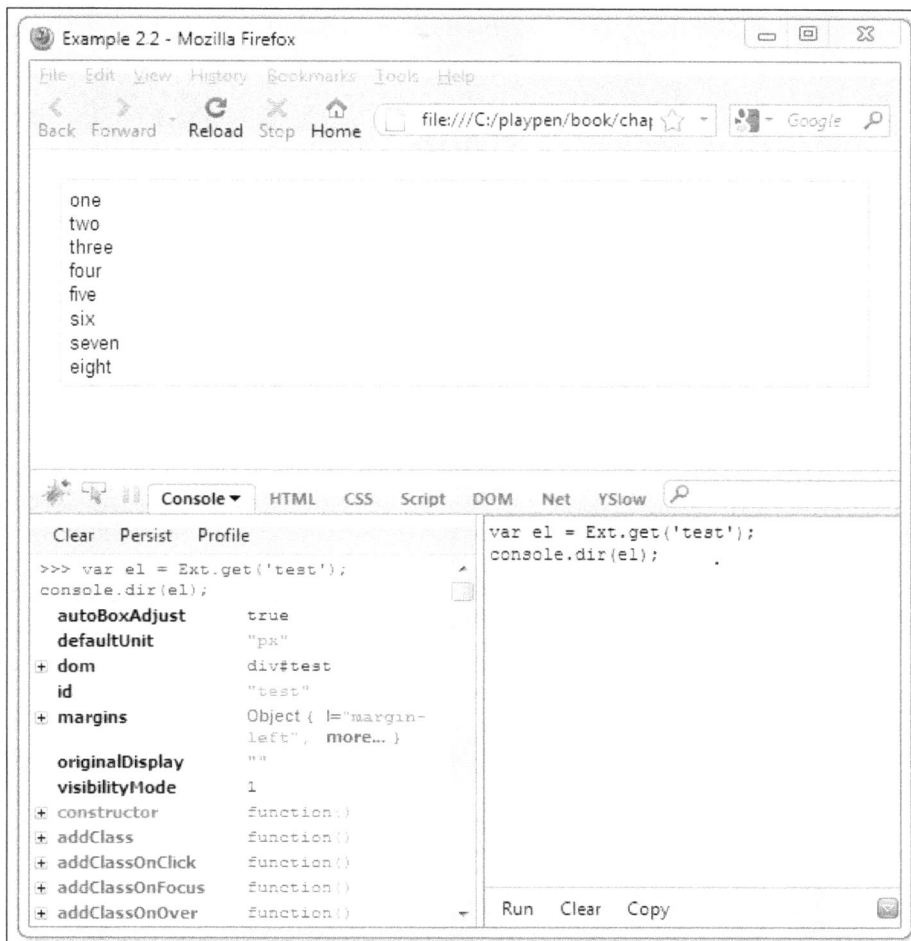

You should see something similar to screenshot we just saw, where we've constructed an `Ext.element` `el` using the `Ext.get` command, and then used the Firebug `console.dir` command to display the `el` object on the bottom left.

Firebug shows the properties in a black font, the methods/functions in a green font, and constructor classes in a red font. When using Firebug to display JavaScript objects, be aware that you are seeing the raw JavaScript object, so both public and private methods are exposed.

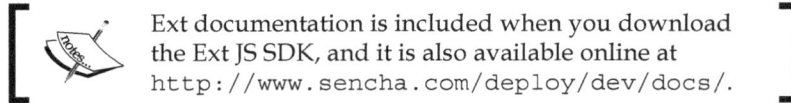

> Ext documentation is included when you download the Ext JS SDK, and it is also available online at http://www.sencha.com/deploy/dev/docs/.

You should always consult the Ext documentation if you are unsure whether or not a method is private, as calling a private method out of context may have undesirable side effects.

Heavyweight versus flyweight

`Ext.get` accepts an ID of the node, a DOM Node, or an existing `Ext.Element` as a parameter, and returns an `Ext.Element` (or null when unmatched), so the following statements are all valid:

```
// string Id
var el1 = Ext.get('test');

// DOM node
var el2 = Ext.get( document.getElementById('test') );

// Ext Element
var el3 = Ext.get(el1);
```

Let's try using one of the `Ext.Fx` methods `highlight`, which is automatically applied to the `Ext.Element` interface, to highlight an element briefly:

```
var el = Ext.get('test');
el.highlight();
```

The test `div` should change its background color to yellow and then fade out to its original color.

We could have written the same instruction using JavaScript chaining as follows:

```
Ext.get('test').highlight();
```

If all we are doing with our test div is highlighting it once, the overhead of creating an `Ext.Element` is a wasteful of memory resources. The Ext team recognized this, and created the `Ext.fly` method (shorthand for `Ext.Element.fly`), which uses a global shared flyweight `Ext.Element` across the library.

`Ext.fly` takes the same arguments as `Ext.get`, but should only ever be used for one-time references to DOM elements that are not going to be used again. So, for our previous example, we can write instead:

```
Ext.fly('test').highlight();
```

For an example of using `Ext.fly` incorrectly:

```
/*** example showing incorrect use of Ext.fly ***/
var el = Ext.fly('el-5');

Ext.fly('test').setWidth(400);
Ext.fly('test').center();

el.highlight();
```

Here, we have assigned a variable to the global flyweight element for Dom element `el-5`, then used the flyweight to manipulate another DOM element `test`. When we apply the highlight method to our variable, it is accessing the global flyweight, no longer pointing at our original DOM element. This results in the wrong element being highlighted.

> `Ext.fly` should only ever be used for one-time references to DOM elements, which are not going to be used again.

Sizing and positioning

`Ext.Element` provides methods for sizing and positioning elements. Let's try a few of them out using the Firebug console.

Set the width of the `test` element:

```
Ext.fly('test').setWidth(400);
```

Determine the height of the `test` element and conditionally resize it:

```
var ht = Ext.fly('test').getHeight();
console.log('ht = %s', ht);
if (ht < 200) {
    Ext.fly('test').setHeight(200);
}
```

Center the `test` element in the middle of the page:

```
Ext.fly('test').center();
```

Move the `test` element to a specific location at x=100, y=50 using animation:

```
Ext.fly('test').setLocation(100,50,true);
```

Hide the `test` element:

```
Ext.fly('test').hide();
```

Show the `test` element, with some animation:

```
Ext.fly('test').show(true);
```

Relocate the `test` element to its original position:

```
Ext.fly('test').clearPositioning();
```

As you can see, it's very easy to manipulate the size and positioning of DOM elements using `Ext.Element`. We haven't explored all the features here, but if you refer to the `Ext.Element` documentation at http://dev.sencha.com/deploy/dev/docs/?class=Ext.Element, you will find comprehensive methods for getting and setting the margin, border, padding, and position of an element.

CSS classes and styling

`Ext.Element` also has a set of methods for manipulating DOM elements using CSS classes and styles, allowing you to query, add, remove, and replace classes and styles. Let's try a few.

First, refresh your page, and resize and center the `test` div:

```
Ext.fly('test').setWidth(400);
Ext.fly('test').center();
```

To add a class to an element:

```
Ext.fly('el-5').addClass('ux-selected');
```

Your page should look like the following screenshot:

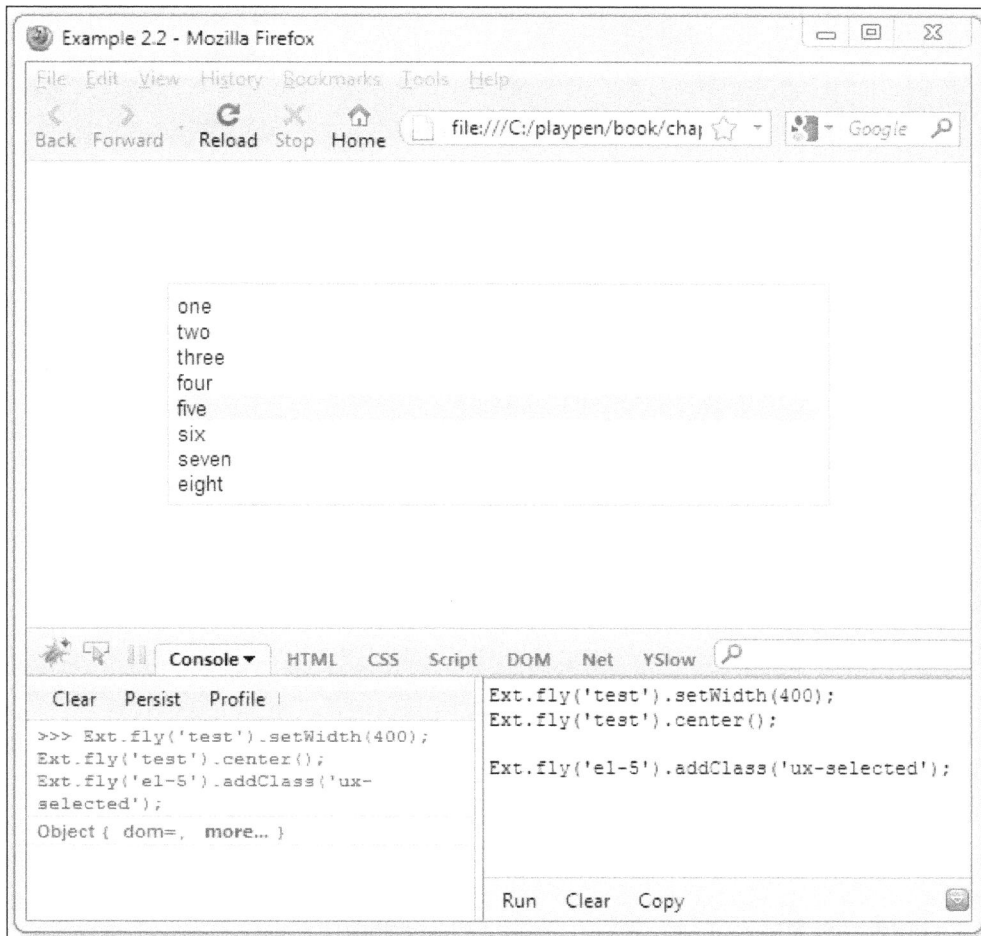

To remove a class:

```
Ext.fly('el-5').removeClass('ux-selected');
```

To alternately add and remove a class, you can toggle it:

```
Ext.fly('el-5').toggleClass('ux-selected');
```

To "stripe" the test elements' child elements so each alternate row is highlighted, and toggle the striping effect on and off:

```
Ext.fly('test').select('div:even').toggleClass('ux-selected');
```

The result is shown in the following screenshot:

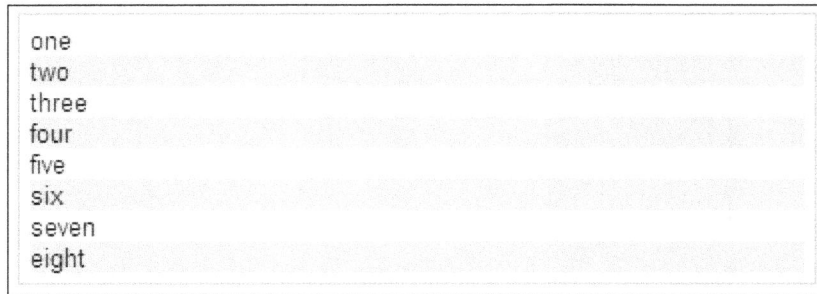

```
one
two
three
four
five
six
seven
eight
```

To add a class to one element, and remove the same class from all siblings:

```
Ext.fly('el-5').radioClass('ux-selected');
```

Methods also exist for styles, for example:

```
Ext.fly('el-5').setStyle('border', '1px solid #FF0000');
```

DOM traversal

In order to be able to navigate around the DOM tree from any given position, traversing both up and down the DOM in a browser, Ext provides a traversal API using CSS selectors to locate elements. Ext supports most of the CSS3 selectors, along with custom selectors and basic XPath. For a complete list of supported selectors, refer to the Ext API documentation for `Ext.DomQuery` at `http://dev.sencha.com/deploy/dev/docs/?class=Ext.DomQuery`.

Open `chapter02\Example 2.3.html`, which includes all of the content of the earlier `Example 2.2.html`, along with the body containing additional HTML markup for an unordered list and a paragraph (`ul` and `p` elements).

```html
<body>
    <!-- body content -->
    <div id="test" class="box">
        <div id="el-1">one</div>
        <div id="el-2">two</div>
        <div id="el-3">three</div>
        <div id="el-4">four</div>
        <div id="el-5">five
            <ul id="foo">
                <li>5.1</li>
                <li>5.2</li>
                <li>5.3</li>
```

```
            <li>5.4</li>
         </ul>
         <p>a paragraph</p>
      </div>
      <div id="el-6">six</div>
      <div id="el-7">seven</div>
      <div id="el-8">eight</div>
   </div>
</body>
```

Using the Firebug console once again, let's try some of the DOM traversal methods available in `Ext.Element`.

Let's toggle a class for the first and last child elements of `foo`:

```
Ext.fly('foo').first().toggleClass('ux-selected');
Ext.fly('foo').last().toggleClass('ux-selected');
```

The result is shown in the following screenshot:

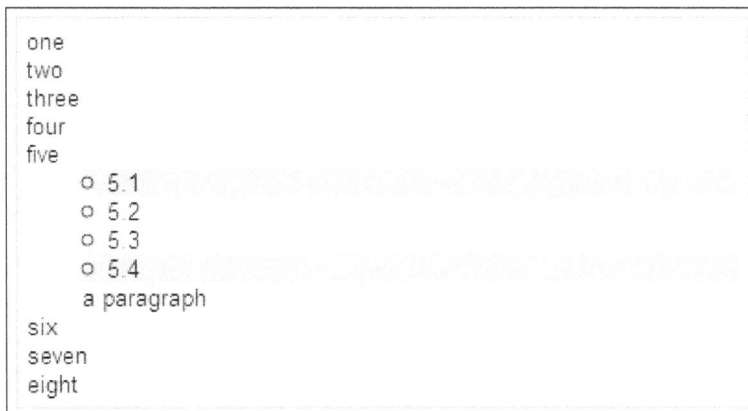

```
one
two
three
four
five
      o  5.1
      o  5.2
      o  5.3
      o  5.4
      a paragraph
six
seven
eight
```

Passing a selector filters for that selector:

```
// no selector the toggles the list
Ext.fly('el-5').first().toggleClass('ux-selected');

// using a selector, the paragraph is toggled instead
Ext.fly('el-5').first('p').toggleClass('ux-selected');
```

To return the first child at any depth below the current element based on a passed in selector, we use the `child` method; whereas for the first direct child (1 level down), we use the `down` method:

```
// child method finds the first list item
Ext.fly('el-5').child('li').toggleClass('ux-selected');

// down method does not find the first list item
Ext.fly('el-5').down('li').toggleClass('ux-selected');
```

Navigating between siblings is done using the `next` and `prev` methods; once again you can optionally pass selectors to filter for that selector:

```
// toggle previous sibling
Ext.fly('el-5').prev().toggleClass('ux-selected');

// toggle next sibling
Ext.fly('el-5').next().toggleClass('ux-selected');

// toggle next sibling that is a div with class "pickme"
// does not exist in the example file!!
Ext.fly('el-5').next('div.pickme').toggleClass('ux-selected');
```

Traversing up the DOM path is just as easy using `up` and `parent` methods, which provide similar functionality but accept different parameters.

To select the immediate parent:

```
var el = Ext.get('foo').first();
el.parent().toggleClass('ux-selected');
```

Walking up the DOM, looking for a parent that matches the passed simple selector:

```
// up( String selector, [Number/Mixed maxDepth] )
el.up('div.box').toggleClass('ux-selected');
```

This is equivalent to:

```
// parent( [String selector], [Boolean returnDom] )
el.parent('div.box').toggleClass('ux-selected');
```

Selecting multiple elements

In our DOM traversal examples so far, we have fetched only a single element to manipulate. More often than not, we are going to be more interested in interacting with multiple elements, which is where `Ext.select` and `Ext.query` come into play.

`Ext.select` takes a query and returns an `Ext.CompositeElement` or an array of `Ext.Elements`. This allows you to interact easily with every element returned by `Ext.select` without looping and modifying each one separately.

For example, we saw earlier to "stripe" the test elements' child elements, and toggle them on and off, is a one line command:

```
Ext.fly('test').select('div:even').toggleClass('ux-selected');
```

Another way of writing the same command could be:

```
Ext.select('div:even',false,'test').toggleClass('ux-selected');
```

To add and remove a CSS class when the mouse is over an element is just as easy:

```
Ext.select('div',false,'test').addClassOnOver('ux-over');
```

Sometimes we may want to make several changes to the elements, so you can use the `Ext.each` method to iterate through an Array/NodeList:

```
function doSomething() {
   this.highlight();
}

var els = Ext.select('div',true,'test');
els.each(function(el) {
    // several commands..
    el.on('click',doSomething, this);
    console.log(el.id);
});
```

> It is important point to note the second parameter in `Ext.select` syntax: `Ext.select( String/Array selector, [Boolean unique], [HTMLElement/String root] )`. `unique`, when true, returns a unique `Ext.Element` for each element (defaults to `false`, returning a shared flyweight object).

Try running the previous `Ext.each` example as is, then refresh the page and run the example replacing true with false. Note the changed behavior; regardless of which `div` you click, the last `div` is highlighted. Are you able to explain why this happens?

`Ext.query` accepts CSS selector and root node like `Ext.select`, but instead returns an array of DOM nodes.

Reworking our previous example to use `Ext.query`:

```
function doSomething() {
  this.highlight();
}

var els = Ext.query('div','test');
Ext.each(els,function(el) {
    // el is a DOM node here
    Ext.get(el).on('click',doSomething);
    console.log(el.id);
});
```

DOM manipulation

Ext provides a strong API to allow us to add, modify, and remove elements in the DOM easily. We will be using `chapter02\Example 2.3.html` to test the Ext API once again.

Let's start by creating some DOM elements:

```
Ext.fly('test').createChild('<div id="el-9">nine</div>');
Ext.fly('test').createChild({tag:'div',id:'el-10', html:'ten'});
```

Here, we used the `Ext.Element.createChild` method to create and append two div elements to the test element, each containing a text string. For the first div, we simply passed the HTML to include. The second example shows an alternative method using a `Ext.DomHelper` config, which provides an abstraction of the DOM allowing you to build up complex HTML fragments programmatically before applying them to the DOM.

When using `Ext.Element.createChild`, an `Ext.Element` is returned, allowing you to do additional processing:

```
var el = Ext.fly('test').createChild({tag:'div', html:'eleven'});

el.addClass('ux-selected');
console.log(el.id);
```

In this example, an id for the `div` tag wasn't specified, instead `Ext.Element`, returned to the `el` variable, was used for additional processing. Take a moment to inspect the new `div` using the Firebug HTML inspector. You should see the div tag has automatically been assigned an id, as shown in the following screenshot:

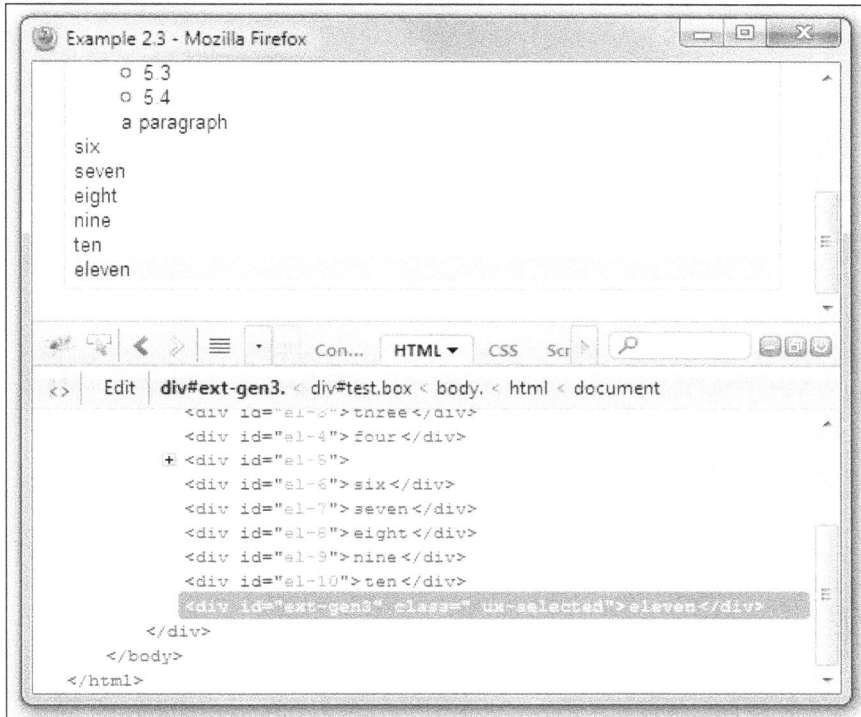

Adding of elements relative to an existing DOM node is done using `insertHTML`, `insertSibling`, or using convenience methods `insertBefore`, `insertAfter`, `insertFirst`. Refresh the page, and let's try a few.

Before we do, refresh the page and run the following code to add a border and some space around the div elements within the test dev:

```
// add styling to existing div elements
Ext.fly('test').select('div')
  .setStyle('border','1px solid #c0c0c0')
  .setStyle('margin','2px');
```

Run the following code:

```
// create a reusable template for text substitution
var html = ' <span class="ux-selected">{text}</span> ';
var tpl = new Ext.DomHelper.createTemplate(html);

// show insertHtml placement options
var el = Ext.get('el-4');
el.insertHtml('beforeBegin',tpl.apply({text:'beforeBegin'}));
el.insertHtml('afterBegin' ,tpl.apply({text:'afterBegin'}));
el.insertHtml('beforeEnd'  ,tpl.apply({text:'beforeEnd'}));
el.insertHtml('afterEnd'   ,tpl.apply({text:'afterEnd'}));

// show insertSibling placement options
var obj = Ext.get('el-7');
obj.insertSibling(tpl.apply({text: 'before Sib'}), 'before');
obj.insertSibling(tpl.apply({text: 'after Sib'}), 'after');
```

The result is shown in the following screenshot:

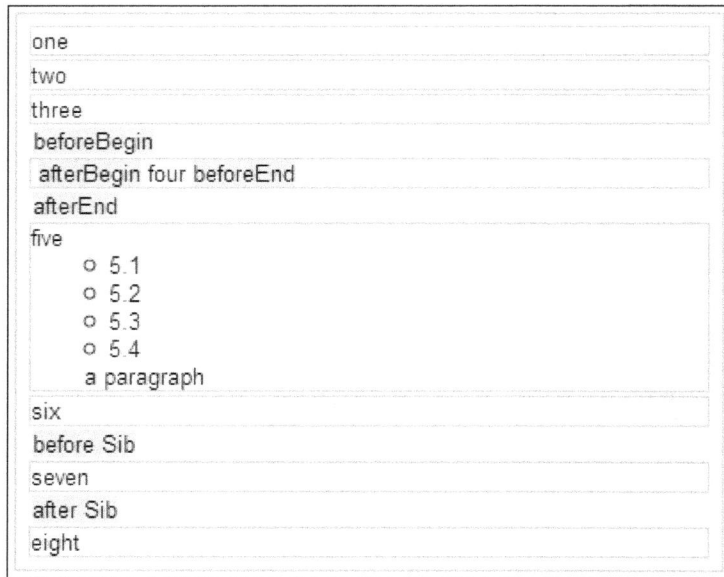

```
one
two
three
beforeBegin
 afterBegin four beforeEnd
afterEnd
five
        o 5.1
        o 5.2
        o 5.3
        o 5.4
        a paragraph
six
before Sib
seven
after Sib
eight
```

Notice the use of `Ext.DomHelper.createTemplate` in the code; it's something not previously mentioned. An `Ext.Template` defines a fragment of HTML code with some embedded placeholder tags, allowing you to substitute values quickly and easily. This is done repeatedly further down in the code using the `apply` method, which returns the HTML fragment with the substituted values.

The `insertHtml` method has four different locations to insert the HTML in relation to this element-beforeBegin, afterBegin, beforeEnd, afterEnd. The previous screenshot shows the difference between beforeBegin and afterBegin: beforeBegin creates a sibling node, whereas afterBegin creates a child node. The beforeEnd and afterEnd locations work similarly.

As you would expect, `insertSibling` locations of before and after insert HTML as their names imply.

The methods mentioned before for creating new elements — insertBefore, insertAfter, insertFirst — can also be used for relocating existing elements. Refresh your page and try these out:

```
Ext.fly('el-7').insertBefore('el-5');
Ext.fly('test').select('div:even').insertBefore('el-1');
Ext.fly('test').insertFirst('el-6');
Ext.fly('el-2').insertAfter('el-4').highlight();
```

Removing nodes is trivial, either referring to the node ID or using CSS selectors:

```
Ext.fly('test').select('div:even').remove();
Ext.fly('el-8').remove();
```

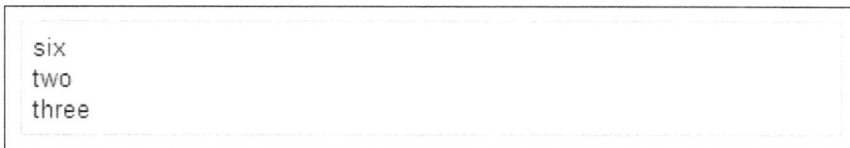

Another useful method is `wrap` that creates and wraps the element with another element:

```
Ext.fly('foo').wrap({tag: 'div', class:'box'});
```

> Wrapping an element is a very useful technique used many times within Ext components.

The `Ext.Element.boxWrap` wraps the specified element with a special 9-element markup/CSS block that renders by default as a gray container with a gradient background, rounded corners, and a four-way shadow.

This special mark-up is used throughout Ext when box wrapping elements. Examples of elements using it include the `Ext.Button`, `Ext.Panel` when attribute `frame=true` is set, and `Ext.Window`. To see this in action, run the following code:

```
Ext.get("el-5").boxWrap();
Ext.get("foo").boxWrap().addClass("x-box-blue");
```

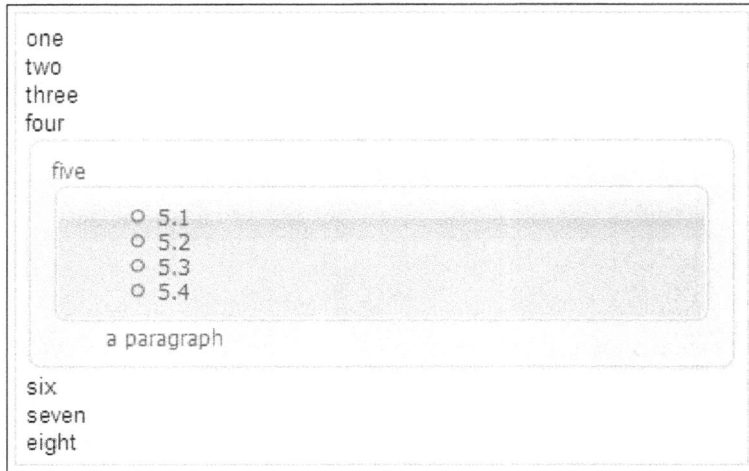

```
one
two
three
four

   five

          ○ 5.1
          ○ 5.2
          ○ 5.3
          ○ 5.4

       a paragraph

six
seven
eight
```

This screenshot shows the expected output, where `el-5` has been wrapped with the default gray container, and a four-way shadow. Element `foo` has been wrapped, and a class `x-box-blue` has been applied to the wrapper, resulting in a blue container. The x-box-blue CSS rules are included with Ext; to use an alternate class, you would need to provide the necessary CSS rules also.

Defining event handlers

Event-driven programming is supported in web browsers through the use of JavaScript to register event handlers and listeners on page elements in the DOM tree. Event handlers provide a mechanism to make a HTML page interactive, so when you click on page elements, or hover over something, JavaScript is executed, and the appearance or behavior of the page changes.

Historically, developers used the **Inline model** to add event handlers directly to an element as an attribute of the element:

```
<div id="test" onclick="alert(this.id + ' was clicked');">Click me</
div>
```

Or developers also used the **Traditional model** to add event handlers via scripts, for example:

```
<div id="test">Click me</div>

<script type="text/javascript">
var dom = document.getElementById('test');
dom.onclick = function () {
    alert(this.id + ' was clicked');
};
</script>
```

This event-handling model is known as **DOM Level 0**, and allows only a single event handler for each event to be attached to a DOM node.

The W3C designed a more flexible event handling model in **DOM Level 2**, to allow multiple events to be attached to a DOM node and uses methods including addEventListener, removeEventListener, and dispatchEvent. Unfortunately, Microsoft does not follow the W3C model, instead uses their own model using methods including attachEvent, detachEvent, and fireEvent, to provide similar functionality.

Ext removes the need to deal with different browser event models by wrapping the browser's native event-object into Ext.EventObject, to provide normalized event processing, freeing us from dealing with cross-browser differences.

Let's take a look at the ExtEventObject API. Open chapter02\Example 2.4.html, which includes all of the content of the earlier Example 2.3.html, with some additional formatting added to the div elements, and a new messages region included above, as shown in the following screenshot:

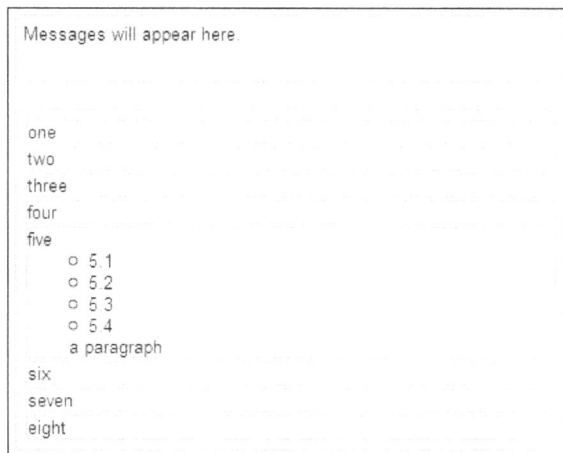

To add an event handler or listener to an element, we use the `addListener` method, or preferably use the `on` method, which is shorthand for `addListener`:

```
function handleClick(e, t){
    e.preventDefault();
    var target = Ext.get(t);
    target.highlight();

    var msg = Ext.get('msg-ct');
    msg.update('You clicked ' + target.id +
        ', with innerHtml ' + target.dom.innerHTML);
    msg.highlight();
}

// add a click event to div el-6
Ext.fly('el-6').on('click',handleClick);
```

In this example, we added an event handler for a mouse-click event on a specific DOM element, `el-6`, to execute an action handler function `handleClick`. The `handleClick` function accepts two parameters: `e`, which is an `Ext.EventObject`, and `t`, the DOM element that was the target of the event. Our `handleClick` function is used here to highlight the target element and update the messages region with information about the target element and highlight the messages region.

The `preventDefault` method is used to prevent the default handling of the event by a browser. It's not really necessary here, but if we had attached an event to a DOM link, it would prevent the browser opening the link address.

Alternate syntaxes for adding the event handler:

```
Ext.EventManager.on("el-6", 'click', handleClick);
Ext.EventManager.addListener("el-6", 'click', handleClick);
```

To remove an event handler, we use the `removeListener` method, or the shorthand equivalent `un` method:

```
Ext.fly('el-6').removeListener('click',handleClick);
Ext.fly('el-6').un('click',handleClick);
```

You must include a reference to the function passed in the `addListener` call. All listeners attached to an element can be removed using `removeAllListeners`:

```
Ext.fly('el-6').removeAllListeners();
```

Using event delegation to reduce memory consumption

Adding listeners to multiple elements can be done easily using CSS selectors:

```
Ext.select('div:even','test').on('click',handleClick);
```

However, before you do add multiple selectors, you may want to consider event delegation. Rather than registering multiple event handlers for each element in a group of elements, you can register an event to a container element and take advantage of events bubbling up the DOM hierarchy.

So, in `Example 2.4.html`, our HTML looks like this:

```
<div id="test" class="box">
    <div id="el-1">one</div>
    <div id="el-2">two</div>
    <div id="el-3">three</div>
    <div id="el-4">four</div>
    <div id="el-5">five
        <ul id="foo">
            <li>5.1</li>
            <li>5.2</li>
            <li>5.3</li>
            <li>5.4</li>
        </ul>
        <p>a paragraph</p>
    </div>
    <div id="el-6">six</div>
    <div id="el-7">seven</div>
    <div id="el-8">eight</div>
</div>
```

We could use event delegation as follows:

```
function handleClick(e, t){
    e.preventDefault();
    var target = Ext.get(t);
    target.highlight();

    var msg = Ext.get('msg-ct');
    msg.update('You clicked ' + target.id +
        ', with innerHtml ' + target.dom.innerHTML);
    msg.highlight();
}
```

```
Ext.fly('test').on(
    'click',                //event name
    handleClick,            //function
    this,                   //scope
    {delegate: 'div:even'} //options object
);
```

Here, we have the optional `scope` and `options` parameters; within the options object we have used the `delegate` attribute to specify a CSS selector to be applied, filtering the descendants of the target, so that only the even `div` elements will fire the event.

> Event delegation reduces memory consumption, and reduces potential memory leaks.

Something else really neat about delegates is that the handler will work for any descendant of the target that matches that CSS selector, even if it is created in the future.

Try adding two more `div` elements within the `test div`:

```
Ext.fly('test').createChild('<div id="el-9">nine</div>');
Ext.fly('test').createChild('<div id="el-10">ten</div>');
```

Clicking on `el-10` will execute the `handleClick` function because it matches the CSS selector.

One-off events

To create a "one off" handler that fires once and then removes itself, we use the options object and single attribute:

```
Ext.fly('test').on(
    'click',                //event name
    handleClick,            //function
    this,                   //scope
    {single: true}         //options object
);
```

You can use the `buffer` option to run a handler after a delay period (in milliseconds). If the event fires again within that period, the original event is cancelled and the new event invoked after the new delay.

```
// buffer the handleClick for 1000ms (1 second)
Ext.fly('test').on('click',handleClick, this,{buffer: 1000});
```

The `delay` option fires the event after the delay period, but does not cancel events:

```
// delay the handleClick for 1000ms (1 second)
Ext.fly('test').on('click',handleClick, this,{delay: 1000});
```

Parameter passing using object notation

Many of the APIs provided by Ext use a `config` object to pass configuration settings to a JavaScript function. So what exactly is this `config` object, and why use it?

The `config` object is an object literal, which we will learn about shortly. We use it because it's more flexible and is self documenting.

Old-school parameters

Using old school JavaScript programming, a typical function looked like this:

```
function show_prompt(title, message, width) {
    // code
}
```

To call that code, you would write:

```
var answer = show_prompt('my title','a short message', 300);
```

While this isn't too bad for this example, as a developer you have to call the function passing parameters in the order specified, and you must pass all parameters. In a few months time, an issue gets raised, and looking at the function call you have absolutely no idea what `300` is about without digging around to find the function definition.

Using object notation

The new way of passing parameters is done using **object literals**, popularized by Douglas Crockford as **JSON (JavaScript Object Notation)**. Its structure is simple; it is a comma separated list of properties wrapped in curly braces. Each property is denoted by listing its name and value separated by a colon character.

Here is a complete example, using object literals:

```
var config = {
    title: 'Contact details',
    msg: 'Please enter your Name:',
    width: 300,
    buttons: Ext.MessageBox.OKCANCEL,
```

```
        multiline: true,
        fn: function (btn, answer, obj) {
            console.log('You typed: ' + answer);
        },
        icon: Ext.MessageBox.INFO
    }

    Ext.Msg.show(config);
```

While this example is a little more complicated, it's more readable because we are passing parameter names and values, so in a few months time it's plain to see that 300 refers to the width.

Object literals don't care about the order of parameters being passed, or whether all parameters are being passed, so the Ext team could add additional parameters to the `Ext.Msg` object and our code will still work. Naturally the Ext team would need to make the additional parameters optional, or assign default values, but they would need to update only the object definition.

One other less obvious benefit is that by wrapping all our variables into an object literal, we aren't defining variables in the global namespace, reducing the chances of overwriting an existing variable. This is an increasingly important consideration as web pages rely more and more on JavaScript, and often include one or more JavaScript libraries as well as custom code.

Basic syntax

An *object literal* is an unordered set of properties using the following syntax rules:

- An object is enclosed by curly braces {}
- Each property lists its name and value separated by a colon character
- Name/value pairs are separated by a comma
- Names can be almost any string except JavaScript-reserved keywords
- Values can be of any data type, including array literals and object literals
- Array literals are enclosed by square brackets, for example, ['a',{b: 100}, ['f','g','h']]

For further information on JSON, refer to `http://www.json.org/`.

> Beware the trailing comma after the last name/value pair. Firefox won't object if you add it, but Internet Explorer will trigger an error: **Expected identifier, string or number.**

Use namespacing to avoid collisions

Something you have to be aware of when doing JavaScript programming is corruption of the global namespace. Every time you define a simple function, or other variable at the top level of a web page, the names you've chosen could potentially come in conflict with names used by other developers or libraries that you are using. In the browser, all global variables become properties of the window object.

So when you declare a variable:

```
var gDebug = false;
```

you're actually declaring:

```
var window.gDebug = false;
```

More often than not, modern web browser applications use one or more JavaScript libraries, snippets of code from multiple sources, and code you've written as well. For our environment, APEX includes jQuery, jQuery UI, and APEX JavaScript libraries, and we've added Ext also. It's not safe to assume you can reference a variable or object in the global namespace without impacting an existing variable or object.

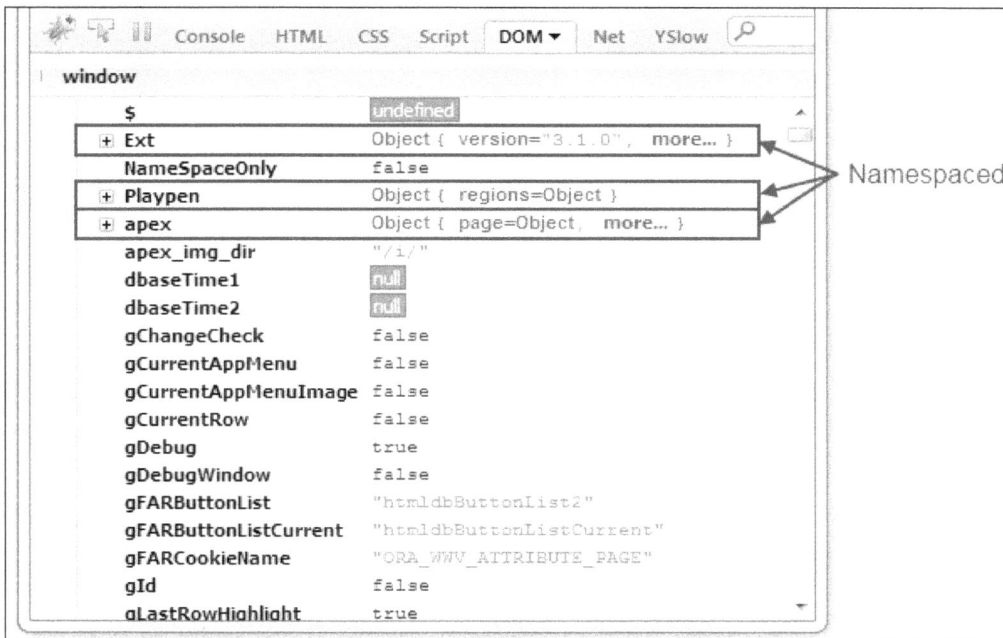

When looking at Firebug's DOM tab in this screenshot, we have a basic APEX application that includes the highlighted `apex`, `Ext`, and `Playpen` namespaced objects. There are also a great many more variables shown that have been declared in the global namespace.

If you expanded the Ext object, you would see Ext consolidates all of its classes into a single namespace of Ext and further organizes its classes into various packages. APEX has made a concerted effort to namespace it's JavaScript objects between the 3.2 and 4.0 releases, so is moving in the right direction, but isn't quite there yet.

> JavaScript rule for namespace collisions are simple:
> Last person to have their code included wins.

To see the impact of namespace collisions, open the `chapter02\Example 2.1.html` example and type into the Firebug console:

```
Ext.Msg.alert('Hello World', 'Ext JS is very cool!');
```

The Ext modal alert should appear. Close it, and type into the Firebug console:

```
var Ext = 'fred';
Ext.Msg.alert('Hello World', 'Ext JS is very cool!');
```

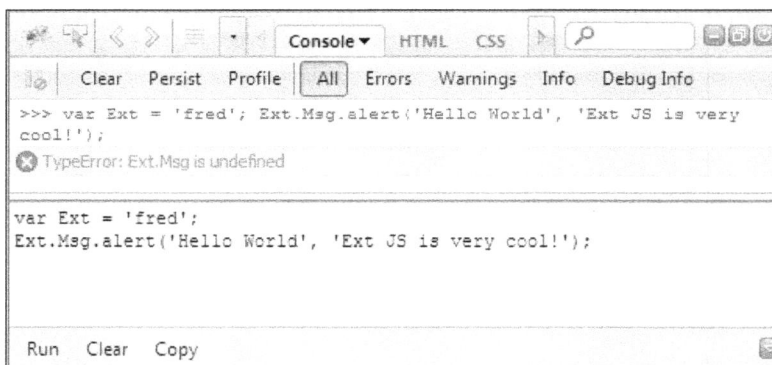

This time we have overwritten the Ext object, the namespace collision has removed the entire Ext object and all its components.

> To avoid namespace collisions, you should create your own namespace, and define all your JavaScript variables and functions within that namespace. Ext provides the `Ext.namespace` method to do this simply.

Ext.namespace

Ext provides the `Ext.namespace` method (or the shorthand `Ext.ns`) which will set up namespaces for you, including checking if the namespace already exists. For example, to set up a namespace of `Playpen` and the packages `regions` and `form`:

```
Ext.namespace('Playpen.regions', 'Playpen.form');
```

Then to define a new class, such as `customerDetails` within `Playpen.regions`:

```
Playpen.regions.customerDetails = new Ext.Panel({
    allowDomMove : false,
    applyTo: 'customerDetails',
    animCollapse: false,
    autoHeight: true,
    ...
    titleCollapse: true
});
```

Ext.BLANK_IMAGE_URL

Ext uses a 1x1 pixel transparent `.gif` image to create inline icons with CSS background images, allowing Ext to size objects correctly in a cross-browser compatible way. In older versions of IE, this defaults to `http://extjs.com/s.gif`, which can cause issues if `extjs.com` is not accessible, or you're using SSL, which will raise security warnings in browsers.

To prevent these issues, you need to set the `Ext.BLANK_IMAGE_URL` to a 1x1 pixel transparent `.gif` image on your local web server. If you're using a standard APEX install, you can reference:

```
Ext.BLANK_IMAGE_URL = '/i/1px_trans.gif';
```

This needs to be included in your page template directly after the Ext JavaScript files, normally included in an external JavaScript file, but could be inline as follows:

```
<html>
<head>
    <title>Example 2.1</title>
    <!-- Ext stylesheet -->
    <link rel="stylesheet" type="text/css"
        href="../../extjs/resources/css/ext-all.css" />
    <!-- Application stylesheet goes here -->
    <!-- Ext adapter and library -->
    <script type="text/javascript"
        src="../../extjs/adapter/ext/ext-base.js">
```

```
        </script>
        <script type="text/javascript"
            src="../../extjs/ext-all.js">
        </script>
        <!-- Application javascript library goes here -->
        <script type="text/javascript">
            Ext.BLANK_IMAGE_URL = '/i/1px_trans.gif';
        </script>
    </head>
    <body>
        <!-- body content -->
    </body>
</html>
```

Summary

In this chapter we have spent time familiarizing ourselves with some of the underlying concepts and functionality Ext provides for manipulating the Document Object Model (DOM).

By using simple standalone testing pages, we have done isolated testing without worrying about interaction with APEX, or trying to build end solutions. Using the Firebug Console, HTML, and DOM tabs, we have executed Ext code snippets and inspected the results both in the browser and within Firebug.

We have investigated the `Ext.Element` component, exploring how it allows us to easily manipulate and navigate the DOM. We have used CSS3 selectors provided by `Ext.DomQuery` to retrieve elements of interest, and then modified them by using the `Ext.Element` API to add and remove classes, attach event handlers, and add or remove elements around them.

We have explored more advanced event techniques such as delegation and one-off events, as well as modern JavaScript programming concepts such as object notation and the need for namespacing variables.

Enough with the theory! Let's start building some APEX templates with Ext JS.

3
Building a Ext JS Theme into APEX

This chapter starts our journey building a theme based application on Ext JS into APEX. It provides a background on APEX themes and discusses how to create an APEX theme from scratch. Instructions on how to integrate the Ext JS library into the page template are provided, together with potential issues you may encounter.

This chapter includes:

- An overview of APEX themes, explaining the template types that make up a theme, as well as the benefits of separating the APEX engine, templates, and application functionality from each other.
- Starting out creating a APEX Theme.
- Building a Page Template based on the **Ext.Viewport** component. This covers the process of creating a template using a standalone prototype and integrating it into an APEX page template.
- Discussion on how JavaScript DOM manipulation can result in input items appearing outside the form element, and the consequences that result. A customized version of the **Ext.Viewport** is created to ensure that input items always remain with the form.

Theme basics

Out of the box, APEX comes with twenty themes, each theme comprising a collection of templates used to define the layout and appearance of an entire application. An application can have many themes, but only one theme is active at any time; switching themes is done at design time only.

You can create custom themes, which may be published, either within a workspace by a Workspace Manager or for the whole APEX instance by an Internal Workspace Manager. Publishing a theme encourages consistency across applications.

A theme comprises nine template types: breadcrumb, button, calendar, label, list, page, popup list of values, region, and report. A theme must have at least one of each of the nine template types.

Within each template type are a set of predefined classes and eight custom classes. For example, the label template has the following classes:

- - Not Identified -
- No Label
- Optional Label
- Optional Label with Help
- Required Label
- Required Label with Help
- Custom 1... Custom 8

Programmers use these templates to construct the HTML pages that make up an application. Each page is declaratively defined using metadata to select templates to be used for the presentation.

The APEX engine dynamically renders an HTML page using the metadata, assembling relevant templates and injecting dynamic data into placeholders within the templates. The HTML page is viewed when you request a page through a web browser. When you submit a page, the APEX engine performs page processing, once again using declaratively defined metadata to perform computations, validations, processes, and branching.

This type of processing is a typical **Model-View-Controller**(MVC) pattern, where the **view** is the HTML generated using the application templates. The APEX engine is the **controller** and receives the GET or POST input and decides what to do with it, handing over to domain objects. The domain objects **model** is encapsulated in the page definition and contains the business rules and functionality to carry out specific tasks.

Separation of concerns

The MVC pattern also promotes another good design principle—separation of concerns. APEX has been designed so that the APEX engine, templates, and the application functionality can be optimized independently of each other.

Clearly, the process of assembling and sequencing the steps necessary to render a page, and process a page are important to the overall solution. By separating this out and letting Oracle deal with the complexities of this through the APEX engine, it allows programmers to concentrate on providing business functionality.

Equally, by separating presentation templates from the business logic, it allows each aspect to be maintained separately. This provides a number of advantages including ease of design change, allowing templates to be modified either by different people or at different times to enhance the interface without breaking the application.

An excellent example of this is the standard themes provided in APEX, which have been designed to be completely interchangeable. Switching standard themes is simply a matter of loading a theme from the repository and then switching the active theme. APEX then remaps components to the new active theme using the template class identifiers.

Standard themes

We will be building our own custom theme rather than using one of the twenty pre-built ones. Nevertheless, it's worthwhile knowing what they provide, as we will build our custom theme by using one of them as a "starter".

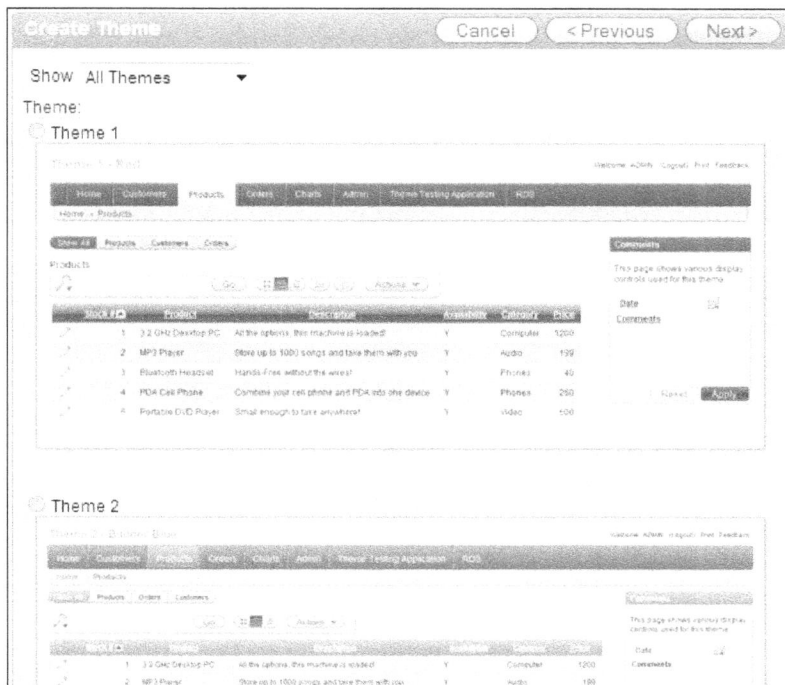

Looking at this image, we can see a preview of the standard APEX themes. Each theme provides a similar interface, so really each standard theme is just a visual variation on the others. The colors used are a little different, or the HTML layout is tweaked slightly, but in reality they are all much the same.

Theme 4 is used by APEX as the "starter" theme and contains one template for each template class for all the template types—a total of 69 templates. Theme 19 is also worth noting as it's designed for mobile devices. Each of these themes are full of good HTML practices and show how and where to use the substitution strings.

Creating a theme

When creating a theme, you can choose to copy one from the repository, create one from scratch or from an export file. The repository and export file options copy the entire theme, and you start editing the template to suit. Creating a theme from scratch creates a theme without any templates. You then need to define templates for each different type before you can switch from the active theme.

In my opinion, the easiest way to build a new theme is to take the approach that the application should always be in a working state, and the way to do this is to create a new empty TEMPLATE application using a standard theme and build from there.

From this working base, you can progressively convert the templates to use Ext functionality, building simple test pages as you go to verify the templates. These test pages also form part of your template documentation, allowing team members to examine and understand specific functionality in isolation.

Once a theme has templates for each of the nine template types, you can publish the theme into the workspace to be used by your business applications.

The following screenshot shows a dialog named **Create Workspace Theme** from the APEX wizard. Notice that you can change the theme number when you publish a theme, providing a very simple mechanism for you to version control your themes.

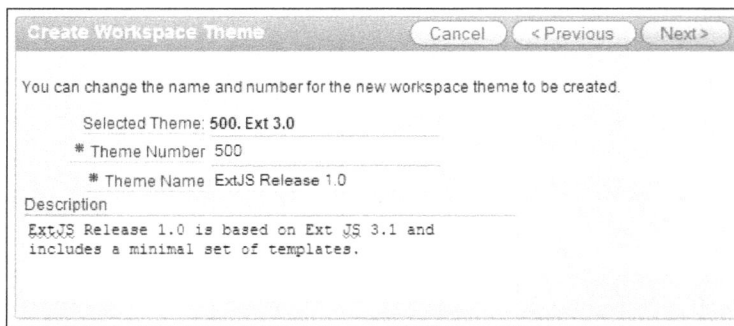

A published theme can't be edited directly once it has been created, but using a TEMPLATE application, you can republish it using a different theme number. Applications can have multiple themes, but only one active theme. By switching themes, applications can easily test a new version, safe in the knowledge that changing back to the earlier version is just a matter of switching back to the prior theme.

So before we go any further, create a new TEMPLATE application based on Theme 4, and let's begin the process of creating our Ext JS theme.

Building a Viewport Page template

Several of the examples provided with Ext feature the Viewport utility container, including the RSS Feed Viewer shown in the screenshot below. The Viewport automatically renders to the document body, sizing itself to the browser viewport and dividing the page into up to five distinct regions; the center region is mandatory, with north, south, east, and west regions being optional.

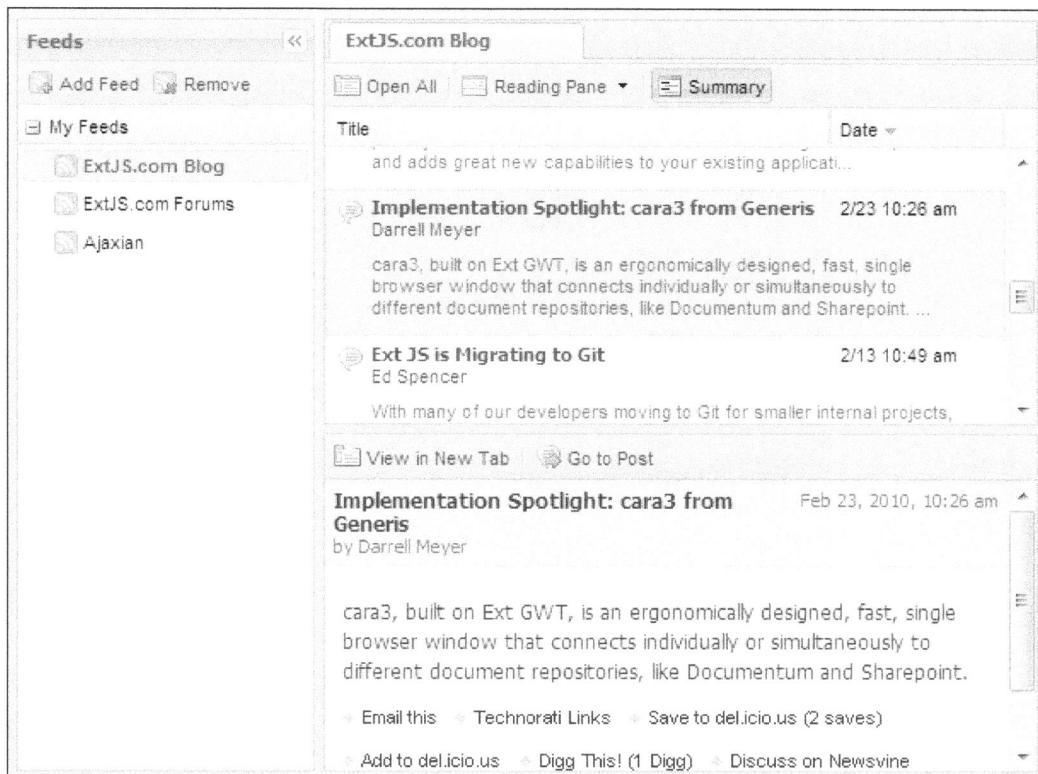

Viewport regions are configurable, and by setting a few simple attributes, you quickly find yourself with a very interactive page, with expanding/collapsing regions and splitters to resize regions by clicking and dragging with the mouse.

We are going to build a basic viewport for our APEX page template including all five regions.

Starting with a standalone template

Once again we're going to take a prototyping approach to building an APEX page template. It's easier to build a standalone HTML page and make sure we've got the JavaScript right, and then load it into APEX.

```html
<html>
  <head>
    <title>#TITLE#</title>
    <link rel="icon" href="#IMAGE_PREFIX#favicon.ico"
        type="image/x-icon">
    <link rel="shortcut icon"
        href="#IMAGE_PREFIX#favicon.ico"
        type="image/x-icon">

    <!-- css includes -->
    <link rel="stylesheet" type="text/css"
        href="../../extjs/resources/css/ext-all.css">
    <link rel="stylesheet" type="text/css"
        href="ex3-1-local-viewport.css">

    <!-- js includes -->
    <script type="text/javascript"
        src="../../extjs/adapter/ext/ext-base.js">
    </script>
    <script type="text/javascript"
        src="../../extjs/ext-all.js">
    </script>
    <script type="text/javascript"
        src="ex3-1-local-viewport.js">
    </script>
  </head>
  <body>
    <div id="app-north-panel">
      <div id="app-logo"><a href="&HOME_LINK.">#LOGO#</a>
      </div>
      <div id="app-navigation-bar">
```

```
            #NAVIGATION_BAR# #CUSTOMIZE# &APP_USER.
        </div>
        #REGION_POSITION_01#
    </div>
    <div id="app-west-panel">#REGION_POSITION_02#</div>
    <div id="app-center-panel">
        #FORM_OPEN#
            <div id="app-messages"> #GLOBAL_NOTIFICATION##SUCCESS_
MESSAGE##NOTIFICATION_MESSAGE#
            </div>
            <div id="app-content">#BOX_BODY#</div>
        #FORM_CLOSE#
    </div>
    <div id="app-east-panel">#REGION_POSITION_03#</div>
    <div id="app-south-panel">footer contents go here</div>
    </body>
</html>
```

The code shows the content of the standalone HTML page located in chapter03/
ex3-1-local-viewport.html, which contains a mixture of HTML elements and
APEX substitution tags (key words are enclosed by # characters).

Looking at the header section enclosed by HEAD tags, you can see the standard Ext
components: stylesheet ext-all.css, adapter layer ext-base.js, and library ext-
all.js are present. Also included are our application CSS and JavaScript files: ex3-
1-local-viewport.css and ex3-1-local-viewport.js.

The body section, enclosed by BODY markup tags, contains a series of DIV tags
with region IDs, for example, app-north-panel, which will become panels in our
viewport. APEX uses #FORM_OPEN# and #FORM_CLOSE# substitution tags to define the
HTML form element wwvFlowForm used for all APEX pages.

In this template, region tags #REGION_POSITION_01#, #REGION_POSITION_02#,
and #REGION_POSITION_03# are outside of the #FORM_OPEN# and #FORM_CLOSE#
substitution tags, so they cannot be used for APEX input items, which we will cover
in more depth shortly in the *Issue when input items are outside the form* section.

The accompanying JavaScript located in ex3-1-local-viewport.js is:

```
Ext.onReady(function(){
    Ext.BLANK_IMAGE_URL = '../../extjs/resources/images/default/s.
gif';

    new Ext.Viewport({
        layout: 'border',
        defaults: {
```

```
                  animCollapse: false,
                  autoScroll: true
              },
              items: [{
                  applyTo: 'app-north-panel',
                  autoHeight: true,
                  autoScroll: false,
                  region: 'north',
                  style: {padding: '0 5px'},
                  xtype: 'box'
              }, {
                  contentEl: 'app-south-panel',
                  height: 30,
                  region: 'south',
                  style: {padding: '0 5px'},
                  xtype: 'box'
              }, {
                  contentEl: 'app-west-panel',
                  //collapseMode: 'mini',
                  collapsible: true,
                  margins: '0 0 0 5',
                  maxSize: 500,
                  minSize: 100,
                  region: 'west',
                  split: true,
                  title: 'Navigation',
                  width: 275
              }, {
                  contentEl: 'app-center-panel',
                  region: 'center',
                  title: document.title,
                  xtype: 'panel'
              }, {
                  contentEl: 'app-east-panel',
                  collapseMode: 'mini',
                  collapsible: true,
                  margins: '0 5 0 0',
                  maxSize: 500,
                  minSize: 100,
                  region: 'east',
                  split: true,
                  title: 'Actions',
                  width: 275
              }]
          });
      });
```

The JavaScript could be summarized as follows:

```
Ext.onReady(function(){
    Ext.BLANK_IMAGE_URL = '../../extjs/resources/images/default/s.
gif';

    new Ext.Viewport({ configuration });
});
```

Looking at the summarized version, we are passing an anonymous function to `Ext.onReady`, which executes the function after waiting for **only** the document structure to be fully parsed and the HTML converted into a DOM tree. This performs better than the traditional `window.onload` handler, which waits for the entire page to be fully loaded before executing.

The anonymous function contains two statements; the first assigns the location image of the 1x1 pixel transparent spacer image using the following code:

```
Ext.BLANK_IMAGE_URL = '../../extjs/resources/images/default/s.gif';
```

The second statement instantiates a new `Ext.Viewport` object passing its configuration settings as a config object:

```
new Ext.Viewport({ ..configuration.. });
```

`Ext.Viewport` is a specialized container that renders to the document body, automatically resizing when the browser window is resized. Viewports contain up to five pre-defined regions (or panels) defined in the items object, with the center region being mandatory. Each of these panels is separately configured, and can inherit default configurations from the viewport.

```
new Ext.Viewport({
    layout: 'border',
    defaults: {
        animCollapse: false,
        autoScroll: true
    },
    items: [{
        applyTo: 'app-north-panel',
        autoHeight: true,
        autoScroll: false,
        region: 'north',
        style: {padding: '0 5px'},
        xtype: 'box'
    }, {
```

```
            contentEl: 'app-south-panel',
            autoScroll: false,
            height: 30,
            region: 'south',
            style: {padding: '0 5px'},
            xtype: 'box'
        },
```

Looking at the first part of the Viewport configuration, you can see that defaults are set for `animCollapse` to switch off animation for collapsing regions, and `autoScroll` set to `true`, enabling scrollbars to appear in regions. These defaults are applied to all of the regions defined within `items`, unless specifically overridden, as shown in the **north region**.

When using north or south regions, you must specify a height; similarly for east and west regions, you must specify a width. For the south region here, I've set the height property in pixels, and for the north region I've used set `autoHeight: true` to show an alternative method.

Notice that the north region is using `applyTo: 'app-north-panel'`, whereas the south region is using `contentEl: 'app-south-panel'`. The attributes produce a subtly different outcome when rendered; one takes an existing HTML element and places it into the layout of the viewport, where the other uses the existing DOM element as part of the layout. Can you work out which attribute does what? Consult the Ext documentation and inspect the HTML using Firebug and verify.

> In this example, the difference between using `applyTo` and `contentEl` doesn't adversely impact the behavior, but it's a little reminder to take a little extra time to understand what's happening.

In the **west** region is a commented-out line `//collapseMode: 'mini'`. Try collapsing and expanding the panel before comparing the behavior to the **east** region. When in `mini` mode the regions split bar displays a small collapse button appears in the center of the bar, and the region collapses to a thinner bar than in normal mode. Which collapseMode do you prefer?

Finally, the CSS file `ex3-1-local-viewport.css` contains the following CSS:

```
#app-navigation-bar {
    color:grey;
    position:absolute;
    right:5px;
}
```

There is almost nothing in our CSS file; just one rule to right align the app-navigation-bar DIV element in our template. With so little content in our CSS file, it's hardly worth having a separate file; we could instead just include it within the page.

Remember here that we're taking the first step in building our application CSS, and we are going to be adding more rules as we go. So let's start a good habit and include the CSS that is going to be used by every page request using the template in a separate file, taking advantage of static file caching by the browser and reducing the size of our dynamically generated page.

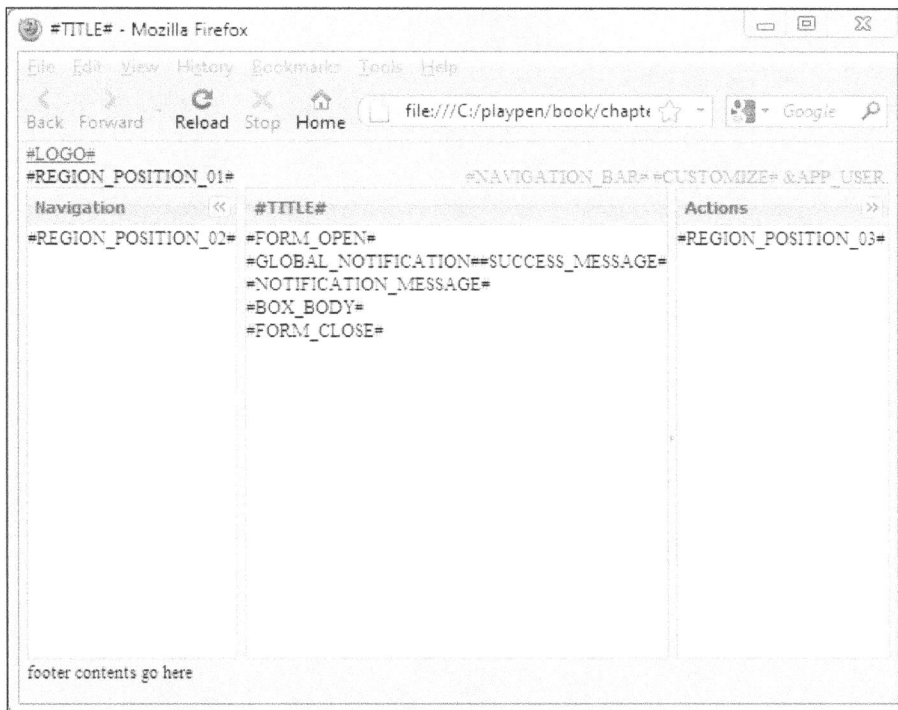

This screenshot shows what our prototype looks like in the browser window.

The north region on the left-hand side contains APEX substitution tags #LOGO# for the application logo, and #REGION_POSITION_01# for breadcrumbs. The right-hand side contains substitution tags for #NAVIGATION_BAR#, #CUSTOMIZE#, and &APP_USER.

The west region is titled **Navigation,** and contains the #REGION_POSITION_02# substitution tag. As the name suggests, you would include links in this panel to navigate your application. Similarly, the east region contains the #REGION_POSITION_03# substitution tag, and could be used for actions specific to the page.

The center region's title is dynamically assigned in our viewport definition to use JavaScript document.title property, which in our page is the #TITLE# substitution tag. The center region body contains the #FORM_OPEN# and #FORM_CLOSE# tags that enclose the notification and message substitution tags #GLOBAL_NOTIFICATION#, #SUCCESS_MESSAGE#, #NOTIFICATION_MESSAGE#, along with the #BOX_BODY# substitution tag for our page content.

The south region here contains some plain text, and would typically be used for page referencing and copyright information.

Loading the page template into APEX

So all that remains is to transfer the prototype into APEX as a page template, and then make a couple of minor adjustments.

Currently the path to our included JavaScript and CSS files is:

```
<!-- css includes -->
<link rel="stylesheet" type="text/css"
    href="../../extjs/resources/css/ext-all.css">
<link rel="stylesheet" type="text/css"
    href="ex3-1-local-viewport.css">

<!-- js includes -->
<script type="text/javascript"
    src="../../extjs/adapter/ext/ext-base.js">
</script>
<script type="text/javascript"
    src="../../extjs/ext-all.js">
</script>
<script type="text/javascript"
    src="ex3-1-local-viewport.js">
</script>
```

You will need to modify the path for the src attributes to suit the location of the files on your web server.

> If you are using a hosted APEX environment, such as apex. oracle.com, you can reference Ext JS files using the CacheFly content delivery network, described in *Chapter 1, Setting up an Oracle APEX and Ext JS Environment*. For example, for ext-all.js, use http://extjs.cachefly.net/ext-3.3.1/ext-all.js.

The #HEAD# substitution tag needs to be added in the HTML header to include the standard APEX JavaScript in the page template. APEX will automatically add JavaScript and CSS includes replacing the substitution tag. It is best to add the tag **before** our JavaScript and CSS files, as it allows our custom code to override both CSS rules and JavaScript functions when needed.

For this book the Ext library is stored on the web server under /ux/extjs/, and application assets under /ux/playpen/, so the path looks like:

```
#HEAD#

<!-- css includes -->
<link rel="stylesheet" type="text/css"
    href="/ux/extjs/resources/css/ext-all.css">
<link rel="stylesheet" type="text/css"
    href="/ux/playpen/ex3-1-local-viewport.css">

<!-- js includes -->
<script type="text/javascript"
    src="/ux/extjs/adapter/ext/ext-base.js">
</script>
<script type="text/javascript"
    src="/ux/extjs/ext-all.js">
</script>
<script type="text/javascript"
    src="/ux/playpen/ex3-1-local-viewport.js">
</script>
```

The other change you will need to make is to change the ex3-1-local-viewport. js file modifying the location of the 1x1 pixel transparent spacer image to: Ext Ext. BLANK_IMAGE_URL = '/i/1px_trans.gif';.

Here, we are referencing a blank image that is part of the standard APEX install.

Now, open one of the existing page templates. This example uses the No Tabs with Sidebar template. Replace content of the header, body, and footer regions with the updated content from the prototype, as shown in the following screenshot:

```
Definition

# Header
<html>
<head>
    <title>#TITLE#</title>
    <link rel="icon" href="/ux/playpen/resources/favicon.ico"
        type="image/x-icon">
    <link rel="shortcut icon" href="/ux/playpen/resources/favicon.ico"
        type="image/x-icon">
    #HEAD#

    <!-- css includes -->
    <link rel="stylesheet" type="text/css"
        href="/ux/extjs/resources/css/ext-all.css">
    <link rel="stylesheet" type="text/css"
        href="/ux/playpen/ex3-1-local-viewport.css">

    <!-- js includes -->
    <script type="text/javascript" src="/ux/extjs/adapter/ext/ext-base.js">
    </script>
    <script type="text/javascript" src="/ux/extjs/ext-all.js"></script>

    <script type="text/javascript" src="/ux/playpen/ex3-1-local-viewport.js">
</script>
</head>
<body>

# Body
    <div id="app-north-panel">
        <div id="app-logo"><a href="&HOME_LINK.">#LOGO#</a></div>
        <div id="app-navigation-bar">
            #NAVIGATION_BAR# #CUSTOMIZE# &APP_USER.
        </div>
        #REGION_POSITION_01#
    </div>
    <div id="app-west-panel">#REGION_POSITION_02#</div>
    <div id="app-center-panel">
        #FORM_OPEN#
            <div id="app-messages">
                #GLOBAL_NOTIFICATION##SUCCESS_MESSAGE##NOTIFICATION_MESSAGE#
            </div>
            <div id="app-content">#BOX_BODY#</div>
        #FORM_CLOSE#
    </div>
    <div id="app-east-panel">#REGION_POSITION_03#</div>
    <div id="app-south-panel">footer contents go here</div>

Footer
</body>
</html>
```

Rename the template to **EXTJS No Tabs with Sidebar**, so it's easy to recognize the updated template and apply the changes.

Finally, copy the ex3-1-local-viewport.js and ex3-1-local-viewport.js files onto your web server in the location referenced in the page template.

Create a blank page using the newly created template, and run the page. It should look the next screenshot:

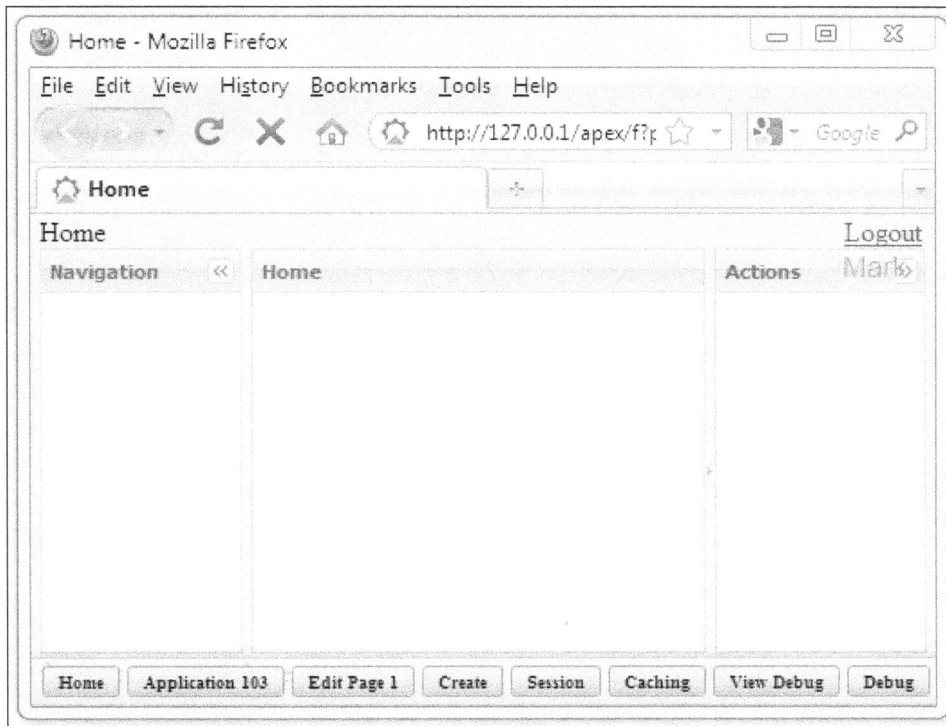

Looking at the North panel, we haven't specified a logo in the **Application** properties so the #LOGO# substitution tag has been replaced with an empty value. The layout issues on the right-hand side with the navigation bar and user name are caused by additional HTML included in the Subtemplate section of the page template. The appearance of the links in the header needs further refinement, which we will do a little later under breadcrumb templates. So, although we have made a good start on the page template, there is still more to do.

To fix the navigation bar on the right-hand side so that the user name is on the same line, update the page template, changing the **Subtemplate** as follows.

Navigation Bar - remove the div tag	
Before	`<div class="t4NavigationBar">#BAR_BODY#</div>`
After	`#BAR_BODY#`

Navigation Bar Entry- remove the class attribute	
Before	`<a href="#LINK#" class="t4NavigationBar">#TEXT#</a>`
After	`<a href="#LINK#">#TEXT#</a>`

While we are working on the Subtemplate, we might as well modify the Success Message and the Notification entries also.

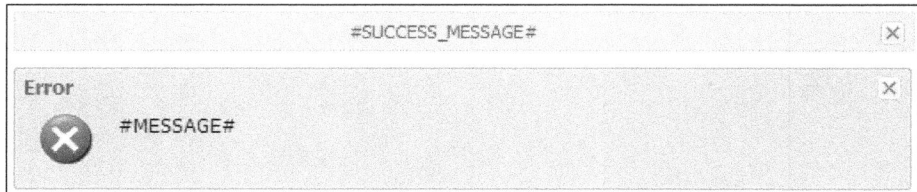

The **Success Message**, shown at the top of the preceding screenshot, uses the following HTML:

```
<div id="app-notification" class="app-success">
  <div class="x-tool x-tool-close"
       onclick="Ext.fly('app-notification').remove();"
       style="display: block; margin-left:5px"> </div>
  <div>#SUCCESS_MESSAGE#</div>
</div>
```

And it requires the following CSS rule to be included in the CSS file:

```
.app-success {
    background:none repeat scroll 0 0 #DFE8F6;
    border:1px dotted #99BBE8;
    color:#15428B;
    cursor:default;
    clear: both;
    font:normal 11px tahoma,arial,sans-serif;
    padding:5px 0;
    text-align:center;
    margin:10px 30%; width:40%;
}
```

Functionally, it is the same as the standard APEX content it replaces; a DIV region displaying a message, with an image that deletes the region when clicked. JavaScript purists may complain about including JavaScript code in the highlighted `onclick` attribute.

The "better" way would be to remove the `onclick` attribute and adding the following code to add a listener in your application JavaScript:

```
Ext.onReady(function(){
    /*… application code before…*/

    if (Ext.fly('app-notification')) {
        Ext.fly('app-notification').on('click', function(){
            this.remove();
        });
    }
});
```

Both ways achieve the desired outcome; it's just a matter of personal preference which way you want to code.

The **Notification** entry in the previous screenshot is a more complicated layout based on the HTML created by Ext.Alert, allowing the reuse of existing Ext CSS rules. It provides similar functionality to the **Success Message**; the HTML source is in `chapter03/ex3-2-local-viewport.html`.

The page template now has all the page definition and also the Subtemplate sections completed. But that's not the end of the page template just yet! There is a nasty issue potentially lurking in the template, where input items can appear outside the FORM element, which needs to be addressed.

Issue when input items are outside the form

As web developers, we are becoming more reliant on using JavaScript to manipulate the page layout to provide functionality such as tab panels, accordion regions, popup dialogs, and the like. This leads to existing elements in the DOM being relocated to new positions, and form INPUT items can end up outside the FORM element.

Irrespective of what JavaScript library you use, DOM manipulation can lead to form INPUT items appearing outside the FORM element. In fact, you don't even need to use JavaScript at all to cause the issue, as we will show in this example.

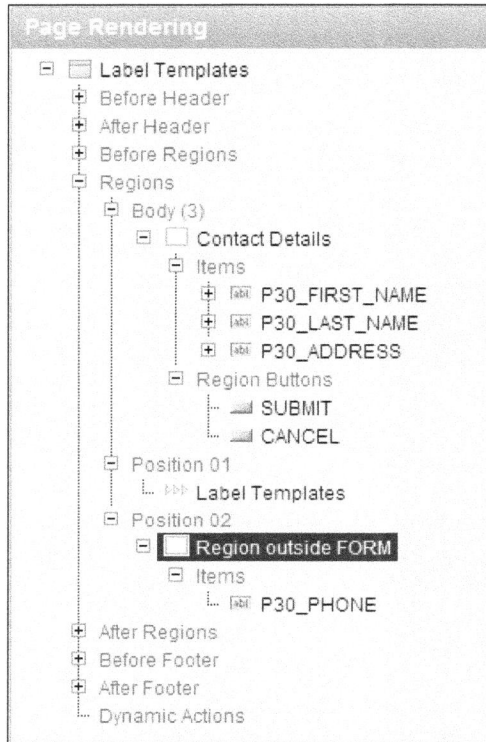

This screenshot shows the Page Definition within APEX Builder for a simple page containing the following items of interest:

- The **Contact Details** region to be rendered in location Body (3) [#BOX_ BODY#], with input items P30_FIRST_NAME, P30_LAST_NAME, and P30_ ADDRESS.

- The **Region outside FORM** region to be rendered in location Position 2 [#REGION_POSITION_02#], containing item P30_PHONE.

If you refer to the earlier page template, it shows the #REGION_POSITION_02# clearly outside the #FORM_OPEN# and #FORM_CLOSE# substitution tags.

When the page is rendered, and after the layout has been changed using JavaScript, a simplified view of the HTML looks like this:

```
<html>
<body>
<input type="text" name="p_t01" value="" id="P30_PHONE"/>

<form action="wwv_flow.accept" method="post" name="wwv_flow"
id="wwvFlowForm">
    <input type="text" name="p_t02" value="" id="P30_FIRST_NAME"/>
    <input type="text" name="p_t03" value="" id="P30_LAST_NAME"/>
    <textarea name="p_t04" id="P30_ADDRESS"></textarea>
</form>
</body>
</html>
```

This shows the highlighted input item, where ID P30_PHONE is clearly outside the FORM tags.

From the HTML code shown, you can see the action for the form is wwv_flow. accept and the item names are p_t01 .. p_t04, corresponding to the database package procedure and parameters being executed by the mod_plsql HTTP request.

When the form is submitted, the values for the inputs are loaded into session state, page processing occurs, and the APEX engine branches to a page. In this example, there is no processing, simply branching to the same page, so the page is rendered again with the passed values.

So, given the P30_PHONE item is not in the form it shouldn't be processed, but what about the items within the form? The following is the result of submitting the form, showing submitted and returned values:

ID	Name	Submitted value	Returned value
P30_PHONE	p_t01	aaa	-
P30_FIRST_NAME	p_t02	bbb	-
P30_LAST_NAME	p_t03	ccc	bbb
P30_ADDRESS	p_t04	ddd	ccc

So as expected, no value is returned for P30_PHONE, because it was outside the form. However, there is an unexpected displacement of the values, shifting them down, so the P30_FIRST_NAME submitted value of bbb is returned in P30_LAST_NAME, and similarly the value for P30_LAST_NAME is returned in P30_ADDRESS. The whereabouts of the value for P30_ADDRESS is unknown and is not easily explained.

Without having access to the source code for the APEX engine, it is only possible to speculate on why this occurs. Nevertheless, we still need to deal with the issue and come up with a strategy to prevent it from occurring.

Ensuring that input items always remain with the form

To ensure form items always remain within the `FORM` element, we need to address both the static HTML issue and potential JavaScript DOM manipulation.

Modify the page template so that all region substitution tags are contained within the `#FORM_OPEN#` and `#FORM_CLOSE#` substitution tags, as shown in the following screenshot:

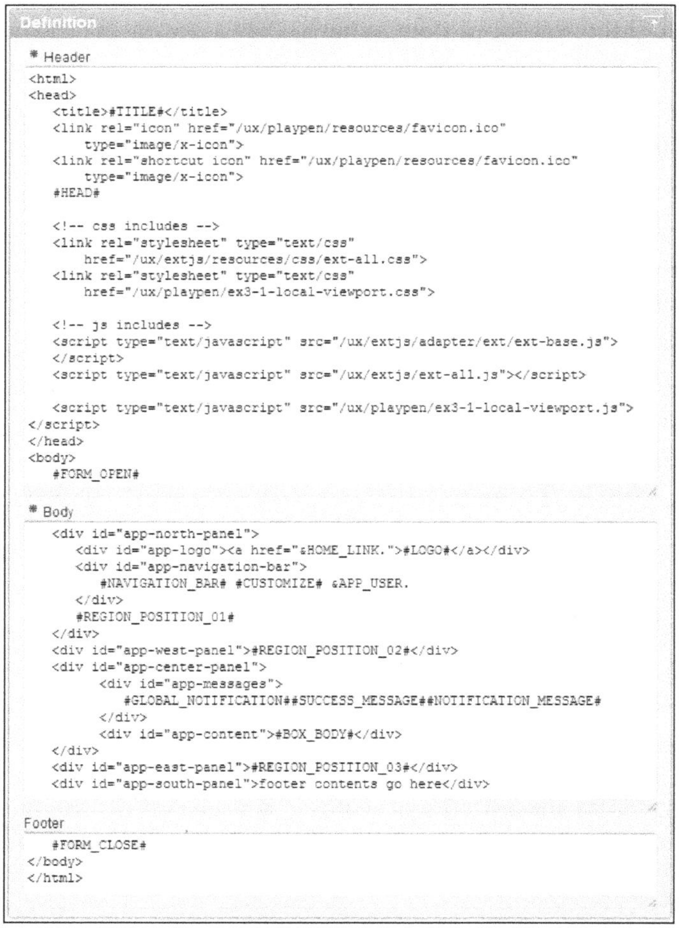

Definition

* Header

```
<html>
<head>
   <title>#TITLE#</title>
   <link rel="icon" href="/ux/playpen/resources/favicon.ico"
       type="image/x-icon">
   <link rel="shortcut icon" href="/ux/playpen/resources/favicon.ico"
       type="image/x-icon">
   #HEAD#

   <!-- css includes -->
   <link rel="stylesheet" type="text/css"
       href="/ux/extjs/resources/css/ext-all.css">
   <link rel="stylesheet" type="text/css"
       href="/ux/playpen/ex3-1-local-viewport.css">

   <!-- js includes -->
   <script type="text/javascript" src="/ux/extjs/adapter/ext/ext-base.js">
   </script>
   <script type="text/javascript" src="/ux/extjs/ext-all.js"></script>

   <script type="text/javascript" src="/ux/playpen/ex3-1-local-viewport.js">
</script>
</head>
<body>
   #FORM_OPEN#
```

* Body

```
   <div id="app-north-panel">
      <div id="app-logo"><a href="&HOME_LINK.">#LOGO#</a></div>
      <div id="app-navigation-bar">
         #NAVIGATION_BAR# #CUSTOMIZE# &APP_USER.
      </div>
      #REGION_POSITION_01#
   </div>
   <div id="app-west-panel">#REGION_POSITION_02#</div>
   <div id="app-center-panel">
         <div id="app-messages">
            #GLOBAL_NOTIFICATION##SUCCESS_MESSAGE##NOTIFICATION_MESSAGE#
         </div>
         <div id="app-content">#BOX_BODY#</div>
   </div>
   <div id="app-east-panel">#REGION_POSITION_03#</div>
   <div id="app-south-panel">footer contents go here</div>
```

Footer

```
   #FORM_CLOSE#
</body>
</html>
```

The previous screenshot shows the updated Viewport template, addressing the static HTML side of the issue. The #FORM_OPEN# tag now appears immediately after the `<body>` markup, and the #FORM_CLOSE# tag immediately before the `</body>` markup.

The only other change is that the application JavaScript file is now `ex3-1-custom-viewport.js`, which addresses the JavaScript DOM manipulation.

To ensure form items always remain within the form element, we can use a customized version of **Ext.Viewport**, which uses the APEX form element `wwvFlowForm` as the container for the viewport, instead of the body element.

```
// create custom namespace if doesn't exist
Ext.ns('Ext.apex');

// custom container
Ext.apex.Viewport = Ext.extend(Ext.Container, {
  initComponent : function() {
    Ext.apex.Viewport.superclass.initComponent.call(this);

    // APEX specific code
    this.el = Ext.get('wwvFlowForm');
    if(this.el){
      this.el.addClass('x-viewport');
      var debug = Ext.getDom('pdebug');
      if (!(debug && (debug.value == 'YES'))) {
        document.getElementsByTagName('html')[0].className += '
x-viewport';
      }
    } else {
      this.el = Ext.getBody();
      document.getElementsByTagName('html')[0].className   += '
x-viewport';
    }

    this.el.setHeight = Ext.emptyFn;
    this.el.setWidth = Ext.emptyFn;
    this.el.setSize = Ext.emptyFn;
    this.el.dom.scroll = 'no';
    this.allowDomMove = false;
    this.autoWidth = true;
    this.autoHeight = true;
    Ext.EventManager.onWindowResize(this.fireResize, this);
    this.renderTo = this.el;
  },
```

```
    fireResize : function(w, h){
      this.fireEvent('resize', this, w, h, w, h);
    }
});

    // Register container so that lazy instantiation may be used
    Ext.reg('apex-viewport', Ext.apex.Viewport);
```

The script starts by creating a custom namespace, `Ext.apex`, to ensure that we don't pollute the global namespace. The `Ext.apex.Viewport` is then defined, which is a direct copy of the `Ext.Viewport`, excepting the highlighted APEX specific code.

For APEX, the code checks to see if the APEX form element with the `wwvFlowForm` ID is present in the page, and if yes, whether it uses this as containing item for the Viewport. When `wwvFlowForm` is not present, it reverts to standard Ext.Viewport functionality, using the document body instead. This is useful when previewing the page template, or selecting the location for a region in the APEX Builder.

Finally, the container is registered so that lazy instantiation can be used using the xtype attribute value of `apex-viewport`. See the panel definitions in the application code for examples of xtypes box and panel.

A check is also done to see if APEX is in debug mode, and if yes, it ensures the HTML page allows scrolling, otherwise scrolling is disabled for the page and scrolling is managed within the viewport using Ext features.

To use the custom viewport, we simply replace calls to `Ext.Viewport` with `Ext.apex.Viewport` like this:

```
Ext.onReady(function(){
    Ext.BLANK_IMAGE_URL = '../../extjs/resources/images/default/s.
gif';

    new Ext.apex.Viewport({ configuration });
});
```

The custom viewport needs to appear before the application code in the JavaScript file. The application code has also been modified to show the east panel only when its container app-east-panel has child nodes other than text.

```
Ext.onReady(function(){
    var items = [];

    Ext.BLANK_IMAGE_URL = '/i/1px_trans.gif';

    items.push({
```

```
        applyTo: 'app-north-panel',
        autoHeight: true,
        autoScroll: false,
        region: 'north',
        style: {padding: '0 5px'},
        xtype: 'box'
    }, {
        contentEl: 'app-south-panel',
        autoScroll: false,
        height: 30,
        region: 'south',
        style: {padding: '0 5px'},
        xtype: 'box'
    }, {
        contentEl: 'app-west-panel',
        //collapseMode: 'mini',
        collapsible: true,
        margins: '0 0 0 5',
        maxSize: 500,
        minSize: 100,
        region: 'west',
        split: true,
        title: 'Navigation',
        width: 275
    }, {
        contentEl: 'app-center-panel',
        region: 'center',
        title: document.title,
        xtype: 'panel'
    });

// conditionally add east panel if it contains child nodes
if (Ext.fly('app-east-panel') &&
    Ext.fly('app-east-panel').first()) {
    items.push({
        contentEl: 'app-east-panel',
        collapseMode: 'mini',
        collapsible: true,
        margins: '0 5 0 0',
        maxSize: 500,
        minSize: 100,
        region: 'east',
        split: true,
        title: 'Actions',
```

```
            width: 275
        });
    }

    new Ext.apex.Viewport({
        layout: 'border',
        defaults: {
            animCollapse: false,
            autoScroll: true
        },
        items: items
    });
});
```

The page template is now complete and the issue of input items appearing outside the form element has been resolved.

Summary

We have seen how APEX page processing fits a typical Model-View-Controller (MVC) pattern, where the **view** is the HTML generated using the application templates. The APEX engine is the **controller** and receives the GET or POST input and decides what to do with it, handing it over to domain objects. The domain objects **model** is encapsulated in the page definition and contains the business rules and functionality to carry out specific tasks.

This separation of concerns provided by the MVC pattern allows APEX to easily swap themes for an application. The publishing mechanism allows new versions of a theme to be built separately from the application. By switching themes, applications can easily test a new version, safe in the knowledge that we can revert to the earlier version if required.

We then set about creating a page template, using a standalone prototype initially to make sure the markup and JavaScript works correctly before loading it into APEX. Once a few adjustments were made to load it, the page template was up and running in APEX. This revealed some layout issues with the navigation sub-template (which was corrected), as along with the success and error notifications.

Finally, the issue of JavaScript DOM manipulation potentially causing input items appearing outside the form element was demonstrated. A custom version of Ext. Viewport was developed to ensure that this would never happen in our page template.

While we won't be going through any more page templates here, it is very worthwhile to put some time into the "Login" template before you preview your application to anyone. After all, first impressions count, and the first page people will see is the Login page.

In the next chapter we turn our attention to other APEX template types used within the page template for regions, labels, and lists.

4
Ext Themed Regions, Labels, and Lists

This chapter continues building a theme based on Ext into APEX, developing templates for the regions, labels, and lists.

Regions act as the basic building block for content within a page. Each page can hold an unlimited number of regions. The appearance of regions is controlled using Region templates, which can use a mixture of HTML markup, CSS, and JavaScript to control the visual and structural layout.

HTML lists are enormously versatile when combined with CSS layouts, due to their graphically flexible nature. In this chapter we will develop list templates, which use traditional CSS styling, as well as using list templates to act as a JavaScript generator to integrate with the Ext JS TreePanel component.

In this chapter we will cover:

- Creating region templates using Ext JS panels
- Adding JavaScript functionality to region templates
- Creating simple label templates
- Using Ext JS QuickTips for error messages
- Styling simple list templates relying on just HTML and CSS
- Using list templates to integrate the Ext JS TreePanel component

Region templates

The APEX Theme 4 we are using as our "starter" theme contains 22 region templates, one for each of the region template classes. Using this many template classes in an application can only lead to confusion and inconsistencies. Oracle has provided so many alternatives to give you a wide range of templates from which to pick and choose when designing your application layout, but don't expect that you would use them all.

Well-designed APEX applications will typically rationalize this down to a small number of region templates used for the everyday functionality covering most of the application, and then perhaps add a few "specialized" region templates.

Region templates must contain a #BODY# token; all other allowable tokens are optional. Tokens for the title #TITLE#, #REGION_ID# or #REGION_STATIC_ID#, and #REGION_ATTRIBUTES# are commonly included.

Button position names, such as #EDIT#, #CLOSE#, #CREATE#, #CREATE2#, #EXPAND#, #HELP#, #DELETE#, #COPY#, #NEXT#, and #PREVIOUS# are also commonly included. Similar to reducing the number of template types, it's a good idea to rationalize the number of button position names to just a few. Because buttons can be assigned to any button position name, the ordering of buttons can be mostly managed through sequencing of buttons within the page region.

Report Region

The Ext Basic Panel works well here for the Report Region template, which is typically used for "classic" reports.

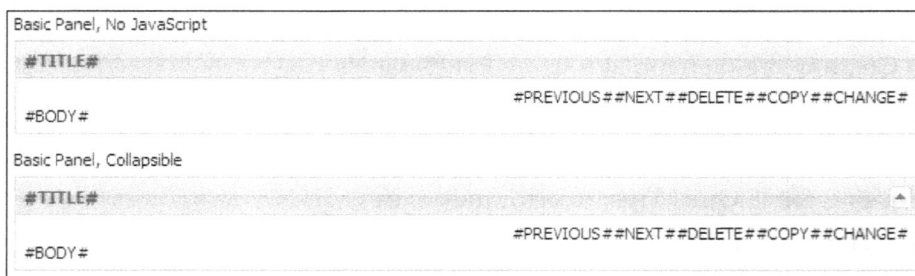

To construct the "Basic Panel, No JavaScript" template shown in the previous screenshot, the following HTML has been used:

```
<div id="#REGION_STATIC_ID#" class="x-panel ux-panel">
    <div class="x-panel-header">
        <span class="x-panel-header-text">#TITLE#</span>
```

```
        </div>
        <div class="x-panel-bwrap">
            <div class="x-panel-body">
                <div class="x-panel-tbar" align="right">
                    #PREVIOUS##NEXT##DELETE##COPY##CHANGE#
                </div>
                <p>#BODY#</p>
            </div>
        </div>
    </div>
```

If you refer the Ext documentation for **Ext.Panel - frame** config option, available at http://dev.sencha.com/deploy/dev/docs/?class=Ext.Panel, you will see the same HTML is generated for a dynamically constructed panel. We are including the panel-specific structural markup to reproduce the visual appearance of the Ext. Panel component.

Two minor additions to the Ext markup have been included, both shown in bold.

Adding the ux-panel CSS class to the outer DIV allows customization of the DIV and its child components without affecting other objects using the Ext CSS classes. For example, the following CSS adds a margin at the bottom of the Panel to create a vertical spacing between panels. Also added is some padding to the body of the panel, so contained elements are not hard up against the border.

```
.ux-panel {margin-bottom: 10;}
.ux-panel .x-panel-body {padding: 5px}
```

The other change included is the align="right" attribute to the x-panel-tbar DIV, used to right align button elements.

To make the Report Region template collapsible, simply add the following JavaScript immediately after the HTML in the template body:

```
<script type="text/javascript">
Ext.onReady(function(){
    new Ext.Panel({
        allowDomMove : false,
        applyTo: '#REGION_STATIC_ID#',
        animCollapse: false,
        autoHeight: true,
        collapsible:true,
        titleCollapse: true
    });
});
</script>
```

Setting config option `applyTo` with the `#REGION_STATIC_ID#` tag will render the Panel to the corresponding DOM node. When `applyTo` is used, the `Ext.Panel` code checks the DOM node for constituent parts of the panel specified by CSS class names within the main element. The panel will automatically create those components from that markup. Any required components not specified in the markup will be auto-generated if necessary.

The following class names are supported (baseCls defaults to x-panel):

- `baseCls + '-header'`
- `baseCls + '-header-text'`
- `baseCls + '-bwrap'`
- `baseCls + '-tbar'`
- `baseCls + '-body'`
- `baseCls + '-bbar'`
- `baseCls + '-footer'`

The other config options make the panel collapsible, adding a collapse icon in the top right of the header bar. When the icon is clicked, the panel body collapses to be completely hidden. The icon inverts, and clicking on it again restores the panel body. Setting the `titleCollapse` option to `true` allows you to click anywhere in the title to collapse the panel body.

Form Region

In case of Form Regions, it is useful to distinguish them visually from non-editable regions. Once again we will use the Ext Basic Panel, this time using the "framed" look.

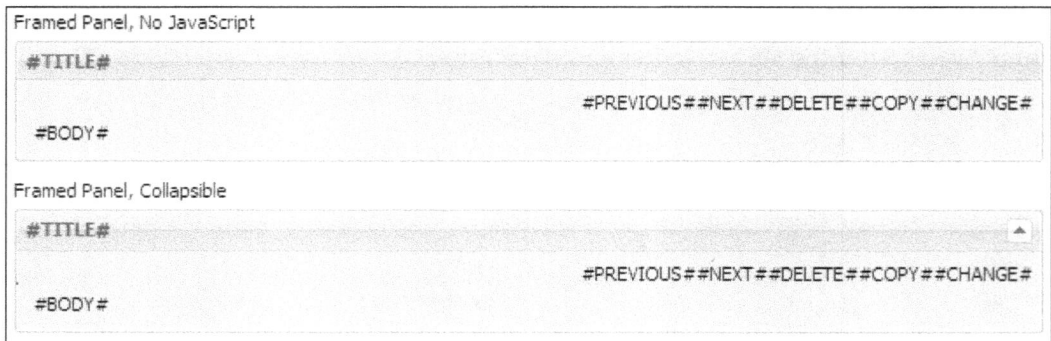

The following is the HTML code for the **Framed Panel, No JavaScript,** shown in the previous screenshot:

```
<div id="#REGION_STATIC_ID#" class="x-panel ux-panel">
  <div class="x-panel-tl">
    <div class="x-panel-tr">
      <div class="x-panel-tc">
        <div class="x-panel-header">
          <span class="x-panel-header-text">#TITLE#</span>
        </div>
      </div>
    </div>
  </div>

  <div class="x-panel-bwrap">
    <div class="x-panel-ml">
      <div class="x-panel-mr">
        <div class="x-panel-mc">
          <div class="x-panel-tbar" align="right">
            #PREVIOUS##NEXT##DELETE##COPY##CHANGE#
          </div>
          <div class="x-panel-body">
            <p>#BODY#</p>
          </div>
        </div>
      </div>
    </div>

    <div class="x-panel-bl x-panel-nofooter">
      <div class="x-panel-br">
        <div class="x-panel-bc"></div>
      </div>
    </div>
  </div>
</div>
```

Like the Basic Panel used for the Reports Region template, it contains the same basic "structural" DIV elements, with the addition of a series of DIVs to provide the rounded corners. The CSS rules applied to the panel body are different, providing the blue background color, and more significant visual difference, we are after.

The HTML code for the **Framed Panel, Collapsible** region is much simpler. It is quite similar to that used for the Basic Panel in the Reports Region template.

```
<div id="#REGION_STATIC_ID#" class="x-panel ux-panel">
    <div class="x-panel-header">
        <span class="x-panel-header-text">#TITLE#</span>
    </div>
    <div class="x-panel-tbar" align="right">
        #PREVIOUS##NEXT##DELETE##COPY##CHANGE#
    </div>
    <div  class="x-panel-body"><p>#BODY#</p></div>
</div>
```

The differences being the `x-panel-bwrap` DIV is not present, and the `x-panel-tbar` DIV is a sibling instead of a child node of the `x-panel-body` DIV.

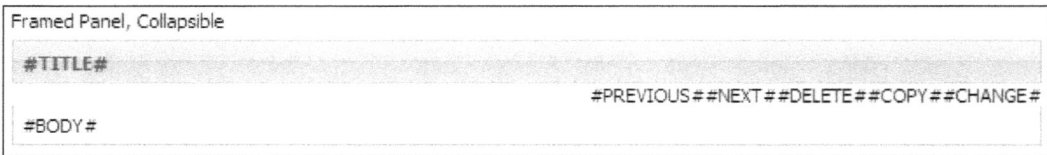

The previous screenshot shows the HTML without the JavaScript to convert it into a Framed Panel. It looks like an imperfect version of the Basic Panel. The reason behind this much simpler HTML gets back to the **applyTo** config option for Ext.Panel, which is looking for the "structural" class names to convert within the main element. If we kept the Framed Panel, No JavaScript version, the Ext.Panel JavaScript does not check for the "visual classes", so they are ignored leading to a questionable result.

The JavaScript to create the Framed Panel is once again almost identical, the only difference being the `frame: true` config option:

```
<script type="text/javascript">
Ext.onReady(function(){
    new Ext.Panel({
        applyTo: '#REGION_STATIC_ID#',
        animCollapse: false,
        autoHeight: true,
        collapsible:true,
        frame: true,
        titleCollapse: true
    });
});
</script>
```

Additional region templates

Undoubtedly you will need more region templates than we have created here. As we progress through the chapters, we will be adding more specialized templates as we go, and revisiting the ones we have created.

For the Form Region and Report Region templates, and some additional variations of both, which include a toolbar region, see `chapter04/ex-4-panels.html`.

Label templates

Label templates have only five predefined classes:

- No Label
- Optional Label
- Optional Label with Help
- Required Label
- Required Label with Help

Probably the only real decision required for which classes you need to define templates is whether or not your application is going to use item-level help.

The need to distinguish between optional and mandatory labels visually, as well as the need to easily hide labels, indicates that you will need to define a template for each of these classes.

This screenshot shows the optional and mandatory labels we will be creating, with the mandatory label including a red asterisk to differentiate it visually. The appearance of the labels is similar to that used for Ext labels; however, the HTML markup and CSS used has to be completely customized because APEX uses HTML tables to layout items and labels.

Optional label

The HTML for the optional label is as follows:

Before label:

```
<span id="#CURRENT_ITEM_NAME#-label"
      class="ux-form-item-label">
<label for="#CURRENT_ITEM_NAME#">
```

After label:

```
</label>
</span>
```

On error before label:

```
<div class="ux-status-error" ext:qclass="x-form-invalid-tip"
ext:qtip="#ERROR_MESSAGE#">
```

On error after label:

```
</div>
```

The CSS that is used with the label is:

```
.ux-form-item-label{
    font:normal 11px tahoma,arial,helvetica,sans-serif;
}

.ux-status-error {
    background: transparent no-repeat 3px 2px;
    background-image: url(/ux/extjs/resources/images/default/form/
exclamation.gif);
    color: #CC3333;
    cursor: pointer;
    display: inline;
    line-height:16px;
    padding:2px 2px 2px 25px;
}
```

The HTML used for the label is very basic, simply a label element referencing its item using the #CURRENT_ITEM_NAME# tag, which is then enclosed by a span element. The purpose for wrapping the label with a span element is that it allows more CSS rules to be applied than the label element. For example, you could specify a CSS rule setting a fixed width for the span, but if you tried to do the same for the label element, the rule would simply be ignored.

QuickTips for error messages

Looking at following screenshot, you can see one of the issues faced when displaying inline error messages. The input items have been pushed to the right, the length of the error message forcing the input item to be partially obscured.

So, how can we overcome this problem while still providing meaningful inline error messages?

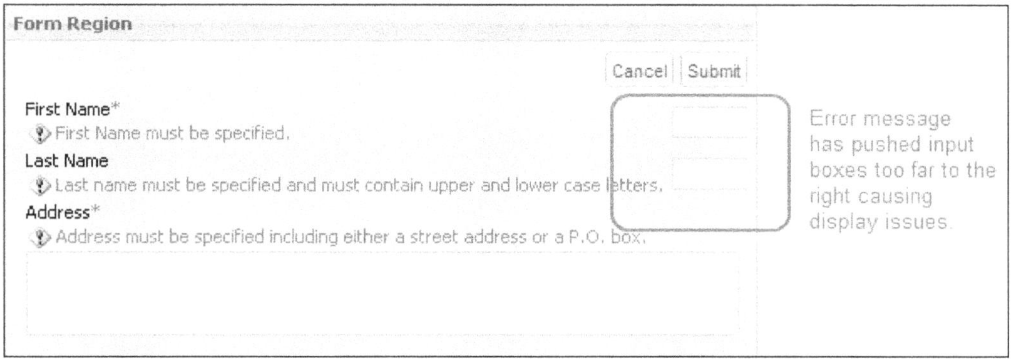

One way is to include a small error image and include the error message in the title and alt attributes, so when the mouse hovers over it the message is revealed as a tooltip. Ext has taken this concept and improved it with **Ext.QuickTips**, as shown in the following screenshot:

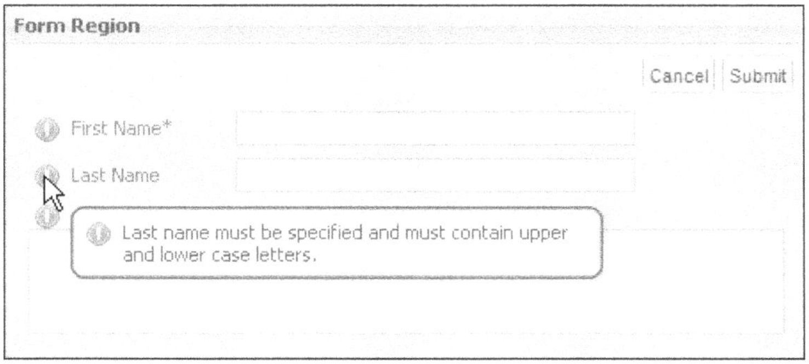

Ext.QuickTips provides attractive and customizable tooltips for any element, and can be configured via tag attributes directly in markup.

Ext documentation summarizes the supported attributes (optional unless otherwise noted).

- `hide`: Specifying "user" is equivalent to setting `autoHide = false`. Any other value will be the same as `autoHide = true`.

- `qclass`: A CSS class to be applied to the quick tip (equivalent to the "cls" target element config).

- `qtip` (required): The quick tip text (equivalent to the "text" target element config).

- `qtitle`: The quick tip title (equivalent to the "title" target element config).

- `qwidth`: The quick tip width (equivalent to the "width" target element config).

You can also configure the QuickTips singleton in addition to the supported attributes.

To enable Ext.QuickTips, you need to include a call to `Ext.QuickTips.init` in your application JavaScript.

```
Ext.onReady(function(){

    // Init the singleton.
    // Any tag-based quick tips will start working.
    Ext.QuickTips.init();

    // Apply a set of config properties to the singleton.
    // Use interceptTitles to pick up title attribute,
    // excepting IE as cannot prevent tooltip appearing also.
    Ext.apply(Ext.QuickTips.getQuickTip(), {
        interceptTitles: (!Ext.isIE),
        maxWidth: 300,
        minWidth: 100,
        showDelay: 50,
        trackMouse: true
    });

    // more code
});
```

For the example provided in the previous screenshot, the markup for the Last Name label with its error message looks like:

```
<div class="ux-status-error" ext:qclass="x-form-invalid-tip"
ext:qtip="Last name must be specified and must contain upper and lower
case letters.">
   <span id="P30_LAST_NAME-label" class="ux-form-item-label">
     <label for="P30_LAST_NAME">Last Name</label>
   </span>
</div>
```

The DIV element has a class attribute of ux-status-error, which displays a background image, padding the element sufficiently to display the image and provide some spacing before the label text.

Specifying the ext:qclass="x-form-invalid-tip" attribute means the QuickTip will use an Ext CSS rule specifically designed for errors, rather than the standard QuickTip styling.

Optional label with help

The HTML is identical to that of the optional label, with an additional link element:

Before label:

```
<span id="#CURRENT_ITEM_NAME#-label"
      class="ux-form-item-label">
<label for="#CURRENT_ITEM_NAME#">
<a href="javascript:popupFieldHelp('#CURRENT_ITEM_ID#', '&SESSION.')">
```

After label:

```
</a>
</label>
</span>
```

On error before label:

```
<div class="ux-status-error" ext:qclass="x-form-invalid-tip"
ext:qtip="#ERROR_MESSAGE#">
```

On Error after label:

```
</div>
```

The CSS that is used with the label is:

```
.ux-form-item-label a {
    color:#1E4176;
    cursor:pointer;
    text-decoration:none;
    -moz-outline: none;
    outline: none;
}

.ux-form-item-label a:hover {
    text-decoration:underline;
}
```

The HTML used here is the same as for the optional label, with the inclusion of a link `<a href="javascript:popupFieldHelp('#CURRENT_ITEM_ID#', '&SESSION.')"></a>`, which calls the APEX JavaScript to display item help in a popup window.

Additional CSS has been included to make the link visually similar, but not the same as the optional label, with a subtle color difference and different cursor to provide visual cues for a different behavior. When the mouse hovers over the label, it is underlined, reinforcing again the cue for a different behavior.

Mandatory label

The HTML for the mandatory label is almost identical to the optional label:

Before label:

```
<span id="#CURRENT_ITEM_NAME#-label"
      class="ux-form-item-label">
<label for="#CURRENT_ITEM_NAME#">
```

After label:

```
<em>*</em>
</label>
</span>
```

On error before label:

```
<div class="ux-status-error" ext:qclass="x-form-invalid-tip"
ext:qtip="#ERROR_MESSAGE#">
```

On error after label:

```
</div>
```

The only difference between the optional and mandatory labels is the addition of the * markup in the After Label section, and the additional CSS rule to make the asterisk red:

```
.ux-form-item-label em {color:#CC3333;}
```

Mandatory label with help

The HTML is identical to that of the mandatory label, with an additional link element used to display field-level, context-sensitive help:

Before label:

```
<span id="#CURRENT_ITEM_NAME#-label"
      class="ux-form-item-label">
<label for="#CURRENT_ITEM_NAME#">
<a href="javascript:popupFieldHelp('#CURRENT_ITEM_ID#', '&SESSION.')">
```

After label:

```
<em>*</em>
</a>
</label>
</span>
```

On error before label:

```
<div class="ux-status-error" ext:qclass="x-form-invalid-tip"
ext:qtip="#ERROR_MESSAGE#">
```

On error after label:

```
</div>
```

No additional CSS is required for the link element, which uses the same CSS rules as the optional label with help.

Hidden label

The HTML for the hidden label is even simpler:

Before label:

```
<span class="x-hidden">
```

After label:

```
</span>
```

On error before label:

```
<div class="ux-status-error" ext:qclass="x-form-invalid-tip"
ext:qtip="#ERROR_MESSAGE#">
```

On error after label:

```
 </div>
```

For this label, we are using a SPAN element with an Ext class named `x-hidden` to hide the label text. The On error label markup remains the same as the optional label, allowing errors to be displayed even when no label is visible. An extra HTML string (` `) has been added to ensure the error icon displays correctly when no text has been provided for the label.

This wraps up the section on Label templates, which really are quite straightforward, just requiring a minimal amount HTML markup and some CSS styling. The addition of `Ext.QuickTips` here neatly solves the problem of error messages ruining region layouts while retaining APEX provided functionality for item-level, context-sensitive help.

List templates

Lists are one of the most versatile HTML elements, providing a way to display content and information in a very easy way to scan and read. APEX contains a great variety of lists already with its built-in themes, as is evident by the template classes for lists:

- Button List
- Hierarchical Expanded
- Hierarchical Expanding
- Horizontal Images with Label List
- Horizontal Links List
- Pull Down Menu
- Pull Down Menu with Image
- Tabbed Navigation List
- Vertical Images List
- Vertical Ordered List

- Vertical Sidebar List
- Vertical Unordered List with Bullets
- Vertical Unordered List without Bullets
- Wizard Progress List

The list templates display data defined in APEX lists, and may be flat or hierarchical in structure. A list is considered to be hierarchical when a parent-child relationship has been defined in the list for one or more entries.

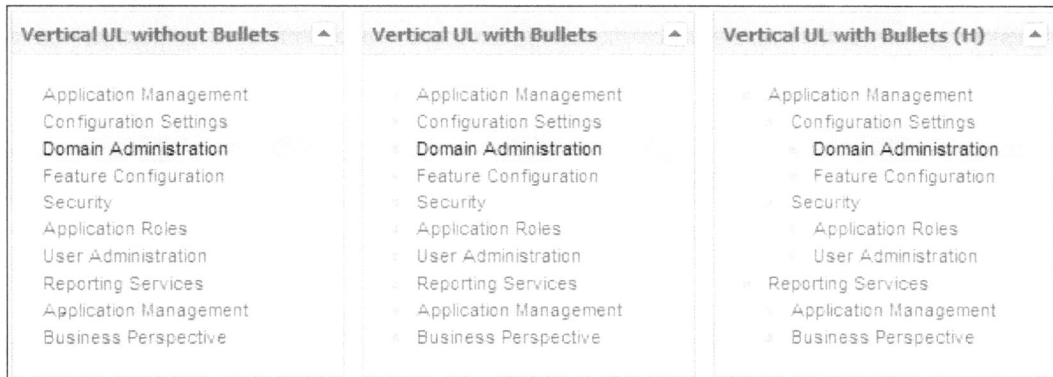

If your lists become overly complicated or lose their simplicity, you will have lost the essence of the list and will lose your visitors' interest as well. To start with, let's create the list templates shown in previous screenshot.

Vertical unordered list without bullets

The list template has a large number of fields available to use; only the ones being populated are shown here.

- Name: EXTJS vertical unordered list without bullets
- Template Class: Vertical unordered list without bullets

List template before rows:

```
<div class="ux-list">
<ul>
```

List template current:

```
<li class="ux-list-selected"><a href="#LINK#">#TEXT#</a></li>
```

List template current with sub list items:

```
<li class="ux-list-selected"><a href="#LINK#">#TEXT#</a></li>
<ul>
```

List template noncurrent:

```
<li><a href="#LINK#">#TEXT#</a></li>
```

List template noncurrent with sub list items:

```
<li><a href="#LINK#">#TEXT#</a></li>
<ul>
```

Sublist template current:

```
<li class="ux-list-selected"><a href="#LINK#">#TEXT#</a></li>
```

Sublist template current with sub list items:

```
<li class="ux-list-selected"><a href="#LINK#">#TEXT#</a></li>
<ul>
```

Sublist template noncurrent:

```
<li><a href="#LINK#">#TEXT#</a></li>
```

Sublist template noncurrent with sub list items:

```
<li><a href="#LINK#">#TEXT#</a></li>
<ul>
```

Sublist template after rows:

```
</ul>
</div>
```

For a flat list, the sublist fields are unnecessary, and removing the sublist markup would make absolutely no difference. However, not having the sublist markup would mean a hierarchical list would only display the top-level list items. For this reason, it's a good practice to define the sublist markup and apply CSS styling to suit.

Ext includes some CSS rules to "reset" unordered lists and list items, removing margins, padding, and list item indicators; so, before we add any CSS rules of our own, both a flat list and a hierarchical list look like **Before CSS styling** list in the following screenshot, which is close to the desired result:

Before CSS styling | After CSS styling

The following CSS will produce the look of the **After CSS styling** list shown earlier in previous screenshot:

```
.ux-list {
  background:#fff;
  padding:10px;
  text-align:left;
  border:0 none transparent;
}

.ux-list li {
    color:#ccc;
    line-height:16px;
    font-family: helvetica,arial,tahoma,sans-serif !important;
    font-size:11px;
}

.ux-list .ux-list-selected {
    background-color:#D9E8FB;
}

.ux-list a {
    color:#555555;
    padding-left:2px;
}

.ux-list a:link, .ux-list a:visited, .ux-list a:active {
    color:#555555;
    text-decoration:none;
```

```
}

.ux-list a:hover {
    color:#0464BB;
    text-decoration:underline;
}

.ux-list .ux-list-selected a {
    color:#000000;
}
```

By wrapping a DIV tag around the list and assigning a class name of `ux-list` to the DIV tag, all unordered list and list items within don't need any class attributes. This reduces the size of the generated markup slightly, and also makes it easy to restyle the list by changing the class name for the DIV, as we will see in the next template.

For the "Current" fields, the `ux-list-selected` class has been added, but because the corresponding CSS rules are prefixed by `ux-list`, changing the class name for the DIV will follow on to any "current" list item.

Vertical unordered list with bullets

To create this template, all we need to do is copy the "EXTJS vertical unordered list without bullets" template using the APEX copy feature on the **Shared Components | Templates** page within APEX Application Builder and make the following edits:

Name: EXTJS Vertical Unordered List **with** Bullets

Template Class: Vertical Unordered List **with** Bullets

List Template Before Rows:

```
<div class="ux-list ux-list-bullet">
<ul>
```

Surprised at how little was changed?

Because the structure of the list isn't being changed, only the CSS class needs to be modified and additional CSS rules added:

```
.ux-list-bullet ul {
    list-style-type: square;
    margin-left:13px;
}
```

In this case, the original class `ux-list` was kept and a second class name `ux-list-bullet` added. For CSS styling it means the original classes are applied and any new classes have their attributes added.

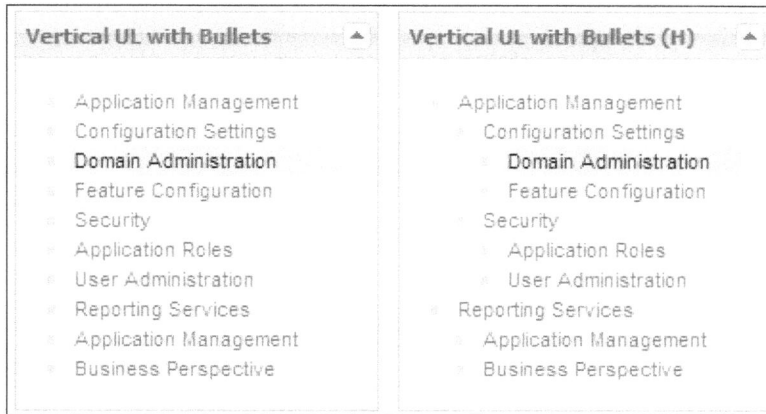

The addition of the one CSS rule adds the square bullet to the list, with the left margin indenting the list, and for hierarchical sublists, the indent is multiplied by the number of levels. The previous screenshot shows the difference between a flat list and a hierarchical list using the template.

Building an Ext JS tree template using lists

Every computer user is immediately familiar with using a tree view for navigating in an application. Tree components allow hierarchical data to be presented in a compact and structured manner, allowing the user to interact to hide or show information.

APEX hierarchical lists are ideal for presenting static data, and using the built-in lists to store and display the data provide some advantages over a custom table-based solution.

Built-in lists allow you to use conditional logic when displaying list entries using either the "Conditions" fields, or "Authorization Scheme". This means you can conditionally show items depending on security privileges, or show or hide items based on some application state.

A second advantage is the list data is part of the APEX application export, so you don't need to remember to migrate data from application tables.

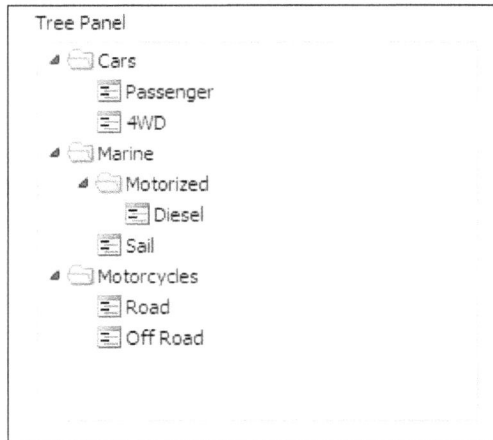

Let's take a look at the prototype, `chapter04/ex-4-tree-panel.html`, shown in previous screenshot, and examine the JavaScript used to construct the tree.

```
<div id="tree-div"></div>

<script type="text/javascript">
Ext.onReady(function(){

  // define tree data as an object
  var treeData = {text:"Root Node", expanded:true, children:[
  {id:"L01",text:"Cars",        href:"#",leaf:false,children: [
  {id:"L02",text:"Passenger",   href:"#",leaf:true},
  {id:"L03",text:"4WD",         href:"#",leaf:true}]},
  {id:"L04",text:"Marine",      href:"#",leaf:false,children: [
  {id:"L05",text:"Motorized",   href:"#",leaf:false,children: [
  {id:"L06",text:"Diesel",      href:"#",leaf:true}]},
  {id:"L07",text:"Sail",        href:"#",leaf:true}]},
  {id:"L08",text:"Motorcycles", href:"#",leaf:false,children: [
  {id:"L09",text:"Road",        href:"#",leaf:true},
  {id:"L10",text:"Off Road",    href:"#",leaf:true}]}
  ]};

  // create the tree
  new Ext.tree.TreePanel({
      renderTo:'tree-div',
      useArrows:true,
```

```
        autoScroll:true,
        animate:true,
        border:false,
        rootVisible: false,
        root: treeData
    });

});
</script>
```

Looking at the prototype code, you can see two separate code blocks, the first being a JavaScript object of tree node definitions. Each tree node has the id, text, href, and leaf properties defined, except the root node, which just has the text and expanded properties defined.

Ext JS automatically assigns an ID to each tree node if it doesn't already have an ID assigned, so the ID is optional. The generated ID is a text string in the form **ext-genN**, with N being replaced with a number. The reason behind assigning an ID to the other elements is the fact that we are interacting with the backend server, asynchronously loading tree nodes or manipulating nodes, and those nodes are associated with backend data such as a database records primary key, so it's very useful to be able to match nodes with the backend data.

However, the root node is an artificial construct, required by Ext.tree.TreePanel, because every tree must have only one root node.

The second code block instantiates an Ext.tree.TreePanel object, passing a configuration block. Along with configuring how the tree is to be displayed, it also assigns the root to the treeData object defined in the first code block, and sets the renderTo:'tree-dev' property to use the DIV markup immediately before the script block.

APEX 4.0 tree template

Release 4 of APEX added the "Template Definitions for First Entry" section to the List Template, including four new fields:

- **List Template Current (First)**
- **List Template Current with Sub List Items (First)**
- **List Template Noncurrent (First)**
- **List Template Noncurrent with Sub List Items (First)**

These new fields assist in generating a unique ID for the target DIV tag, used to render the tree. I will show you an alternative version for earlier releases of APEX shortly, but let's first look at the APEX 4 version.

List template current:

```
{id:"#LIST_ITEM_ID#",text:"#TEXT#",href:"#LINK#",leaf:true,
isCurrent:true}
```

List template current with sub list items:

```
{id:"#LIST_ITEM_ID#",text:"#TEXT#",href:"#LINK#",leaf:false,
isCurrent:true, children:[
```

List template noncurrent:

```
{id:"#LIST_ITEM_ID#",text:"#TEXT#",href:"#LINK#",leaf:true}
```

List template noncurrent with Sub List Items:

```
{id:"#LIST_ITEM_ID#",text:"#TEXT#",href:"#LINK#",leaf:false,
children:[
```

Between List Elements:

```
,
```

List template current (first):

```
<div id="tree#LIST_ITEM_ID#"></div>

<script type="text/javascript">
Ext.onReady(function(){

var treeRegion = 'tree#LIST_ITEM_ID#';

var treeData = {text:"Root Node", expanded:true, children:
[{id:"#LIST_ITEM_ID#",text:"#TEXT#",href:"#LINK#",leaf:true,
isCurrent:true }
```

List template current with sub list items (first):

```
<div id="tree#LIST_ITEM_ID#"></div>

<script type="text/javascript">
Ext.onReady(function(){

var treeRegion = 'tree#LIST_ITEM_ID#';
```

```
var treeData = {text:"Root Node", expanded:true, children:
[{id:"#LIST_ITEM_ID#",text:"#TEXT#",href:"#LINK#",leaf:false,
isCurrent:true, children:
[
```

List template noncurrent (first):

```
<div id="tree#LIST_ITEM_ID#"></div>

<script type="text/javascript">
Ext.onReady(function(){

var treeRegion = 'tree#LIST_ITEM_ID#';

var treeData = {text:"Root Node", expanded:true, children:
[{id:"#LIST_ITEM_ID#",text:"#TEXT#",href:"#LINK#",leaf:true}
```

List template noncurrent with sub list items (first):

```
<div id="tree#LIST_ITEM_ID#"></div>

<script type="text/javascript">
Ext.onReady(function(){

var treeRegion = 'tree#LIST_ITEM_ID#';

var treeData = {text:"Root Node", expanded:true, children:
[{id:"#LIST_ITEM_ID#",text:"#TEXT#",href:"#LINK#",leaf:false,
children:
[
```

Sub list template current:

```
{id:"#LIST_ITEM_ID#",text:"#TEXT#",href:"#LINK#",leaf:true,
isCurrent:true }
```

Sub list template current with sub list items:

```
{id:"#LIST_ITEM_ID#",text:"#TEXT#",href:"#LINK#",leaf:false,
isCurrent:true, children: [
```

Sub list template noncurrent:

```
{id:"#LIST_ITEM_ID#",text:"#TEXT#",href:"#LINK#",leaf:true}
```

Sublist template noncurrent with sub list items:

```
{id:"#LIST_ITEM_ID#",text:"#TEXT#",href:"#LINK#",leaf:false, children:
[
```

Between sub list items:

```
,
```

Sublist template after rows:

```
]}
```

List template after rows:

```
]};
new Ext.tree.TreePanel({
    renderTo:treeRegion,
    useArrows:true,
    autoScroll:true,
    animate:true,
    border:false,
    rootVisible: false,
    root: treeData
});
});
</script>
```

Traditionally, templates contain HTML markup and occasionally a little JavaScript. Here we are doing exactly the opposite with just a single DIV element, and using the rest of the template to generate JavaScript code.

Despite appearances, the template is close to our original prototype; however, there is one adjustment that had to be made.

In the prototype, the DIV tag the `TreePanel` component will be rendered into is specified by the `renderTo` attribute as a string:

```
// create the tree
new Ext.tree.TreePanel({
    renderTo:'tree-div',
    useArrows:true,
    autoScroll:true,
    animate:true,
    border:false,
    rootVisible: false,
    root: treeData
});
```

In the APEX template, a variable has been defined and referenced:

```
<div id="tree#LIST_ITEM_ID#"></div>

<script type="text/javascript">
Ext.onReady(function(){

var treeRegion = 'tree#LIST_ITEM_ID#';

  // code...

new Ext.tree.TreePanel({
    renderTo:treeRegion,
    useArrows:true,
    autoScroll:true,
    animate:true,
    border:false,
    rootVisible: false,
    root: treeData
});
```

The reason for doing this is that the list template does not allow #REGION_ID# or some equivalent substitution tag to be used in the **List template before rows** field. To generate a unique ID for DIV, the #LIST_ITEM_ID# has been used in the first list item. Because this cannot be referenced later in the **List Template After Rows** field, the ID has to be passed by variable reference.

In case you're wondering, the treeRegion variable is local to the anonymous function enclosed by **Ext.onReady**, so you could have multiple instances of the variable without any issue.

Prior APEX versions tree template

APEX versions prior to APEX 4.0 don't have the "Template Definitions for First Entry" section, so it is a two-part solution to create a tree component using a list template. The tree definition remains mostly unchanged in the list template, the code in the "First Entry" field needs to be moved to a customized region template.

The markup for the "EXTJS Tree Panel" region is as follows:

```
<div id="#REGION_STATIC_ID#" #REGION_ATTRIBUTES#></div>
<script type="text/javascript">
Ext.onReady(function(){
var treeRegion = '#REGION_STATIC_ID#';
```

```
// define tree data as an object
var treeData = {text:"Root Node", expanded:true, children:[
#BODY#
]};

new Ext.tree.TreePanel({
    renderTo:treeRegion,
    useArrows:true,
    autoScroll:true,
    animate:true,
    border:false,
    rootVisible: false,
    root: treeData
});

});
</script>
```

The region creates a DIV element with an ID populated by the #REGION_STATIC_ID# substitution tag. The #BODY# tag will be populated by the list definition:

List template current:

```
{id:"#LIST_ITEM_ID#",text:"#TEXT#",href:"#LINK#",leaf:true,
isCurrent:true}
```

List template current with sub list items:

```
{id:"#LIST_ITEM_ID#",text:"#TEXT#",href:"#LINK#",leaf:false,
isCurrent:true, children:[
```

List template noncurrent:

```
{id:"#LIST_ITEM_ID#",text:"#TEXT#",href:"#LINK#",leaf:true}
```

List template noncurrent with sub list items:

```
{id:"#LIST_ITEM_ID#",text:"#TEXT#",href:"#LINK#",leaf:false,
children:[
```

Between list elements:

```
,
```

Sub list template current:

```
{id:"#LIST_ITEM_ID#",text:"#TEXT#",href:"#LINK#",leaf:true,
isCurrent:true}
```

Sub list template current with sub list items:

```
{id:"#LIST_ITEM_ID#",text:"#TEXT#",href:"#LINK#",leaf:false,
isCurrent:true, children: [
```

Sub list template noncurrent:

```
{id:"#LIST_ITEM_ID#",text:"#TEXT#",href:"#LINK#",leaf:true}
```

Sublist template noncurrent with sub list items:

```
{id:"#LIST_ITEM_ID#",text:"#TEXT#",href:"#LINK#",leaf:false, children:
[
```

Between sub list items:

```
,
```

Sublist template after rows:

```
]}
```

The only differences between this and the APEX 4.0 version are that the **Template Definitions for First Entry** section doesn't exist, and the **List Template After Rows** field is blank.

Highlighting the current node

To highlight the "current" node in our tree, as shown in the following screenshot, the list template use the attribute `isCurrent:true` for the current entries.

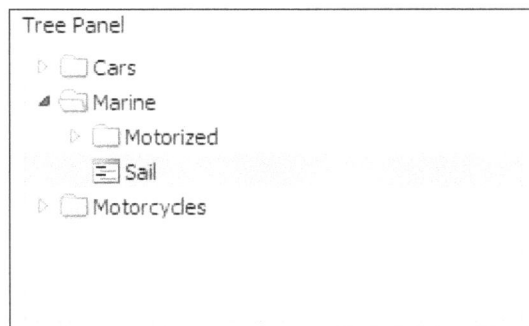

For example the "Sub List Template Current" looks like:

```
{id:"#LIST_ITEM_ID#", text:"#TEXT#", href:"#LINK#", leaf:true,
```
isCurrent:true}

Now we need to modify the JavaScript to detect this attribute and use built-in Ext. tree.treePanel functionality to select the node. Because you're most likely to be using the tree regularly, it's worthwhile creating a custom component and saving it to your application JavaScript file, rather than embedding the code within the page. A nice way of doing this is by extending the Ext JS component.

The code shown here is in `chapter04/Ext.apex.tree.TreePanel.js`.

```javascript
// create custom namespace if doesn't exist
Ext.ns('Ext.apex.tree');

/**
 * @class Ext.apex.tree.TreePanel
 * @extends Ext.tree.TreePanel
 * <p>The APEX TreePanel highlights the first node with "isCurrent"
set to true.</p>
 */
Ext.apex.tree.TreePanel = Ext.extend(Ext.tree.TreePanel, {
  afterRender: function(){
    Ext.apex.tree.TreePanel.superclass.afterRender.call(this);
    this.highlightCurrentNode();
  },

  highlightCurrentNode: function(){
    var path = this.getCurrentNodePath(this.root.attributes);

    this.expandPath(path, 'id', function(isSuccess, currentNode){
      if (isSuccess) {
        currentNode.select();
        currentNode.ensureVisible();
      }
    });
  },

  getCurrentNodePath: function(node){
    if (node.isCurrent) {
      return this.pathSeparator + node.id;
    }
    else {
      if (node.children) {
        for (var i = 0; node.children.length > i; i += 1) {
          var result = this.getCurrentNodePath(node.children[i]);
          if (result) {
            return this.pathSeparator + node.id + result;
          }
        }
```

```
            }
         }
      }
      // not found
      return null;
   }
});

// Register container so that lazy instantiation may be used
Ext.reg('apex-treepanel', Ext.apex.tree.TreePanel);
```

Ext uses lazy loading an Ext.tree.TreeNode's child nodes, meaning the child nodes are loaded only when a tree node is expanded. This reduces the number of DOM nodes rendered by the initial tree load and improves performance, particularly for large trees.

However, it's somewhat inconvenient here, as the Ext.tree.treePanel API doesn't provide a mechanism to search for nodes that haven't been rendered yet. As the data for the tree is contained within the page, and not being fetched by an AJAX request, it's safe to extend the Ext.tree.treePanel to search the tree data for the unrendered nodes.

And that's what we are doing—searching down the hierarchy path of the root node:

```
highlightCurrentNode: function(){
   var path = this.getCurrentNodePath(this.root.attributes);


   this.expandPath(path, 'id', function(isSuccess, currentNode){
      if (isSuccess) {
         currentNode.select();
         currentNode.ensureVisible();
      }
   });
},
```

Once the current node is detected, we use the Ext.tree.treePanel API call currentNode.select(); to select (and render) the node, and then scroll it into view using currentNode.ensureVisible();.

To call the extension, just modify the template replacing the reference to Ext.tree.TreePanel with Ext.apex.tree.TreePanel.

Customizing individual nodes

APEX provides spare substitution tags #A01#...#A10# for list items, allowing you to add additional content to list items if your list template supports it. It is good practice to use these spare tags for special templates, and use the standard tags for lists so that you can easily swap templates on a page-by-page basis.

So, modify all the template items to include #A02# after the leaf tag, for example:

```
{id:"#LIST_ITEM_ID#", text:"#TEXT#", href:"#LINK#", leaf:true#A02#}
```

Now you have a list item field that stores 2000 characters of additional data.

For example, to change the appearance of a node:

Define a CSS rule for the node icon in your application CSS file, using the !important attribute to override the normal node icon:

```
.ux-lock {
    background-image: url(/ux/extjs/resources/images/default/grid/
hmenu-lock.gif) !important;
}
```

Then add the following text in the A02 field for a node (note the leading comma):

```
,iconCls: "ux-lock"
```

The nodes appearance is now a padlock, as shown in the following screenshot:

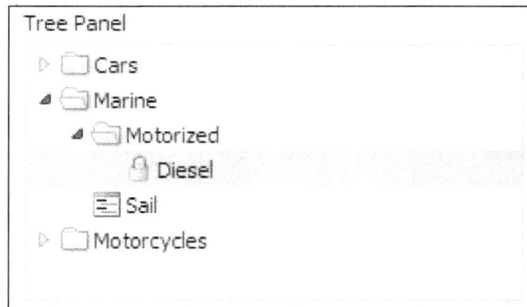

With 2000 characters available with which to play, you can do quite a bit, and if that's not enough, you still have nine of the remaining #A01#..#A10# substitution tags up your sleeve.

Here's another example, attaching a click handler to a node:

```
,iconCls:'ux-lock',
listeners:{click:function(node, e){
    // stop standard event
    e.stopEvent();
    Ext.MessageBox.show({
        title: 'Credits',
        msg: 'Website developed by Snazzy Websites',
        buttons: Ext.MessageBox.OK
    });
}}
```

We will be covering much more on Ext trees in later chapters, but as you can see, you can do quite a bit just using the list template as your data source.

Summary

In this chapter we've covered Region templates, showing how to create static versions of the Ext.Panel with framed and unframed variants. Then, to make the regions collapsible, a few lines of JavaScript were added with minor modifications to the static templates.

For Label templates, we created simple HTML templates using custom CSS to approximate the Ext look. Inline error messages can create display issues, pushing items off the display area. By modifying the error attributes for labels to make use of **Ext.QuickTips**, a small error icon is displayed instead; when the mouse hovers over the icon, an error message is revealed.

For List templates, we started by creating some very simple templates relying on just HTML and CSS, all using the same list structure. By modifying only the class of a DIV wrapper element, different appearances could be achieved with minimal additional CSS rules.

APEX lists are ideal for presenting static data, and using the built-in lists has advantages over a custom table-based solution. Built-in lists allow you to display entries conditionally based on "Conditions" fields, or "Authorization Scheme". List data is also part of the application export, so you don't need to remember to include data from database tables as part of your application promotions.

Using List templates, we implemented the **Ext.tree.TreePanel**, showing how templates can also be used to produce JavaScript code and JSON objects, and not just HTML. Two versions of the Tree Template were created—one for APEX 4.0 and the other for earlier versions of APEX. Using the current list item template field to identify the current tree node, the **Ext.tree.TreePanel** was extended to create a custom component, allowing the current tree node to be selected and scrolled into view.

Finally, we saw how to customize the appearance of individual tree nodes using the A01#..#A10# substitution tags available for each list item, as well as add specific JavaScript code.

In the next chapter we continue developing templates for the remaining template types, emphasizing a rich and responsive interface for buttons, popups, calendars, and reports.

5
Ext Themed Buttons, Popups, Calendars, and Reports

Have you ever stopped and asked yourself "What's the difference between a link and button"?

You press a button when you want something to happen, just as in everyday life. You press a button to switch on a light, change channels on TV, or start your computer, washing machine, car, and so on. The BRB, or big red button, is often featured in movies with the person in charge sweating over the decision of triggering a self-destructive process. "Whatever you do, do not press the big red button." When you press a button, there are consequences!

On the other hand, the main purpose of a link is to navigate to another location, not really affecting anything and no real consequences. In other words, the humble button on your web application is a really important component and needs to be given serious design consideration.

We continue building up a theme based on Ext into APEX, developing templates for the remaining template types: buttons, popup list of values, breadcrumbs, calendars, and reports.

The modern website user experience is now about rich and responsive user interfaces, with interfaces displaying intuitive visual cues to communicate the status of the users' interaction with the system. For instance, clicking on a button often changes the appearance from "normal" to a "pressed" look, giving immediate feedback to the user, confirming their action has triggered an action with the system.

By the end of the chapter, you will have a "minimal" theme ready to publish.

Button templates

APEX allows you to create three styles of buttons: HTML, Template, and Image.

The HTML button creates the native browser-based button with attributes you can specify; the rendered appearance differs based on your operating system and browser. The HTML button is lightweight for HTTP requests, but limited in how you can manipulate its appearance.

The Image button allows you to control the appearance by specifying the image used and the image attributes. A significant limitation of image-based buttons is that you have to specify the image details every time you create a button—a real productivity killer. For this reason alone, I would strongly encourage you not to use image-based buttons, but rather create a template-based button with the image details included.

The Template button provides you with far greater design flexibility, allowing you to duplicate the HTML generated by either the HTML or Image style buttons, or create something with greater functionality.

The additional flexibility Template buttons offer, without the drawbacks of either of the other button styles, make it the obvious choice for all your buttons.

Over the next few pages, we will explore the following alternative approaches to buttons:

- Creating a custom markup button using Sliding Doors and CSS sprites
- An Ext static markup template button
- JavaScript enabling the Ext button
- Toolbar buttons using pure JavaScript

Sliding doors meet CSS sprites

Here, we are creating a custom markup button using the sliding doors method to provide horizontal scalability and creating multiple states by applying different background images contained in a sprite image. The following screen shows what we are trying to achieve—a normal button appearance, that is, a light blue background when the mouse hovers over, and a darker blue background when the button is pressed. The **Apply Changes** button shows the appearance of the button is maintained for variable widths.

A standalone example of the finished buttons can be found in `chapter05/ex-5-buttons.html`.

The Sliding Doors technique was first introduced on A List Apart (http://www.alistapart.com/articles/slidingdoors/). The principle involves making two images slide over each other, allowing the button to stretch horizontally to accommodate the button content, as shown in the following diagram. By making one of the images sufficiently wide, you can accommodate a large range of button widths.

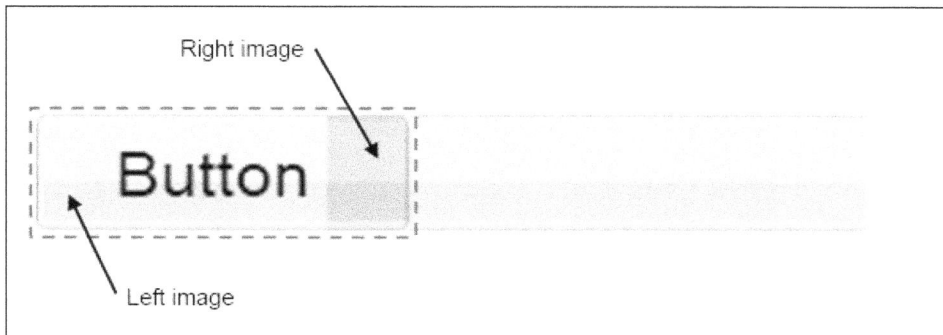

The simplified HTML for this button is:

```
<button class="ux-btn-alt ux-btn-markup">
  <span><em>Button</em></span>
</button>
```

To hide the buttons border and a ensure consistent layout for different browsers, the following CSS rules are applied:

```
button.ux-btn-alt{
  border:0;
  background:none;
  cursor: pointer;
  padding:0;
  margin:0;
  width:auto;
  overflow: visible; /* removes extra side padding in IE */
  text-align:center;
```

```
  white-space:nowrap;
  height: 22px;
  }

.ux-btn-alt span, .ux-btn-alt span em {
  display: block;
  height: 22px;
  line-height: 22px;
}

/* override extra padding in Firefox */
.ux-btn-alt::-moz-focus-inner {
  border: 0;
  padding: 0;
}

/* prevent RH edge disappearing when pressed */
.ext-opera .ux-btn-alt span {
  margin-right:2px;
  margin-bottom:1px;
}

.ux-btn-alt em{
  color:#333333;
  font:11px arial,tahoma,helvetica,sans-serif;
  }
```

The `border:0` setting removes the border from the button; the remaining settings ensure the height of the button is the same as the images used and ensure that the text positioning and appearance is consistent across different browsers.

One way of minimizing HTTP requests is to combine multiple images into a single image, or sprite, and using the CSS `background-image` and `background-position` properties to display the desired image segment. Here, we are using the sprite shown in the following figure, which holds left and right images for the button on a transparent background. The button positions for the "Normal" state are shown with the left button at (0,0) and the right button at (right,-100px).

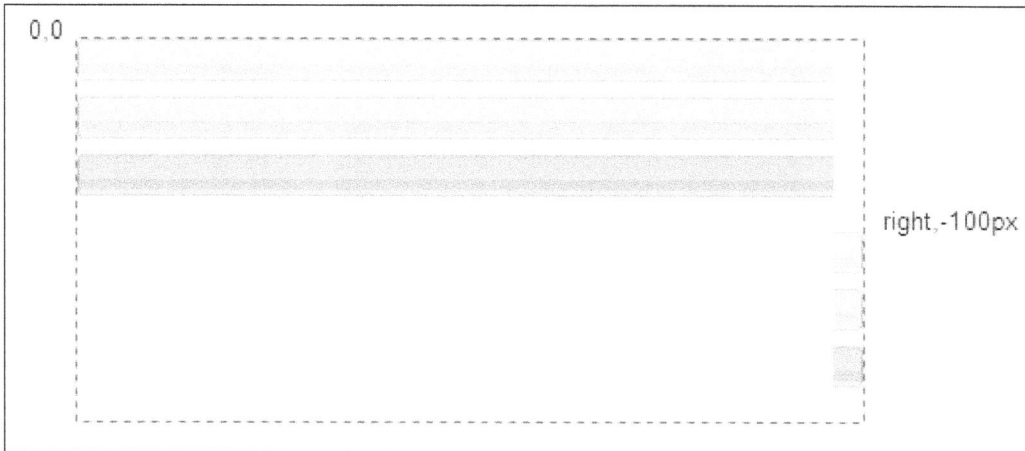

```
.ux-btn-alt em{
  padding-left:10px;
  background:url(btn-sprite.gif) no-repeat 0 0;
  }

.ux-btn-alt span{
  padding-right:0 10px 0 0;
  background:url(btn-sprite.gif) no-repeat right -100px;
  }
```

The images for the button are specified using the CSS background property, a shorthand way of specifying background-image and background-position properties. The EM element is used for the left image, and the SPAN element is used for right image. Here, both images have been combined into a single image, using CSS offsets to reference the right image.

To create the "hover" and "active" appearance for the buttons, we use the CSS selectors of the same name with the !important attribute to override the background-position of the SPAN and EM elements:

```
.ux-btn-alt:hover em, .ux-btn-alt-over em {
  background-position: 0 -30px !important;
}

.ux-btn-alt:hover span, .ux-btn-alt-over span {
  background-position: right -130px !important;
}

.ux-btn-alt:active em, .ux-btn-alt-click em{
```

```
    color:#000000;
    background-position: 0 -60px !important;
}

.ux-btn-alt:active span, .ux-btn-alt-click span {
    background-position: right -160px !important;
}
```

All modern browsers support the :active pseudo selector; however, when it comes to supporting the :hover pseudo selector, there is an exception of IE6 and IE7. The additional ux-btn-alt-over selector was added to be able to include JavaScript to address this deficiency.

For toolbars, the button borders can be hidden until the mouse hovers over using:

```
.x-toolbar .ux-btn-alt span, .x-toolbar .ux-btn-alt em {
    background-position: 0 -100px;
}
```

APEX sliding door CSS sprite button template

To include this little gem as an APEX button template, add the CSS rules and button sprite to your resource files, and create the following button template:

```
<button type="button" class="ux-btn-alt ux-btn-markup"
onclick="#LINK#" value="#LABEL#" #BUTTON_ATTRIBUTES#>
    <span><em>#LABEL#</em></span>
</button>
```

The complete CSS for the button can be found in chapter05/ex-5-buttons.html, and is shown below. Just add the images to your resources, and include the CSS in your project CSS file, adjusting the paths for the images as necessary.

```
button.ux-btn-alt{
    border:0;
    background:none;
    cursor: pointer;
    padding:0;
    margin:0;
    width:auto;
    overflow: visible; /* removes extra side padding in IE */
    text-align:center;
    white-space:nowrap;
    height: 22px;
    }
```

```css
.ux-btn-alt span, .ux-btn-alt span em {
  display: block;
  height: 22px;
  line-height: 22px;
}

/* override extra padding in Firefox */
.ux-btn-alt::-moz-focus-inner {
  border: 0;
  padding: 0;
}

/* prevent RH edge disappearing when pressed */
.ext-opera .ux-btn-alt span {
  margin-right:2px;
  margin-bottom:1px;
}

.ux-btn-alt em{
  color:#333333;
  font:11px arial,tahoma,helvetica,sans-serif;
}

.ux-btn-alt em{
  padding-left:10px;
  background:url(btn-sprite.gif) no-repeat 0 0;
  }

.ux-btn-alt span{
  padding:0 10px 0 0;
  background:url(btn-sprite.gif) no-repeat right -100px;
  }

.ux-btn-alt:hover em, .ux-btn-alt-over em {
  background-position: 0 -30px !important;
}

.ux-btn-alt:hover span, .ux-btn-alt-over span {
  background-position: right -130px !important;
}

.ux-btn-alt:active em, .ux-btn-alt-click em{
  color:#000000;
  background-position: 0 -60px !important;
```

```
}

.ux-btn-alt:active span, .ux-btn-alt-click span {
  background-position: right -160px !important;
}

.x-toolbar .ux-btn-alt span, .x-toolbar .ux-btn-alt em {
  background-position: 0 -100px;
}
```

So, there you have it, a cross-browser method for custom styling button elements using sliding door sprites to provide interactive feedback on hover and when clicked.

Let's have a look now at how we can create an Ext.Button from markup.

Building a hideous Ext.Button

The markup used for the standard Ext.Button is made up using in the Ext team's own words "a hideous table template". Hideous it may be, but the advantage of using this complex table structure is that it provides enormous flexibility in its dimensions. The following screenshot shows some of the layouts that can be created using an Ext.Button:

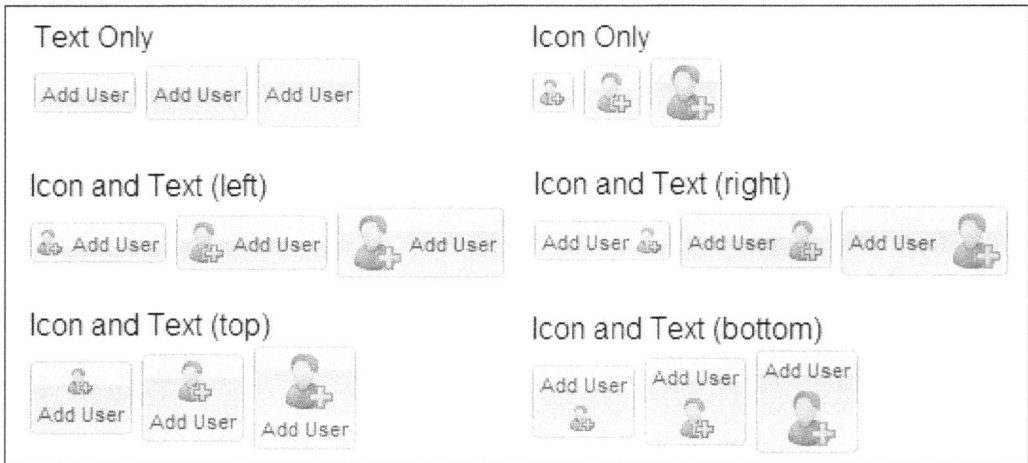

To create a button template duplicating the Ext layout, the first thing we need to do is get the markup generated for an Ext.button. This can be done quite easily using Firebug.

Open an example page that has the Ext JavaScript files attached, and run the following commands from the Firebug console:

```
Ext.get(document.body).update('<div id="test"></div>');

new Ext.Button({
    text: '#TITLE#',
    scale:'small',
    renderTo: 'test'
});
```

The first command replaces the entire HTML document body, with a single DIV element having an ID of test. The second command renders an Ext.Button into the DIV. I'm using the small scaled button here, but you may prefer the "medium" or "large" buttons for your application.

From there, locate the test DIV in the Firebug HTML tab, as shown in the following screenshot. select it, and using the right-click menu, choose the **Copy innerHTML** option and paste it into your favorite text editor.

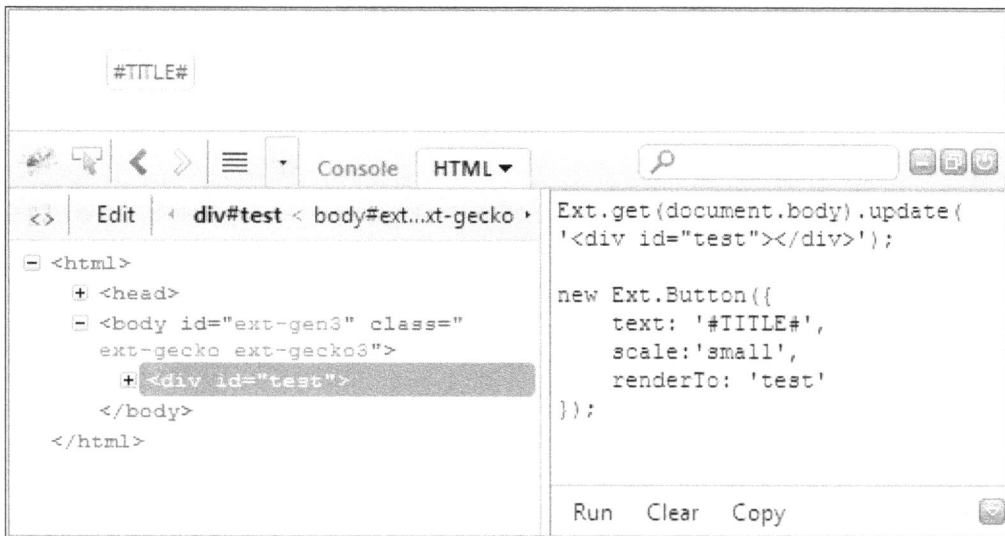

With a little formatting, the markup looks something like this:

```
<table style="width: auto;" id="ext-comp-1013" class="x-btn    x-btn-
noicon " cellspacing="0">
<tbody class="x-btn-small x-btn-icon-small-left">
<tr>
  <td class="x-btn-tl"><i> </i></td>
```

```
    <td class="x-btn-tc"></td>
    <td class="x-btn-tr"><i> </i></td>
  </tr>
  <tr>
    <td class="x-btn-ml"><i> </i></td>
    <td class="x-btn-mc">
      <em class="" unselectable="on">
        <button class=" x-btn-text" id="ext-gen15"
type="button">#TITLE#</button>
      </em>
    </td>
    <td class="x-btn-mr"><i> </i></td>
  </tr>
  <tr>
    <td class="x-btn-bl"><i> </i></td>
    <td class="x-btn-bc"></td>
    <td class="x-btn-br"><i> </i></td>
  </tr>
  </tbody>
  </table>
```

To convert this into an APEX button template only requires us to strip out the ID attributes, and add in the APEX substitution tags for #LINK# and #BUTTON_ATTRIBUTES#. Like every good lazy programmer, I had already included the #LABEL# tag when creating the button.

The finished markup for the **EXTJS Button** template is:

```
<table onclick="#LINK#" cellspacing="0" class="ux-btn ux-btn-markup
x-btn x-btn-noicon" style="width:auto;" #BUTTON_ATTRIBUTES#>
<tbody class="x-btn-small x-btn-icon-small-left">
<tr>
  <td class="x-btn-tl"><i> </i></td>
  <td class="x-btn-tc"></td>
  <td class="x-btn-tr"><i> </i></td>
</tr>
<tr>
  <td class="x-btn-ml"><i> </i></td>
  <td class="x-btn-mc">
    <em unselectable="on" class="">
      <button type="button" class="x-btn-text">#LABEL#</button>
    </em>
  </td>
  <td class="x-btn-mr"><i> </i></td>
</tr>
```

```
<tr>
  <td class="x-btn-bl"><i> </i></td>
  <td class="x-btn-bc"></td>
  <td class="x-btn-br"><i> </i></td>
</tr>
</tbody>
</table>
```

The opening TABLE element highlighted in the template needs some explanation.

First, using the `onclick="#LINK#"` attribute allows the button to work quite happily using standard APEX functionality without any further JavaScript manipulation whatsoever. This provides robustness to the design. As soon as the button has been rendered, a user can click on the button, and it will execute. For very simple pages, such as wizards with sensible default values, an experienced user will click through the page rapidly.

The `class="ux-btn ux-btn-markup x-btn x-btn-noicon"` has two non-standard class attributes:

`ux-btn-markup` acts as a marker that will be used shortly to add some JavaScript functionality. `ux-btn` is used to apply the following CSS rules, ensuring standard Ext buttons created using tables (which are block level elements) are changed to inline-block elements to allow side-by-side layout.

Ext usually renders buttons in separate table cells to avoid this issue; we need to allow for this not being the case. IE provides support only for **inline-block** in version 8 and upwards in some modes, so for IE, use **inline** instead.

```
table.ux-btn {display:inline-block}
.ext-ie table.ux-btn {display:inline}
```

Finally, the `#BUTTON_ATTRIBUTES#` substitution tag allows the developer to assign a specific ID attribute to a button. The following shows how you assign the ID in the **Button Display Attributes** section of the button:

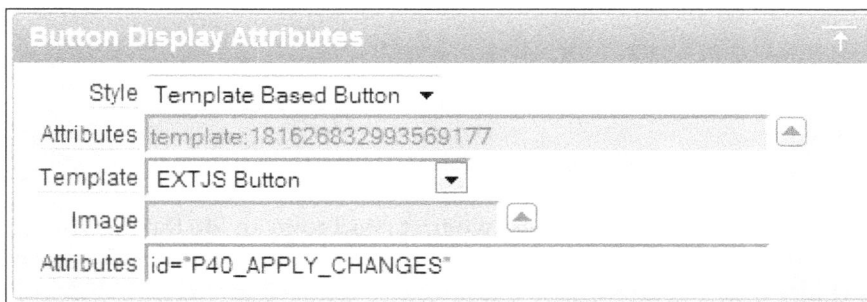

> APEX supports a #BUTTON_ID# substitution tag, but performs substitutions only for buttons in Region positions and not for button items.
>
> Use button attributes instead to assign a specific ID.

So now we have a functioning button that looks just like an Ext button, but doesn't behave like one. The "hover" and "active" effects aren't happening, and they aren't registered Ext components, so we can't manipulate them easily. We also haven't covered adding icons and menus to the buttons.

It's time to convert the button to take advantage of the rich Ext API.

Converting our buttons

Before we look at the JavaScript to convert our static markup buttons to Ext buttons, it is worthwhile discussing why we want to convert them in the first place. The "hover" and "active" effects for our buttons are a nice to have feature, rather than a must have.

Converting buttons to Ext buttons opens additional display and functional options, with the rich Ext API allowing you to add icons easily, or make buttons toggle on and off. Ext also provides menus so that clicking a menu button displays a drop-down menu, or in the split button case, provides a "primary action" when you click the main button region and shows a drop-down menu when the drop-down region is clicked. You can see these features in the following screenshot.

When you create an **Ext.Button**, it is automatically registered with the **Ext.ComponentMgr**, providing a mechanism to easily access all Ext components by component ID. So, you could easily disable or enable buttons based on the state of some page item, or show or hide items based on a button's state.

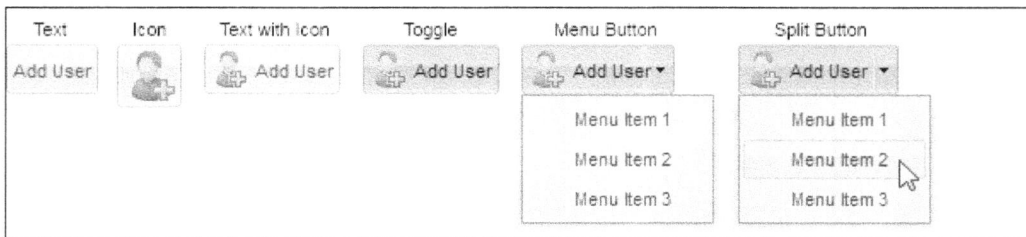

To convert our buttons to Ext buttons, we first need to override the **Ext.Button** object to modify its functionality, in order to allow the button object to be applied to our markup.

In *Chapter 4, Ext Themed Regions, Labels, and Lists*, we saw **Ext.Panel** detect panel-specific structural markup when using the `applyTo` configuration attribute, converting static APEX region templates into an **Ext.Panel**. The Ext.Button, however, does not provide equivalent functionality to detect structural markup, so we need to add it ourselves.

Ext contains `Ext.Extend` and `Ext.Override` utility functions, providing the mechanism for simulating class inheritance. Using these functions gives you the ability to modify or extend the base functionality of any JavaScript class without making code changes directly to the class.

If you are adding or changing the behavior of a class, usually you would use `Ext.Extend` to create a new class; however, in this case I've chosen to override the `Ext.Button` class because I want the changes to flow through to its child classes. The following screenshot, taken from the Ext documentation, shows the inheritance path for `Ext.SplitButton`; observe that `SplitButton` extends `Button`.

By using `Ext.Override`, the changes to the `Button` class will be inherited by `SplitButton`, which in turn subclasses `CycleButton`.

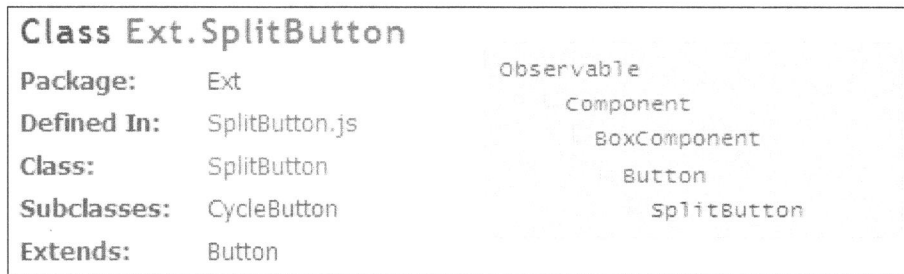

Class Ext.SplitButton

Package:	Ext	Observable
Defined In:	SplitButton.js	Component
Class:	SplitButton	BoxComponent
Subclasses:	CycleButton	Button
Extends:	Button	SplitButton

The code for the button override is contained in `chapter05/Override.Ext.Button.js` and includes commenting, which has been stripped out here for brevity.

```
Ext.override(Ext.Button, {
    // private
    isRendered: false,
    arrowSelector: 'em',

    initComponent: function(){
        if (this.transformEl) {
            this.isRendered = true;
            this.applyTo = this.transformEl;
            delete this.transformEl;
        }
        Ext.Button.superclass.initComponent.call(this);
```

```
                this.addEvents(
                    'click',
                    'toggle',
                    'mouseover',
                    'mouseout',
                    'menushow',
                    'menuhide',
                    'menutriggerover',
                    'menutriggerout'
                );
                if(this.menu){
                    this.menu = Ext.menu.MenuMgr.get(this.menu);
                }
                if(Ext.isString(this.toggleGroup)){
                    this.enableToggle = true;
                }
            },
```

So, here we can see a couple of additional variables, isRendered and
arrowSelector, being declared. In the initComponent function, a small piece
of code has been added to detect when a button has been instantiated, with a
transformEl attribute identifying the markup button to be converted. After setting
the isRendered variable to true, the transformEl variable is reassigned to the
applyTo variable, to be used by the standard Ext.Button code.

```
            onRender: function(ct, position){
                if (!this.template) {
                    if (!Ext.Button.buttonTemplate) {
                        // hideous table template
                        Ext.Button.buttonTemplate = new Ext.Template(
                        '<table id="{4}" cellspacing="0" class="x-btn {3}">',
                            '<tbody class="{1}">',
                            '<tr><td class="x-btn-tl"><i> </i></td>',
                            '<td class="x-btn-tc"></td>',
                            '<td class="x-btn-tr"><i> </i></td></tr>',
                            '<tr><td class="x-btn-ml"><i> </i></td>',
                            '<td class="x-btn-mc">',
                            '<em class="{2}" unselectable="on">',
                            '<button type="{0}"></button></em></td>',
                            '<td class="x-btn-mr"><i> </i></td></tr>',
                            '<tr><td class="x-btn-bl"><i> </i></td>',
                            '<td class="x-btn-bc"></td>',
                            '<td class="x-btn-br"><i> </i></td></tr>',
                            '</tbody></table>');
                        Ext.Button.buttonTemplate.compile();
```

```
    }
    this.template = Ext.Button.buttonTemplate;
}

var btn, targs = this.getTemplateArgs();

if (this.isRendered) {
    btn = this.el;

    // remove class from transformed btn
    btn.removeClass('ux-btn-markup');

    // remove onclick from DOM and make button event
    var clickString = btn.getAttribute('onclick');
    if (clickString) {
        btn.dom.onclick = null;

        // config handler overrides onclick attribute
        if (!this.handler) {
            if (Ext.isIE) {
                eval("this.on('click', " + clickString +
                    ");");
            }
            else {
                eval("this.on('click', function(){ " +
                    clickString + "});");
            }
        }
    }

    // assign config text or markup when not specified
    if (!this.text) {
        this.btnEl = btn.child(this.buttonSelector);
        this.text = this.btnEl.dom.innerHTML;
    }

    btn.child('tbody').dom.className = targs[1];

    // Menu - assign class if specified
    if (this.menu && targs[2]) {
        btn.child(this.arrowSelector).addClass(targs[2]);
    }
} else {
    if (position) {
```

```
            btn = this.template.insertBefore(position, targs, true);
        }
        else {
            btn = this.template.append(ct, targs, true);
        }
    }

    this.btnEl = this.btnEl || btn.child(this.buttonSelector);
    this.mon(this.btnEl, {
        scope: this,
        focus: this.onFocus,
        blur: this.onBlur
    });

    this.initButtonEl(btn, this.btnEl);

    Ext.ButtonToggleMgr.register(this);
    }
});
```

While there is quite a lot of code in the listing, we need to focus only on the highlighted code, as everything else has been copied directly from Ext.Button. The isRendered variable is picked up in the onRender function, executing our custom code.

> Overrides to Ext components should be included in a script immediately after the Ext library, and before application scripts. This ensures the overrides are applied and available to your application scripts.

Let's not get bogged down in the detail of the onRender function. Basically, we are converting the markup button including the onclick attribute into an Ext.Button, unless the configuration for the new button overrides the markup.

Whew — that saved some time explaining the boring bits!

Much more interesting is looking at an example usage shown in previous screenshot, and found in `chapter05/ex-5-buttons-transform.html`:

```
Ext.onReady(function(){
    // Page specific code
    new Ext.SplitButton({
        transformEl: 'P40_APPLY_CHANGES',
        id:'P40_APPLY_CHANGES',
        iconCls: 'ux-icon-tick',
        menu: {
            // dropdown menu items when the arrow is clicked
            items: [{
                text: 'Item 1',
                request:'ITEM1',
                handler: onMenuItemClick
            }, {
                text: 'Item 2',
                request:'ITEM2',
                handler: onMenuItemClick
            }]
        }
    });

    function onMenuItemClick(item){
        //apex.submit(item.request);
        Ext.Msg.alert('Menu Item Click', 'You clicked the "' +
          item.text + '" item with request "' +
          item.request + '".');
    }
});

// Application code
Ext.onReady(function(){
    // Convert remaining markup buttons to Ext components
    // assigns id if exists, otherwise Ext will generate
    var els = Ext.select("table.ux-btn-markup", true);
    els.each(function(el){
        new Ext.Button({transformEl: el, id:el.dom.id});
    });

});
```

This shows some page-specific code, which is doing the task of transforming the `P40_APPLY_CHANGES` button, assigning the same ID to the button component, and adding an icon and a menu with a function to process the menu items.

In this example, an icon is added using:

```
iconCls: 'ux-icon-tick',
```

Ext assigns the class to the button as part of the transform; you just need to include a CSS rule specifying the background-image attribute for your image:

```
.ux-icon-tick {
    background-image:url(tick-square.gif) !important;
}
```

The `!important` attribute used here raises the specificity of the CSS rule, ensuring that this background is used in preference to the Ext-supplied rule.

A menu has also been added to the button using:

```
menu: {
    // dropdown menu items when the arrow is clicked
    items: [{
        text: 'Item 1',
        request:'ITEM1',
        handler: onMenuItemClick
    }, {
        text: 'Item 2',
        request:'ITEM2',
        handler: onMenuItemClick
    }]
}
```

In this case, a separate click-handler function has been assigned to each menu item, so you could call completely different functions for each item.

Ext also lets you assign default values for the menu, which are applied to every menu item unless overridden at the menu item level:

```
menu: {
    // defaults for all menu items, unless overridden
    defaults: {
        handler: doSomethingDifferent
    },
    items: [{
        text: 'Item 1',
        request:'ITEM1'
    }, {
        text: 'Item 2',
        request:'ITEM2',
        handler: onMenuItemClick
    }]
}
```

In this code snippet, `Item 1` uses the menu's default click handler to `doSomethingDifferent`, whereas `Item 2` uses `onMenuItemClick`.

The `onMenuItemClick` function is showing an Ext alert, but notice the commented line:

```
function onMenuItemClick(item){
    //apex.submit(item.request);
    Ext.Msg.alert('Menu Item Click', 'You clicked the "' +
        item.text + '" item with request "' +
        item.request + '".');
}
```

Uncommenting this would pick up the standard APEX page submit code, passing a request matching the menu items request attribute. This is how you would tie your menu items in to your APEX page processing.

Finally, at the end of the script is the application code:

```
// Application code
Ext.onReady(function(){
    // Convert remaining markup buttons to Ext components
    // assigns id if exists, otherwise Ext will generate
    var els = Ext.select("table.ux-btn-markup", true);
    els.each(function(el){
        new Ext.Button({transformEl: el, id:el.dom.id});
    });

});
```

This code would be included in your application JavaScript file and executed after any page specific scripts. The code converts any buttons using the table-based template that haven't already been converted—a set and forget feature.

We've spent quite a bit of time looking at buttons. Initially, we saw how to use a HTML and CSS-only approach using Sliding Doors and CSS Sprites to create your own custom buttons. We then covered creating a static version of an Ext button as an APEX template, showing how the button can work without any further changes. And finally, we looked at how to convert the static Ext button into a fully functioning button, opening up a range of possibilities that the Ext.Button API offers.

Let's move on to the remaining template types.

Popup List of Values template

The Popup List of Values template controls how the popup list of values items are displayed in the APEX application for all items of type POPUP. Unlike other template types, only one popup template is allowed per theme.

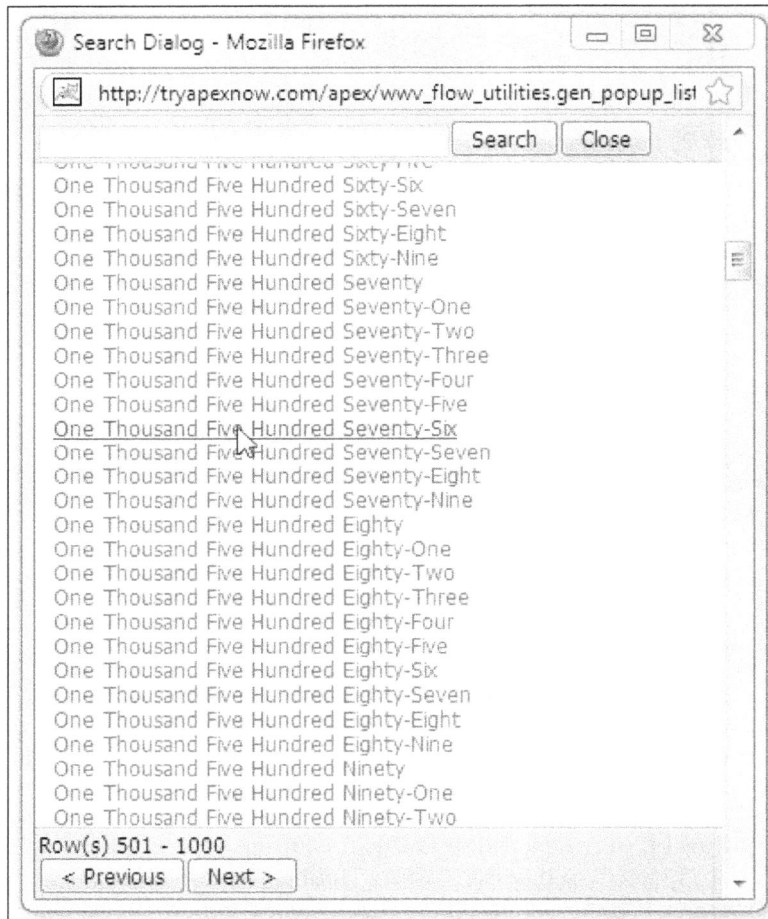

The popup template is more restricted than other templates in how you can modify the layout, but it is still possible to change its appearance to give it an Ext look, and make some minor functional improvements. The previous screenshot shows the popup page in use. The header and footer regions use Ext styling, and use fixed CSS positioning to ensure that both regions are always visible when scrolling large lists.

The template responsible to make this happen is:

Before field text:

```
<div class="ux-top-toolbar">
```

Filter text attributes:

For pre APEX 4.0, versions only, add the following line:

```
id="search-item"
```

In APEX 4.0 this value is automatically included.

After field text:

```
</div>
```

This wraps a DIV tag around the search field, and assigns an ID to the field, so we can modify the appearance using CSS.

Pagination result row X of Y:

```
Row(s) #FIRST_ROW# - #LAST_ROW#
```

Before result set:

```
<div style="padding: 20px 10px 40px">
```

After result set:

```
</div>
<div class="ux-btm-toolbar">
```

Page body attributes:

```
onload="first_field()"
```

Page footer text:

```
</div>
```

Similarly, wrapping the result set with a DIV tag allows padding to be added using an inline style attribute. A DIV tag for the bottom toolbar is also added, and the Pagination Result Row X of Y has all HTML tags removed, leaving just the text.

At this point, all that remains to be done is to add the CSS rules. Because the popup page has only a few elements to style, rather than linking to an external CSS file, you can embed the styles directly in the page header instead.

Page HTML Head:

```css
<style type="text/css">
body {background-color:#FFFFFF;margin:0}
* {font: normal 12px tahoma,arial,helvetica,sans-serif;}

a:link, a:visited, a:active {
  font: normal 12px tahoma,arial,helvetica,sans-serif;
  color: #0464BB;
  text-decoration:none;
}
a:hover {
  color: #1C417C;
  text-decoration: underline;
}

.ux-top-toolbar   {
    background-color:#D0DEF0;
    background:none repeat-x scroll left top transparent;
    background-image: url("/ux/extjs/resources/images/default/toolbar/
bg.gif");
    border-color:#A9BFD3;
    border-style:solid;
    display:block;
    overflow:hidden;
    padding:2px;
    width:100%;
    border-width:0 0 1px;
    left:0;
    position:fixed;
    top:0;
}
.ux-btm-toolbar   {
    background-color:#D0DEF0;
    background:none repeat-x scroll left top transparent;
    background-image: url("/ux/extjs/resources/images/default/toolbar/
bg.gif");
    border-color:#A9BFD3;
    border-style:solid;
    display:block;
    overflow:hidden;
    padding:2px;
    width:100%;
    border-width:1px 0 0;
    top:auto;
```

```
      left:0;
      position:fixed;
      bottom:0;
}

#search-item {
background-color:#FFFFFF;
background-image: url("/ux/extjs/resources/images/default/form/text-
bg.gif");
border:1px solid #B5B8C8;
line-height:normal;
padding:3px 3px 0;
vertical-align:middle;
}
</style>
```

The CSS styles the body search item and link elements, as well as uses fixed positioning to ensure that the top and bottom toolbars remain in position regardless of scrolling.

Popup List of Values are fine to use, but we will see better alternatives in later chapters when we look at AJAX-enabled combo boxes.

Breadcrumb templates

Breadcrumbs or breadcrumb trails provide a navigation aid to assist in identifying the user's location in a website. Breadcrumbs typically are used as a **secondary navigation scheme**, and appear horizontally near the top of a page, showing the path taken to reach the current page.

Typical breadcrumbs look like this:

```
Home page > Section page > Subsection page
```

There are three types of web breadcrumbs:

- **Path breadcrumbs** are dynamic, and show the user the exact steps they have taken to arrive at their current location.
- **Location breadcrumbs** are static, showing where the page is located in the website hierarchy.
- **Attribute breadcrumbs** give information that categorizes the current page, for example, Electronics > Televisions > Plasma TV.

APEX supports only location and attribute breadcrumbs, because it uses static hierarchies to define breadcrumbs.

Benefits of using breadcrumbs

Breadcrumbs work well in websites that have a large amount of content organized in a hierarchical manner, such as e-commerce websites, in which a large variety of products are grouped into logical categories.

Some of the benefits of using a breadcrumb trail are:

- **Reduced clicks to return to higher-level pages:** APEX-generated pages often use a **Cancel** or **Back** button to return to an earlier page. Using breadcrumbs, users can return to a higher-level page with a single click instead of navigating back through the pages, saving multiple page loads.

- **Consumption of minimal screen real estate:** Typically, breadcrumbs are horizontally oriented and use plain styling, consuming minimal screen space and minimal overhead to page content.

- **Alternative uses:** Breadcrumbs can be used for specific page groups, such as wizards or guided tours. The following screenshot shows how Flickr uses a breadcrumb trail, indicating the number of sections in the Flickr tour:

When not to use breadcrumbs

Breadcrumb trails have a linear structure, so using them will be difficult if your pages can't be classified into neat categories. Deciding whether to use breadcrumbs largely depends on how you've designed your website hierarchy. If you can navigate to a lower-level page from more than one location or category, breadcrumb trails are ineffective, inaccurate, and confusing to the user.

Basic horizontal breadcrumb template

The breadcrumb template shown in the next screenshot uses a simple unordered list and some CSS to define a horizontal breadcrumb trail:

The source for the breadcrumb template is:

Start with: Parent to Leaf

Before first:

```
<div class="breadcrumb">
  <ul>
```

Current page breadcrumb entry:

```
<li>#NAME#</li>
```

Non-current page breadcrumb entry:

```
<li><a href="#LINK#" title="#LONG_NAME#">#NAME#</a></li>
```

After last:

```
  </ul>
</div>
```

Maximum Levels: 12

The template is just the minimal markup required to define an unordered list, with non-current pages containing a link element with a title attribute. The list is wrapped by a DIV element with a class attribute.

So, the only thing controlling the horizontal layout of the list is the CSS:

```
.breadcrumb {
    color: grey;
    display:block;
    left:0;
    overflow:hidden;
    padding:2px;
    position:relative;
    top:0;
}
.breadcrumb li {
    float: left;
    display: inline;
    margin-right: 4px;
}
.breadcrumb a {
    color: #222;
    background: url(/i/r_arrow.gif) no-repeat scroll right center;
    padding-right: 12px;
    text-decoration: none;
}
```

Using `display: inline` changes the list from a vertical to a horizontal list. Everything else is visual styling.

Breadcrumbs are usually contained in a Region template of type "Breadcrumb Region". As the template defined here is self contained, the region template is just a wrapper:

Template Class: Breadcrumb Region

Template:

```
<div id="#REGION_STATIC_ID#" #REGION_ATTRIBUTES#>#BODY#</div>
```

Breadcrumbs are simple to implement and effective to use; let's move onto something a little more challenging in Report templates.

Report templates

APEX has two report types, the "Classic Report" and the "Interactive Report".

Classic reports have been in APEX since its inception, and are the formatted result of the `SELECT` statement of SQL language. The report templates used to control the layout of a classic report can either be "Generic Column" or "Named Column" templates. The main difference being that Generic Column templates render every column using the same column sub-template, whereas Named Column templates allow you to render each column differently, but need to define each column in the template.

The overwhelming majority of APEX applications will predominantly use Generic Column templates, reserving Named Column templates for very specific report layouts. We will be looking only at the Generic Column Report template in this chapter, as this will give you the maximum benefit in creating your initial Ext JS theme.

Interactive Reports were first introduced in APEX 3.1, providing the user with the ability to customize the appearance of the data through a searching, filtering, sorting, column selection, highlighting, and other data manipulations. They were the "killer feature" of the APEX 3.1 release, causing both developers and application users to clamor at managers doors demanding to "Upgrade immediately!".

In APEX 4.0, a whole series of new features have been added to Interactive Reports, including icon and detail views, the ability to have multiple "saved reports", e-mailing reports, and more. While all this makes Interactive Reports even more compelling to use, they don't have templates, so we won't be covering them here.

Another limitation of Interactive Reports is that you are limited to one Interactive Report per page, leaving a huge hole to be filled by Classic reports.

It's a classic

The Ext Grid is one of the most advanced and widely used components of Ext JS. You can use it to simply display and paginate tabular data using AJAX, edit data inline, drag–and-drop columns, hide and show columns, have expanding and collapsing rows, and so on.

In this template we are going to "fake it", using the built-in functionality of an APEX Classic report and combining it with some CSS, so it looks like a read-only Ext Grid with AJAX paging.

The following screenshot shows what our report template looks like, sitting inside a collapsible Report Region template. Notice how some of the elements we have already covered are all coming together—the report is sitting very nicely within a collapsible panel, looking very integrated with the panel. The buttons for the pagination and the CSV download use CSS sprite techniques we also covered earlier in this chapter.

Customers						
Id	First Name ▾	Last Name	Logon Name	Email Address		Last Logon
457	Andrew	Rowe	arowe	arowe@nowhere.com.au		13-MAR-2010
404	Angela	Stevens	astevens	astevens@nowhere.com.au		02-MAY-2010
539	Angela	Hayes	ahayes	ahayes@nowhere.com.au		07-MAY-2010
622	Angela	Parsons	aparsons	aparsons@nowhere.com.au		06-MAY-2010
475	Anita	Barrett	abarrett	abarrett@nowhere.com.au		17-APR-2010
512	Ann	Cowen	acowen	acowen@nowhere.com.au		19-APR-2010
469	Anna	Harrison	aharrison	aharrison@nowhere.com.au		07-MAY-2010
460	Anne	Whelan	awhelan	awhelan@nowhere.com.au		23-MAY-2010
306	Anthony	Hawkins	ahawkins	ahawkins@nowhere.com.au		03-APR-2010
544	Barbara	Davey	bdavey	bdavey@nowhere.com.au		18-MAY-2010
◀ Displaying 21 - 30 ▶						🗐

Create a new report template, populating the fields shown here.

Report Template Name: EXTJS Standard

Template Class: Standard

Before rows:

```
<div class="x-panel-body ux-report">
<table id="report-#REGION_STATIC_ID#" cellpadding="0" cellspacing="0"
class="ux-table" #REPORT_ATTRIBUTES#>
```

Before column heading:

```
<thead>
```

Column heading template:

```
<td id="#COLUMN_HEADER_NAME#" class="ux-cell-hd x-grid3-header"
#ALIGNMENT# #COLUMN_WIDTH#>#COLUMN_HEADER#</td>
```

When using a version prior to APEX 4.0, leave out the #COLUMN_WIDTH# attribute.

After column heading:

```
</thead>
<tbody>
```

Before each row:

```
<tr #HIGHLIGHT_ROW#>
```

Column template 1:

```
<td class="ux-cell valign="top" #ALIGNMENT#>#COLUMN_VALUE#</td>
```

Column template 1 condition:

Use for odd numbered rows

Column template 2:

```
<td class="ux-cell-alt" valign="top" #ALIGNMENT#>#COLUMN_VALUE#</td>
```

Column template 2 condition:

Use for even numbered rows

After each row:

```
</tr>
```

After rows:

```
</tbody>
</table>
</div>
<div class="x-panel-bbar">
  <div class="x-toolbar x-small-editor x-toolbar-layout-ct">
    <table cellspacing="0" class="x-toolbar-ct"><tbody><tr>
      <td align="left" class="x-toolbar-left">
        <table cellspacing="0">#PAGINATION#</table>
      </td>
```

```
        <td class="x-toolbar-right">
            <table cellspacing="0" align="right"
                 class="x-toolbar-right-ct"><tbody>
               <tr>
                  <td class="pagination">
                      <span class="xtb-sep"></span>
                  </td>
                  <td class="pagination">#CSV_LINK#</td>
                  <td class="pagination">#EXTERNAL_LINK#</td>
               </tr></tbody>
            </table>
        </td>
    </tr></tbody></table>
  </div>
</div>
```

Background color for checked row:

```
#cfe0f1
```

Background color for current row:

```
#efefef
```

Pagination template:

```
Displaying #TEXT#
```

Next page template:

```
<a onclick="#LINK#" ext:qtip="#PAGINATION_NEXT#"><span>
  <img src="/i/1px_trans.gif" width="16px" height="16px"  class="x-
tbar-page-next"/>
</span></a>
```

Previous page template:

```
<a onclick="#LINK#" ext:qtip="#PAGINATION_PREVIOUS#"><span>
  <img src="/i/1px_trans.gif" width="16px" height="16px"  class="x-
tbar-page-prev"/>
</span></a>
```

Next set template:

```
<a href="#LINK#" ext:qtip="#PAGINATION_NEXT_SET#"><span>
  <img src="/i/1px_trans.gif" width="16px" height="16px"  class="ux-
tbar-pageset-next"/>
</span></a>
```

Previous set template:

```
<a href="#LINK#" ext:qtip="#PAGINATION_PREVIOUS_SET#"><span>
  <img src="/i/1px_trans.gif" width="16px" height="16px"  class="ux-
tbar-pageset-prev"/>
</span></a>
```

Looking at the earlier fields for the template, you can see we are using a very standard table layout, integrating the relevant APEX substitution tags as we go. It's really all quite ordinary in fact!

If you are using APEX versions earlier than APEX 4.0 for the **Column Heading Template,** the #COLUMN_WIDTH# substitution tag is not available. You can fix column widths without it anyway, using CSS rules picking up the table ID and column ID. So for this template, if the region used a static region name of customer and the column name was first_name you could set the column width using a CSS rule in the page header:

```
#report-customer #first_name {width: 80px}
```

The After Rows field looks quite complicated, but that's only because APEX insists on creating the #PAGINATION# sub-template as a table row, using table cells with a "pagination" class attribute. To get this to fit into the Ext toolbar markup and right align the #CSV_LINK# on the same line, some fancy footwork has been done, introducing some additional embedded tables as a means to achieving a result.

For the **Pagination** components, starting at **After Rows** all the way down to **Previous Set Template**, two techniques have been repeatedly used to create the pagination icons and the CSV download icon.

For the button outline, the CSS sprite technique discussed at the beginning of the chapter has been reused, this time with a fixed width image, as all the icons used are of a known size. Once again the "hover" and "active" appearance for the buttons have been achieved using the CSS `background-image` and `background-position` properties to display the desired image segment. The following diagram shows the image used for the button outline:

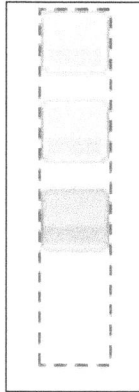

The icons for the "next" and "previous" indicators and CSV download use a transparent image with a fixed size of 16x16 pixels, and a class specifying the CSS **background-image** attribute for the icon. For example, the "next" page indicator uses the following markup for the image:

```
<img src="/i/1px_trans.gif" width="16px" height="16px"  class="x-tbar-page-prev"/>
```

The `x-tbar-page-prev` class attribute picks up the Ext CSS rule for the icon:

```
.x-tbar-page-prev{
    background-image: url(../images/default/grid/page-prev.gif)
!important;
}
```

It is worth remembering that by using the `background-image` attribute instead of directly assigning the image source, you can easily update the image by modifying the CSS file once, rather than in every place you reference the image source.

A better sorting indicator

For the column-sorting indicator, APEX gives you some predefined choices, and if you don't like those choices it can be difficult to reference another image.

The reason behind it being difficult is that APEX prefixes whatever image name you specify in the **Ascending Image** and **Descending Image** fields in the Sorting section of the Report Attributes for a Report Region with /i/, and not the #IMAGE_PREFIX# substitution tag as you would expect.

Fortunately, among the standard images supplied with APEX in that folder is a one-pixel transparent image, allowing you to use the CSS background-image technique to use the transparent image once again, and specify a class to pick up the image you want to use. The following screenshot shows how to assign the image and classes:

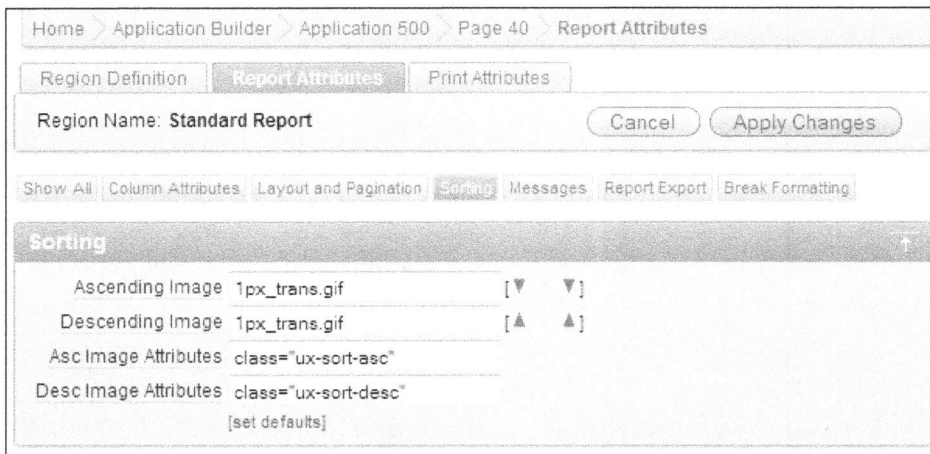

The CSS for the sorting indicator is:

```
.ux-sort-asc {
    background-image:url(/ux/extjs/resources/images/default/grid/sort_
asc.gif);
    background-repeat:no-repeat;
    display:inline;
    height:4px;
    margin-left:3px;
    vertical-align:middle;
    width:13px;
}
.ux-sort-desc {
    background-image:url(/ux/extjs/resources/images/default/grid/sort_
desc.gif);
```

```
    background-repeat:no-repeat;
    display:inline;
    height:4px;
    margin-left:3px;
    vertical-align:middle;
    width:13px;
}
```

CSS for the standard report

There is quite a lot of CSS behind this report template, so rather than showing it all here, I will just refer you to the CSS file located in `chapter5/playpen-book.css`. Look for the section under "Reports".

Calendar templates

Calendar templates are unusual because they contain multiple layouts within a single template. Within a Calendar template, there are separate templates for monthly, weekly, and daily calendars, and in APEX 4.0 there is an additional custom calendar template.

The calendar we will be creating is shown in the following screenshot. It scales to the width of the enclosing region, and scales vertically based on the content of the calendar items. To restrict the size of the calendar, set the enclosing regions width in the **Region Attributes** field for the region.

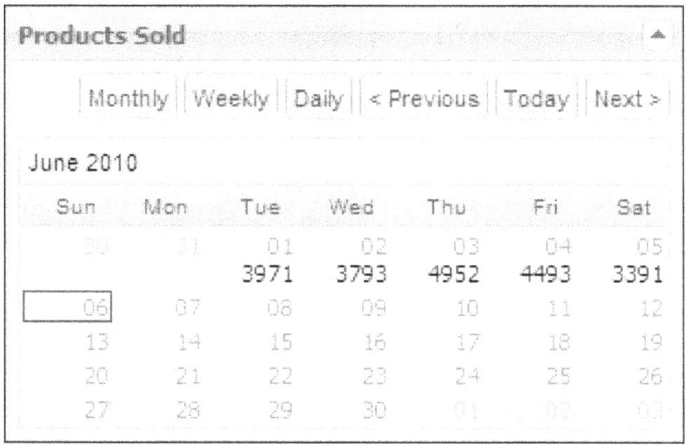

Create a new Calendar template, name it EXTJS Calendar, and populate the fields for the Monthly Calendar:

Month formats:

Month title format

```
<div class="ux-calendar x-list-wrap"> <div class="x-list-header">
<div class="x-list-header-inner"> <div><em style="border-left-
width:0">#IMONTH# #YYYY#</em></div> </div> </div>
```

Day of week format

```
<th><span>#IDY#</span></th>
```

Month open format

```
<table border="0" cellpadding="0" cellspacing="1px" summary="0"
class="x-date-inner">
```

Month close format

```
</table>
</div>
```

Week formats:

Week open format

```
<tr>
```

Week close format

```
</tr>
```

Weekday formats:

Day title format

```
<div>#DD#</div>
```

Day open format

```
<td class="x-date-active" title="">
```

Day close format

```
</td>
```

Today open format

```
<td valign="top" class="x-date-active x-date-today">
```

Non-day formats:

Non-day title format

```
<div>#DD#</div>
```

Non-day open format

```
<td class="x-date-disabled" title="">
```

Non-day close format

```
</td>
```

Weekend formats:

Weekend title format

```
<div>#DD#</div>
```

Weekend open format

```
<td class="x-date-active" title="">
```

Weekend close format

```
</td>
```

The weekly and daily calendars are very similar; the main differences to note is the enclosing DIV element has an additional class attribute—ux-calendar-weekly or ux-calendar-daily.

The weekly template is:

Month title format

```
<div class="ux-calendar ux-calendar-weekly x-list-wrap"> <div
class="x-list-header"> <div class="x-list-header-inner"> <div><em
style="border-left-width:0">#WTITLE#</em></div> </div> </div>
```

Day of week format

```
<th><span>#IDY#<br>#MM#/#DD#</span></th>
```

Month open format

```
<table border="0" cellpadding="0" cellspacing="1px" summary="0"
class="x-date-inner">
```

Month close format

```
</table> </div>
```

Hour formats

Hour open format

```
<tr>
```

Hour close format

```
</tr>
```

Weekday formats:

Day open format

```
<td class="x-date-active" title="">
```

Day close format

```
</td>
```

Today open format

```
<td valign="top" class="x-date-active">
```

Time formats:

Time title format

```
#TIME#
```

Time open format

```
<th>
```

Time close format

```
</th>
```

Weekend formats:

Weekend open format

```
<td>
```

Weekend close format

```
</td>
```

And the Daily Calendar template is:

Month formats:

Month title format

```
<div class="ux-calendar ux-calendar-daily x-list-wrap"> <div
class="x-list-header"> <div class="x-list-header-inner"> <div><em
style="border-left-width:0">#IMONTH# #DD#, #YYYY#</em></div> </div> </
div>
```

Day of week format

```
<th width="100%"><div>#IDAY# #DD#/#MM#</div></th>
```

Month open format

```
<table border="0" cellpadding="0" cellspacing="1px" summary="0"
class="x-date-inner">
```

Month close format

```
</table> </div>
```

Hour formats:

Hour open format

```
<tr>
```

Hour close format

```
</tr>
```

Weekday formats:

Day open format

```
<td class="x-date-active" title="">
```

Day close format

```
</td>
```

Today open format

```
<td valign="top" class="x-date-active">
```

Time formats:

Time title format

```
#TIME#
```

Time open format

```
<th class="c1">
```

Time close format

```
</th>
```

So finally, after three whole chapters, we have created each type of template, and now have a "minimal" theme. Hooray!! Let's clean up and publish our theme.

Removing unused templates quickly

Now is the time to go through your templates deciding, which ones to keep and which ones aren't needed for the time being. We will temporarily remove all those we don't need before we publish our APEX theme. Throughout the book, all the templates have been created using EXTJS as a prefix, making it easy to identify which ones to keep; hopefully you've done something similar.

In *Chapter 1*, *Setting up an Oracle APEX and Ext JS Environment*, two APEX utilities included in the source were mentioned – the **APEXExport** and **APEXExportSplitter** Java classes located in the Oracle APEX distribution in `utilities/oracle/apex` directory. At the time we set up a batch script to run the APEXExport utility. We are now going to make use of the **APEXExportSplitter**.

First, export your theme from **Application Builder | Export**, as shown in the following screenshot:

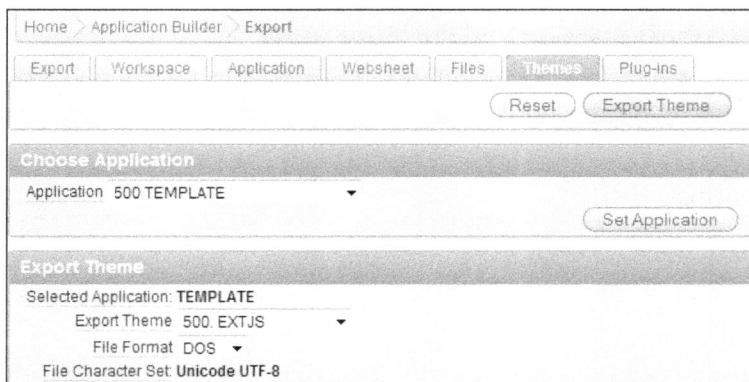

Save the file onto your computer and copy it to a second file, which I'll name `theme.sql` here.

From the command prompt, you then need to set your Java CLASSPATH and run the APEXExportSplitter. I'm doing it here from a DOS prompt; Unix users will need to adjust accordingly.

If you're using database 11g, set the **CLASSPATH** to `ojdbc6.jar`.

```
set CLASSPATH=%CLASSPATH%;<path>\ojdbc6.jar
```

For database 10g, set the **CLASSPATH** to `classes12.jar`.

```
set CLASSPATH=%CLASSPATH%;<path>\classes12.jar
```

Also, set the CLASSPATH to include the utilities directory containing the APEXExportSplitter.

```
set CLASSPATH=%CLASSPATH%;<path>\utilities
```

Now you can run the splitter.

In case of my local environment:

```
set CLASSPATH=%CLASSPATH%;C:\playpen\oracle\instantclient_10_2\
classes12.jar
set CLASSPATH=%CLASSPATH%;C:\playpen\oracle\utilities

java oracle.apex.APEXExportSplitter theme.sql
```

This splits the file into the individual components in subfolders, as shown in the following screenshot:

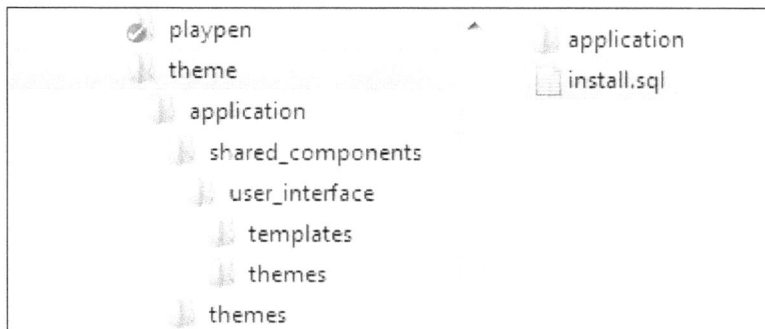

Locate the `install.sql` file in the top folder and edit it, commenting out all the unwanted templates. I've modified the text replacing `shared_components/user_interface/templates` with ... in following code for layout purposes. You simply need to comment out the lines containing unwanted templates.

```
@application/init.sql
@application/themes/300.sql
@application/.../page/login.sql
@application/.../page/extjs_no_tabs_with_sidebar.sql
-- @application/.../page/no_tabs.sql
-- @application/.../page/one_level_tabs.sql
-- @application/.../page/one_level_tabs_with_sidebar.sql
@application/.../page/extjs_popup.sql
-- @application/.../page/printer_friendly.sql
-- @application/.../page/two_level_tabs.sql
-- @application/.../page/two_level_tabs_with_sidebar.sql
@application/.../page/extjs_viewport.sql
@application/.../button/extjs_button.sql
@application/.../button/extjs_button_alternative_1.sql
-- @application/.../button/button_alternative_2.sql
-- @application/.../button/button_alternative_3.sql
```

Now, if you run the `install.sql` script from a SQL*Plus session as the database user for your APEX workspace, the theme will be deleted and recreated with just the uncommented components.

If you missed a file or two, you can edit and rerun this script as often as you like.

Publishing your theme

You are now in a position to publish your "minimal" theme. At this point you have at least one template for each of the template types (breadcrumb, button, calendar, label, list, page, popup list of values, region, and report), but lack templates for every template class within each template type.

Publishing a theme takes a copy of your theme and stores it in the theme repository for the workspace. The published theme cannot be edited directly; to modify it you need to create an application with the theme, modify it, and then publish it to the theme repository.

Having a TEMPLATE application, where you keep the current version of your theme within your workspace, is a really good idea. Apart from having the latest copy on hand, it also lends weight to the argument if you have a policy of no changes to be made to templates within an application without thorough testing. By ensuring that template changes are made in your TEMPLATE application, you can have all your use cases and developer usage documentation in a tidy little bundle — also useful when bringing in new people to your team.

The actual process of publishing a theme is very simple. From within Application Builder, navigate to **Shared Components | Themes | Manage Workspace Themes**. From there, you step through a simple wizard to publish your theme. The following screenshot shows the most complicated step—coming up with a name for your theme!

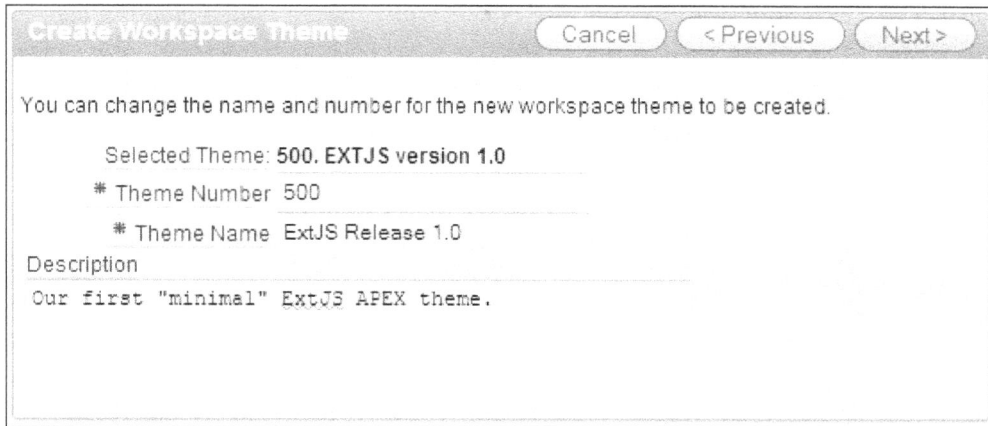

APEX Instance Administrators can publish your theme as a **public theme**. Public themes are available to all workspaces. Generally, it's advisable to have templates for each of the template types, as well as each of the classes within each type, before making a theme public.

Summary

In this chapter, we had a good long look at buttons, creating a custom markup button using the sliding doors method to provide horizontal scalability, and creating multiple states by applying different background images contained in a sprite image.

We then integrated the "horrible" Ext button, starting out using static markup, showing how the button can work without any further changes. After that we converted the static Ext button into a fully functioning button, opening up a range of possibilities that the Ext.Button API offers, including transforming it to include drop-down menus and icons.

Popup list of values and breadcrumbs were covered next, tweaking the template types to create the Ext look, with some simple changes.

The Classic report template was then given a makeover, "faking it" so it looks and behaves like a basic Ext Grid, using the built-in APEX functionality. The report template demonstrated how some of the earlier templates and techniques covered are all coming together, with the report working very nicely within a collapsible panel.

The Calendar template was covered next, once again adding some visual polish to an already functional APEX component.

You saw how to delete all the unwanted templates quickly from the APEX theme using the **APEXExportSplitter** Java class, and discussed the process of publishing the theme.

Also pointed out are the benefits of maintaining a TEMPLATE application, providing a place to modify your theme templates, and also have all your use cases and developer usage documentation in a tidy little bundle.

Now have our working theme up and running. The next chapter starts introducing some Ext widgets into our application.

6
Adding Ext Layout Elements

In consulting circles the term "low-hanging fruit" is often used to describe quick-win solutions, where a minor change significantly improves some aspect of an application with a broad impact across the entire application.

Consultants and developers in general love "low-hanging fruit" solutions because they are easy to reach, and help keep the forward momentum of a project going. With estimating task complexity and duration in software development not being an exact science, some activities take far longer than originally estimated while others come in well under time. Having a few "low-hanging fruit" solutions available means you can smooth out some of the overruns and buy some time by reporting "feature X was held back this release because we implemented feature Y across the entire application".

Having said that, the term evokes visual imagery of fruit-laden trees and ironically in orchards, picking the low-hanging fruit first is the worst thing to do. Experienced pickers start at the top of the tree where the fruit is ripest. Starting at the top makes the job easier, as you rest the bag, which is around your neck and shoulders on the ladder. You fill as you go down, so the bag is full when you get to the bottom.

In this chapter, we will cover the following "low-hanging fruit":

- Converting APEX Classic dates to the Ext.DatePicker
- Making all text areas resizable, or better still, auto-sizing
- Transforming select lists to auto-completing combo boxes
- Building tab panels using subregions
- Building toolbars and menus

Speed dating with a Date Picker

In versions prior to APEX 4.0, the Date Picker component displays a text field with a calendar icon next to it. When clicked, the icon displays a small calendar in a pop-up window as a separate page request. Selecting a date passes back the value to the text field, and closes the pop-up window. This date picker still exists in APEX 4.0, as the **Date Picker** (**Classic**), shown on the left of the following screenshot:

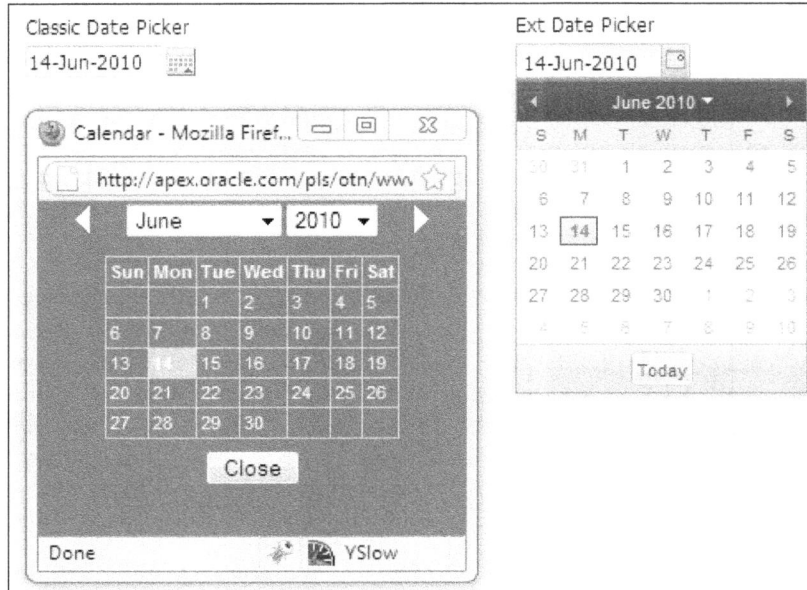

The Ext alternative to this classic date picker is the **Ext.DatePicker**, a highly configurable component, which dynamically constructs a calendar within the page when the icon is clicked. It also allows you to rapidly scroll through months and years using keyboard shortcuts; it also features auto-complete functionality, allowing you to type partial dates or use alternative date formats, which are automatically converted when you tab out of the field.

In APEX 4.0, the Date Picker item type uses the jQuery UI Datepicker as the replacement for the Date Picker (Classic). It offers similar functionality to the Ext. DatePicker component, rendering a calendar dynamically within the page and uses keyboard shortcuts to rapidly scroll through months and years.

It comes with the added advantage that as a native APEX item, it has a number of settings that can be applied declaratively by the developer, as can be seen in the following screenshot:

APEX 4.0 Date Picker

◀		June 2010				▶		Settings	

Sun Mon Tue Wed Thu Fri Sat

		1	2	3	4	5
	6	7	8	9	10	11	12
	13	14	15	16	17	18	19
	20	21	22	23	24	25	26
	27	28	29	30

Value Required   No ▼
Format Mask
Highlighted Date   +0d
Minimum Date
Maximum Date
Show   on icon click ▼
Show other Months   No ▼
Navigation List for   None   ▼

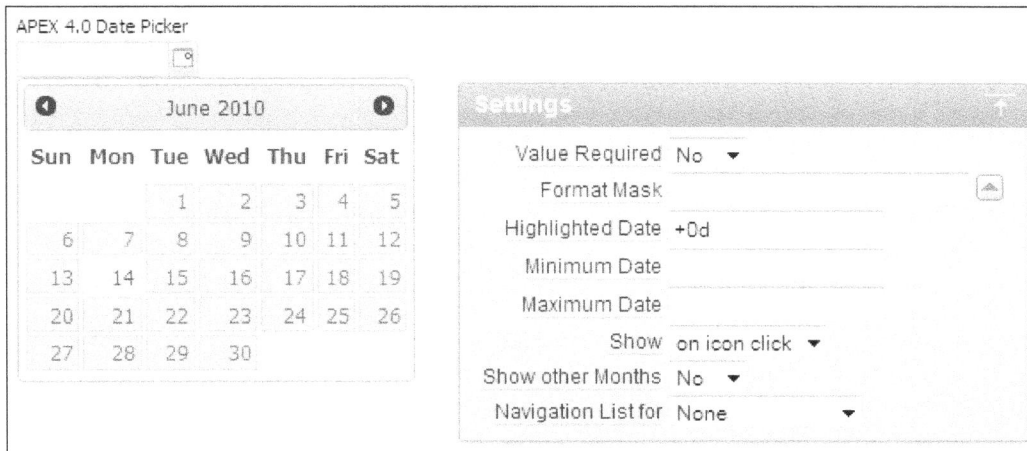

Applications upgrading to APEX 4.0 can easily upgrade Date Picker (Classic) items to the new Date Picker using the **Application Builder | Utilities | Upgrade Application | "Upgrade Date Picker (Classic) to new Date Picker"** interface.

For APEX versions prior to APEX 4.0, the Ext.DatePicker makes very good sense to use in preference to the Date Picker (Classic), whereas in APEX 4.0, the new Date Picker offers similar functionality with better declarative support.

So, if you're currently using a version prior to APEX 4.0, converting to the Ext. DatePicker is very worthwhile. The conversion approach simply adds a little generic JavaScript to the application, resulting in minimal effort to add, and minimal effort to remove. When you eventually upgrade to APEX 4.0, you can decide whether or not to switch to the new APEX Date Picker.

For new applications in APEX 4.0, unless you're hell-bent on using the Ext. DatePicker and write an APEX plugin to give you similar declarative functionality, the APEX Date Picker is the way to go. If you like the look of the date item, you can duplicate it using CSS anyway, as I've done in the previous screenshot and in the included `playpen-book.css` file.

Converting Classic Dates to the Ext. DatePicker

The technique described will convert all Classic Dates to use the Ext.DatePicker, so we are making the assumption that you use the same date format for all your dates in your application. Usually this is done by setting the **Application Date Format**, found in Application Builder under **Shared Components | Globalization Attributes**.

For most applications, this is a reasonable assumption, but if you're using multiple date formats, you can alter the code to include or exclude items with a specific class only, which you assign to individual date items in the HTML form element attributes.

Classic Dates are rendered in a HTML table like this:

```
<table cellspacing="0" cellpadding="0" border="0" id="P80_DATE_PICKER_
holder" summary="" class="datepicker">
<tbody>
<tr>
<td class="datepicker">
  <input type="hidden" value="3813216463288336"
   name="p_arg_names">
  <input type="text" id="P80_DATE_PICKER" value="23-Mar-2010"
   maxlength="2000" size="12" name="p_t08">
</td>
<td>
  <a href="JavaScript:void($p_DatePicker(
    'P80_DATE_PICKER','0',
    'DD-Mon-YYYY','#666666','','','','','2010',
    'en-us','N','103',
    '1038420889063720','06','210'));">
  <img align="absmiddle" alt="Calendar" src="/i/asfdcldr.gif"
    id="P80_DATE_PICKER_IMG">
  </a>
</td>
</tr>
</tbody>
</table>
```

The key points to note here is that the date is rendered in a table with `class="datepicker"`, and the input item holding the date is in the first TD element, and the icon is in the second TD element.

To use the Ext.DatePicker, you would include the following code in your application JavaScript file:

```
Ext.onReady(function(){
    var els = Ext.select("table.datepicker", true);

    els.each(function(el){
        // remove the datepicker class, to remove any styling
        el.removeClass('datepicker');
        Ext.fly(el).child('.datepicker').removeClass('datepicker');
```

```
        // remove the icon's table cell
        el.select('td:even').remove();

        // retrieve the date item as a dom node
        var dt = Ext.fly(el).child('input[type=text]', true);

        // convert to date
        new Ext.form.DateField({
            id: dt.id,
            applyTo: dt,
            "format": 'd-M-Y',
            "altFormats": 'j|j/n|j/n/y|j/n/Y|j-M|j-M-y|j-M-Y'
        });
    })
});
```

The code starts out by parsing the DOM, retrieving any tables with the
class="datepicker" attribute, and saving the results in an array els. Each table is
then processed in a loop:

```
var els = Ext.select("table.datepicker", true);

els.each(function(el){
    // process each datepicker...
})
```

Within the loop, each datepicker table is modified, removing the datepicker class
from the table and any child elements:

```
// remove the datepicker class, to remove any styling
el.removeClass('datepicker');
Ext.fly(el).child('.datepicker').removeClass('datepicker');

// remove the icon's table cell
el.select('td:even').remove();
```

Then the input item is selected and converted to an Ext.DatePicker; the item name
and values are retained as part of the conversion:

```
// retrieve the date item as a dom node
var dt = Ext.fly(el).child('input[type=text]', true);

// convert to date
new Ext.form.DateField({
    id: dt.id,
    applyTo: dt,
    "format": 'd-M-Y',
    "altFormats": 'j|j/n|j/n/y|j/n/Y|j-M|j-M-y|j-M-Y'
});
```

The database date format I'm using is DD-Mon-YYYY, which corresponds to the Ext date format d-M-Y. For a complete list of format masks available, consult the Ext documentation at http://www.extjs.com/deploy/dev/docs/?class=Date.

The "altFormats" attribute shown in the preceding code snippet includes a number of alternative formats, which can be used for data entry. So, for example, typing 1 and then tabbing out of the date would automatically be converted to the first day of the current month and year. Similarly, typing 1/3 would convert to the first of March for the current year.

If you prefer the format DD-MON-YYYY for your dates, it's not available using the date formats listed for Ext, but can be done by overriding the default Ext date names with the following line of JavaScript at the beginning of your application JavaScript file:

```
Date.monthNames =["JANUARY","FEBRUARY","MARCH","APRIL","MAY",
"JUNE","JULY","AUGUST","SEPTEMBER","OCTOBER","NOVEMBER",
"DECEMBER"];
```

This is the Ext way of internationalizing dates, so it's fully supported, and forces the JavaScript date format "d-M-Y" to return the month in uppercase.

So there you have it, a simple "drop in" solution that you can incorporate into existing pre-APEX 4.0 applications and give them enhanced functionality. The more interesting question is once you have moved to APEX 4.0, are you going to keep the Ext DatePicker, or switch to the APEX jQuery version?

Resizable text areas

In APEX 4.0, text areas have a resizable option, when enabled allowing users to resize text areas, so they can see all the text. I'm sure you're already too familiar with how frustrating it is using the APEX Builder when you're trying to edit code in a text area much smaller than your code.

As developers, we normally have local administration rights on our computers, so it's very easy to overcome this issue by using a browser add-on, such as the Firefox "Text Area Resizer and Mover", available at https://addons.mozilla.org/en-US/firefox/addon/8287. Our corporate users aren't usually so lucky, with locked-down computers, so they can't alter their set up.

The following screenshot shows the Ext version of the resizable text area compared with the APEX 4.0 resizable text area—quite similar visually, and provides similar functionality.

Ext Text Area

APEX Text Area

The Google browser has similar functionality built into the browser, making all text areas resizable. I believe this is a very sensible approach; after all, why should only some text areas be resizable?

To convert your text areas, just include the following code in your application JavaScript:

```
Ext.onReady(function() {
  var els=Ext.select('textarea',true);
  els.each(function(el){
    new Ext.Resizable(el, {
        wrap:true,
        pinned:true,
        handles: 's',
        width:el.getWidth(),
        height:el.getHeight(),
        minWidth:el.getWidth(),
        minHeight: el.getHeight()
    });
  })
});
```

The script finds all text area elements on the page, and then applies the Ext. Resizable class to the element. This applies drag handles to the element to make it resizable, the original text area remains unchanged—very handy if you have enabled the character counter on a text area!

As usual, Ext provides a number of configuration options, allowing you to set which handles to include, either 'all' or any of 'n s e w ne nw se sw', whether the handles "pinned" to ensure they are always visible, or only visible when the user mouses over the resizable borders, or transparent so the handles don't appear at all.

The `Ext.Resizable` class can be used on more than just text areas; resizable images are very effective also. In the examples provided with the Ext JS SDK library, the `examples/resizable/basic.html` file demonstrates the full range of options available, including options such as animated transitions, preserved ratios, and snapping.

Auto-sizing text areas

Having implemented resizable text areas over three years ago in some APEX applications, my application users take this feature very much for granted. So much so, that they started to complain about having to resize the text area every time they visited a page to see the full content.

If like my users, you spend your entire day in an application racking up over 2000 page hits individually, you can understand how something little like this really starts to be too much effort for a minor detail.

Having scoured the Internet looking for a solution at the time, it appears Facebook was the first website to introduce an auto-growing text area that gets bigger as you type into it. After spending some time looking at some of the different solutions available, I cobbled together a solution for Ext using techniques borrowed from other people's great ideas.

Now you don't have to, it's a configuration option in the Ext.form.TextArea

To make all your text areas automatically grow, add the following code to your application JavaScript:

```
Ext.onReady(function() {
  var els=Ext.select("textarea",true);
  els.each(function(el){
      new Ext.form.TextArea({
          applyTo: el,
          grow: true,
          width: el.getWidth()
      });
  })
});
```

Setting the width configuration option retains the original width of the text area.

To limit the size of your text areas, Ext.form.TextArea includes configuration options `growMax` to set maximum height to allow when grow=true (defaults to 1000), and `growMin` to set the minimum height to allow when grow=true (defaults to 60).

No more messing about with grab handles to resize your text boxes; they are always sized to the content. Now my users are happy, for a little while.

Auto-completing text fields

The **Ext.Combo** provides an alternative to the text field with auto-complete item type, which was introduced in APEX 4.0. The text field with auto complete item type shows a list of possible values when the user starts typing in the field, progressively filtering the data as more keys are typed.

The following screenshot shows an example of the text field with auto-complete item type displaying a list of countries, with the field on the right showing that the additional character has further reduced the list of matching values.

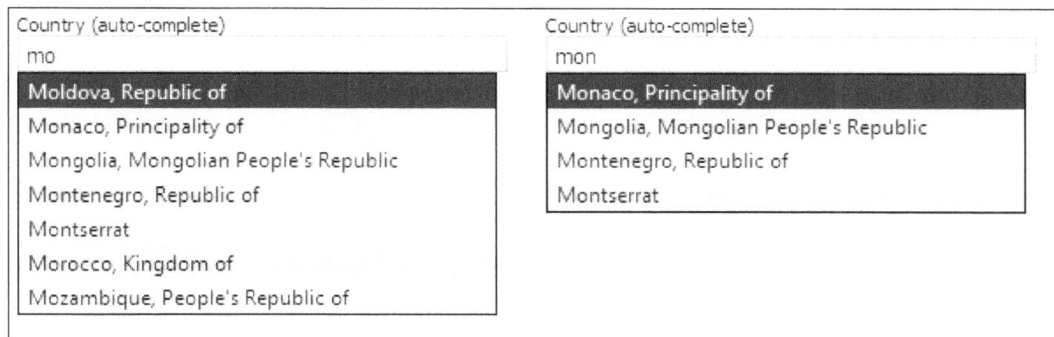

The values are based on the defined **List of Values** (LOV) SQL statement returning a single column, for example:

```
SELECT country_name
  FROM countries
 ORDER BY country_name
```

As the text field with auto-complete item type does not prevent additional values not already in the LOV SQL statement being entered, it is your responsibility as the developer to determine how existing and new values are processed.

Assume we are processing a purchase order (PO) record in the PURCHASE_ORDERS table, and currently looking up the country names from the COUNTRIES table using the earlier query.

Consider the following options for the country field from the preceding screenshot when the page is submitted to the APEX engine for processing:

Use Case	Action
Existing value entered, country stored	Verify existing country. Process PO record.
Existing value entered, country ID stored	Fetch country ID using country name. Process PO record.
New value entered, country stored New values for country are allowed	Verify existing country => NOT FOUND. Add country to COUNTRIES table. Process PO record.
New value entered, country ID stored New values for country are allowed	Fetch country ID using country name => NOT FOUND. Add country to COUNTRIES table, returning country ID. Process PO record.
Change LOV SQL to query PO table New value entered, country stored New values for country are allowed	Process PO record.

Looking at the Use Cases, it becomes evident that most of the time you need to do additional validation and processing for the *text field with auto complete* item type. If it is used as a free-text field, which accepts any input, including new values not already in the LOV SQL statement, then this is an appropriate choice.

For most applications, this is a less common scenario, much more typically you want to limit allowable values for an item to a pre-determined set, only allowing additional values to be added through administration forms by privileged users, if at all.

For this typical lookup scenario, the humble select list is appropriate for relatively short lists of values, and the Popup LOV item type for longer lists. In fact, for the internal APEX applications, which make up the APEX Application Builder, the select list is by far the most commonly used input item, being used for roughly 25% of all input items.

Select Lists have a display value and a returned value for each option.

Continuing our purchase order example for the country field, the values could be based on the defined LOV SQL statement:

```
SELECT country_name d
       ,id r
  FROM countries
 ORDER BY country_name
```

The APEX engine would generate HTML markup for the select list as:

```
<select size="1" id="P70_SELECT_LIST" name="p_t08">
  <option value="65">Afghanistan</option>
  <option value="131">Aland Islands</option>
  <option value="118">Albania, Republic of</option>

  <!-- many more options... -->

  <option value="117">Yemen</option>
  <option value="64">Zambia, Republic of</option>
  <option value="54">Zimbabwe</option>
</select>
```

The results in a user-friendly country description displayed to the user, and the ID value returned when the page is submitted. Looking at the highlighted code, the displayed value is Yemen and the returned value is 117.

The Action for our earlier Use Cases when the APEX engine processes the page is simply "Process PO record", because we have the value we wish to store.

Select lists are very useful for limiting inputs to a set of allowable values, but don't have auto-complete functionality. This is where the **Ext.form.ComboBox** comes into play.

Adding auto-complete to select lists

The **Ext.form.ComboBox** can be used as a direct replacement for the HTML select list. It provides the same drop-down list of values, as well as auto-completing filtering functionality, enabling users to find and select a value quickly.

The following screenshot shows a select list with a large set of values, and a combo box showing the same set of values filtered on the first 3 characters using the auto-complete functionality.

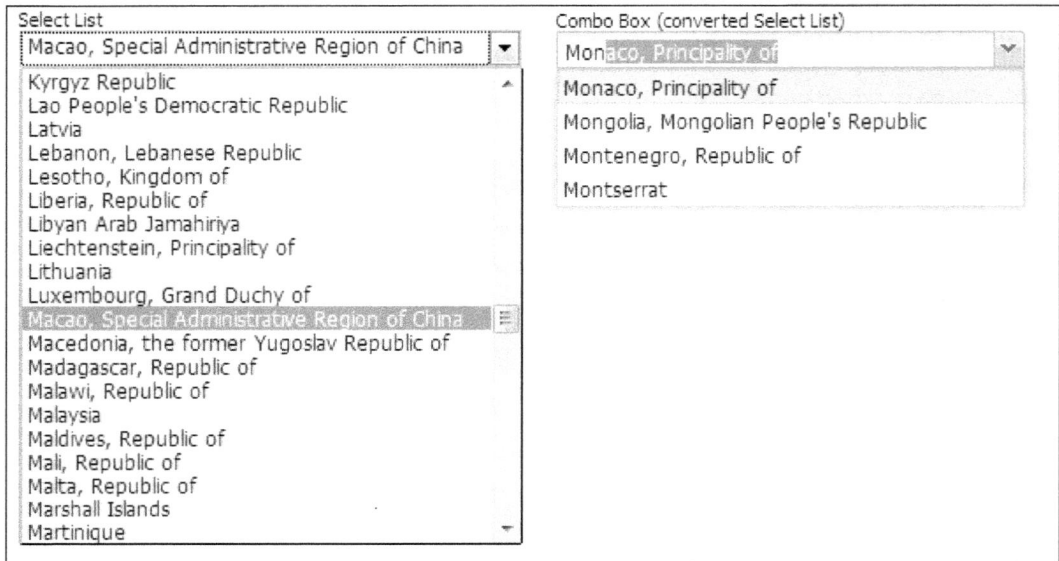

Select List	Combo Box (converted Select List)
Macao, Special Administrative Region of China ▾	Monaco, Principality of ▾
Kyrgyz Republic	Monaco, Principality of
Lao People's Democratic Republic	Mongolia, Mongolian People's Republic
Latvia	Montenegro, Republic of
Lebanon, Lebanese Republic	Montserrat
Lesotho, Kingdom of	
Liberia, Republic of	
Libyan Arab Jamahiriya	
Liechtenstein, Principality of	
Lithuania	
Luxembourg, Grand Duchy of	
Macao, Special Administrative Region of China	
Macedonia, the former Yugoslav Republic of	
Madagascar, Republic of	
Malawi, Republic of	
Malaysia	
Maldives, Republic of	
Mali, Republic of	
Malta, Republic of	
Marshall Islands	
Martinique	

To convert select lists without an onchange attribute to combo boxes is very simple:

```
Ext.onReady(function() {
    var els=Ext.select("select[multiple!='multiple']",true);
    els.each(function(el){
        new Ext.form.ComboBox({
            id: 'cb-'+el.id,
            hiddenId: el.id,
            disabled: el.dom.disabled,
            typeAhead: true,
            triggerAction: 'all',
            transform:el,
            width:el.getWidth(),
            forceSelection:true
        });
    })
});
```

Once again we are using the `Ext.select` function to retrieve all single-line select lists. All of the work to convert each select list into a combo box is done using the highlighted `transform` configuration option to identify the select list. The other configuration options define the behavior we want for the combo box.

However, we have only solved part of the problem!

The APEX 4.0 Application Builder has five different page actions when a select list item type is changed, as shown in the following screenshot:

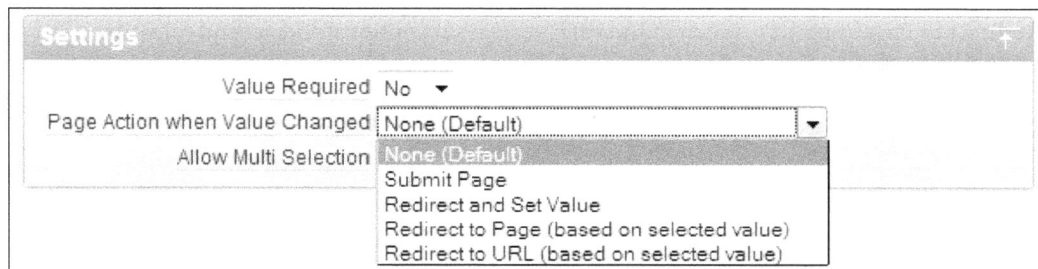

Apart from the "None (Default)" option, each of the options adds an `onchange` attribute to the HTML markup for the select list.

For example, the APEX engine would generate HTML markup for the Submit page select list as:

```
<select class="selectlist"
onchange="apex.submit('P90_SL_SUBMIT');"
size="1" id="P90_SL_SUBMIT" name="p_t05">
  <option value="65">Afghanistan</option>
  <option value="131">Aland Islands</option>
  <option value="118">Albania, Republic of</option>

  <!-- many more options... -->

  <option value="117">Yemen</option>
  <option value="64">Zambia, Republic of</option>
  <option value="54">Zimbabwe</option>
</select>
```

The following table shows an example of the onchange HTML markup for each option:

Option	onchange
None (Default)	
Submit Page	apex.submit('P90_SL_SUBMIT');
Redirect and Set Value	location.href='f?p=103:90:2624308855119166::NO::P90_SL_REDIRECT:'+this.options[selectedIndex].value;
Redirect to Page (based on selected value)	location.href='f?p=103:'+this.options[selectedIndex].value+':2624308855119166::NO';
Redirect to URL (based on selected value)	location.href=this.options[selectedIndex].value;

The auto-sizing text area we modified previously simply adds JavaScript events to the existing DOM element, so existing onchange attributes and existing JavaScript events are retained.

When the select list is transformed to a Ext.form.ComboBox, the JavaScript code creates new DOM elements to make up the Ext.form.ComboBox, and then deletes the select list DOM element together with its onchange attributes.

To convert select lists including logic from onchange attributes to combo boxes:

```
Ext.onReady(function() {
  var els=Ext.select("select[multiple!='multiple']",true);
  els.each(function(el){
    // save attribute as a string
    var attr = el.dom.getAttribute('onchange');
    if (attr && attr.indexOf('this.options[selectedIndex].value') !=
    -1 ) {
      // replace Select List logic with ComboBox equivalent
      attr = attr.replace('this.options[selectedIndex].value',
      'this.getValue()');
    }

    // transform Select List to ComboBox
    var cb = new Ext.form.ComboBox({
      id: 'cb-'+el.id,
      hiddenId: el.id,
      disabled: el.dom.disabled,
      typeAhead: true,
      triggerAction: 'all',
      transform:el,
```

```
    width:el.getWidth(),
    forceSelection:true
  });


  // add on select event
  if (attr) {
    eval( "cb.on('select', function(){ " + attr + "});" );
  }
 })
});
```

Looking at the highlighted code, we first save the value of the `onchange` attribute into a variable and then replace any instance of the string `'this.options[selectedIndex].value'` with `'this.getValue()'`:

```
if (attr && attr.indexOf('this.options[selectedIndex].value') !=
-1 ) {
  // replace Select List logic with ComboBox equivalent
  attr = attr.replace('this.options[selectedIndex].value',
   'this.getValue()');
}
```

Replacing the string changes the logic to fetch the selected value within the select list with its Ext equivalent to fetch the selected value for the combo box.

Once we transform the select list into a combo box, we then conditionally add a listener that executes a function when the `'select'` event is fired:

```
// add on select listener
if (attr) {
  eval( "cb.on('select', function(){ " + attr + "});" );
}
```

The listener is added using the JavaScript `eval` command, which evaluates the concatenated string and executes the statement.

For example, from the earlier table for the redirect to URL option, the `onchange` attribute value was originally `location.href=this.options[selectedIndex].value;`, which was modified to the string `location.href=this.getValue();`.

The string was then concatenated into the statement `cb.on('select', function(){location.href=this.getValue();});`, which was finally executed to add a select listener to the combo box.

Hopefully, I haven't lost you in all the detail. We now are able to transform select lists, including those with `onchange` attributes, into combo boxes. Are we done yet?

No, we're still not done! There's one more thing to take into account.

For pre-APEX 4.0 versions, we have covered all the out-of-the-box scenarios, so unless you have written custom JavaScript, you are reasonably safe. However, APEX 4.0 introduced new functionality, such as *cascading select lists* and *dynamic actions*, resulting in far more JavaScript based interaction between different elements on the page.

Consequently, there will be some circumstances where you don't want to convert specific select lists. A simple way to manage this is by adding a class to the select list, and coding to not transform select lists with this class.

In the following screenshot, the class attribute has been added with the `noTransform` class, along with another class in the HTML form element attributes field for a select list page item within the APEX Application Builder.

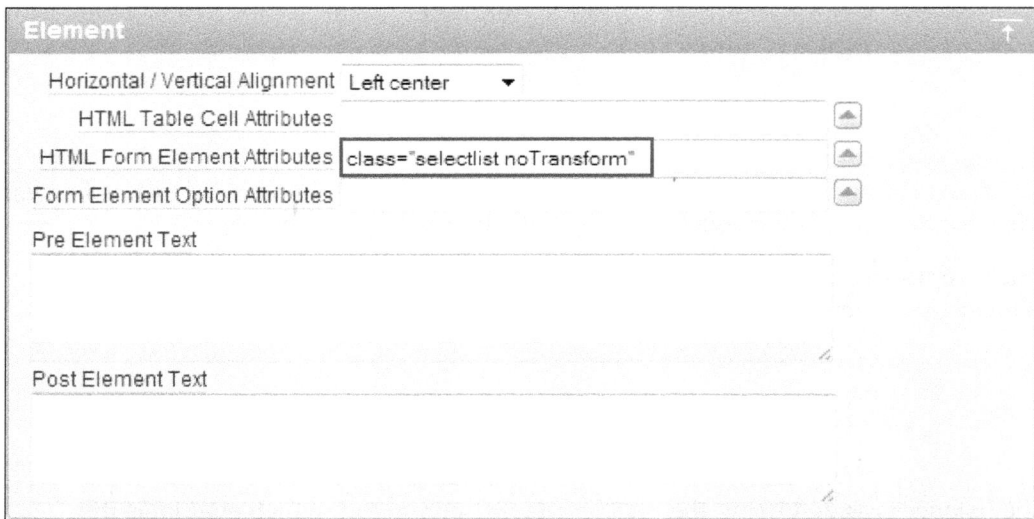

Finally, a check is added to the code to skip select lists with the `noTransform` class:

```
Ext.onReady(function() {
  var els=Ext.select("select[multiple!='multiple']",true);
  els.each(function(el){
    if (!el.hasClass('noTransform')) {
      // save attribute as a string
      var attr = el.dom.getAttribute('onchange');
      if (attr && attr.indexOf('this.options[selectedIndex].value') !=
-1 ) {
        // replace Select List logic with ComboBox equivalent
```

```
        attr = attr.replace('this.options[selectedIndex].value',
'this.getValue()');
      }

      // transform Select List to ComboBox
      var cb = new Ext.form.ComboBox({
        id: 'cb-'+el.id,
        hiddenId: el.id,
        disabled: el.dom.disabled,
        typeAhead: true,
        triggerAction: 'all',
        transform:el,
        width:el.getWidth(),
        forceSelection:true
      });

      // add on select event
      if (attr) {
        eval( "cb.on('select', function(){ " + attr + "});" );
      }
    }
  })
});
```

So at last, we now have a complete solution, which can be dropped into your Application JavaScript.

Building tab panels using subregions

APEX 4.0 introduced subregions, allowing regions to be nested within other regions in a parent-child relationship. This provides display opportunities, such as breaking up large forms into a series of separate sections while still maintaining visual coherence.

Support for subregions was also included in region templates. Adding sections for **subregion header templates**, together with **subregion header entry templates**, provide the possibility to generate a list of region titles of all the subregions of the current region. Mix in a little JavaScript with your subregion templates, and building tab panels like the one shown in the following screenshot becomes very easy:

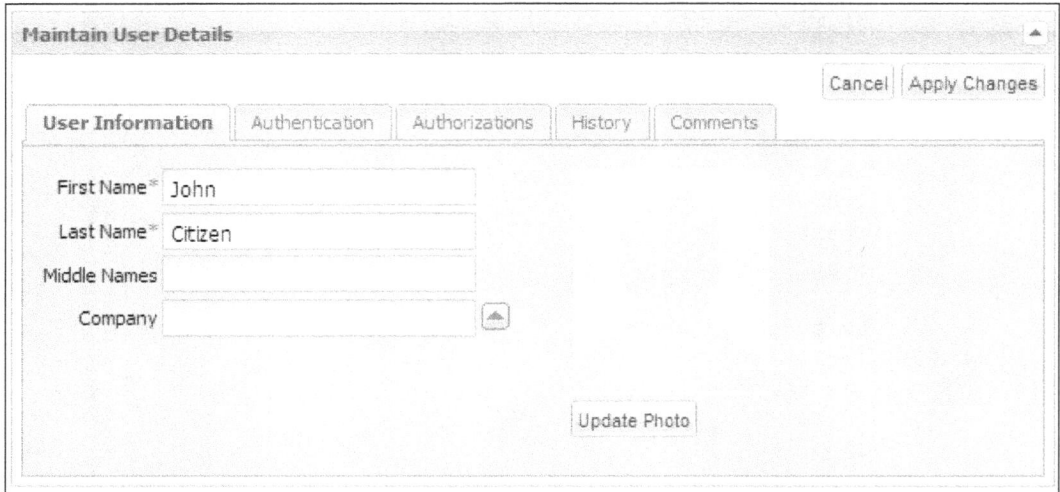

Creating Ext.TabPanels from existing HTML markup can be done using:

- Pre-structured markup: A container DIV with one or more nested tab DIVs with class 'x-tab'. Setting the Ext.TabPanel configuration option of autoTabs to true will automatically query and convert the nested DIVs.

- Un-structured markup: A tab panel can be rendered from markup that is not strictly structured by specifying by ID the elements making up the container and the tabs. Using this method, tab content can be pulled from different elements within the page by ID regardless of the page structure.

We will be using the un-structured markup approach, mainly because the IDs for each of the tab panels are known.

> Specifying the IDs directly instead of querying the DOM to find DIVs with the class 'x-tab' has a slight performance advantage when the browsers JavaScript engine is manipulating the page.

Using the un-structured markup approach, the JavaScript shown:

```
Ext.onReady(function(){
    new Ext.TabPanel({
        renderTo: 'my-tabs',
        activeTab: 0,
        items:[
            {contentEl:'tab1', title:'Tab 1'},
            {contentEl:'tab2', title:'Tab 2'}
        ]
    });
});
```

would convert this markup into a tab panel:

```
<div id="my-tabs"></div>
<div id="tab1" class="x-hide-display">A simple tab</div>
<div id="tab2" class="x-hide-display">Another one</div>
```

Adding the class "x-hide-display" to each of the DIVs stops them from being displayed outside the tabs, and reduces your page content from jumping around when it's being rendered and then manipulated by the page JavaScript. Ext uses this same class to hide or show the tab panels.

Building the tab panel template

The easiest approach to building the template is to start by constructing a page with some nested subregions, and building a solution from there. This way, you can check your progress as you go.

Start off by creating a simple page with several regions, with one for the tab panel; assign the others as subregions of the tab panel. Assigning a region as a subregion is done in Application Builder by setting the parent region attribute, as shown in the following screenshot:

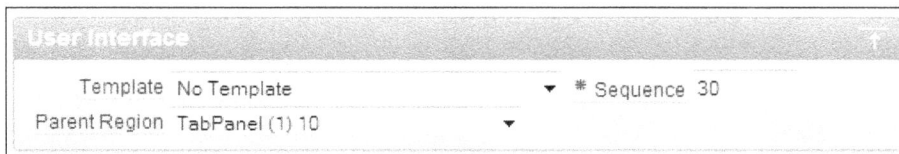

You don't need to assign a template to the subregions for this solution. If you do, it will change the appearance for the content of the individual tab, but not the tab panel itself.

The following screenshot shows the Application Builder view of the tab panel example shown earlier:

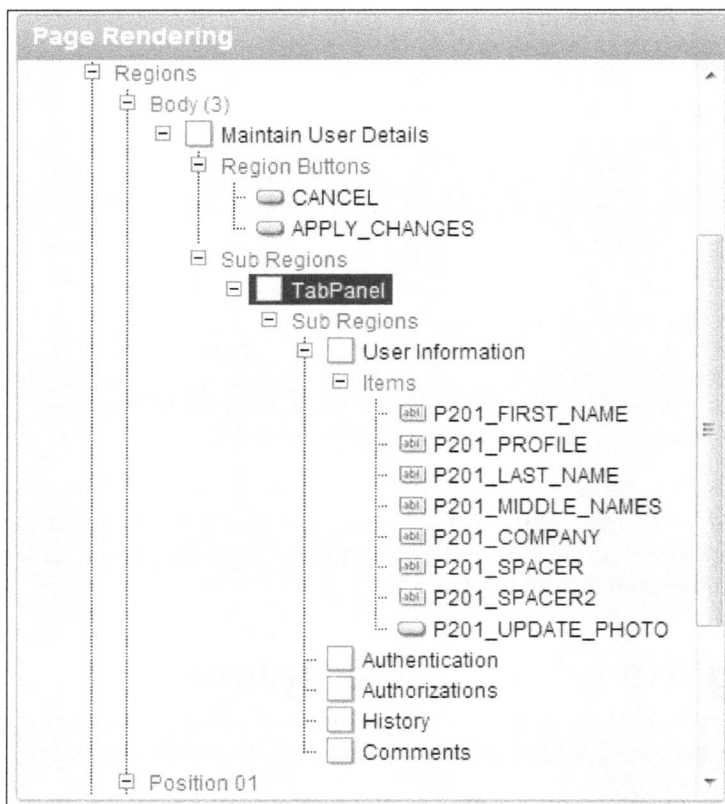

Within the **Maintain User Details** region are some region buttons and a tab panel region as a subregion. The tab panel region in turn contains five subregions and some items within those regions.

No items are included in the tab panel, as the template we are creating is designed simply to be a container for the panels within.

Next, create a new region template with the following properties:

Name:

```
EXTJS TabPanel
```

Template class:

```
Custom 1
```

Template:

```
<div id="#REGION_STATIC_ID#" #REGION_ATTRIBUTES#></div>
#SUB_REGIONS#
#SUB_REGION_HEADERS#
```

For the subregion elements:

Header template:

```
<pre>
Ext.onReady(function(){
    var subs = [];
#ENTRIES#

    new Ext.TabPanel({
        renderTo: '#REGION_STATIC_ID#',
        activeTab: 0,
        items:subs
    });
});
</pre>
```

Header entry template:

```
        subs.push({
            contentEl:'#SUB_REGION_ID#-tab',
            title:'#SUB_REGION_TITLE#'
        });
```

Subregion template:

```
<div id="#SUB_REGION_ID#-tab" class="x-hide-display">
#SUB_REGION#
</div>
```

Rather than my explaining the code we have just added to the template immediately, you should assign the template to the tab panel region in the test form you created earlier. Then run the page to view the output. Did it look like what you expected?

The output for the example used throughout this section is shown in the following screenshot. It shows the contents of the **Maintain User Details** panel and its buttons, but instead of a tab panel, there is just some JavaScript code. No sign of the fields from the first tab panel subregion at all.

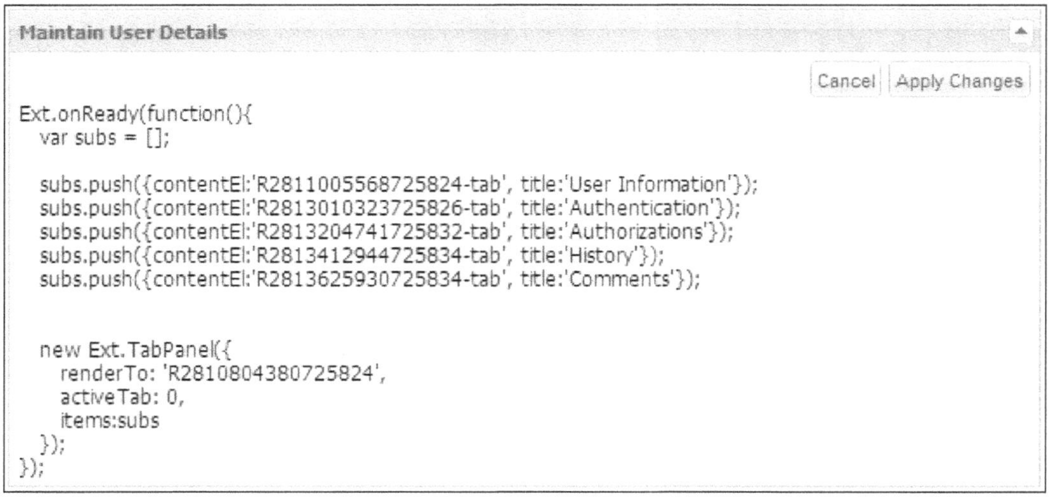

```
Maintain User Details                                                                    ▲

                                                           Cancel   Apply Changes

Ext.onReady(function(){
  var subs = [];

  subs.push({contentEl:'R2811005568725824-tab', title:'User Information'});
  subs.push({contentEl:'R2813010323725826-tab', title:'Authentication'});
  subs.push({contentEl:'R2813204741725832-tab', title:'Authorizations'});
  subs.push({contentEl:'R2813412944725834-tab', title:'History'});
  subs.push({contentEl:'R2813625930725834-tab', title:'Comments'});


  new Ext.TabPanel({
    renderTo: 'R2810804380725824',
    activeTab: 0,
    items:subs
  });
});
```

> Replacing `script` tags with `pre` tags around the JavaScript components in the template allows us to view the generated content.

Now for some explanation, **working our way from the bottom of the template up:**

Subregion template:

```
<div id="#SUB_REGION_ID#-tab" class="x-hide-display">
#SUB_REGION#
</div>
```

Here we are wrapping the subregions with additional HTML code. In this case, a DIV tag encloses the #SUB_REGION# substitution tag. The DIV tag uses the #SUB_REGION_ID# substitution tag with -tab appended to create a unique ID. Assigning the class x-hide-display hides the contents of the subregion until the Ext.TabPanel code is ready to display the subregion.

Header entry template:

```
subs.push({
    contentEl:'#SUB_REGION_ID#-tab',
    title:'#SUB_REGION_TITLE#'
});
```

Subregion header entry templates can be used to construct a list of region titles of all the subregions for the current region. We are adding our own twist by constructing JavaScript instead of HTML. The command is pushing an object literal onto an array, the object literal containing the name of the DIV we wrapped around each subregion, together with the subregion title. This is done by using the #SUB_REGION_ID# and #SUB_REGION_TITLE# substitution tags.

Header template:

```
<script type="text/javascript">
Ext.onReady(function(){
    var subs = [];
#ENTRIES#

    new Ext.TabPanel({
        renderTo: '#REGION_STATIC_ID#',
        activeTab: 0,
        items:subs
    });
});
</script>
```

The subregion header template is mainly used to assemble the accumulated results from the header entry template in the #ENTRIES# substitution tag.

Also included here is the JavaScript to create the Ext.TabPanel, which is rendered into the DIV in the template using the ID generated from the #REGION_STATIC_ ID# substitution tag. This time the pre tags have been replaced with the script tags.

Template:

```
<div id="#REGION_STATIC_ID#" #REGION_ATTRIBUTES#></div>
#SUB_REGIONS#
#SUB_REGION_HEADERS#
```

The template is a simple DIV element the Ext.TabPanel will be rendered into. The #REGION_STATIC_ID# is used to identify the region; the #REGION_ATTRIBUTES# allows attributes to be assigned from the Edit Region Form. This is very useful for sizing the DIV region, for example style="width:595px; height:240px".

The #SUB_REGIONS# and #SUB_REGION_HEADERS# are used to hold the content of the subregions and the JavaScript we have created in the subregion header template.

Now that the script tags are in place, the tab panel will render properly using the minimal configuration we provided.

Configuring the tab panel template

The Ext.TabPanel is highly configurable; so far we have used a minimal configuration when creating the tab panel in the template definition.

Our minimal configuration means the individual tab panel's size to their contents. Looking at the following screenshot, you can see the height of the User Information tab is much larger than the empty **History** tab shown below it. Depending on your requirements, that may be perfectly fine. Let's look at a couple of alternative configurations.

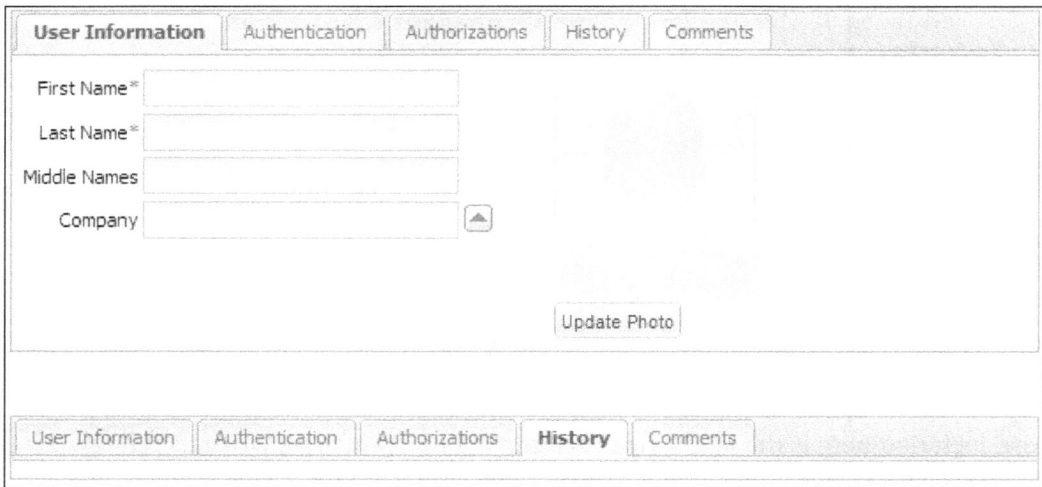

Setting the tab panel's attributes value to `style="width:450px; height:240px"`, as shown in the following screenshot, controls the height and width of the containing DIV the tab panel is rendered into through the `#REGION_ATTRIBUTES#` substitution tag:

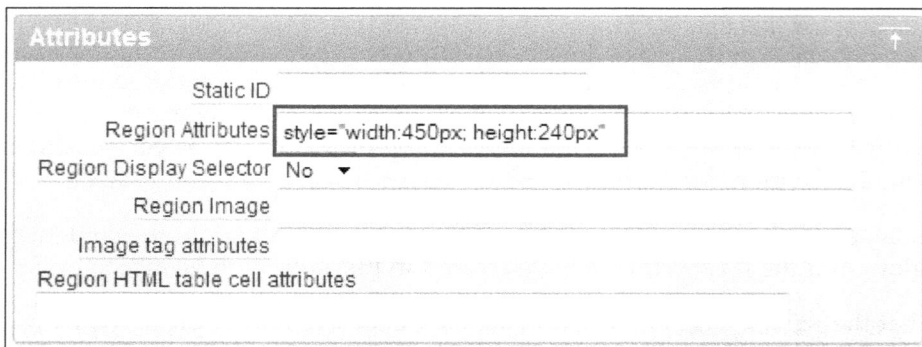

This automatically limits the width of the tab panel, which sizes to the parent container. Using the following configuration allows the height of the individual tabs to be set to the same value:

```
new Ext.TabPanel({
    renderTo: '#REGION_STATIC_ID#',
    activeTab: 0,
    height: Ext.fly('#REGION_STATIC_ID#').getHeight()||'auto',
    defaults: {autoScroll:true, boxMinHeight: 100},
    cls: 'blue-tabs',
    plain: true,
    items:subs
});
```

The `height` config option is set to the height of the containing `DIV` if specified, otherwise falls back to the `'auto'` setting and uses the height of the tabs contents.

The `defaults` config option sets all tabs to include a scrollbar automatically if the content overflows the fixed tab region instead of clipping the content, and specifying `boxMinHeight` sets a minimum height if the `'auto'` setting is applied.

Adding `cls: 'blue-tabs'` picks up the custom CSS style:

```
.blue-tabs .x-panel-bwrap .x-panel-body {
    background-color:#e0ecfc; padding:10px
}
```

Setting `plain: true` removes the background from the tab strip. The result of all these configuration options is the very different looking tab panel in the following screenshot:

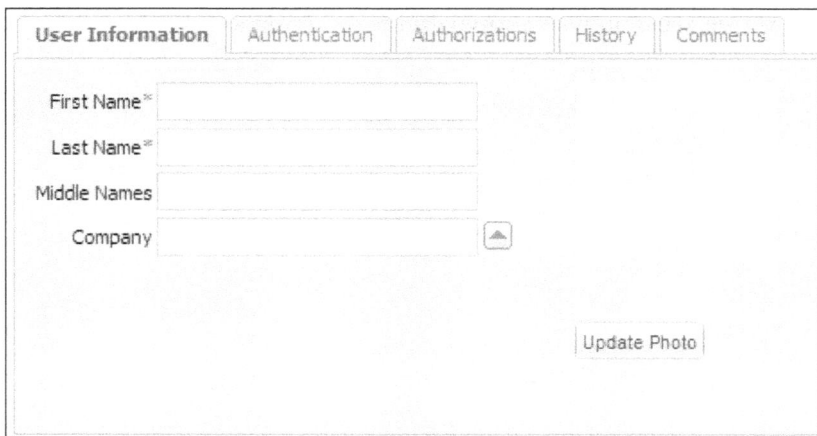

Flipping the tab strip from the top of the tab panel to the bottom is done by simply setting the configuration option `tabPosition: 'bottom'`; the result is shown in the following screenshot:

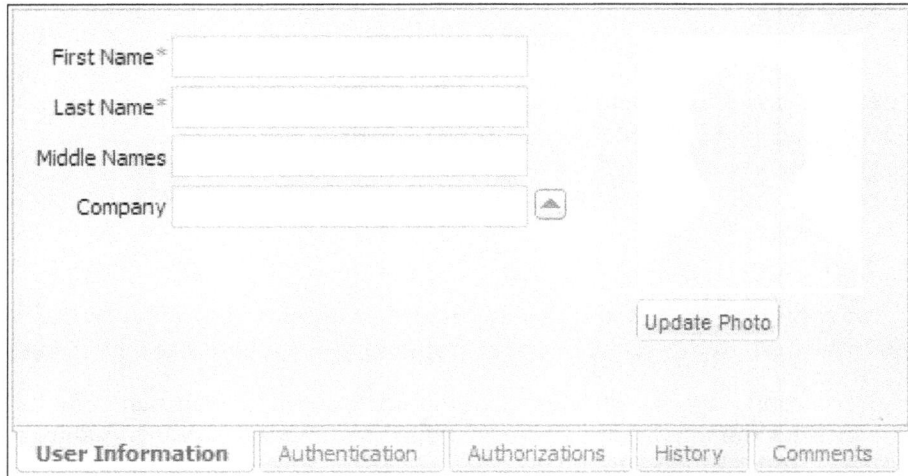

There are still a large number of configuration options we haven't explored here, so it's well worth spending some time experimenting to work out what suits your application best.

Toolbars and menus

Back in *Chapter 4, Ext Themed Regions, Labels, and Lists*, we went through a solution to creating a hierarchical tree component using a list template to build a script and generate an Ext.tree.TreePanel, as shown on the left-hand side of the following figure:

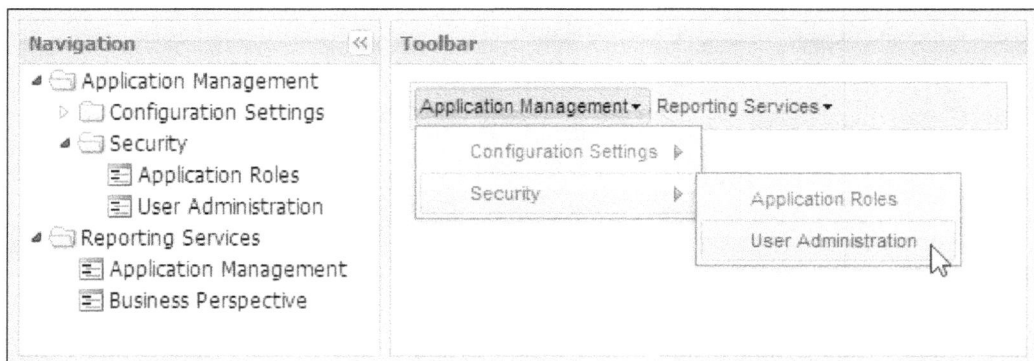

This time we are going to use much the same approach to produce the toolbar on the right hand side of the preceding figure. One thing really nice about this solution is that the tree and toolbar are using the same list as the data source.

As the solution is so similar to the Ext.tree.TreePanel solution in *Chapter 4*, we will only cover the APEX 4.0 solution. If you are still using an earlier APEX version, you can easily adapt the pre APEX 4.0 solution in *Chapter 4* in the same manner.

Create a new List Template:

Name: EXTJS Toolbar List

Template class: Hierarchical Expanding

List template current:

```
{id:"#LIST_ITEM_ID#",'text":"#TEXT#","href":"#LINK#"#A02#}
```

List template current with sub list items:

```
{id:"#LIST_ITEM_ID#",'text":"#TEXT#","href":"#LINK#"#A02#,menu:{
items:[
```

List template noncurrent:

```
{id:"#LIST_ITEM_ID#","text":"#TEXT#","href":"#LINK#"#A02#}
```

List template noncurrent with sub list items:

```
{id:"#LIST_ITEM_ID#","text":"#TEXT#","href":"#LINK#"#A02#,menu:{
items:[
```

Between list elements:

```
,
```

List template current (first):

```
<div id="menu#LIST_ITEM_ID#"></div>
<script type="text/javascript">
Ext.onReady(function() {
  var menuRegion = 'menu#LIST_ITEM_ID#';

  var menuData = [{id:"#LIST_ITEM_ID#","text":"#TEXT#",
"href":"#LINK#"#A02#,menu:{
items:[
```

List template current with sublist items (first):

```
<div id="menu#LIST_ITEM_ID#"></div>
<script type="text/javascript">
Ext.onReady(function(){
  var menuRegion = 'menu#LIST_ITEM_ID#';

  var menuData = [{id:"#LIST_ITEM_ID#","text":"#TEXT#",
"href":"#LINK#"#A02#}
```

List template noncurrent (first):

```
<div id="menu#LIST_ITEM_ID#"></div>
<script type="text/javascript">
Ext.onReady(function(){
  var menuRegion = 'menu#LIST_ITEM_ID#';

  var menuData = [{id:"#LIST_ITEM_ID#","text":"#TEXT#",
"href":"#LINK#"#A02#}
```

List template noncurrent with sublist items (first):

```
<div id="menu#LIST_ITEM_ID#"></div>
<script type="text/javascript">
Ext.onReady(function(){
  var menuRegion = 'menu#LIST_ITEM_ID#';

  var menuData = [{id:"#LIST_ITEM_ID#","text":"#TEXT#",
"href":"#LINK#"#A02#,menu:{
```

items:[

Sublist template current:

```
{id:"#LIST_ITEM_ID#","text":"#TEXT#","href":"#LINK#"#A02#}
```

Sublist template current with sublist items:

```
{id:"#LIST_ITEM_ID#","text":"#TEXT#", "href":"#LINK#"#A02#,menu:{
items:[
```

Sublist template noncurrent:

```
{id:"#LIST_ITEM_ID#","text":"#TEXT#","href":"#LINK#"#A02#}
```

Sublist template noncurrent with sublist items:

```
{id:"#LIST_ITEM_ID#","text":"#TEXT#", "href":"#LINK#"#A02#,menu:{
items:[
```

Between sublist items:

```
,
```

Sublist template after rows:

```
]}}
```

List template after rows:

```
];

  new Ext.Toolbar({
    renderTo: menuRegion,
    style: {border: '1px solid #99BBE8'},
    items: menuData
  });

});
</script>
```

We won't go through a detailed explanation of the code here; it really is just
repeating what was covered in *Chapter 4*, with minor adjustments to produce an Ext.
toolbar instead of an Ext.tree.TreePanel.

The main points to remember:

Using APEX lists allow conditions on individual entries,
allowing you to show items conditionally depending on security
privileges of application state.

APEX lists are automatically included in exports, so you don't
need to migrate data manually.

The #A02# substitution tag allows you to add extra JavaScript
code against individual menu items, for example, to change the
appearance or add a custom 'click' action.

Attaching the toolbar to the center panel

If you want to integrate the toolbar into the center panel so it is directly attached to the header of the center panel, as shown in the following screenshot, there are a few simple changes to make:

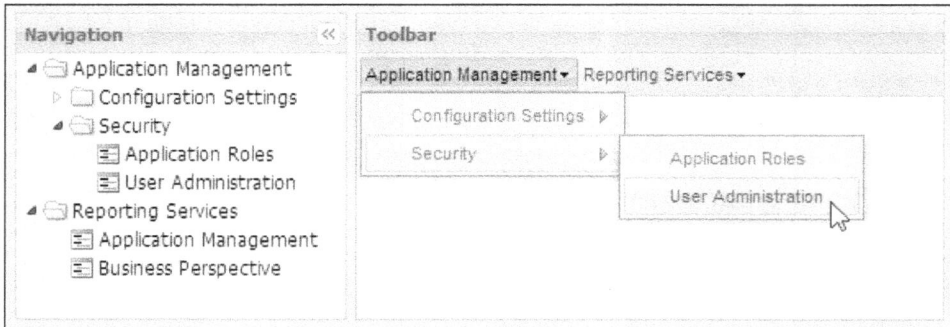

First, you will need to change your page template to include an empty toolbar in the center region. This is necessary because Ext cannot add a toolbar to a panel once it has been rendered.

So, for a simplified Viewport, the highlighted line adds a hidden toolbar to the center panel:

```
new Ext.Viewport({
    layout: 'border',
    defaults: {
        animCollapse: false,
        autoScroll: true
    },
    items: [{
        contentEl: 'app-west-panel',
        collapsible: true,
        region: 'west',
        split: true,
        title: 'Navigation',
        width: 275
    }, {
        id: 'gen-center-panel',
        contentEl: 'app-center-panel',
        region: 'center',
        title: document.title,
        tbar: {hidden:true, items:[]},
        xtype: 'panel'
    }]
});
});
```

The other item to note is that we have set the ID `'gen-center-panel'` for the center panel, making it easy to reference later.

Then either copy or modify the toolbar list template, changing the following section:

List template after rows:

```
];

var tb = Ext.getCmp('gen-center-panel').getTopToolbar();

tb.add(menuData);
if (!tb.isVisible()) tb.setVisible(true);
tb.doLayout();
});
</script>
```

Now, instead of rendering the toolbar to a DIV element, we are looking up the existing toolbar using the ID of the center panel. Once we have this, the menu items in the array `menuData` are added to the toolbar. Finally, we set the toolbar to `visible` and update the layout.

The references to the DIV element the menu was originally rendered into can also be removed from the template.

We have barely scratched the surface of what you can do with the Ext.toolbar here. There are many more features and options available, so spend some time exploring the toolbar examples included with the Ext library.

Summary

In this chapter, we have introduced some "low-hanging fruit" Ext JS components that add functionality to applications with minimal effort to set them up.

For the date picker, resizable or auto-sizing text areas, and the combo boxes, we have simply improved existing HTML components. The tab panels and toolbar menus introduce new functionality not previously available in our theme.

In some ways, using the template approach is ultimately limited, because you are restricted to hard-coding your configuration options into the template. We saw for the tab panels to have several different variations requires you to have multiple templates.

Plugins, also introduced in APEX 4.0, offer much more flexibility, which we will see in the next chapter.

7
Working with Plug-ins and Dynamic Actions

Plug-ins and dynamic actions are the two most exciting new features for developers in APEX 4.0. Combining them with Ext JS components is a recipe for success.

For the first time we now have the ability to add custom "widgets" directly into APEX that can be used declaratively in the same way as native APEX components. Plug-ins and dynamic actions are supported with back end integration, allowing developers to make use of APEX provided PL/SQL APIs to simplify component development.

Plug-ins give developers a supported mechanism to enhance the existing built-in functionality by writing custom PL/SQL components for item types, regions, and processes.

Dynamic actions provide developers with a way to define client-side behavior declaratively without needing to know JavaScript. Using a simple wizard, developers can select a page item and a condition, enter a value, and select an action (for example, Show, Hide, Enable, and Show Item Row).

Most APEX developers come from a database development background. So, they are much more comfortable coding with PL/SQL than JavaScript. The sooner work is focused on PL/SQL development the more productive APEX developers become.

The ability to create plug-ins that can be used declaratively means developers don't have to write page-specific JavaScript for items on a page, or use messy "hacks" to attach additional JavaScript functionality to standard APEX items.

Ext JS provides a rich library of sophisticated JavaScript components just waiting to be integrated into APEX using plug-ins.

Over the next chapters, we will be looking at plug-ins and dynamic actions and how they interact together. This chapter will cover in detail the development process for creating a simple NumberField plug-in, allowing you to focus on the process rather than the widget.

A home for your plug-ins and dynamic actions

APEX allows you to create plug-ins for item, region, dynamic action, and process types. Like templates and themes, plug-ins are designed to be shared, so they can be easily exported and imported from one workspace application to another. Plug-ins can also be subscribed, providing a way to easily share and update common attributes between plug-ins.

In *Chapter 3 Building a Ext theme into APEX*, I discussed the benefits of building your theme in a dedicated TEMPLATE application, and building simple test pages as you go to verify the templates. These test pages also form part of your template documentation, allowing team members to examine and understand specific functionality in isolation. The same principle applies for building plug-ins and dynamic actions.

Building a better Number Field

APEX 4.0 introduced the Number Field as a new item type, allowing you to configure number-range checks by optionally specifying minimum and maximum value attributes. It also automatically checks that the entered value is a number, and performs NOT NULL validation as well. You can also specify a format mask for the number as well, presumably to enforce decimal places.

This all sounds great, and it does work as described, but only after you have submitted the page for processing on the server.

The following screenshot shows the APEX and Ext versions of the Number Field, both setup with a valid number range of 1 to 10,000. The APEX version allows you to enter any characters you want, including letters. The Ext version automatically filters the keys pressed to only accept numbers, conditionally the decimal separator, and the negative sign. It also highlights invalid values when you go outside the valid number range.

Simple Form Inputs	
APEX Number Field	999abc999
ExtJS Number Field	99999

The maximum value for this field is 10000

We are going to build a better Number Field using APEX plug-ins to provide better functionality on the client side, and still maintain the same level of server-side validation.

The Number Field is quite a simple example, allowing us to be introduced to how APEX plug-ins work without getting bogged down in the details.

The process of building a plug-in requires the following:

- Creating a plug-in in your application workspace
- Creating a test page containing your plug-in and necessary extras to test it
- Running your application to test functionality
- Repeating the build/test cycle, progressively adding more features until satisfied with the result.

Creating a plug-in item

For our Number Field, we will be creating an item plug-in.

So, navigate to the plug-ins page in Application Builder, found under **Application Builder | Application xxx | Shared Components | Plug-ins**, and press **Create** to open the Plug-in Create/Edit page.

Start filling in the following fields:

- **Name**: Ext.form.NumberField. Here, I'm using the Ext naming for the widget, but that's just for a convenience.
- **Internal Name**: Oracle's recommendation here is to use your organization's domain name as a prefix. So for example, a company domain of mycompany. com would prefix a plug-in named Slider, would result in an internal name of COM.MYCOMPANY.SLIDER.

- **File Prefix**: As we are referencing the Ext JavaScript libraries in our page template, we can skip this field completely. For specialized plug-ins that are only used on a handful of specific pages, you would attach a JavaScript file here.

- **Source**: For the PL/SQL source code required to implement our plug-in, you can either enter it as a PL/SQL anonymous block of code that contains functions for rendering, validating and AJAX callbacks, or refer to code in a PL/SQL package in the database.

You get better performance using PL/SQL packages in the database, so that's the smart way to go. Simply include your package function names in the Callbacks section, as shown in the following screenshot, noting that no AJAX function name is specified as no AJAX functionality is required for this plug-in. The package doesn't need to exist at this time—the form will submit successfully anyway.

Source	
PL/SQL Code	
☐ Do not validate PL/SQL code (parse PL/SQL code at runtime only).	

Callbacks	
Render Function Name	plug_ext_form_numberfield.render
AJAX Function Name	
Validation Function Name	plug_ext_form_numberfield.validate

Standard attributes:

In addition to being able to create up to ten custom attributes, the APEX team has made the standard attributes available for plug-ins to use. This is really useful, because the standard attributes comprise elements that are useful for most components, such as width and height. They also have items such as List of Values (LOV), which have more complicated validation rules already built-in, checking SQL queries used for the LOV source are valid queries, and so on.

For the Number Field, only a few attributes have been checked:

- Is Visible Widget: Indicating the element will be displayed

- `Session State Changeable`: So that APEX knows to store the value of the item in session state

- `Has Read Only Attribute`: So that conditional logic can be used to make the item read only

- `Has Width Attributes`: Allowing the width of the item to be set

Notice that some of the attributes are disabled in the following screenshot. This is because the APEX Builder conditionally enables the checkboxes that are dependent on another attribute. So, in this screenshot the **List of Values Required**, **Has LOV Display Null Attributes**, and **Has Cascading LOV Attributes** checkboxes are disabled, because they are dependant on the **Has List of Values** checkbox. Once it is checked, the other checkboxes are enabled.

Custom attributes:

Defining the custom attributes for our Number Field is largely an exercise in reviewing the configuration options available in the documentation for Ext.form. NumberField, and deciding which options are most useful to be included.

You need to also take into account that some configuration options are already included when you define an APEX item using your plug-in. For example, Item Label is included with an APEX item, but is rendered separately from the item, so don't need to be included. Likewise `Value Required` is a validation rule, and is also separate when rendering the APEX item.

The following next screenshot shows some Ext.form.NumberField configuration options, overlaid with the custom attributes defined in APEX for the plug-in:

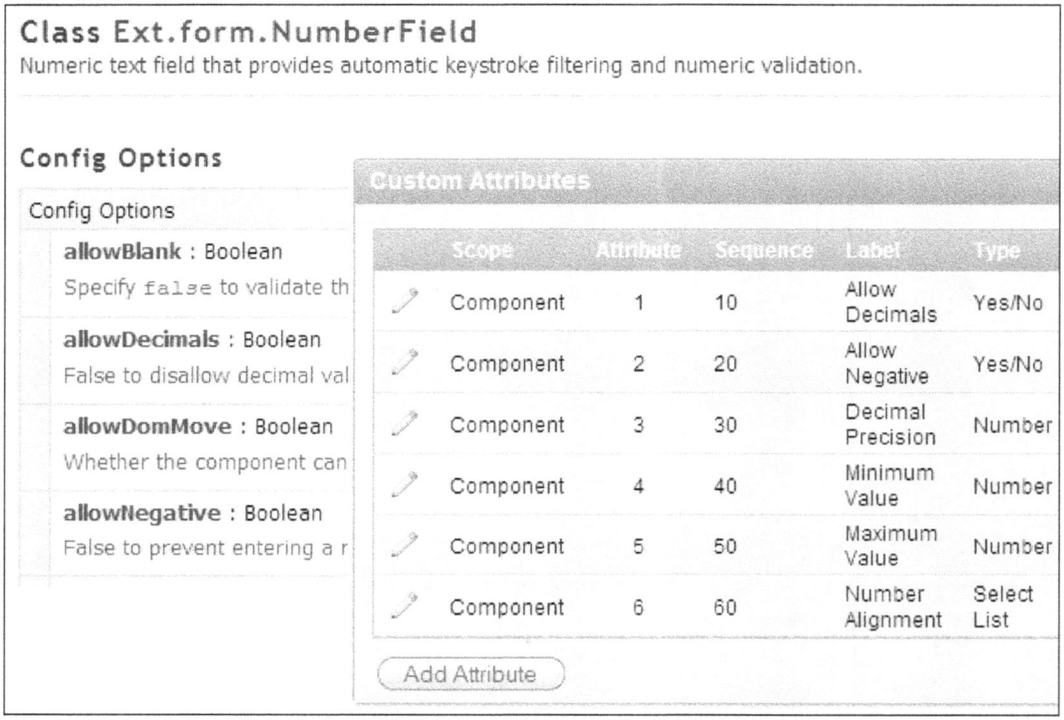

I've chosen not to include the `allowBlank` config option as a custom attribute, simply because this can be determined by the APEX `Value Required` property. Other Configuration options, such as `allowDecimals` and `allowNegative`, are included as custom attributes as Yes/No types.

The custom attributes created are listed in the following table:

Label	Type	Required	Depending on	Values
Allow Decimals	Yes/No	Yes		
Allow Negative	Yes/No	Yes		
Decimal Precision	Number	No	Allow Decimals	
Minimum Value	Number	No		
Maximum Value	Number	No		
Number Alignment	Select List	No		left, center, right

Custom events:

Custom events are used to define JavaScript event that can be exposed to dynamic actions. For this simple plug-in, there is no need to define any custom events.

At this point, we are done defining the Number Field in APEX; it's time to turn our attention to building the database package to execute the Callbacks to render and validate the plug-in.

Defining the plug-in Callback functions

Plug-ins must implement a fixed interface, defined for the plug-in type (item, region, dynamic action) and the Callback function (Render, AJAX, Validation).

For example, the item type plug-in Render Functions must implement the following interface:

```
function <name of function> (
    p_item              in apex_plugin.t_page_item,
    p_plugin            in apex_plugin.t_plugin,
    p_value             in varchar2,
    p_is_readonly       in boolean,
    p_is_printer_friendly in boolean )
    return apex_plugin.t_page_item_render_result
```

So, for the Number Field plug-in, I'm using a package name `plug_ext_form_numberfield`, and function names `render`, `ajax`, and `validate`.

The PL/SQL package specification becomes:

```
CREATE OR REPLACE PACKAGE plug_ext_form_numberfield AS

function render (
    p_item              in apex_plugin.t_page_item,
    p_plugin            in apex_plugin.t_plugin,
    p_value             in varchar2,
    p_is_readonly       in boolean,
    p_is_printer_friendly in boolean )
    return apex_plugin.t_page_item_render_result;

function ajax (
    p_item   in apex_plugin.t_page_item,
    p_plugin in apex_plugin.t_plugin )
    return apex_plugin.t_page_item_ajax_result;

function validate (
```

```
      p_item    in    apex_plugin.t_page_item,
      p_plugin  in    apex_plugin.t_plugin,
      p_value   in    varchar2 )
      return apex_plugin.t_page_item_validation_result;

END;
/
```

For the PL/SQL package body, we'll start out by building working stubs for the functions, and fill in the details, as we work through the solution.

```
CREATE OR REPLACE PACKAGE BODY plug_ext_form_numberfield AS

FUNCTION render (
  p_item              in apex_plugin.t_page_item,
  p_plugin            in apex_plugin.t_plugin,
  p_value             in varchar2,
  p_is_readonly       in boolean,
  p_is_printer_friendly in boolean )
  return apex_plugin.t_page_item_render_result
IS
  l_result apex_plugin.t_page_item_render_result;

  subtype attr is
    apex_application_page_items.attribute_01%type;

  -- assign local names to attributes
  l_allow_decimals    attr := p_item.attribute_01;
  l_allow_negative    attr := p_item.attribute_02;
  l_decimal_precision attr := p_item.attribute_03;
  l_min_value         attr := p_item.attribute_04;
  l_max_value         attr := p_item.attribute_05;
  l_align             attr := p_item.attribute_06;

  -- Only use escaped value for the HTML output!
  l_code          varchar2(32767);
  l_escaped_value varchar2(32767)
                    := sys.htf.escape_sc(p_value);
  l_name          varchar2(30);
BEGIN
  -- Debug information
  if apex_application.g_debug then
    apex_plugin_util.debug_page_item (
      p_plugin          => p_plugin,
      p_page_item       => p_item,
```

```
        p_value               => p_value,
        p_is_readonly         => p_is_readonly,
        p_is_printer_friendly => p_is_printer_friendly );
end if;

if p_is_readonly or p_is_printer_friendly then
  -- emit hidden field if necessary
  apex_plugin_util.print_hidden_if_readonly (
    p_item_name           => p_item.name,
    p_value               => p_value,
    p_is_readonly         => p_is_readonly,
    p_is_printer_friendly => p_is_printer_friendly );

  -- emit display span with the value
  apex_plugin_util.print_display_only (
    p_item_name           => p_item.name,
    p_display_value       => p_value,
    p_show_line_breaks    => false,
    p_escape              => true,
    p_attributes          => p_item.element_attributes );

else
  -- If a page item saves state, we have to call the
  -- get_input_name_for_page_item to render the internal
  -- hidden p_arg_names field. It will also return the
  -- HTML field name which we have to use when we render
  -- the HTML input field.
  l_name := apex_plugin.get_input_name_for_page_item(false);
  sys.htp.p('<input type="text" name="'||l_name||
      '" id="'||p_item.name||'" '||
      'value="'||l_escaped_value||
      '" size="'||p_item.element_width||'" '||
      'maxlength="'||p_item.element_max_length||'" '||
      coalesce(p_item.element_attributes,
              'class="x-form-text"')||' />');


  -- ****************************************************
  -- @todo - write code for widget here
  -- ****************************************************
  l_code := 'Ext.onReady(function(){'||
            'alert("@todo - write widget code");'||
            '});';
```

```
            -- Initialize page item when the page has been rendered.
            apex_javascript.add_onload_code(p_code => l_code);

            -- Tell APEX engine that field is navigable, in case
            -- it's the first item on the page, and APEX page is
            -- configured to navigate to first item (by default).
            l_result.is_navigable := true;
        end if;

    return l_result;
END render;



FUNCTION ajax (
    p_item   in apex_plugin.t_page_item,
    p_plugin in apex_plugin.t_plugin )
    return apex_plugin.t_page_item_ajax_result
IS
    l_result apex_plugin.t_page_item_ajax_result;
BEGIN
    -- @note - not using AJAX for this widget
    -- usually logic goes here

    -- not used by APEX yet
    return l_result;
END ajax;



FUNCTION validate (
    p_item   in      apex_plugin.t_page_item,
    p_plugin in      apex_plugin.t_plugin,
    p_value  in      varchar2 )
    return apex_plugin.t_page_item_validation_result
IS
    l_result apex_plugin.t_page_item_validation_result;
BEGIN
    -- Debug information
    if apex_application.g_debug then
        apex_plugin_util.debug_page_item (
            p_plugin    => p_plugin,
            p_page_item => p_item );
    end if;

    -- @todo - write validation code
```

```
    return l_result;
END validate;

END plug_ext_form_numberfield;
/
```

Once the PL/SQL package specification and body has been compiled in the same schema as the parsing schema for the APEX Application, you have a fully functional "stub" for an item plug-in. The "stub" is a basic template pattern for item plug-ins; you simply insert the relevant code for your particular plug-in where the @todo comments are shown.

I'm not going to spend much time going through this PL/SQL code; that would be like "teaching your Grandmother how to suck eggs", as the saying goes.

There are a few important points worth noting though.

The APEX plug-in engine does a lot of work for you before it calls the plug-in code to render, validate, or execute AJAX processing on an item. The engine gathers the relevant metadata for the specific APEX page item, performing substitutions along the way before passing that information through to the plug-in as record-type parameters.

So, looking at the render function specification,

```
FUNCTION render (
   p_item              in apex_plugin.t_page_item,
   p_plugin            in apex_plugin.t_plugin,
   p_value             in varchar2,
   p_is_readonly       in boolean,
   p_is_printer_friendly in boolean )
   return apex_plugin.t_page_item_render_result
```

you can see the the function is being passed record types `apex_plugin.t_page_item` and `apex_plugin.t_plugin`, and returning `t_page_item_render_result`.

The definitions for the record types are contained in the APEX_PLUGIN (APEX_040000.WWV_FLOW_PLUGIN) package specification, and include the following type declarations:

```
type t_plugin is record (
    name          varchar2(45),
    file_prefix   varchar2(4000),
    attribute_01  varchar2(32767),
    ...
    attribute_10  varchar2(32767) );
```

```
type t_page_item is record (
    id                          number,
    name                        varchar2(255),
    label                       varchar2(4000),
    plain_label                 varchar2(4000),
    format_mask                 varchar2(255),
    is_required                 boolean,
    lov_definition              varchar2(4000),
    lov_display_extra           boolean,
    lov_display_null            boolean,
    lov_null_text               varchar2(255),
    lov_null_value              varchar2(255),
    lov_cascade_parent_items    varchar2(255),
    ajax_items_to_submit        varchar2(255),
    ajax_optimize_refresh       boolean,
    element_width               number,
    element_max_length          number,
    element_height              number,
    element_attributes          varchar2(2000),
    element_option_attributes   varchar2(4000),
    escape_output               boolean,
    attribute_01                varchar2(32767),
    ...
    attribute_10                varchar2(32767) );

type t_page_item_render_result is record (
    is_navigable      boolean default false,
    navigable_dom_id varchar2(255) );
```

As you can see, there is a fairly substantial amount of metadata available for you to use when generating code for your plug-in.

Once you start writing, your plug-in the package APEX_PLUGIN_UTIL (APEX_040000. WWV_FLOW_PLUGIN_UTIL) contains some very useful procedures to help you build plug-ins quickly. A number of them have already been included in our stub plug-in.

One of the utility procedures most useful when starting out building your plug-in is the debugging procedure, called using the following code:

```
if apex_application.g_debug then
  apex_plugin_util.debug_page_item (
      p_plugin    => p_plugin,
      p_page_item => p_item );
end if;
```

With debugging enabled for a page containing your plug-in, the debugging page shows the parameters values being passed to your plug-in package, as can be seen in the following screenshot:

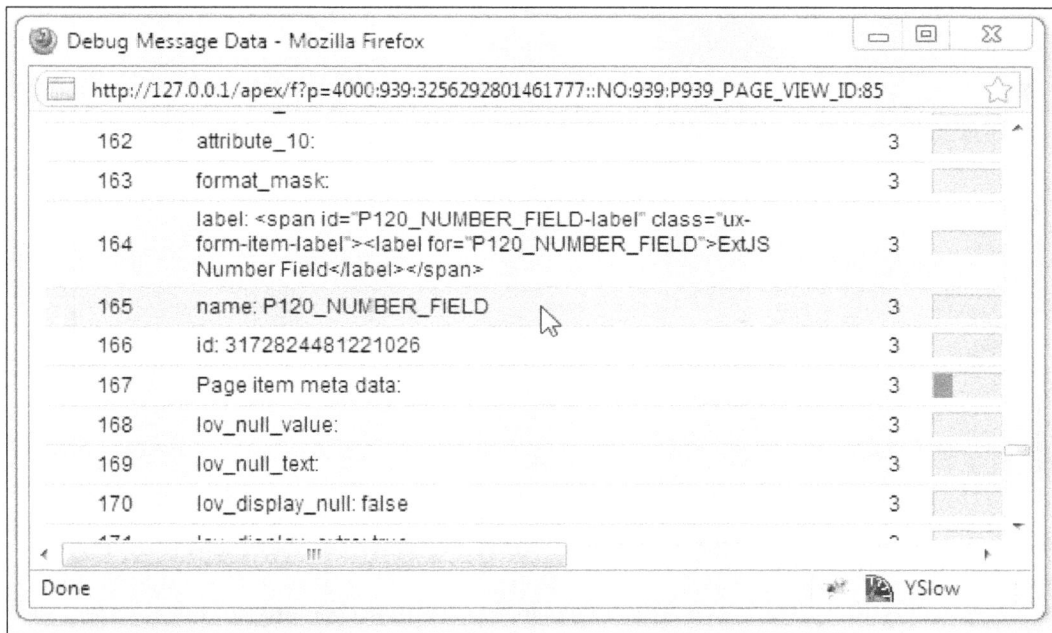

At this point, it's a good time to create a page and include the number plug-in, so we can do some testing and progressively add functionality to the plug-in.

Creating a page item based on the Number Field plug-in

Creating a page item based on your plug-in is done exactly the same way you would any standard APEX item. Simply create the item, then select your plug-in under the **Display** option, and start filling in the details for the item as usual.

The standard attributes available are determined by the plug-in definition; we didn't select the standard attribute `Has List of Values` for the plug-in earlier, so that section isn't available for our Number Field. The custom attributes we defined for the Number Field appear in the **Settings** section, as you can see in the following screenshot:

So, go ahead and create a test page with your shiny new Number Field plug-in, and give it a test run. If everything is working as expected, then it should look and behave exactly like a standard APEX Text Field. It will accept any text you enter, submit and store the result in Session state, and render it as a read-only field if you set the Read-Only Condition.

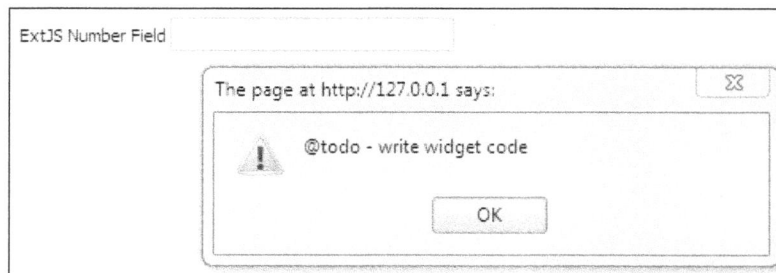

The only inconvenient thing about it is that annoying JavaScript alert shown in preceding screenshot, reminding us that we haven't finished writing the plug-in source. Let's remedy that now.

Render functionality for the Number Field plug-in

Our stub function already includes enough logic to behave as a standard APEX Text field. To make it behave as an Ext.form.NumberField, providing automatic keystroke filtering and number validation, we need to generate JavaScript code to convert it.

The generated JavaScript will look similar to the following:

```
Ext.onReady(function(){
    new Ext.form.NumberField({
        applyTo:          'P120_NUMBER_FIELD',
        allowDecimals:    false
        allowNegative:    false,
        decimalPrecision: 2,
        minValue:         1,
        maxValue:         10000,
        value:            54
    });
});
```

You can easily test this on your test page by pasting the preceding code into the Firebug console in Firefox, changing the `applyTo` value to match your page item, and running it.

Looking at the generated JavaScript, it's readily apparent that the code generator simply needs to build up the text, adding the parameters and dynamic values as it goes.

The final version of the `render` function is as follows:

```
FUNCTION render (
  p_item                in apex_plugin.t_page_item,
  p_plugin              in apex_plugin.t_plugin,
  p_value               in varchar2,
  p_is_readonly         in boolean,
  p_is_printer_friendly in boolean )
  return apex_plugin.t_page_item_render_result
IS
  l_result apex_plugin.t_page_item_render_result;
```

```
subtype attr is
  apex_application_page_items.attribute_01%type;

-- assign local names to attributes
l_allow_decimals     attr := p_item.attribute_01;
l_allow_negative     attr := p_item.attribute_02;
l_decimal_precision  attr := p_item.attribute_03;
l_min_value          attr := p_item.attribute_04;
l_max_value          attr := p_item.attribute_05;
l_align              attr := p_item.attribute_06;

-- Only use escaped value for the HTML output!
l_code               varchar2(32767);
l_escaped_value varchar2(32767)
                     := sys.htf.escape_sc(p_value);
l_name               varchar2(30);
```

To improve the readability of your code, it's worthwhile assigning the `p_item` attribute values to local variables.

Also highly recommended is escaping any values passed from the HTML page using the Oracle provided `sys.htf.escape_sc` function to prevent SQL injection attacks. A malicious person can easily circumvent any HTML page protection using developer tools, such as Firebug, to force the page to submit SQL injection text.

```
BEGIN
  -- Debug information
  if apex_application.g_debug then
    apex_plugin_util.debug_page_item (
      p_plugin            => p_plugin,
      p_page_item         => p_item,
      p_value             => p_value,
      p_is_readonly       => p_is_readonly,
      p_is_printer_friendly => p_is_printer_friendly );
  end if;

  if p_is_readonly or p_is_printer_friendly then
    -- emit hidden field if necessary
    apex_plugin_util.print_hidden_if_readonly (
      p_item_name         => p_item.name,
      p_value             => p_value,
      p_is_readonly       => p_is_readonly,
      p_is_printer_friendly => p_is_printer_friendly );

    -- emit display span with the value
```

```
apex_plugin_util.print_display_only (
  p_item_name        => p_item.name,
  p_display_value    => p_value,
  p_show_line_breaks => false,
  p_escape           => true,
  p_attributes       => p_item.element_attributes );

else
  -- If a page item saves state, we have to call the
  -- get_input_name_for_page_item to render the internal
  -- hidden p_arg_names field. It will also return the
  -- HTML field name which we have to use when we render
  -- the HTML input field.
  l_name := apex_plugin.get_input_name_for_page_item(false);
  sys.htp.p('<input type="text" name="'||l_name||
      '" id="'||p_item.name||'" '||
      'value="'||l_escaped_value||
      '" size="'||p_item.element_width||'" '||
      'maxlength="'||p_item.element_max_length||'" '||
      coalesce(p_item.element_attributes,
            'class="x-form-text"')||' />');
```

The first section of the procedure remains exactly the same as the earlier version.
Now we remove the stubbed code:

```
-- ****************************************************
-- @todo - write code for widget here
-- ****************************************************
l_code := 'Ext.onReady(function(){'||
          'alert("@todo - write widget code");'||
          '});';
```

The stubbed code is replaced with the following highlighted code:

```
-- build Ext.form.NumberField properties
l_code := wwv_flow_javascript.add_attribute(
    'applyTo', p_item.name)
||wwv_flow_javascript.add_attribute(
    'allowDecimals'
    ,case when l_allow_decimals = 'N' then 'false' end)
||wwv_flow_javascript.add_attribute(
    'allowNegative'
    ,case when l_allow_negative = 'N' then 'false' end)
||wwv_flow_javascript.add_attribute(
    'decimalPrecision', l_decimal_precision)
```

```
      ||wwv_flow_javascript.add_attribute(
          'minValue',l_min_value)
      ||wwv_flow_javascript.add_attribute(
          'maxValue',l_max_value)
      ||wwv_flow_javascript.add_attribute(
          'value',l_escaped_value);

      -- can't use add_attribute() as it escapes double quotes
      if l_align is not null then
          l_code := l_code||'"style": {"text-align":"'
          ||l_align||'"},';
      end if;

      l_code := l_code||wwv_flow_javascript.add_attribute(
          p_name      => 'ajaxIdentifier',
          p_value     => apex_plugin.get_ajax_identifier,
          p_add_comma => false);

      l_code :=
        'Ext.onReady(function(){new Ext.form.NumberField({'
        ||l_code||'});});';

      -- Initialize page item when the page has been rendered.
      apex_javascript.add_onload_code(p_code => l_code);

      -- Tell APEX engine that field is navigable, in case
      -- it's the first item on the page, and APEX page is
      -- configured to navigate to first item (by default).
      l_result.is_navigable := true;
   end if;

   return l_result;
END render;
```

The highlighted code shows the changes to the stubbed version, simply replacing the alert message with the final JavaScript we want, dynamically assigning the property values using the APEX items metadata. Once again, APEX has provided utilities in the APEX_JAVASCRIPT (APEX_040000.WWV_FLOW_JAVASCRIPT) package to simplify the process.

Validation functionality for the Number Field plug-in

Currently, the validation function for the Number Field plug-in does absolutely nothing; it's just a stub that compiles and nothing more. Even so, APEX does some validation for us, checking for mandatory items.

The final code for the validation function verifies the page item value is a number with a value conforming to the rules specified for the page item:

```
FUNCTION validate (
  p_item    in     apex_plugin.t_page_item,
  p_plugin  in     apex_plugin.t_plugin,
  p_value   in     varchar2 )
  return apex_plugin.t_page_item_validation_result
IS
  subtype attr is
    apex_application_page_items.attribute_01%type;

  -- assign local names to attributes
  l_allow_decimals attr    := p_item.attribute_01;
  l_allow_negative attr    := p_item.attribute_02;
  l_precision      number := to_number(p_item.attribute_03);
  l_min_value      number := to_number(p_item.attribute_04);
  l_max_value      number := to_number(p_item.attribute_05);

  n number;
  l_result apex_plugin.t_page_item_validation_result;
BEGIN
  -- Debug information
  if apex_application.g_debug then
    apex_plugin_util.debug_page_item (
        p_plugin    => p_plugin,
        p_page_item => p_item );
  end if;

  -- Nothing to do when null (APEX checks for mandatory items)
  if p_value is null then return l_result; end if;

  -- verify value is numeric
  begin
    n := to_number(p_value);
  exception
  when value_error then
```

```
        l_result.message := 'Value for '||
          p_item.plain_label||' must be a number';
        return l_result;
    end;

    case when l_allow_decimals = 'N' and n <> trunc(n) then
            l_result.message := 'Decimals not allowed for '||
              p_item.plain_label;
        when l_precision is not null
            and n <> trunc(n,l_decimal_precision) then
            l_result.message := 'Decimals places cannot exceed '||
              l_precision||' for '||p_item.plain_label;
        when l_allow_negative = 'N' and n <> abs(n) then
            l_result.message := 'Negative numbers not allowed'||
              ' for '||p_item.plain_label;
        when l_min_value is not null and n < l_min_value then
            l_result.message := 'The minimum value for '||
              p_item.plain_label||' is '||l_min_value;
        when l_max_value is not null and n > l_max_value then
            l_result.message := 'The maximum value for '||
              p_item.plain_label||' is '||l_max_value;
    else null;
    end case;

    -- return l_result with error message, success => null
    return l_result;
END validate;
```

That wraps up the implementation for the Number Field Plug-in; the final package specification and package body are found in the files included with the book under Chapter 7.

Summary

In this chapter, we have covered the development process for creating an item type plug-in, showing how to define the plug-in and its parameters in APEX.

We initially created a "stub" PL/SQL package for the Plug-in, allowing us to create a test page for our Plug-in and start using it as a standard APEX text item. Once the stub was working, we then were able to add in the enhanced JavaScript functionality progressively on the web page, before completing the Plug-in by adding the server-side validation.

Since the NumberField is just enhancing a standard HTML input field and does not add additional HTML elements, the standard Dynamic Actions will work quite happily without change. We haven't implemented any AJAX functionality because there hasn't been any requirement.

Chapter 8 implements a much more sophisticated component, the **Ext.form. ComboBox**, as a Plug-in, and deals with both AJAX functionality and Dynamic Actions, so we will have a look at that next.

8

Data Stores, AJAX-enabled Plug-ins, and Dynamic Actions

Data Stores provide the Ext JS framework with the ability to store data on the browser client acting much like an in-memory database. This provides enormous flexibility for data-aware components, such as the ComboBox, GridPanel, and TreePanel, as it logically separates the component from the data.

This makes the process of integrating AJAX functionality into plug-ins far simpler, because the AJAX processes will be focused on just passing data between the browser client and the database. The Ext components already contain the client-side functionality to update the display.

On the database side, APEX provides rich PL/SQL APIs to speed up the development of plug-ins. We will be making good use of the APEX-provided PL/SQL APIs to simplify component development.

In this chapter we will cover:

- Storing data on the browser client using **Ext.data.Store**
- Creating a complex ComboBox Plug-in, dealing with more advanced plugin concepts including AJAX processing and interacting with dynamic actions
- Overriding standard Ext.form.ComboBox functionality to work within the APEX Dynamic Actions framework
- Creating APEX Custom Events for the ComboBox plugin

It makes for an interesting chapter, by really bringing the client-side Ext JS framework together with the server-side capabilities of APEX to harness their full potential.

Storing data on the browser client

The `Ext.data.Store` class is used to store data on the browser client acting much like an in-memory database. The `Store` class caches Record objects that are used by data-aware components such as the ComboBox, GridPanel, and TreePanel.

Data is loaded into a Store using different formats such as JavaScript Arrays, XML, or JSON through the `Ext.data.DataReader` class. The `DataReader` class has subclasses `ArrayReader`, `JsonReader`, and `XmlReader` that read structured data from a data source in a specific format, converting it into Record objects and metadata for use by a Store object.

A number of Store types are available such as ArrayStore, JsonStore, and XmlStore, customized and pre-configured for use with a specific `DataReader`. These custom store types act as a helper class to provide a simpler shorthand way of implementing the same solution.

For example, a basic Data Store to consume an Array looks like:

```
// data array of records
var countryData = [
    ["Afghanistan","65"]
    ,["Aland Islands","131"]
    ,["Albania, Republic of","118"]
        /*..snipped..*/
    ,["Zambia, Republic of","64"]
    ,["Zimbabwe","54"]
    ];

// define the record type structure
var countryRecord = Ext.data.Record.create([
{ name: 'countryName', mapping : 1 },
{ name: 'countryId',   mapping : 2 }
]);

// create a reader, assigning the record type
var arrayReader = new Ext.data.ArrayReader({}, countryRecord);

// create a store, assigning the reader
var store = new Ext.data.Store({
```

```
        reader : arrayReader
});

// manually load the store
store.loadData(countryData);
```

It can be re-written using the `Ext.data.ArrayStore`, when it simply becomes:

```
// data array of records
var countryData = [
    ["Afghanistan","65"]
    ,["Aland Islands","131"]
    ,["Albania, Republic of","118"]
       /*..snipped..*/
    ,["Zambia, Republic of","64"]
    ,["Zimbabwe","54"]
    ];

// create the store, assigning fields
var store = new Ext.data.ArrayStore({
    fields: ["countryName", "countryId"],
    data: countryData
});
```

We will be using `Ext.data.ArrayStore` when data is locally defined in the page. The ArrayStore is configured with an `Ext.data.ArrayReader` that automatically calls the store's load method after creation to load the data into the store.

The following function should be included as part of a database package to render the ArrayStore:

```
FUNCTION render_local_store (
  p_item    in apex_plugin.t_page_item,
  p_plugin  in apex_plugin.t_plugin,
  p_value   in varchar2 )
  RETURN sys.dbms_sql.desc_tab2
IS

  l_sql_handler    apex_plugin_util.t_sql_handler;
  l_col_value_list apex_plugin_util.t_column_value_list;
  l_col_count      number;

BEGIN
  -- open sql cursor and get description for sql statement
  l_sql_handler := apex_plugin_util.get_sql_handler (
    p_sql_statement  => p_item.lov_definition,
```

```
      p_min_columns     => 1,
      p_max_columns     => 999,
      p_component_name => p_item.id
);


l_col_count := l_sql_handler.column_list.count();

-- binds all page item bind variables
apex_plugin_util.prepare_query (
  p_sql_handler      => l_sql_handler );

-- fetch the data
l_col_value_list := apex_plugin_util.get_data (
  p_sql_handler => l_sql_handler );

-- close the open cursor created by get_sql_handler
apex_plugin_util.free_sql_handler(l_sql_handler);

-- start script
sys.htp.p('<script type="text/javascript">');
sys.htp.p('Ext.onReady(function(){');
sys.htp.p('var ns = Ext.ns("Ext.apex.'||p_item.name||'");');

-- print data
if l_col_value_list.exists(1) then
  sys.htp.p('ns.data = [');
  for i in 1 .. l_col_value_list(1).count loop
    sys.htp.prn(case when i > 1 then ',' else ' ' end||'[');
    for j in 1 .. l_col_count loop
      sys.htp.prn(case when j > 1 then ',' end||
        '"'||apex_plugin_util.escape(
              l_col_value_list(j)(i),true)||'"');
    end loop;
    sys.htp.p(']');
  end loop;
  sys.htp.p('];');
else
  sys.htp.p('ns.data = [];');
end if;

-- print store
sys.htp.p('// simple array store');
sys.htp.p('ns.store = new Ext.data.ArrayStore({');
sys.htp.prn('    fields: [');
```

```
    for i in 1 .. l_col_count loop
      sys.htp.prn(case when i > 1 then ',' end||
                '"'||l_sql_handler.column_list(i).col_name||'"');
    end loop;
    sys.htp.p('],');
    sys.htp.p('    data : ns.data');
    sys.htp.p('});');

    -- end script
    sys.htp.p('});');
    sys.htp.p('</script>');

    return l_sql_handler.column_list;
EXCEPTION
    when others then
      apex_plugin_util.free_sql_handler(l_sql_handler);
      raise;
END render_local_store;
```

The render_local_store uses the APEX_PLUGIN_UTIL (WWV_FLOW_PLUGIN_UTIL) package to prepare the SQL query, bind session state variables, and retrieve the data. That's quite a bit of work done for you by APEX, leaving you to render the data in the desired format, in this case as a data store.

The JavaScript produced by the render_local_store function looks like the following:

```
<script type="text/javascript">
Ext.onReady(function(){

  var ns = Ext.ns("Ext.apex.P120_COMBO");

  ns.data = [
    ["Afghanistan","65"]
   ,["Aland Islands","131"]
   ,["Albania, Republic of","118"]
      /* ..snipped .. */
   ,["Zambia, Republic of","64"]
   ,["Zimbabwe","54"]
  ];

  // simple array store
  ns.store = new Ext.data.ArrayStore({
      fields: ["CODE_DESCRIPTION","ID"],
      data : ns.data
```

```
        });
    });
    </script>
```

The only difference from our earlier example of an ArrayStore is that the store has been namespaced:

```
    var ns = Ext.ns("Ext.apex.P120_COMBO");
...
    ns.store = new Ext.data.ArrayStore({
        fields: ["CODE_DESCRIPTION","ID"],
        data : ns.data
    });
```

The `Ext.apex.P120_COMBO` namespace has been defined using the `Ext.ns` (namespace) function. By assigning local variable `ns` to the namespace, an "alias" has been defined, allowing you to code using the generic, abbreviated version. The `store` is an object within this namespace, and can be referenced from JavaScript elsewhere in a page using the fully qualified name `Ext.apex.P120_COMBO.store`.

Using Data Stores with large datasets

It's not practical for large datasets to be stored locally in the page, so when returning large datasets, the sensible approach is to fetch only a subset of data using an AJAX request, letting the user remotely load the data and use pagination and filtering functionality to filter the results.

For large datasets, we will use `Ext.data.JsonStore`, which is automatically configured with `Ext.data.JsonReader`, and implicitly creates `Ext.data.HttpProxy` if a URL is specified. The `HttpProxy` uses the browser's XHR (XML Http Request) object to perform generic AJAX requests.

For APEX plug-ins, a JsonStore would look like:

```
    var store = new Ext.data.JsonStore({
        url: 'wwv_flow.show',
        root: 'rowset',
        idProperty: 1,
        fields: ["countryName", "countryId"],
        baseParams: {
            p_flow_id: Ext.getDom('pFlowId').value,
            p_flow_step_id: Ext.getDom('pFlowStepId').value,
            p_instance: Ext.getDom('pInstance').value,
            p_request: 'PLUGIN=4A6E248DAACFAED09B96..7261F1E1F7E'
        },
```

```
        paramNames: {
            start:'p_widget_action_mod',
            limit:'p_widget_action'
        }
    });
```

The JsonStore calls the named url, passing parameter names and values sourced from the baseParams and paramNames config options.

The following PL/SQL function render_remote_store generates the JavaScript for a remote store definition, and should be included in a database package:

```
FUNCTION render_remote_store (
   p_item     in apex_plugin.t_page_item,
   p_plugin   in apex_plugin.t_plugin,
   p_value    in varchar2 )
   RETURN sys.dbms_sql.desc_tab2
IS

   l_sql_handler     apex_plugin_util.t_sql_handler;
   l_col_value_list  apex_plugin_util.t_column_value_list;
   l_col_count       number;
   l_col_names       varchar2(32767);

   l_script  varchar2(32767) := q'^
Ext.onReady(function(){
  var ns = Ext.ns('Ext.apex.#ITEM_NAME#');

  // simple array store
  ns.store = new Ext.data.JsonStore({
      url: 'wwv_flow.show',
      root: 'rowset',
      fields: [#FIELD_LIST#],
      baseParams: {
          p_flow_id: Ext.getDom('pFlowId').value,
          p_flow_step_id: Ext.getDom('pFlowStepId').value,
          p_instance: Ext.getDom('pInstance').value,
          p_request: 'PLUGIN=#AJAX_IDENTIFIER#'
      },
      paramNames: {
          start:'p_widget_action_mod',
          limit:'p_widget_action'
      }
  });
 });
^';
```

The `baseParams` specified are all required by APEX to perform AJAX processing successfully. These parameters identify the application, page, session, and plugin on the page. Specifying them in the `baseParams` attribute ensures they are passed to the server with every AJAX request for this component.

> Parameter names passed by the Ext AJAX process must correspond to parameter names for the APEX database procedure `wwv_flow.show`, otherwise APEX will error, raising a **HTTP Status 500 - System Unavailable** message.

Overriding the names passed by the JsonStore to identify the starting record and limit records returned to `'p_widget_action_mod'` and `'p_widget_action'` is necessary to match the parameter names of the called database procedure `wwv_flow.show`, identified here in the `url` attribute.

```
BEGIN
  -- for remote store we only need to describe the store

  -- open sql cursor and get description for sql statement
  l_sql_handler := apex_plugin_util.get_sql_handler (
    p_sql_statement  => p_item.lov_definition,
    p_min_columns    => 1,
    p_max_columns    => 999,
    p_component_name => p_item.id
  );

  -- close the open cursor created by get_sql_handler
  apex_plugin_util.free_sql_handler(l_sql_handler);

  l_col_count := l_sql_handler.column_list.count();

  -- build comma separated string list of column names
  for i in 1 .. l_col_count loop
    l_col_names := l_col_names||
      case when i > 1 then ',' end||
      '"'||l_sql_handler.column_list(i).col_name||'"';
  end loop;

  -- substitute values into placeholders
  wwv_flow_utilities.fast_replace(l_script,
    '#ITEM_NAME#',p_item.name);

  wwv_flow_utilities.fast_replace(l_script,
```

```
      '#FIELD_LIST#',l_col_names);

   wwv_flow_utilities.fast_replace(l_script,
     '#AJAX_IDENTIFIER#',apex_plugin.get_ajax_identifier);

   -- add JS to bottom of page
   apex_javascript.add_onload_code (
     p_code => l_script );

   return l_sql_handler.column_list;
EXCEPTION
   when others then
     apex_plugin_util.free_sql_handler(l_sql_handler);
     raise;
END render_remote_store;
```

Again, the APEX_PLUGIN_UTIL package is used to parse the query and retrieve the column names. This time we don't need to return any data because this will be done by the Ext data-aware component when it initiates a XHR request. Instead, we are just defining the structure of the records held in the data store, and defining the parameters for the HttpRequest object.

The code to retrieve the data will be dependent on each custom plug-in and handled by the PL/SQL code for AJAX requests, so we won't provide the details here. For a simple tabular component such as a ComboBox or Grid, data returned would look like:

```
{"total":20,"rowset":[
 {"CODE_DESCRIPTION": "Bahamas, Commonwealth of the","ID": "170"}
,{"CODE_DESCRIPTION": "Bahrain, Kingdom of","ID": "67"}
,{"CODE_DESCRIPTION": "Bangladesh, People's Republic of","ID": "68"}
,{"CODE_DESCRIPTION": "Barbados","ID": "171"}
,{"CODE_DESCRIPTION": "Belarus","ID": "124"}
,{"CODE_DESCRIPTION": "Belgium, Kingdom of","ID": "121"}
,{"CODE_DESCRIPTION": "Belize","ID": "173"}
,{"CODE_DESCRIPTION": "Benin, People's Republic of","ID": "20"}
,{"CODE_DESCRIPTION": "Bermuda","ID": "172"}
,{"CODE_DESCRIPTION": " Belize","ID": "173"}
]}
```

Here, the total number of records is shown for the filtered result set for the query. This example shows countries starting with "B". There are a total of 20 matching records; the records shown are the first results returned for a pageSize limit of 10 records.

Data Stores are a critical component for data-aware components, but are quite straightforward to understand once you start using them. Let's move onto the ComboBox plug-in to see them in action.

Building a ComboBox plug-in

We introduced `Ext.form.ComboBox` in *Chapter 6, Adding Ext Layout Elements*, showing how it can be used as a direct replacement for the HTML Select List. It provides the same drop-down list of values, as well as auto-completing filtering functionality, enabling users to find and select a value quickly.

But that's only scratching the surface of what the ComboBox can do!

In this section, we will cover creating a plug-in ComboBox, enabling functionality for it to do both local and remote loading of data. The ComboBox can use all of the Ext data store classes for its input data, so we will cover using the ArrayStore for local ComboBoxes, and the JsonStore for remote ComboBoxes.

Unlike the new APEX 4.0 Auto-complete item type and the HTML Select List, ComboBoxes are not limited to just one or two columns for data. We will also cover how to use the Ext.XTemplate to provide enhanced formatting options to show more information to your application users. The example in the following screenshot shows a person's name, address fields, and a credit limit using CSS-formatted text and images — all displayed using conditional logic.

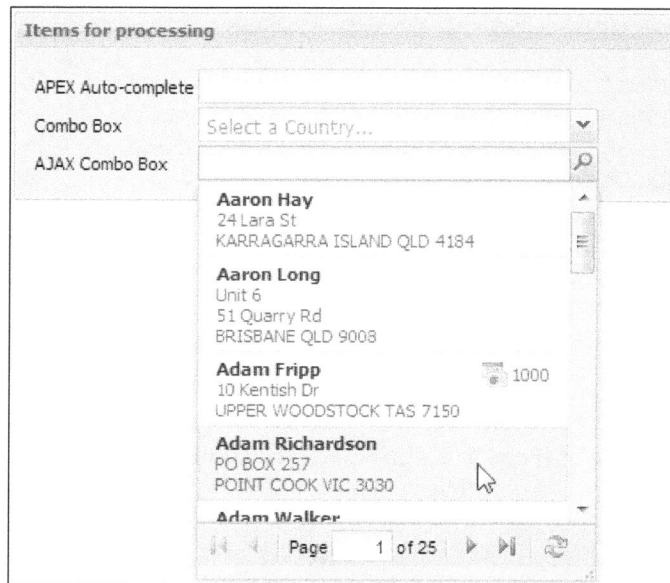

The ComboBox can also be used as a direct replacement for the native APEX Popup List of Values. Those clunky popups in a separate browser window will be a thing of the past!

Finally, we will cover how Dynamic Actions interact with widgets made up of multiple DOM elements like the ComboBox.

Defining the ComboBox plug-in

We will be picking up the pace in our ComboBox definition, as defining plug-ins is about following a pattern. The new functionality will be covered in greater detail; the full source for the database package is included in the Chapter 8 source code files available on Packt's site .

Plugin name:

`Ext.form.ComboBox`

Callbacks:

- Render function name: `plug_ext_form_combo.render`
- AJAX function name: `plug_ext_form_combo.ajax`
- Validation function name: `plug_ext_form_combo.validate`

Standard attributes:

Standard Attributes		
Attributes:		
☑ Is Visible Widget	☑ Session State Changeable	☑ Has Read Only Attribute
☑ Has Escape Output Attribute	☐ Has Quick Pick Attributes	☑ Has Source Attributes
☐ Format Mask Date Only	☐ Format Mask Number Only	☑ Has Element Attributes
☑ Has Width Attributes	☐ Has Height Attribute	☑ Has Element Option Attribute
☑ Has Encrypt Session State Attribute	☑ Has List of Values	☑ List of Values Required
☑ Has LOV Display Null Attributes	☐ Has Cascading LOV Attributes	

Minimum Columns   2 Maximum Columns   998

SQL Examples

```
<pre>select description
      ,id
      ,col3
      ...
      ,col998
  from <tables>
  order by 1
</pre>
```

Having the List of Values enabled is the key to defining the query for our ComboBox. We will be adding an extra column as part of the solution, limiting the number of allowable columns to just 998 columns!

As a design choice, I've decided a minimum of two columns are required, these columns are the description and value fields.

Custom attributes:

Label	Type	Required	Depending on	Values
Mode	Select List	Yes		remote, local
Empty text	Text	No		
Template config	Textarea	No		
Page size	Number	No	Mode	
Min. characters	Integer	No	Mode	

Events:

Name	Internal name
onSelect	select

Defining the ComboBox plug-in callback functions

The PL/SQL package specification for the ComboBox is identical to the NumberField package specification, apart from the changing of the name:

```
CREATE OR REPLACE PACKAGE plug_ext_form_combo AS
function render (
    p_item               in apex_plugin.t_page_item,
    p_plugin             in apex_plugin.t_plugin,
    p_value              in varchar2,
    p_is_readonly        in boolean,
    p_is_printer_friendly in boolean )
    return apex_plugin.t_page_item_render_result;

function ajax (
    p_item   in apex_plugin.t_page_item,
    p_plugin in apex_plugin.t_plugin )
    return apex_plugin.t_page_item_ajax_result;
```

```
function validate (
    p_item   in  apex_plugin.t_page_item,
    p_plugin in  apex_plugin.t_plugin,
    p_value  in  varchar2 )
    return apex_plugin.t_page_item_validation_result;

END;
/
```

Once again we will look at the details of each function separately; the full package body and specification are included in the Chapter 8 source files available for download on Packt's site.

Rendering functionality for the ComboBox plug-in

The PL/SQL render function uses the metadata passed to it to generate HTML and JavaScript to fulfill the following requirements:

- For a display-only item, create a stateful HTML element as a SPAN element

OR

- Create an HTML element that will be transformed into a ComboBox
- Generate JavaScript defining a data store either locally with the data in a JavaScript array, or as a remote data store with parameters for an XHR request
- Generate JavaScript code defining the ComboBox and referencing the store

The PL/SQL code for the render function is as follows:

```
FUNCTION render (
    p_item              in apex_plugin.t_page_item,
    p_plugin            in apex_plugin.t_plugin,
    p_value             in varchar2,
    p_is_readonly       in boolean,
    p_is_printer_friendly in boolean )
    return apex_plugin.t_page_item_render_result
IS
  l_result apex_plugin.t_page_item_render_result;

  subtype attr is
    apex_application_page_items.attribute_01%type;
```

```
       -- assign local names to attributes
       l_mode       attr := p_item.attribute_01;
       l_emptyText  attr := p_item.attribute_02;
       l_tpl        attr := p_item.attribute_03;
       l_pageSize   number := to_number(p_item.attribute_04);
       l_minChars   number := to_number(p_item.attribute_05);

       -- Only use escaped value for the HTML output!
       l_code            varchar2(32767);
       l_escaped_value   varchar2(32767)
                         := sys.htf.escape_sc(p_value);
       l_name            varchar2(30);
       l_columns         sys.dbms_sql.desc_tab2;
     BEGIN
       -- Debug information
       if apex_application.g_debug then
         apex_plugin_util.debug_page_item (
           p_plugin             => p_plugin,
           p_page_item          => p_item,
           p_value              => p_value,
           p_is_readonly        => p_is_readonly,
           p_is_printer_friendly => p_is_printer_friendly );
       end if;

       if p_is_readonly or p_is_printer_friendly then
         -- emit hidden field if necessary
         apex_plugin_util.print_hidden_if_readonly (
           p_item_name          => p_item.name,
           p_value              => p_value,
           p_is_readonly        => p_is_readonly,
           p_is_printer_friendly => p_is_printer_friendly );

         -- emit display span with the value
         apex_plugin_util.print_display_only (
           p_item_name       => p_item.name,
           p_display_value   => p_value,
           p_show_line_breaks => false,
           p_escape          => true,
           p_attributes      => p_item.element_attributes );

       else
         -- If a page item saves state, we have to call the
         -- get_input_name_for_page_item to render the internal
         -- hidden p_arg_names field. It will also return the
```

```
-- HTML field name which we have to use when we render
-- the HTML input field.
l_name
  := apex_plugin.get_input_name_for_page_item(false);

-- emit the input item to be transformed
sys.htp.p('<input type="text" name="'||l_name||
    '" id="'||p_item.name||'" '||
    'value="'||l_escaped_value||
    '" size="'||p_item.element_width||'" '||
    'maxlength="'||p_item.element_max_length||'" '||
    coalesce(p_item.element_attributes,
          'class="x-form-text"')||' />');

-- call store rendering routine
if l_mode = 'local' then
   l_columns := render_local_store (
     p_item    => p_item,
     p_plugin  => p_plugin,
     p_value   => p_value );
else
   l_columns := render_remote_store (
     p_item    => p_item,
     p_plugin  => p_plugin,
     p_value   => p_value );
end if;


-- build combo properties
-- local procedure PUSH adds values to associative array
-- (index by table)
-- use convention ext-xxx, where xxx is the item name
-- makes it easy to lookup components using Ext.getCmp().
push('id'           ,'''ext-'||p_item.name||'''');
push('hiddenName'   ,''''||l_name||'''');
push('hiddenValue'  ,''''||l_escaped_value||'''');
push('applyTo'      ,''''||p_item.name||'''');

push('mode'             ,''''||l_mode||'''');
push('forceSelection'   ,'true');
push('triggerAction'    ,'''all''');
push('selectOnFocus'    ,'true');
push('resizable'        ,'true');
```

```
push('store'         ,'Ext.apex.'||p_item.name||'.store');
push('displayField','''''||l_columns(1).col_name||'''');
push('valueField'   ,'''''||l_columns(2).col_name||'''');
push('emptyText'    ,'''''||escape_json(l_emptyText)||'''');

-- detect DOM node disabled
-- allows developers to set element attribute to disabled
push('disabled',
  'Ext.fly('''||p_item.name||''').dom.disabled'
);

-- Can create a customized layout using Ext.XTemplates
-- otherwise uses Ext.form.ComboBox default
if l_tpl is not null then
    push('itemSelector' ,'''div.search-item''');
    push('tpl',
      'new Ext.XTemplate('||CRLF||l_tpl||')'
    );
end if;

-- lookup the display value when the value is not null
if p_value is not null then
    push('value', '"'||escape_json(
    apex_plugin_util.get_display_data (
      p_sql_statement        => p_item.lov_definition,
      p_min_columns          => 2,
      p_max_columns          => 999,
      p_component_name       => p_item.name,
      p_search_string        => p_value,
      p_display_extra        => false) )||'"'
    );
end if;

-- remote combos have extra params
if l_mode = 'remote' then

  -- the APEX ajaxIdentifier is required to
  -- identify the item and session for AJAX processes
  push('ajaxIdentifier',
    ''''||apex_plugin.get_ajax_identifier||''''
  );

  push('queryParam'    ,'''x01''');
  push('idProperty',
```

```
        ''''||l_columns(2).col_name||''''
    );
    push('triggerClass','''x-form-search-trigger''');

    push('pageSize' ,l_pageSize);
    push('minChars' ,l_minChars);
    push('getParams' ,'function(q){var p = {};'||
      'if (this.pageSize) {p[''p_widget_action_mod''] = 0;'||
      'p[''p_widget_action''] = this.pageSize;}return p;}');
end if;


-- assemble the code, retrieving the "pushed" parameters
-- as a varchar2 string
l_code := CRLF||
          'Ext.onReady(function(){'||CRLF||
          '   new Ext.form.ComboBox({'||CRLF||
          get_properties(8)||'    });'||CRLF||
          '});'||CRLF;

-- Initialize page item when the page has been rendered.
apex_javascript.add_onload_code (
    p_code => l_code );

-- Tell APEX engine that field is navigable, in case
-- it's the first item on the page, and APEX page is
-- configured to navigate to first item (by default).
if p_is_readonly or p_is_printer_friendly then
  l_result.is_navigable := false;
else
  l_result.is_navigable := true;
  -- set navigable element when not same as item name
  -- l_result.navigable_dom_id := 'some other DOM id';
end if;

  end if;

  return l_result;
END render;
```

We won't be going into great detail for the render function, as much of the code is very similar to the code for the NumberField plug-in. Some areas are new, which do need some discussion.

Some convenience routines not used in the NumberField example have been added, those being `push`, `escape_json`, and `get_properties`. The `push` procedure temporarily stores name and value attributes in an associative array (index by table) for later retrieval by the `get_properties` function. Using an associative array indexed by the attribute name means the attributes can be sent as output in alphabetical order when it suits later in the code. Having the attributes in alphabetical order isn't necessary, but it does help when debugging JavaScript.

Using custom routines instead of the APEX supplied `wwv_flow_javascript.add_attribute` routine gives a little more control for JSON escaping text, which is done by the `escape_json` function.

The second area of interest is the `render_local_store` and `render_remote_store` functions that build store definitions. The code to render both the local and remote stores was covered earlier in the chapter, so all we are doing here is calling the PL/SQL routines to generate the code.

To show the JavaScript generated, I've created a simple ComboBox item using a local store. The settings and LOV query are shown in the following screenshot:

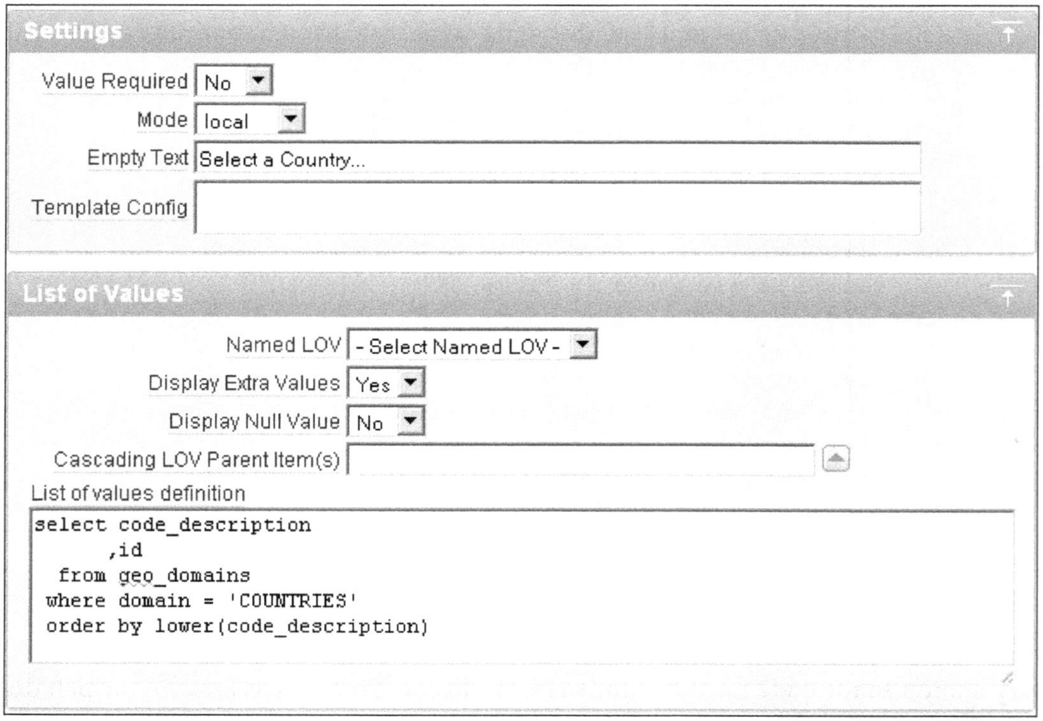

Settings

Value Required `No`

Mode `local`

Empty Text `Select a Country...`

Template Config

List of Values

Named LOV `- Select Named LOV -`

Display Extra Values `Yes`

Display Null Value `No`

Cascading LOV Parent Item(s)

List of values definition

```
select code_description
      ,id
  from geo_domains
 where domain = 'COUNTRIES'
 order by lower(code_description)
```

The JavaScript output for only the ComboBox is:

```
apex.jQuery(document).ready(function(){
(function(){
Ext.onReady(function(){
    new Ext.form.ComboBox({
        applyTo: 'P120_COMBO',
        disabled: Ext.fly('P120_COMBO').dom.disabled,
        emptyText: 'Select a Country...',
        forceSelection: true,
        hiddenName: 'p_t05',
        hiddenValue: '221',
        id: 'ext-P120_COMBO',
        mode: 'local',
        resizable: true,
        selectOnFocus: true,
        triggerAction: 'all',
        value: 'Australia, Commonwealth of',
        displayField: 'CODE_DESCRIPTION',
        store: Ext.apex.P120_COMBO.store,
        valueField: 'ID'
    });
});
})();
});
```

The JavaScript code generated by the ComboBox plug-in has been wrapped by an anonymous function, and a `apex.jQuery(document).ready` function. APEX automatically added these extra functions when we called the `apex_javascript.add_onload_code` procedure to ensure that JavaScript is not executed until the browser has the DOM tree loaded (without waiting for external resources). To ensure that the Ext library has been loaded, I would also like to include the `Ext.onReady` call.

References to the Store have been highlighted; the Store is identified by its fully qualified name `Ext.apex.P120_COMBO.store`, with the ComboBox's display and value fields assigned to use the Store records `CODE_DESCRIPTION` and `ID` columns.

In this example, the `value` and `hiddenValue` attributes have been assigned by the `render` function, performing a lookup on the APEX session state value for the P120_COMBO item.

The final area of interest is around the use of Ext.XTemplate to provide enhanced formatting options, which we will cover together with retrieving data for ComboBox using XHR requests under the AJAX section.

AJAX functionality for the ComboBox plug-in

For large datasets, the ComboBox can be configured to fetch a subset of data using an AJAX request to load the data remotely, and use pagination and type-ahead search functionality to filter the results.

```
FUNCTION ajax (
  p_item    in apex_plugin.t_page_item,
  p_plugin in apex_plugin.t_plugin )
  return apex_plugin.t_page_item_ajax_result
IS
  l_result apex_plugin.t_page_item_ajax_result;
BEGIN
  -- indicate we are returning application/json data
  apex_plugin_util.print_json_http_header;

  emit_json_data (
    p_item    => p_item,
    p_plugin => p_plugin,
    p_value  => null
  );

  -- not used by APEX yet
  return l_result;
END;
```

The AJAX function here just calls an APEX procedure to print a JSON mime-type header, indicating the data being returned is in JSON format and shouldn't be cached. The actual text returned in the HTML Response header is:

```
Content-Type: application/json
Cache-Control: no-cache
Pragma: no-cache
```

The real work is done by the following the EMIT_JSON_DATA procedure:

```
PROCEDURE emit_json_data (
  p_item    in apex_plugin.t_page_item,
  p_plugin in apex_plugin.t_plugin,
  p_value  in varchar2 )
IS
  l_sql_handler    apex_plugin_util.t_sql_handler;
  l_new_sql        varchar2(32767);
  l_col_value_list apex_plugin_util.t_column_value_list;

  /** @todo assign from combo attributes */
```

```
l_search_type    varchar2(20) := 'EXACT_IGNORE';
l_search_col     varchar2(32767);
l_col_count number;

-- assign values from ajax parameters
l_start       number
  := coalesce(apex_application.g_widget_action_mod, 0);

l_limit       number
  := coalesce(apex_application.g_widget_action, 100);

l_search_string varchar2(32767)
  := apex_application.g_x01;
BEGIN
```

Ext Stores need to know the total number of records in the result set, so it's necessary to enclose the original query within a `select` statement to return the total as an extra column named `ext$totalrows`:

```
-- add ext$totalrows column to sql statement
l_new_sql := 'select q.* ,count(*) over () ext$totalrows'||
             '  from ('||p_item.lov_definition||') q';
```

The total number of records is used by the `Ext.PagingToolbar` object, a sub-component of the ComboBox, to provide automatic paging control.

```
l_sql_handler := apex_plugin_util.get_sql_handler (
  p_sql_statement  => l_new_sql,
  p_min_columns    => 1,
  p_max_columns    => 999,
  p_component_name => p_item.name
);

apex_plugin_util.free_sql_handler(l_sql_handler);

l_col_count := l_sql_handler.column_list.count() - 1;


-- can't use APEX search because need to display totals
-- where clause has to be included at this level
if l_search_string is not null then
  l_search_string := apex_plugin_util.get_search_string(
    p_search_type   => l_search_type,
    p_search_string => l_search_string
  );
```

```
            l_search_col := l_sql_handler.column_list(1).col_name;

        l_new_sql := l_new_sql||CRLF||
          case l_search_type
          when 'CONTAINS_CASE'    then
                'where instr('||l_search_col||', '''||
                l_search_string||'''') > 0'

          when 'CONTAINS_IGNORE' then
                'where instr(upper('||l_search_col||'), '''||
                l_search_string||'''') > 0'

          when 'EXACT_CASE'       then
                'where '||l_search_col||' like '''||
                l_search_string||'%'''

          when 'EXACT_IGNORE'     then
                'where upper('||l_search_col||') like '''||
                l_search_string||'%'''

          when 'LOOKUP'           then
                'where '||l_search_col||' = '''||
                l_search_string||''''
          end;
    end if;
```

The where clause needs to be included here to return the correct value for total matching records, because APEX wraps the passed query inside another query to limit the rows returned and the position of the first row returned, for example, returning rows 100 to 110 of the result set.

```
    -- get data based on our new sql statement
    l_col_value_list := apex_plugin_util.get_data (
      p_sql_statement    => l_new_sql,
      p_min_columns      => 1,
      p_max_columns      => 999,
      p_component_name   => p_item.id,
      p_first_row        => l_start,
      p_max_rows         => l_limit
    );

    -- print data
    if l_col_value_list.exists(1) then
      sys.htp.p('{"total":'||
        l_col_value_list(l_col_count + 1)(1)||',"rowset":['
```

```
      );

      for i in 1 .. l_col_value_list(1).count loop
        sys.htp.prn(case when i > 1 then ',' else ' ' end||'{');
        for j in 1 .. l_col_count loop
          sys.htp.prn(case when j > 1 then ',' end||
            '"'||l_sql_handler.column_list(j).col_name||'": '||
            '"'||escape_json(l_col_value_list(j)(i))||'"'
          );
        end loop;
        sys.htp.p('}');
      end loop;

      sys.htp.p(']}');
    else
      sys.htp.prn('{"total":0,"rowset":[]}');
    end if;

  EXCEPTION
    when no_data_found then
      apex_plugin_util.free_sql_handler(l_sql_handler);
      sys.htp.prn('{"total":0,"rowset":[]}');

    when others then
      apex_plugin_util.free_sql_handler(l_sql_handler);
      raise;
  END emit_json_data;
```

Once again, the APEX-provided APIs do most of the work processing the final query, binding any session state variables, and returning the data, which we render using JSON notation.

Using the Ext.XTemplate to provide enhanced formatting

The Ext.XTemplate class provides a templating mechanism that can be used to render arrays of records automatically. It provides advanced functionality such as conditional processing with basic comparison operators, basic math functions, and executing arbitrary inline code using template variables.

To show how the Ext.XTemplate is used for ComboBoxes, I've created a remote ComboBox using the settings shown in the following screenshot:

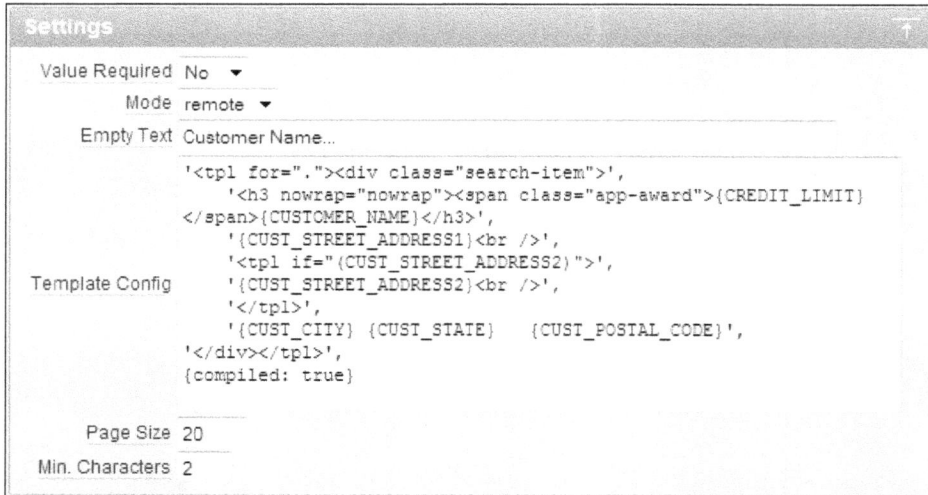

The SQL query used for the LOV on this ComboBox is:

```
select c.cust_first_name||' '||c.cust_last_name customer_name
     ,c.customer_id
     ,c.cust_street_address1
     ,c.cust_street_address2
     ,c.cust_city
     ,c.cust_state
     ,c.cust_postal_code
     ,c.credit_limit
from demo_customers c
order by lower(c.cust_first_name||' '||c.cust_last_name)
```

We are not particularly interested in the query itself; it obeys the rules for our ComboBox plug-in, with the first column returned to be displayField, and the second column valueField. It also retrieves a number of other fields that can also be displayed by using XTemplates.

The PL/SQL PLUG_EXT_FORM_COMBO.RENDER function generates the following JavaScript for our ComboBox on a webpage:

```
Ext.onReady(function(){
    new Ext.form.ComboBox({
        applyTo: 'P120_AJAX_COMBO',
        disabled: Ext.fly('P120_AJAX_COMBO').dom.disabled,
```

```
        displayField: 'CUSTOMER_NAME',
        emptyText: 'Customer Name...',
        forceSelection: true,
        getParams: function(q){
            var p = {};
            if (this.pageSize) {
                p['p_widget_action_mod'] = 0;
                p['p_widget_action'] = this.pageSize;
            }return p;
        },
        hiddenName: 'p_t06',
        hiddenValue: '',
        id: 'ext-P120_AJAX_COMBO',
        idProperty: 'CUSTOMER_ID',
        itemSelector: 'div.search-item',
        minChars: 2,
        mode: 'remote',
        pageSize: 20,
        queryParam: 'x01',
        resizable: true,
        selectOnFocus: true,
        store: Ext.apex.P120_AJAX_COMBO.store,
        tpl: new Ext.XTemplate(
'<tpl for="."><div class="search-item">',
    '<h3 nowrap="nowrap"><span class="app-award">{CREDIT_LIMIT}</
span>{CUSTOMER_NAME}</h3>',
    '{CUST_STREET_ADDRESS1}<br />',
    '<tpl if="(CUST_STREET_ADDRESS2)">',
    '{CUST_STREET_ADDRESS2}<br />',
    '</tpl>',
    '{CUST_CITY} {CUST_STATE}   {CUST_POSTAL_CODE}',
'</div></tpl>',
{compiled: true}),
        triggerAction: 'all',
        triggerClass: 'x-form-search-trigger',
        valueField: 'CUSTOMER_ID'
    });
});
```

The JavaScript shows the ComboBox configuration, including references to the data store and the XTemplate definition, which has been highlighted.

Typing the characters "be" in the ComboBox initiates an AJAX request to load the data store. Two matching records are returned by the `PLUG_EXT_FORM_COMBO.AJAX` function to the browser.

```
{"total":2,"rowset":[
 {"CUSTOMER_NAME": "Benjamin Freeman",
   "CUSTOMER_ID": "25560",
   "CUST_STREET_ADDRESS1": "2",
   "CUST_STREET_ADDRESS2": "19 Princes St",
   "CUST_CITY": "KALPOWAR",
   "CUST_STATE": "QLD",
   "CUST_POSTAL_CODE": "4630",
   "CREDIT_LIMIT": ""}
,{"CUSTOMER_NAME": "Bernard Newman",
   "CUSTOMER_ID": "25649",
   "CUST_STREET_ADDRESS1": "4 Bartlett Gr",
   "CUST_STREET_ADDRESS2": "",
   "CUST_CITY": "FLINDERS LANE",
   "CUST_STATE": "VIC",
   "CUST_POSTAL_CODE": "8009",
   "CREDIT_LIMIT": ""}
]}
```

At this point the data store fires the `datachanged` event, and the ComboBox refreshes its view using the specified XTemplate to render the data.

When a XTemplate is not provided, the ComboBox uses the default template string.

```
'<tpl for="."><div class="x-combo-list-item">{' + this.displayField +
'}</div></tpl>'
```

The XTemplate for this example is:

```
'<tpl for="."><div class="search-item">',
    '<h3 nowrap="nowrap"><span class="app-award">{CREDIT_LIMIT}</
span>{CUSTOMER_NAME}</h3>',
    '{CUST_STREET_ADDRESS1}<br />',
    '<tpl if="(CUST_STREET_ADDRESS2)">',
    '{CUST_STREET_ADDRESS2}<br />',
    '</tpl>',
    '{CUST_CITY} {CUST_STATE}   {CUST_POSTAL_CODE}',
'</div></tpl>',
{compiled: true}
```

The XTemplate `tpl` tag and the `for` operator are used to process the data object for the ComboBox. The `for="."` operator loops through the entire data object starting at the root node.

Each array record is processed, substituting the column values into the column name placeholders, for example {`CUSTOMER_NAME`}.

Conditional logic can be applied using the `tpl` tag and the `if` operator to provide conditional checks to determine whether or not to render parts of the template. Consider the following rule:

```
'<tpl if="(CUST_STREET_ADDRESS2)">',
'{CUST_STREET_ADDRESS2}<br />',
'</tpl>',
```

In this example, this rule is used to produce output text only when the `CUST_STREET_ADDRESS2` field has a value.

When the XTemplate is being used to process multiple records, the `compiled: true` attribute should be set for optimized performance.

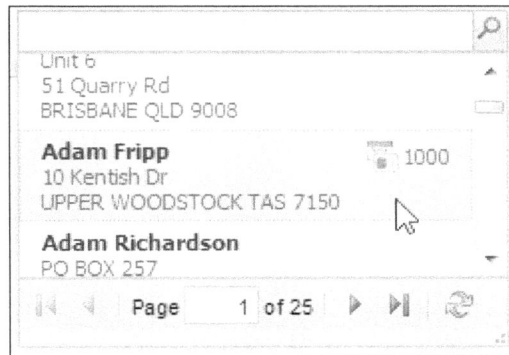

The HTML produced on the browser by the XTemplate for the highlighted record shown in the previous screenshot is:

```
<div class="search-item x-combo-selected">
<h3 nowrap="nowrap"><span class="app-award">1000</span>
Adam Fripp</h3>
10 Kentish Dr<br>UPPER WOODSTOCK TAS     7150
</div>
```

Additional CSS rules need to be provided, either in the APEX page or the application CSS file to produce the actual HTML formatting. The following CSS rules were applied for this example:

```
.search-item {
    border-color:#FFFFFF #FFFFFF #EEEEEE;
    border-style:solid;
    border-width:1px;
    color:#555555;
    font:11px tahoma,arial,helvetica,sans-serif;
    padding:3px 10px;
    white-space:normal;
}
.search-item h3 {
    color:#222222;
    display:block;
    font-weight:bold;
}
.search-item h3 span {
    clear:none;
    display:block;
    float:right;
    font-weight:normal;
    margin:0 0 5px 5px;
    line-height: 18px;
}

.cc-limit {
    color:#c0272b;
    font:normal 11px tahoma, arial, helvetica, sans-serif;
    background: transparent no-repeat 0 2px;
    background-image:url(/ux/playpen/resources/images/icon/
creditcards.gif);
    padding-left:18px;
}
```

So as you can see, XTemplates provide a powerful mechanism to render HTML on the browser client.

For AJAX-based processes, this removes the need to return formatted HTML, or the necessity to have complicated JavaScript coding to render HTML tags inserting values from the JSON data, when returning JSON data only.

Validation functionality for the ComboBox plug-in

After the relatively lengthy code for the RENDER and AJAX functionality, the code to validate the ComboBox is quite trivial:

```
FUNCTION validate (
  p_item    in     apex_plugin.t_page_item,
  p_plugin in      apex_plugin.t_plugin,
  p_value  in      varchar2 )
  return apex_plugin.t_page_item_validation_result
IS
  l_display_value varchar2(32767);
  l_result apex_plugin.t_page_item_validation_result;
BEGIN
  -- Debug information
  if apex_application.g_debug then
    apex_plugin_util.debug_page_item (
        p_plugin     => p_plugin,
        p_page_item => p_item );
  end if;

  -- Nothing to do when null (APEX checks for mandatory items)
  if p_value is null then return l_result; end if;

  -- lookup the display value when the value is not null
  if p_value is not null then
    l_display_value :=
      apex_plugin_util.get_display_data (
        p_sql_statement  => p_item.lov_definition,
        p_min_columns    => 2,
        p_max_columns    => 999,
        p_component_name => p_item.name,
        p_search_string  => p_value,
        p_display_extra  => false);

    -- return error when no display value found
    if l_display_value is null then
      l_result.message :=
        'Error: no display value found for '||
        p_item.name||' value '||p_value||'.';
    end if;
  end if;

  -- populate l_result with error message, otherwise null
  return l_result;
END;
```

The validate function uses the APEX-provided utilities to verify that matching display value exists for the supplied value using the LOV query. If not, it raises an error.

Mixing ComboBoxes with Dynamic Actions

Dynamic Actions provide a declarative mechanism for generating JavaScript to provide client-side behaviors. Native actions include simple actions that show, hide, enable, and disable page elements when a page item's value changes. More advanced native actions include setting item values, executing JavaScript code, and executing PL/SQL code via AJAX calls.

Native actions work immediately for custom plug-ins based on simple DOM elements, such as the NumberField plugin in *Chapter 7, Working with Plug-ins and Dynamic Actions*. For plugins based on multiple DOM elements such as the ComboBox, or the built-in APEX shuttle-box, some additional work has to be done before the native dynamic actions will work correctly.

The following screenshot shows the before and after views of a dynamic action to hide the three items in the region. The **APEX Auto-complete** item uses a simple DOM text item, with the other two items being Ext ComboBoxes, each built using multiple DOM elements.

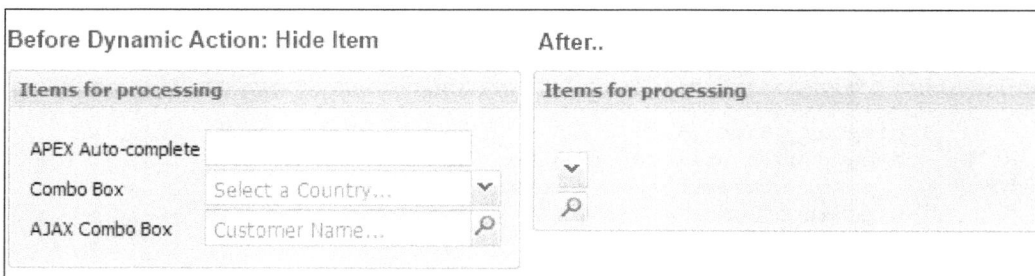

The APEX-generated code for the **Hide Item** dynamic action references the APEX item names, assuming the items are simple DOM elements. For ComboBoxes, this results in the text item component being hidden, leaving the trigger icon visible.

Similarly, when using the Disable Item dynamic action, the text item component is disabled, leaving the trigger icon still enabled! So, despite attempting to restrict users from modifying the item, the trigger icon allows users to change the value.

Fortunately for us, the APEX team has addressed the issue when developing complex native items, building the `apex.widget.initPageItem` function to integrate plug-in items with the Dynamic Actions code seamlessly.

Integrating plugins with the Dynamic Action framework

The `apex.widget.initPageItem` function definition is:

```
apex.widget.initPageItem = function (pName, pOptions) {
    apex.item(pName, pOptions);
};
```

It accepts two parameters—the item name and an object literal containing callback configurations for any or all of the functions: `getValue`, `setValue`, `enable`, `disable`, `show`, `hide`, `nullValue`.

An example initialization for an item `P1_MY_ITEM` is:

```
apex.widget.initPageItem("P1_MY_ITEM", {
    getValue: function(){},
    setValue: function(){},
    nullValue: "%null%"
});
```

You would write suitable code for each of the functions shown to get and set the item values. In this example, the `nullValue` doesn't use a function; instead, it is a simple string value.

The `apex.widget.initPageItem` function is located in the APEX installation files at `apex\images\javascript\uncompressed\apex_widget_4_0.js`. Further examples on its use can be seen in this file for some of the native APEX items.

The `Ext.form.ComboBox` already has methods for `getValue`, `setValue`, `enable`, `disable`, `show`, and `hide`. Our task is to initialize a ComboBox with the Dynamic Action framework, so that any code associated with the APEX item name will be redirected to use functions referencing the ComboBox methods.

Before writing the JavaScript, it's best to build a testing harness so that you can validate your code as you go. The following screenshot shows the test page set up for this example. Each of the Dynamic Actions modifies all of the items in the region below.

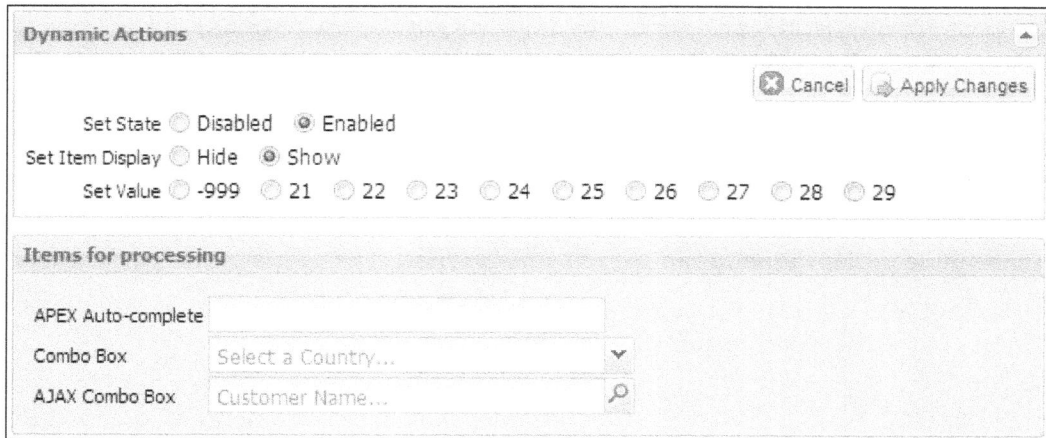

The Dynamic Actions created are summarized in the following table:

Name	When event	When elements	When condition	Actions
Set State	Change (bind)	P120_SET_STATE (Item)	equal to: Enabled	Enable: when true
				Disable: when false
Set Item Display	Change (bind)	P120_SET_DISPLAY (Item)	equal to: Show	Show: when true
				Hide: when false
Set Value	Change (bind)	P120_SET_VALUE (Item)	is not null	JavaScript Expression:
				$v('P120_SET_VALUE')

The ComboBox plugin we have created is rendered by first creating a simple input text item and then using JavaScript to transform it into a ComboBox using the `applyTo` attribute. This becomes the logical place to call the `apex.widget.initPageItem` function.

By overriding the standard ComboBox, this change can be made in the application JavaScript library.

```
Ext.override(Ext.form.ComboBox, {
  applyToMarkup: function(el){
    Ext.form.ComboBox.superclass.applyToMarkup.call(this, el);

    // remove APEX applied class
    Ext.fly(el).removeClass('apex_disabled');

    // get the Ext id for the component
    var x = this.getId();

    // Register customized standard actions for the
    // originating DOM element.
    // Original element has been replaced with ComboBox.
    apex.widget.initPageItem(el, {
      getValue: function(){
        return Ext.getCmp(x).getValue();
      },
      setValue: function(v){
        Ext.getCmp(x).setValue(v);
      },
      enable: function(){
        Ext.getCmp(x).enable();
      },
      disable: function(){
        Ext.getCmp(x).disable();
      },
      show: function(){
        Ext.getCmp(x).show();
        Ext.select(el + '-label').show();
      },
      hide: function(){
        Ext.getCmp(x).hide();
        // Hide label
        // Relies on using label templates, and label naming
        // convention. Could check parent TD for label element
        // for this el, and parent's prev sibling TD for
        // label also.
        Ext.select(el + '-label').hide();
      }
    });
```

```
      // trigger APEX DA event when value selected
      this.on('select', function(o, record, index){
        apex.jQuery('#' + o.el.id).trigger('select');
      });
    }
  });
```

The first few lines perform some basic housekeeping before we register our customized dynamic actions.

```
Ext.override(Ext.form.ComboBox, {
  applyToMarkup: function(el){
    Ext.form.ComboBox.superclass.applyToMarkup.call(this, el);

    // remove APEX applied class
    Ext.fly(el).removeClass('apex_disabled');
```

The highlighted line executes the standard `applyToMarkup` functionality for a ComboBox, which doesn't reside in the ComboBox object, but resides a few levels up the object inheritance hierarchy in the Component object.

APEX may have applied a `apex_disabled` class to the text item to be transformed into a ComboBox, so it is necessary to remove the class.

We then fetch the ID of the ComboBox we are creating to use in subsequent function calls.

```
      // get the Ext id for the component
      var x = this.getId();

      // Register customized standard actions for the
      // originating DOM element.
      // Original element has been replaced with ComboBox.
      apex.widget.initPageItem(el, {
        getValue: function(){
          return Ext.getCmp(x).getValue();
        },
        setValue: function(v){
          Ext.getCmp(x).setValue(v);
        },
```

The `apex.widget.initPageItem` function is called, passing the original APEX item name in the `el` parameter, and defining the callback functions. Because Ext has existing functions to enable/disable, show/hide, and set values, our task is to redirect the code to the ComboBox using the `Ext.getCmp(x)` call to select the component.

Testing shows the ComboBox correctly performs the **enable/disable** and **show/hide** actions. The `setValue` function works correctly for the local ComboBox, but the following screenshot shows it does not retrieve the description for the AJAX ComboBox, which needs to retrieve the data remotely from the database.

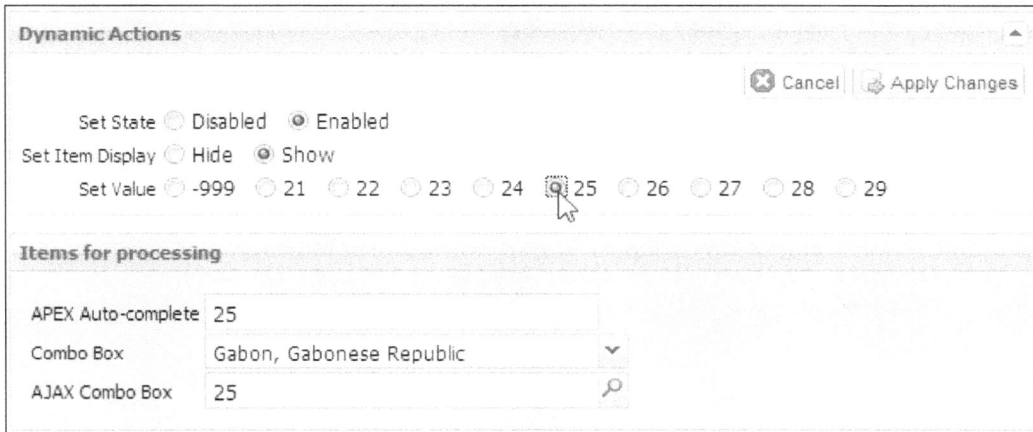

To fix this, a second override needs to be made to the standard `Ext.form.ComboBox`, this time modifying the `setValue` function. Typically, the override would be included with the earlier override, but it can also be applied separately as done here.

```
Ext.override(Ext.form.ComboBox, {
  oneShot: false,
  setValue: function(v){
    var text = v;
    if (this.valueField) {
      var r = this.findRecord(this.valueField, v);
      if (r) {
        this.oneShot = false;
        text = r.data[this.displayField];
      }
      else {
        // do extra step for remote mode
        if (this.mode == 'remote' && this.oneShot == false) {
          this.oneShot = true;
          this.store.on('load',
              this.setValue.createDelegate(this, arguments),
              null, {
                single: true
          });
          this.store.load({
            params: {
              'p_widget_num_return': v
            }
```

```
    });
    return;
  }
  else {
    this.oneShot = false;
    if (Ext.isDefined(this.valueNotFoundText)) {
      text = this.valueNotFoundText;
    }
  }
 }
}
this.lastSelectionText = text;
if (this.hiddenField) {
  this.hiddenField.value = Ext.value(v, '');
}
Ext.form.ComboBox.superclass.setValue.call(this, text);
this.value = v;
return this;
  }
});
```

This time the highlighted code contains the modified functionality. When the `setValue` function doesn't find the value cached in the JavaScript store, ComboBoxes with remote stores will make one attempt to retrieve the display value from the database via an AJAX request, setting `this.oneShot = true;` before loading the data returned for the value passed by the parameter `p_widget_num_return`. The store loads any returned records and executes the `setValue` function again using the `createDelegate` function. Refer to the following screenshot, and you will realize that the AJAX ComboBox now correctly shows the display value:

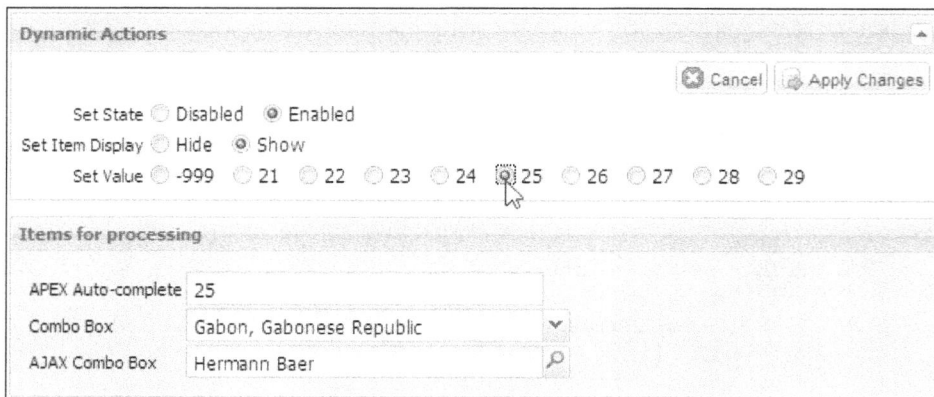

If the display value was still not found, the ComboBox uses default functionality to show the `valueNotFoundText` text if configured, or the hidden value. Submitting this value to the server would result in a validation error.

Defining custom events for the ComboBox

You can create custom events for plug-ins, allowing them to be exposed to dynamic actions. This allows the developer to create custom dynamic actions initiated by a plug-in to interact with other page items on the client. The following screenshot shows a custom event added for the ComboBox:

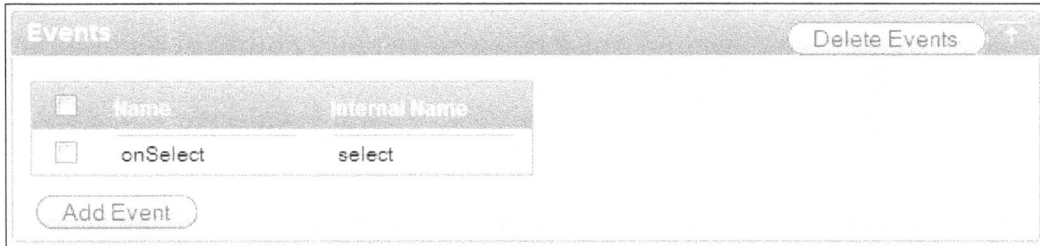

The event is triggered by client-side JavaScript for the plug-in, so for our ComboBox the event would be added to the code as follows:

```
Ext.override(Ext.form.ComboBox, {
  applyToMarkup: function(el){
    Ext.form.ComboBox.superclass.applyToMarkup.call(this, el);

    // ***snipped*** //

    // trigger APEX DA event when value selected
    this.on('select', function(o, record, index){
      apex.jQuery('#' + o.el.id).trigger('select');
    });
  }
});
```

Here, a listener has been added for the `Ext.form.ComboBox select` event, calling a function to trigger the `apex.jQuery select` event for the APEX item. The APEX Dynamic Action framework then executes any dynamic actions listening for the event.

> Note that the event name triggered is the **internal** name for the custom event.

The following screenshot shows a custom `onSelect [Ext.form.ComboBox]` event added to a ComboBox item. It has a single action associated with it, when the event is triggered, setting the value for another page item.

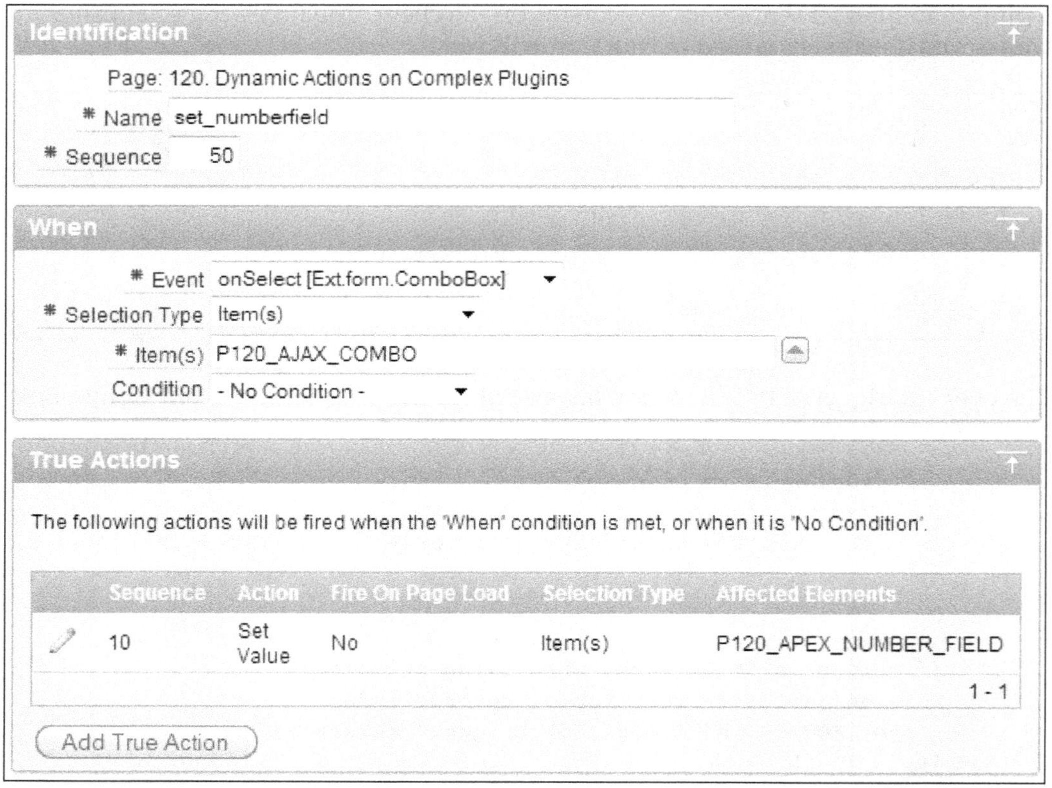

Identification					
Page: 120. Dynamic Actions on Complex Plugins					
* Name	set_numberfield				
* Sequence	50				

When					
* Event	onSelect [Ext.form.ComboBox] ▼				
* Selection Type	Item(s) ▼				
* Item(s)	P120_AJAX_COMBO			⬆	
Condition	- No Condition - ▼				

True Actions

The following actions will be fired when the 'When' condition is met, or when it is 'No Condition'.

	Sequence	Action	Fire On Page Load	Selection Type	Affected Elements
🖊	10	Set Value	No	Item(s)	P120_APEX_NUMBER_FIELD

1 - 1

(Add True Action)

The details for the Set Value action are:

Identification

> Dynamic Action: `set_numberfield`
>
> Action: Set Value

Execution options

> Fire when event result is: True
>
> Fire on page load: Unchecked
>
> Stop execution on error: Checked

Settings

> Set type: JavaScript Expression
>
> JavaScript expression: `Ext.getCmp('ext-' + this.triggeringElement.id).getValue();`

Affected elements

> Selection type: Item(s)
>
> Item(s): `P120_APEX_NUMBER_FIELD`

From the details of the Set Value action, the JavaScript Expression used for settings is slightly unusual. It relies on the naming convention that the ComboBox component ID is the APEX item name prefixed with `ext-`, something set up in the PL/SQL package for our plug-in ComboBox.

Using the ComboBox component name, it returns the value of the ComboBox to the Dynamic Actions framework, which populates the affected elements with the value.

This closes the loop for our ComboBox; it is now fully integrated to use standard dynamic actions, as well as triggering custom actions that can affect other page items.

Summary

In this chapter, we integrated the Ext ComboBox component into APEX. The ComboBox is a data-aware component that uses Ext Data Stores to hold record-based information in the browser client.

The ComboBox utilizes all aspects of creating a custom plug-in, implementing render, AJAX, and validation callbacks. The plug-in makes use of many of the standard attributes available to plug-ins, taking full advantage of the built-in LOV functionality. It also uses custom attributes to expose additional parameters to the developer, as well as a custom event to be used by Dynamic Actions.

The APEX provided PL/SQL APIs for plug-ins greatly sped up the development of the server-side functionality.

On the client side, the Ext ComboBox component was able to be integrated with the Dynamic Actions framework using the `apex.widget.initPageItem` function to declaratively override standard dynamic actions to show/hide, enable/disable and get/set values.

The functionality was integrated using the `Ext.override` method to add custom code, and extend the existing functionality when setting values for ComboBoxes with remote data stores.

We achieved a great deal in this chapter, covering many of the complexities of integrating Ext components into APEX.

For our next challenge, we will look at integrating Ext JS GridPanels into APEX.

9

Getting Interactive with GridPanels

GridPanels are, without doubt, one of the most powerful and most often-used components within the Ext framework. Even the most basic implementations of the GridPanel provide column management features including sorting, resizing, drag-and-drop column reordering, and show/hide columns.

Data presentation is handled separately from data retrieval within GridPanels, with data retrieval done using a Data Store component. For GridPanels with paging and remote sorting enabled, changes made on the client browser, such as hiding or re-ordering columns, are automatically maintained when new data is loaded.

As if that's not impressive enough, GridPanels support plugins (not to be confused with APEX Plug-ins), which allow additional functionality, such as expander rows and "Group By" header menu options, to be integrated.

GridPanels provide a way for you to add functionality to your Classic Reports that's currently only available in Interactive Reports, with the added advantage that you can have multiple Classic Reports on one page.

In this chapter we will cover:

- GridPanel components: Data Store, Column Model, Grid View, and Selection Model
- Key concepts for getting GridPanels into APEX
- Creating a GridPanel Region Plug-in
- Making a GridPanel Stateful
- Using the GridPanel to convert Classic Reports

Components making up a GridPanel

The `Ext.grid.GridPanel` brings together a number of other supporting components to present data in a tabular format. Those components are the **Store, Column model, View,** and **Selection model**.

Let's take a look at standalone example of the **GridPanel** to see how these supporting components each play their part, before we attempt to integrate it into APEX.

Commonwealth Games 2010 Medal Tally						
Rank	Country	Gold	Silver	Bronze	Total	
1	Australia	74	55	48	177	▲
2	India	38	27	36	101	
3	England	37	60	45	142	
4	Canada	26	17	33	76	
5	South Africa	12	11	10	33	
6	Kenya	12	11	9	32	
7	Malaysia	12	10	14	36	
8	Singapore	11	11	9	31	
9	Nigeria	11	8	14	33	
10	Scotland	9	10	7	26	▼

We will be going through the code for the GridPanel shown in the previous screenshot; it's also included in `chapter09/ ex-9-simple-grid.html`.

The overall structure of the page is:

```
<html>
<head>
  <!-- details snipped
        Ext library includes
  -->

</head>
<body>
    <div id="wrapper">
        <div id="gridRegion"></div>
    </div>

<script type="text/javascript">

Ext.onReady(function() {
```

```
    /** details snipped
        localJsonStore, columnModel, gridView, selectionModel
     */

    var grid = new Ext.grid.GridPanel({
        id         : 'my-grid',
        store      : localJsonStore,
        colModel   : columnModel,
        view       : gridView,
        selModel   : selectionModel,
        height     : 260,
        width      : 450,
        renderTo   : 'gridRegion',
        stripeRows : true,
        title      : 'Commonwealth Games 2010 Medal Talley'
    });
});

</script>
</body>
</html>
```

The overall structure of our standalone page is really quite straightforward. The header includes the usual Ext library and CSS includes, and the body of the page contains a DIV region with ID of gridRegion, into which our **GridPanel** will be rendered.

JavaScript code instantiates a new Ext.grid.GridPanel object, specifying parameters in an object literal. The highlighted parameters for store, colModel, view, and selModel reference other Ext components created earlier in the script, but not shown. The entire script is enclosed by a Ext.onReady function call, so that the code is executed as early as possible, ensuring variables are declared in a local namespace.

Okay, so that's the 10,000 feet view of GridPanel; let's look at the referenced components individually.

Defining the Data Store

The first thing we need to do is store our data locally in the HTML page in a Data Store.

```
    var myData = {
      records : [
        {c1:1,  c2:"Australia",
         gold:74, silver:55, bronze:48, total:177},
        {c1:2,  c2:"India",
```

```
        gold:38, silver:27, bronze:36, total:101},
     {c1:3,   c2:"England",
        gold:37, silver:60, bronze:45, total:142},
     {c1:4,   c2:"Canada",
        gold:26, silver:17, bronze:33, total: 76 },
     {c1:5,   c2:"South Africa",
        gold:12, silver:11, bronze:10, total:33 },
                      /** snipped **/
     {c1:35, c2:"Bangladesh",
        gold:0,  silver:0,  bronze:1,  total:1  },
     {c1:35, c2:"Saint Lucia",
        gold:0,  silver:0,  bronze:1,  total:1  }
   ]
};

// Fields definition
var fields = [
  {name: 'rank',   mapping: 'c1' },
  {name: 'name',   mapping: 'c2' },
  {name: 'gold',   mapping: 'gold' },
  {name: 'silver', mapping: 'silver' },
  {name: 'bronze', mapping: 'bronze' },
  {name: 'total',  mapping: 'total' }
];

// create the data store
var localJsonStore = new Ext.data.JsonStore({
  fields : fields,
  data   : myData,
  root   : 'records'
});
```

We first introduced the Data Store in *Chapter 8, Data Stores, AJAX-enabled Plug-ins, and Dynamic Actions,* so this should look very familiar to you. This time we are using Ext.data.JsonStore object, which comes pre-configured with a specific **DataReader** to read data structured in a JSON format.

The JsonStore needs two things—the data itself that we are passing by reference with the myData variable, and a description of the data done using the fields variable.

A reader built into the JsonStore interprets the data using the fields definition. The **root** property in the JsonStore is required by the **DataReader** to identify the name of the property containing the Array of **row** objects.

We have used minimal information in our field definitions here, just including an optional mapping expression to reference the data from an element of the data item's **root** Array.

The `fields` definition could be simplified even further; the `mapping` value defaults to the `name` value, so can be rewritten as:

```
var fields = [
    {name: 'rank',    mapping : 'c1' },
    {name: 'name',    mapping : 'c2' },
    'gold','silver','bronze','total'
];
```

A more complex field definition could contain information such as data type, date format, default value, sort direction, and more; for example:

```
{ name:'myDate', mapping:'d1', type:'date', dateFormat:"Y-m-d g:i:s
A", allowBlank: false }
```

So now that we have defined our data and described how to interpret the data, we need to configure how the data is to be displayed.

Configuring the Column Model

The `Ext.grid.ColumnModel` is used by the GridPanel to configure how and what parts of the data will be displayed.

```
var cols = [
  {header:"Rank",    width:50,  dataIndex:'rank'},
  {header:"Country", width:160, dataIndex:'name', id:'auto-expand'},
  {header:"Gold",    width:50,  dataIndex:'gold'},
  {header:"Silver",  width:50,  dataIndex:'silver'},
  {header:"Bronze",  width:50,  dataIndex:'bronze'},
  {header:"Total",   width:50,  dataIndex:'total'}
];

var cm = new Ext.grid.ColumnModel({
  defaults: {
    sortable: true
  },
  columns: cols
});
```

Display information for the columns is created here using an Array of `Ext.grid.Column` column configuration objects to define the initial layout and display of the columns in the GridPanel.

Here, we have included basic display information, being the **header** and **width** config options, and a **dataIndex** containing the name of the field in the records contained in the GridPanel's Store. As usual, Ext has many more config options, such as **align, editable, fixed width, hidden, resizable, sortable**, and so on.

We have used an object definition to define our **ColumnModel**, passing it the **defaults** config property for all columns to be **sortable,** as well as the columns Array.

Defining the GridView

The `Ext.grid.GridView` encapsulates the user interface of the GridPanel. It is responsible for rendering the outer components of the GridPanel and co-ordinating the rendering of the columns using the **ColumnModel**. It also manages events for the grid such as firing an `update` event when a record is modified or firing the `datachanged` event when the Data Store performs a load.

```
// view is automatically created when not specified
var gridView = new Ext.grid.GridView({
    forceFit: true
});
```

Only one config option has been specified in this example—setting `forceFit` to `true` to ensure that the column widths are automatically sized, so that all displayed columns occupy the full width of the grid at all times. So, if a column is resized manually or programmatically, the other columns are automatically adjusted to fit the grid width.

Most of the time, the config options you will be interested in are `forceFit` and `autoFill`; the remaining config options are more relevant if you are writing a new component extending the GridView. While the GridView is an important piece of the solution, hardly any of the GridPanel examples provided by Sencha include it in their configs; the GridView is always created, even when not explicitly specified.

Defining the Selection Model

The selection model for GridPanels determines how rows and cells are selected, and how many can be selected at a time. Ext provides `RowSelectionModel`, `ColumnSelectionModel`, and a `CheckboxSelectionModel`, which enable selecting records using checkboxes at the beginning of a row.

Each selection model provides methods to retrieve the selected elements. For example, `RowSelectionModel` provides `getSelected` to retrieve the first selected row, and `getSelections` to retrieve an Array of selected records.

```
var selectionModel = new Ext.grid.RowSelectionModel({
    singleSelect:true
});
```

Our example uses a `RowSelectionModel`, with a config option to allow only a single record to be selected.

The choice of selection model will be largely dependent on the needs of your application. It's best to be consistent and limit yourself to only one or two selection models, so it's immediately apparent to the user what model you're using. For example, always limit row selection to a single record, and use the checkbox selection model for multiple rows.

To demonstrate how to use a different Selection Model, change our example to use `CheckBoxSelectionModel` by modifying the following piece of code:

```
var checkboxSM = new Ext.grid.CheckboxSelectionModel();

var cols = [
    checkboxSM,
    {header: "Rank",    width: 50,  dataIndex: 'rank'},
    {header: "Country", width: 160, dataIndex: 'name', id : 'auto-expand'},
    {header: "Gold",    width: 50,  dataIndex: 'gold'},
    {header: "Silver",  width: 50,  dataIndex: 'silver'},
    {header: "Bronze",  width: 50,  dataIndex: 'bronze'},
    {header: "Total",   width: 50,  dataIndex: 'total'}
];
```

Add the line declaring the checkboxSM variable before the cols definition and also include the reference to the checkboxSM in the cols definition. This adds a checkbox column to our list of columns

Then change the GridPanel declaration to use checkboxSM as the selection model.

```
var myGrid = new Ext.grid.GridPanel({
    id              : 'my-grid',
    store           : localJsonStore,
    colModel        : columnModel,
    view            : gridView,
    selModel        : checkboxSM,
    //autoExpandColumn : 'auto-expand',
```

```
height            : 260,
width             : 450,
renderTo          : 'gridRegion',
stripeRows        : true,
title             : 'Commonwealth Games 2010 Medal Talley'
});
```

The result of our changes can be seen in the following screenshot; a checkbox column has been added to the beginning of the grid, shown here with multiple rows selected.

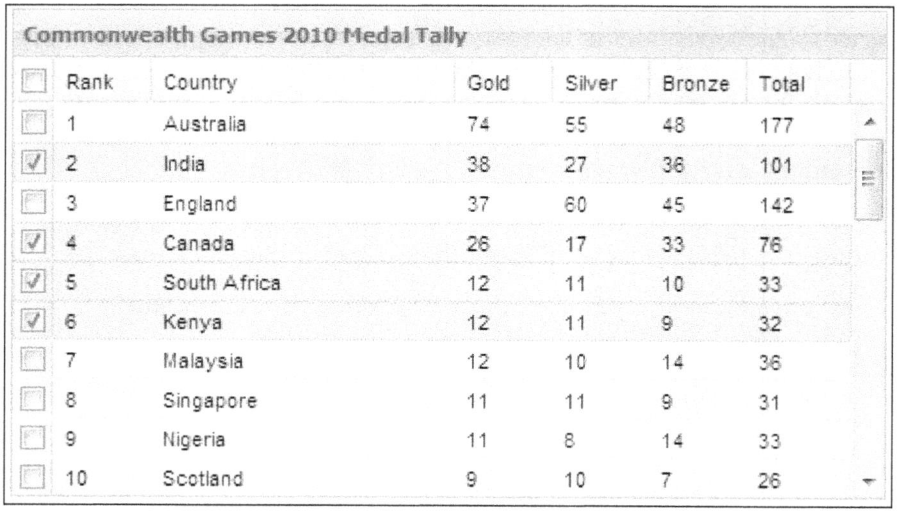

	Rank	Country	Gold	Silver	Bronze	Total	
☐	1	Australia	74	55	48	177	▲
☑	2	India	38	27	36	101	≡
☐	3	England	37	60	45	142	
☑	4	Canada	26	17	33	76	
☑	5	South Africa	12	11	10	33	
☑	6	Kenya	12	11	9	32	
☐	7	Malaysia	12	10	14	36	
☐	8	Singapore	11	11	9	31	
☐	9	Nigeria	11	8	14	33	
☐	10	Scotland	9	10	7	26	▼

Commonwealth Games 2010 Medal Tally

We have now covered each of the major supporting components of a GridPanel:

- **Store**: Model that holds and describes the data records
- **Column model**: Used to describe how the data is displayed in the GridPanel
- **View**: Renders GridPanel and manages GridPanel events
- **Selection model**: Controls the selection behavior when a row or column is selected.

Built-in features

Our basic example of the GridPanel already includes column management features, including sorting, resizing, drag-and-drop column reordering, and show/hide columns.

Commonwealth Games 2010 Medal Tally						
Rank	Country	Gold	Bronze	Silver	Total	
1	Australia		48	55	177	
2	India	38	Total	27	101	
3	England	37		60	142	
4	Canada	26	33	17	76	
5	South Africa	12	10	11	33	
6	Kenya	12	9	11	32	
7	Malaysia	12	14	10	36	
8	Singapore	11	9	11	31	
9	Nigeria	11	14	8	33	
10	Scotland	9	7	10	26	

The preceding screenshot shows the `Total` column being moved to another position using a drag-and-drop action; releasing the mouse would complete the action and relocate the column.

Commonwealth Games 2010 Medal Tally					
Country ▾	Total	Gold	Bronze	Silver	
Australia	A/Z ↓ Sort Ascending		48	55	
India	Z/A ↓ Sort Descending		36	27	
England			45	60	
Canada	Columns ▷		☐ Rank		
South Africa	33	12	☑ Country		
Kenya	32	12	☑ Total		
Malaysia	36	12	☑ Gold		
Singapore	31	11	☑ Bronze		
Nigeria	33	11	☑ Silver		
Scotland	26	9			

The previous screenshot shows the `Total` column in its new position, along with a column header menu containing sorting options and a checkbox list of columns to hide or show columns. Notice that the `Rank` column has been unchecked, and is now hidden.

These features, as well as resizing columns, are out of the box for GridPanels and are configurable to enable/disable the functionality. They really do enhance the user interface, giving a far more interactive experience.

We now need to work out how to integrate the GridPanel into APEX.

Getting the GridPanel into APEX

It's possible to implement GridPanels in APEX in more than one way, with solutions varying from extremes of using almost no APEX functionality to relying mainly on APEX functionality.

- **Almost no APEX approach:**

  An example of an "Almost no APEX" approach would be to create a plug-in region where you define the SQL query, and use no more standard APEX functionality. The solution would rely totally on the plug-in functionality written by you to manage the GridPanel.

  Using the query, you could quite easily generate the datastore, the column headings based on the column aliases for the query. We have mostly written this already in Chapter 8, using the code for the ComboBox.

  So, what about sorting and pagination? Okay, well you would need to write some functionality to pass sorting requests from the GridPanel through to your plug-ins AJAX function, and extend your code to support sorting and pagination.

  Good, so what about format masks on columns—you can do that in Classic Reports. And while we're on the topic, what about column formatting, column links, link validation, authorization, and conditional display logic?

  This is starting to sound like a whole lot of work. Before you know it, you're going to be writing a whole "shadow" API, just to duplicate functionality in APEX.

  Then you will have to figure out some way to maintain it. Are you going to do it declaratively? If so, you will need to build an application to support it, and after that you'll need to build an API to migrate your metadata when you promote it from DEV to TEST to PROD.

  Okay, so maybe this isn't such a great idea—let's look at another alternative.

- **Relying on APEX approach:**

  This approach is built on the simple premise that APEX already provides a lot of functionality for you already. All you are doing is extending what's already there.

  This is the approach I want to show you for the GridPanel. It's a more sustainable solution long term, because you're working within the APEX product, which is supported by a whole team of developers who are trying to make your job easier.

  Perhaps in some future release the functionality we are adding will be native to APEX. Our task then will be to swap over the plug-in with the native component.

Testing the concepts first

Before we embark down the path of building our solution, let's first have a look at the key concepts we are going to use.

Converting APEX-generated table into a GridPanel

One of the Sencha-provided examples is the **From Markup Grid Example**, found in the Ext JS SDK under `/examples/grid/from-markup.html` file. It converts a simple HTML markup table, shown in the left-hand side of the following screenshot, and transforms it into the GridPanel shown on the right-hand side.

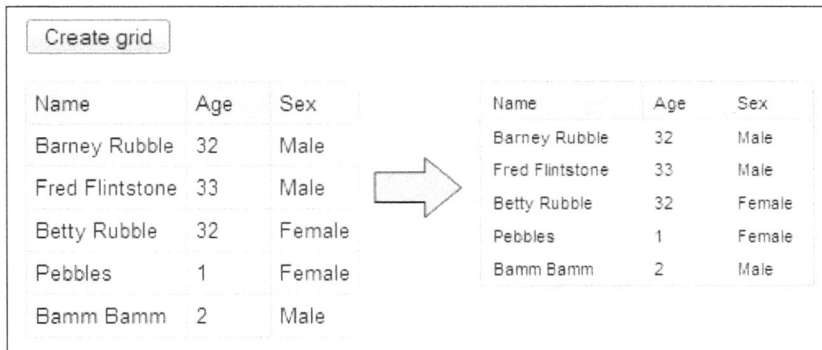

The JavaScript to transform the table is:

```
var grid = new Ext.ux.grid.TableGrid("the-table", {
    stripeRows: true
});
grid.render();
```

It's simply calling a custom `Ext.ux.grid.TableGrid` component, passing the ID of the table to transform and a config object literal.

The smarts are in the TableGrid component, shown here with comments.

```
Ext.ux.grid.TableGrid = function(table, config){
    config = config ||
    {};
    Ext.apply(this, config);
    var cf = config.fields || [], ch = config.columns || [];
    table = Ext.get(table);

    var ct = table.insertSibling();
```

After assigning the config object literal to this object and a reference to the table, a new DIV element is inserted into the DOM as a sibling of the markup table. This will later be used as the target to render the `TableGrid` into.

```
var fields = [], cols = [];
var headers = table.query("thead th");
for (var i = 0, h; h = headers[i]; i++) {
    var text = h.innerHTML;
    var name = 'tcol-' + i;

    fields.push(Ext.applyIf(cf[i] ||
    {}, {
        name: name,
        mapping: 'td:nth(' + (i + 1) + ')/@innerHTML'
    }));

    cols.push(Ext.applyIf(ch[i] ||
    {}, {
        'header': text,
        'dataIndex': name,
        'width': h.offsetWidth,
        'tooltip': h.title,
        'sortable': true
    }));
}
var ds = new Ext.data.Store({
    reader: new Ext.data.XmlReader({
        record: 'tbody tr'
    }, fields)
});

ds.loadData(table.dom);

var cm = new Ext.grid.ColumnModel(cols);
```

The Field model for the Data Store is built by querying the DOM, using the table header cells to generate fields and mapping them to the `innerHTML` of a table cell using: `mapping : 'td:nth(' + (i + 1) + ')/@innerHTML'`.

The Data Store here uses an **XMLReader** to read the table rows in applying the mapping expression to load the data, accomplished using the statement:

```
ds.loadData(table.dom);
```

The Column Model is also built when querying the DOM table header cells.

```
    if (config.width || config.height) {
        ct.setSize(config.width || 'auto', config.height || 'auto');
    }
    else {
        ct.setWidth(table.getWidth());
    }

    if (config.remove !== false) {
        table.remove();
    }


    Ext.applyIf(this, {
        'ds': ds,
        'cm': cm,
        'sm': new Ext.grid.RowSelectionModel(),
        autoHeight: true,
        autoWidth: false
    });
    Ext.ux.grid.TableGrid.superclass.constructor.call(this, ct, {});
};

    Ext.extend(Ext.ux.grid.TableGrid, Ext.grid.GridPanel);
```

The width and height is then determined for the TableGrid—either passed using config properties or using the width of the markup table. The `Ext.applyIf` command is used to configure the TableGrid components if not already specified; the **Datastore**, **Column** model, and **Selection** model components are assigned at this time. Finally, the TableGrid superclass (GridPanel) is called to continue creating a standard GridPanel.

Idea: Use APEX report table as local Data Store

We can use a similar approach to the TableGrid to transform an APEX Classic Report into a GridPanel. To see how well the TableGrid works, include a script reference to the Sencha-provided JavaScript in a page header:

```
<script type="text/javascript" src="/ux/extjs/examples/ux/TableGrid.
js"></script>
```

Then modify the report Id to match your report, and run the following JavaScript from the FireBug console:

```
var grid = new Ext.ux.grid.TableGrid("report_R3369531070222725", {
    stripeRows: true // stripe alternate rows
});

grid.render();
```

The following screenshot shows the result after transforming our "fake" report region template from *Chapter 5, Ext Themed Buttons, Popups, Calendars, and Reports*. Not a bad result for zero effort. Columns now have menus and can be resized, hidden, and swapped around using drag-and-drop.

A few minor issues need fixing, such as the drop-down menu has a sorting indicator next to the ID column. This is because the image was part of the header converted using the innerHTML mapping. The header labels still include the original APEX header hyperlinks making sorting a little confusing, depending on which part of the header is clicked data is either locally sorted, or remote sorted.

Pagination still uses the template links and changes the GridPanel back into a standard report. Any changes to the column layout are lost.

Id ▾	Ranking ▾	Country	Gold	Silver	Bronze	Total
1	1	⤉ Sort Ascending	74	55	48	177
2	19	⤈ Sort Descending	1	1	4	6
3	35		0	0	1	1
4	22	▦ Columns ▸ ☑ Id ▾	0	0	3	4
5	26	Cameroon ☑ Ranking	2	2	4	6
6	4	Canada ☑ Country	17	17	33	76
7	23	Cayman Islands ☑ Gold	0	0	0	1
8	12	Cyprus ☑ Silver	3	3	4	11
9	3	England ☑ Bronze	60	60	45	142
10	27	Ghana ☑ Total	1	1	3	4

Commonwealth Games 2010 Medal Tally

Displaying row(s) 1 - 10 of 36 ▷

Instead of using the table header to determine the Column model, we can query the APEX metadata for the report for the same information. This is more reliable, and also means we don't need to strip out unwanted elements from the header, just like the sort image and the JavaScript calls to do column sorting.

Retrieving the content of a table cell using the DOM innerHTML method means there is no extra work needed to be done regardless of the cells' content. So, if the markup table cell contains a hyperlink defined through the APEX builder, it continues to work unchanged. It's not necessary to do any additional work to define an Ext "select" event.

So, using the TableGrid as a starting point looks very good once we sort out pagination.

GridPanel pagination using APEX Partial Page Refreshes

Our GridPanel will use the rendered table for the initial page load; once transformed, it will continue to use standard APEX **Partial Page Refreshes** (PPR) to retrieve additional records. We need to call the standard APEX pagination routines, retrieving the results to load into the GridPanel's Data Store before presenting the results to the user.

When APEX does a Partial Page Refresh, it executes JavaScript to create an XMLHttpRequest object, issuing an HTTP Post request. Details of the request, including the parameters making up the request can be seen in the Firebug console, as shown in the following screenshot:

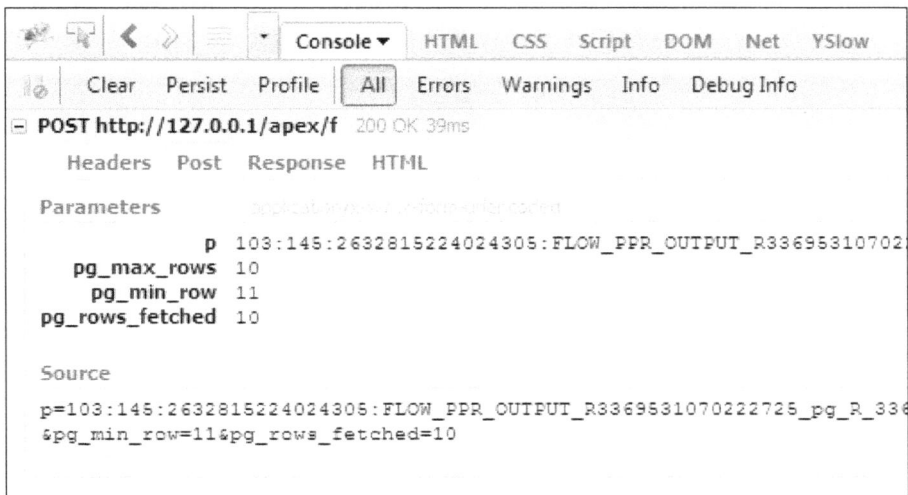

Using this information, we can create an `Ext.Ajax.request`, passing the same parameters and then capturing the server response.

```
var regionId = "3369531070222725";

Ext.Ajax.request({
    url: 'f',
    params: {
        'p': Ext.getDom('pFlowId').value +
        ':' + Ext.getDom('pFlowStepId').value +
        ':' + Ext.getDom('pInstance').value +
        ':FLOW_PPR_OUTPUT_R' + regionId + '_pg_R_' +
            regionId +':NO',
        'pg_max_rows': 10,
        'pg_min_row': 11,
        'pg_rows_fetched': 10
    },
    success: function(response, opts){
        Ext.Msg.show({
            title: 'AJAX Response',
            msg: response.responseText,
            width: 450
        });
    },
    failure: function(response, opts){
        console.log('server-side failure with status code ' +
                    response.status);
    }
});
```

The parameters passed in the HTTP request are built up using the form details on the APEX page, retrieving values for the application, page, and session using `Ext.getDom()` calls.

AJAX server requests are asynchronous, meaning the JavaScript code will have completed before the response is received. A callback function is required to process any returned data. Ext provides config options for both success and failure options; here `responseText` is utilized as a modal `Ext.MessageBox` message for successful responses, as can be seen in the following screenshot:

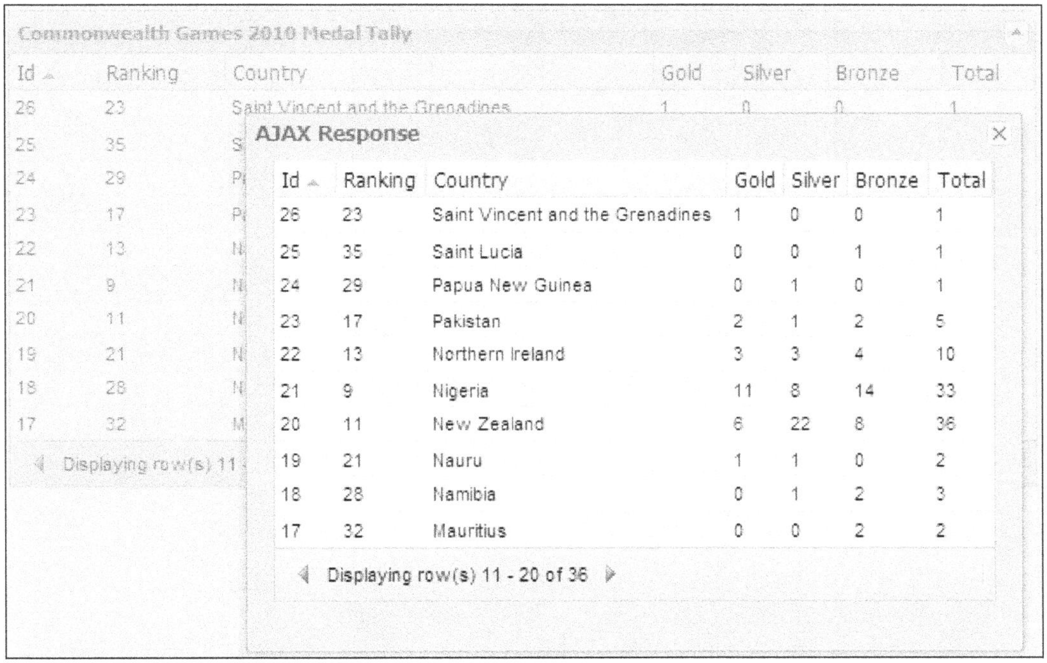

So, with very little effort so far, we have verified that we can transform a Classic Report into a GridPanel using the output of the report, and also execute APEX pagination calls and retrieve the response for further JavaScript manipulation.

It's time to put our solution together.

GridPanel as a region plug-in

We are building a GridPanel as a region plugin, using it as a container for a Classic Report region, as APEX doesn't support defining reports directly into region plugins.

The intention is for the Plug-in to transform a single Classic Report included as a sub-region into a GridPanel, using the metadata for the report and its column definitions to define the columns and data store for the grid. The following screenshot shows an example page in the APEX Application Builder:

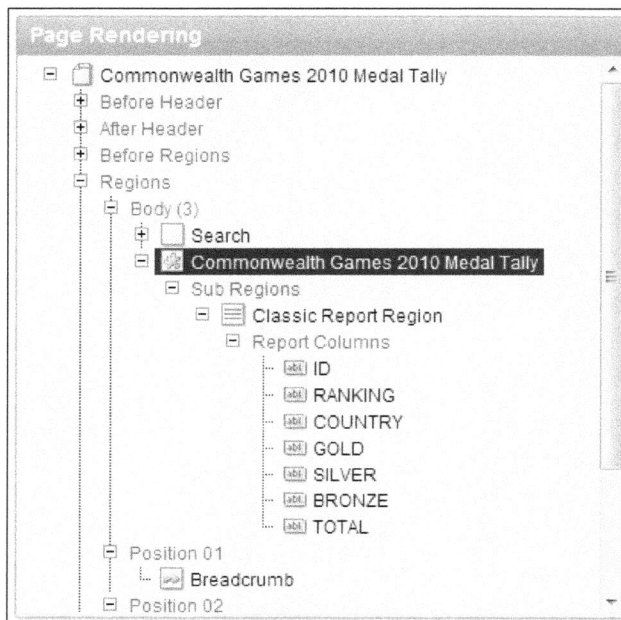

Our GridPanel plug-in has a very simple definition with just a few custom attributes. All the complexity is contained in the database package and the associated JavaScript.

Plug-in definition

The new functionality will be covered in greater detail; the full source for the database package and JavaScript can be found in the Chapter 9 source code files available on the Packt site.

Plugin name:

Ext.apex.TableGrid

Callbacks:

Render Function Name: plug_ext_tablegrid.render

AJAX Function Name: plug_ext_tablegrid.ajax

Standard attributes:

None

Custom attributes:

Label	Type	Required	Depending on	Values	Default
Totals Calculation Method	Select List	Yes		auto, function	auto
Totals Function	PL/SQL Function Body	Yes	Totals Calculation Method		
Width (px)	Number	No			
Collapsible	Select List	Yes		true, false	true

The Totals Calculation Method has two options, `auto` and `function`; these options need a little explaining.

Data Stores with remote data sources need to know the total number of records in the dataset as returned by the server. This is used to manage the pagination bar at the bottom of a GridPanel, shown in the following screenshot:

APEX doesn't publish the total record count for a Classic Report, so the plugin needs to provide this functionality. For the `auto` option, this is done by wrapping the Classic Report's query with a select count(*) statement:

```
select count(*) from (original query)
```

This is done when the page is rendered, adding an additional query to the performance overhead of the page. If the original query is expensive, developers can set the calculation method to `function` and define an anonymous PL/SQL function returning the total rows value using some other calculation method.

Plug-in package

The package specification for a Region plug-in is very similar to an Item plug-in—the differences being the datatypes of the parameters and that Region plug-ins don't have a validation function.

```
CREATE OR REPLACE PACKAGE plug_ext_tablegrid AS

    function render (
       p_region                in apex_plugin.t_region
      ,p_plugin                in apex_plugin.t_plugin
      ,p_is_printer_friendly in boolean
    )
       return apex_plugin.t_region_render_result;

    function ajax (
       p_region in apex_plugin.t_region
      ,p_plugin in apex_plugin.t_plugin
    )
       return apex_plugin.t_region_ajax_result;

END plug_ext_tablegrid;
/
```

We will look at the details of each function separately; the full package body and specification are included in the Chapter 9 files included with the book.

Render functionality for the GridPanel plug-in

The GridPanel render function is used primarily to generate JavaScript to instantiate a TableGrid, passing the column and field mappings, together with some other settings in config object to transform the markup table.

It uses APEX metadata to generate this content; the output will look like the following JavaScript:

```
Ext.onReady(function(){
    new Ext.apex.TableGrid("report_R3369531070222725", {
        apexMinRow:1,
        apexPageSize:10,
        apexPluginId:"20F91201D0AC...1D996C7D5A1A2D36",
        apexTotalRows:36,
        collapsible:true,
        columns:[
            {dataIndex:"c1", header:"Id", width:82, hidden:true},
```

```
            {dataIndex:"c2", header:"Ranking", width:82},
            {dataIndex:"c7", header:"Total", width:82},
            {dataIndex:"c3", header:"Country", width:204},
            {dataIndex:"c4", header:"Gold", width:82},
            {dataIndex:"c5", header:"Silver", width:82},
            {dataIndex:"c6", header:"Bronze", width:82}
        ],
        fields:[
            {name:"c1", mapping:"td:nth(1)/@innerHTML"},
            {name:"c2", mapping:"td:nth(2)/@innerHTML"},
            {name:"c3", mapping:"td:nth(3)/@innerHTML"},
            {name:"c4", mapping:"td:nth(4)/@innerHTML"},
            {name:"c5", mapping:"td:nth(5)/@innerHTML"},
            {name:"c6", mapping:"td:nth(6)/@innerHTML"},
            {name:"c7", mapping:"td:nth(7)/@innerHTML"}
        ],
        id:"my-grid",
        regionId:"3369531070222725",
        sortInfo:{field:"c2", direction:"DESC"},
        title:"Commonwealth Games 2010 Medal Talley",
        width:617
    });
});
```

The JavaScript should look quite familiar, as it is similar to the standalone GridPanel example we saw earlier in the chapter. Here, we are instantiating a custom TableGrid, passing a mix of standard and custom config options in an object literal.

The `fields` array shows the column aliases `c1` to `c7` for the markup table returned by APEX with a simple mapping rule defining how to extract the column data.

Notice that the highlighted line, `dataIndex c7`, is out of sequence, in position 3. The user has re-arranged the column order using drag-and-drop, and this information has been saved to the database for later retrieval. Other stateful attributes include column widths, column hidden attribute, sort information, and the GridPanel width are also included.

The PL/SQL code for the render function is:

```
FUNCTION render (
    p_region             in apex_plugin.t_region
   ,p_plugin             in apex_plugin.t_plugin
   ,p_is_printer_friendly in boolean
)
    return apex_plugin.t_region_render_result is
```

```
type t_type is table of pls_integer index by varchar2(255);
l_default_col_idx t_type;

l_result            apex_plugin.t_region_render_result;

l_rpt_region_id number;
l_total_rows    varchar2(32767);
l_page_size     number;
l_sort          varchar2(4000);

l_script        varchar2(32767);
l_fields        varchar2(32767);
l_column_model  varchar2(32767);

ca              varchar2(255);
j               pls_integer;

-- report column details
l_col_headings  wwv_flow_global.vc_arr2;
l_col_aliases   wwv_flow_global.vc_arr2;
l_col_sortable  wwv_flow_global.vc_arr2;

-- user defined preferences
l_panel_width   varchar2(4000);
l_pref_columns  wwv_flow_global.vc_arr2;
l_pref_widths   wwv_flow_global.vc_arr2;
l_pref_hidden   wwv_flow_global.vc_arr2;

BEGIN
    -- debug info
    if wwv_flow.g_debug then
        wwv_flow_plugin_util.debug_region (
            p_plugin                => p_plugin
            ,p_region               => p_region
            ,p_is_printer_friendly => p_is_printer_friendly
        );
    end if;

    -- TableGrid plugin has Classic Report as a sub-region.
    get_grid_report_properties (
        p_gridpanel_id      => p_region.id
        ,p_rpt_region_id    => l_rpt_region_id
        ,p_page_size        => l_page_size
        ,p_sort_preference  => l_sort
```

```
   ,p_col_headings     => l_col_headings
   ,p_col_aliases      => l_col_aliases
   ,p_col_sortable     => l_col_sortable
);

if l_rpt_region_id is null then
   raise_application_error(-20001,'TableGrid Plugin'||
     ' must have a Classic Report sub-region.'
   );
end if;


-- Define fields for Ext Reader.
-- This identifies the column order APEX returns the data.
for i in 1 .. l_col_aliases.last loop
   l_fields := l_fields||case when i > 1 then ',' end||
       CRLF||'               {'||
       'name: "'||l_col_aliases(i)||'", '||
       'mapping:"td:nth('||i||')/@innerHTML"}';
end loop;

-- Retrieve custom user preferences for grid layout.
-- Users can re-order column layout using drag-and-drop,
-- and save modified layout as a user preference.
fetch_config (
   p_region_id   => p_region.id
  ,p_panel_width => l_panel_width
  ,p_arr_columns => l_pref_columns
  ,p_arr_widths  => l_pref_widths
  ,p_arr_hidden  => l_pref_hidden
);

-- Define Column Model containing display details.
-- May be based on user preferences.
if l_pref_columns.count() = 0 then
   -- no preferences, so use defaults
   for i in 1 .. l_col_aliases.last loop
     l_column_model := l_column_model||
         chr(10)||'               {'||
         'header: "' || l_col_headings(i) || '", '||
         'dataIndex: "'||l_col_aliases(i)||'"},';
   end loop;
   l_column_model := rtrim (l_column_model,',');
```

```
      -- set view to fill table width
      push('viewConfig'    ,'{autoFill: true}');

   else
      -- Index column aliases using associative array,
      -- allowing us to lookup column position by name.
      -- i.e. l_default_col_idx('c4') = 4
      for i in 1 .. l_col_aliases.last loop
         l_default_col_idx(l_col_aliases(i)) := i;
      end loop;

      -- Ext renders columns in the order specified, so need
      -- to specify columns in same order as preferences.
      for i in 1 .. l_pref_columns.last loop
         if l_default_col_idx.exists(l_pref_columns(i)) then
            j  := l_default_col_idx(l_pref_columns(i));

            l_column_model := l_column_model||
               chr(10)||'               {'||
               'dataIndex: "'||l_col_aliases(j)||'", '||
               'header: "'    || l_col_headings(j) || '", '||
                -- saved preferences
               'width: '      || l_pref_widths(i) ||
               case when l_pref_hidden(i) is not null then
                   ', hidden: true' end||
               '},';
         end if;
      end loop;
      l_column_model := rtrim (l_column_model,',');

   end if;

   -- Calculate apexTotalRows
   if p_region.attribute_01 = 'auto' then
      for rec in (select r.region_source
                    from apex_application_page_regions r
                   where r.region_id = l_rpt_region_id
                 )
      loop
         l_total_rows :=
            wwv_flow_plugin_util.get_plsql_function_result(
               p_plsql_function =>
               'declare n number; '||
               'begin select count(*) into n from ('||
```

```
                  rec.region_source||'); return n; end;'
          );
    end loop;
else
    l_total_rows :=
        wwv_flow_plugin_util.get_plsql_function_result(
            p_plsql_function => p_region.attribute_02
        );
end if;

-- Add sortInfo preference
-- e.g. sortInfo: {field: 'c2', direction: 'ASC'}
if l_sort is not null then
    -- stored as fsp_sort_2 or fsp_sort_2_desc
    l_sort := substr(l_sort,10);
    case when substr(l_sort,-4) = 'desc' then
        l_sort := '{field: "c'||
                  substr(l_sort,1,length(l_sort)-5)||
                  '", direction: "DESC"}';
    else
        l_sort := '{field: "c'||l_sort||
                  '", direction: "ASC"}';
    end case;
end if;

-- panel width can be a preference, or default
l_panel_width := nvl(l_panel_width,p_region.attribute_03);

-- Assemble TableGrid config properties
push('columns'    ,'['||l_column_model||CRLF||'        ]');
push('fields'     ,'['||l_fields||CRLF||'        ]');

push('apexTotalRows',l_total_rows);
push('apexMinRow'   ,1);
push('apexPageSize' ,l_page_size);
push('sortInfo'     ,l_sort);

push('id'           ,'"'||p_region.static_id||'"');
push('regionId'     ,'"'||l_rpt_region_id||'"');
push('title'        ,'"'||escape_json(p_region.name)||'"');
push('width'        ,l_panel_width);
push('collapsible'  ,p_region.attribute_04);
push('apexPluginId',
    '"'||wwv_flow_plugin.get_ajax_identifier||'"'
```

```
        );

    l_script := CRLF||
        'Ext.onReady(function(){'||CRLF||
        '    new Ext.apex.TableGrid("report-R'||
            l_rpt_region_id||'", {'||CRLF||
            get_properties(8)||'    });'||CRLF||
        '});'||CRLF;

    -- add JS to bottom of page
    wwv_flow_javascript.add_onload_code (p_code => l_script);

    return l_result;
END;
```

We won't be going into great detail for most of the render function, as much of the code is very similar to earlier code used for the ComboBox and NumberField Plugins. Some convenience routines, such as push, escape_json and get_properties have been reused, so no need to discuss those either.

New subroutines added are get_grid_report_properties and fetch_config.

The get_grid_report_properties procedure retrieves details for the report and report columns by querying the APEX views: APEX_APPLICATION_PAGE_REGIONS and APEX_APPLICATION_PAGE_RPT_COLS. It's very straightforward, so just look at the source code included with this chapter if you want to see the details.

The fetch_config procedure retrieves some custom preferences we will be creating using the plug-in's ajax function, so we will look at that a little later when we discuss the ajax function.

Calculating the number of rows for TableGrid is somewhat of a necessary evil. From an APEX perspective, it's generally recommended not to do this for report regions, as it adds a performance overhead to the query by requiring it to process the entire result set to count the number of records returned. However, we need to do this for the Ext pagination functionality to work for the Data Store.

To address the potential performance issue, we defined two ways of calculating the number of records returned.

```
    -- Calculate apexTotalRows
if p_region.attribute_01 = 'auto' then
    for rec in (select r.region_source
                   from apex_application_page_regions r
                 where r.region_id = l_rpt_region_id
                )
```

```
loop
   l_total_rows :=
       wwv_flow_plugin_util.get_plsql_function_result(
           p_plsql_function =>
           'declare n number; '||
           'begin select count(*) into n from ('||
           rec.region_source||'); return n; end;'
       );
   end loop;
else
   l_total_rows :=
       wwv_flow_plugin_util.get_plsql_function_result(
           p_plsql_function => p_region.attribute_02
       );
end if;
```

The first method automatically calculates total rows returned by wrapping the report query with a `select count(*)` statement in an anonymous function, shown highlighted in the code snippet. The second method allows the developer to specify a custom function possibly to improve performance, as shown in the following screenshot:

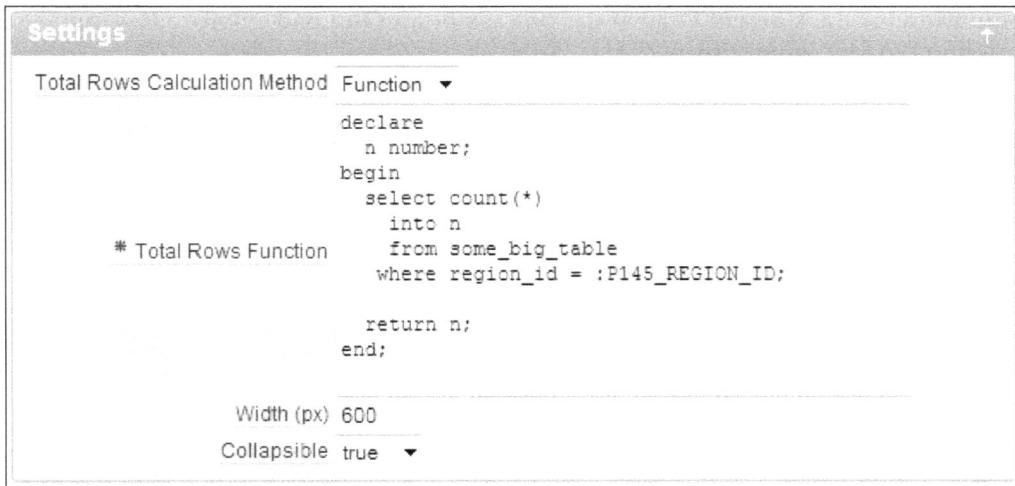

The built-in `WWV_FLOW_PLUGIN_UTIL.GET_PLSQL_FUNCTION_RESULT` function allows developers to use bind variables in exactly the same way as they would for any standard APEX code region.

Minor pagination issue

APEX is stateful when paginating using Partial Page Refresh (PPR) report, but does not make the starting row information accessible to developers in the public APEX PL/SQL packages.

This causes problems if a user has PPR report and paginates to, say page 2 with 10 records per page, and then does a page refresh from the browser. APEX has saved the state of the PPR report, recording that it needs to display records starting from row 11 of the result set.

The PPR report renders the records from row 11 onwards, however, there is no way for our custom plug-in to identify we haven't returned records from the first row. This results in the TableGrid recording incorrect information in its pagination bar.

I've raised this as an issue with the APEX development team, and it is being considered for a release after APEX 4.02.

In the mean time, the workaround is to reset pagination every time the page is refreshed. This changes APEX behavior for a normal report region, but is an acceptable solution.

To do this for a single page, create an unconditional page process to **Reset Pagination** for the **Current Page** at the process point **On Load - Before Regions**, as shown in the following screenshot:

Alternatively, you can create a similar page process on APEX Page 0, to conditionally reset pagination on pages containing the TableGrid plug-in.

AJAX functionality for the GridPanel plug-in

Recall from our earlier investigations for the plug-in that we are going to call the standard APEX routines for pagination and sorting, meaning we don't require any AJAX processing for standard functionality.

However, the TableGrid now supports drag-and-drop column ordering, menu options to show or hide columns, and column resizing. You can imagine your users are very quickly going to demand that APEX remember these settings also!

So, our TableGrid will be using AJAX functionality to remember the layout state. To implement this, we are adding two toolbar items to the panel header, shown in the following screenshot, to save the settings and also restore default settings.

Commonwealth Games 2010 Medal Tally						
Ranking	Country ▾	Gold	Silver	Bronze	Total	Save settings
1	Australia	74	55	48	177	
19	Bahamas	1	1	4	6	
35	Bangladesh	0	0	1	1	
22	Botswana	1	0	3	4	
26	Cameroon	0	2	4	6	
4	Canada	26	17	33	76	
23	Cayman Islands	1	0	0	1	
12	Cyprus	4	3	4	11	
3	England	37	60	45	142	
27	Ghana	0	1	3	4	

Page 1 of 4   Displaying rows 1 - 10 of 36

The PL/SQL code for the AJAX function is:

```
FUNCTION ajax (
   p_region in apex_plugin.t_region
  ,p_plugin in apex_plugin.t_plugin
)
   return apex_plugin.t_region_ajax_result is
   l_result apex_plugin.t_region_ajax_result;
BEGIN
   -- indicate we are returning application/json data
   wwv_flow_plugin_util.print_json_http_header;

   -- direct to sub-routine
   case apex_application.g_widget_action
```

```
        when 'saveConfig' then
            save_config (p_region_id => p_region.id);
        when 'resetConfig' then
            reset_config (p_region_id => p_region.id);
        else
            -- invalid action
            raise_application_error(-20001,'Invalid action: "'||
              apex_application.g_widget_action||'"'
            );
    end case;

    -- not used by APEX yet
    return l_result;

EXCEPTION
    when others then
        htp.p('{success: false,');
        htp.p(' errors: {"sqlCode": "'||
               escape_json(sqlcode)||'",');
        htp.p('          "sqlErrm": "'||
               escape_json(sqlerrm)||'"');
        htp.p('          }');
        htp.p('}');
        return l_result;
END;
```

The AJAX function here just prints a mime-type header, and directs requests to the appropriate subroutine.

Saving modifications is done using the `save_config` procedure:

```
procedure save_config (p_region_id in number) is
    l_prefix varchar2 (255) :=
        'EXT_'||v('APP_ID')||'_'||v('APP_PAGE_ID')||'_'||
        p_region_id||'_';
begin
    wwv_flow_preferences.set_preference (
        p_preference => l_prefix || 'PANEL_WIDTH'
       ,p_value      => apex_application.g_x01
    );
    wwv_flow_preferences.set_preference (
        p_preference => l_prefix || 'COL'
       ,p_value      => wwv_flow_utilities.table_to_string2
                          (apex_application.g_f01)
    );
```

```
    wwv_flow_preferences.set_preference (
       p_preference => l_prefix || 'WIDTH'
      ,p_value      => wwv_flow_utilities.table_to_string2
                       (apex_application.g_f02)
    );
    wwv_flow_preferences.set_preference (
       p_preference => l_prefix || 'HIDDEN'
      ,p_value      => wwv_flow_utilities.table_to_string2
                       (apex_application.g_f03)
    );
    htp.p('{success: true}');
end;
```

Here, we are saving values passed in an AJAX request into the database using the built-in `wwv_flow_preferences.set_preference` procedure. These values are stored by APEX in the `WWV_FLOW_PREFERENCES$` table, and persist across both page requests and sessions.

We are storing the panel width, displayed columns, column widths, and hidden columns. The column-based fields use associative arrays (index by tables), so need to be converted into varchar2 strings using the `wwv_flow_utilities.table_to_string2` procedure.

The preference names and values stored in the database look like those shown in the next table:

Parameter	Value
EXT_103_145_3371020966238884_PANEL_WIDTH	425
EXT_103_145_3371020966238884_COL	c1:c2:c7:c3:c4:c5:c6
EXT_103_145_3371020966238884_WIDTH	82:82:57:121:52:53:56
EXT_103_145_3371020966238884_HIDDEN	true::::::

Interpreting the values shown for the COL parameter, column 7 (c7) has been repositioned next to column 2 (c2). Also, looking at the HIDDEN parameter, the first column (c1) has been hidden.

Complementing the `save_config` procedure are procedures `fetch_config` and `reset_config`; we won't show these here as their purpose is self-evident. These procedures use APEX-supplied procedures `wwv_flow_preferences.set_preference`, `wwv_flow_utilities.string_to_table2`, and `wwv_flow_preferences.remove_preference`.

Let's turn our attention to the JavaScript for our TableGrid.

Building a custom DataReader

Ext provides multiple Readers for reading structured data from a data source and converting it into an object containing **Ext.data.Record** objects and metadata for use by an **Ext.data.Store**.

However, to integrate with APEX, we need to create a custom DataReader. Fortunately, this isn't too hard, because we can extend an existing DataReader to meet our needs:

```
Ext.ns('Ext.apex.data');
Ext.apex.data.HtmlReader = Ext.extend(Ext.data.XmlReader, {
  read: function(response){
    var doc = Ext.DomHelper.createDom({
      html: response.responseText
    });
    if (!doc) {
      throw {
        message: "XmlReader.read: XML Document not available"
      };
    }
    return this.readRecords(doc);
  },
  readRecords: function(doc){
    this.xmlData = doc;

    var root = doc,
        totalRecords = this.meta.apexTotalRecords || 0;

    var records = this.extractData(
        Ext.DomQuery.select(this.meta.record, root), true);
    return {
      success: true,
      records: records,
      totalRecords:  totalRecords || records.length
    };
  }
});
```

In this snippet, we are extending the Ext.data.XmlReader, which expects AJAX responses to be returned with the header in the HTTP response set to text/xml or **application/xml**, and the XML document contained in a property named responseXML.

For the TableGrid paging bar to display the total records and paginate correctly, the custom Reader also needs to have **totalRecords** assigned. This is done when the custom Reader is instantiated using the meta.apexTotalRecords parameter, as APEX doesn't pass this information with the PPR refresh.

Creating a custom TableGrid component

Following through from our earlier "proof of concept", we are modifying the Sencha-provided example **From Markup Grid Example**, to create a custom TableGrid component specifically for APEX.

> The JavaScript for the TableGrid and the HtmlReader are included with the files for Chapter 9 in Ext.apex.TableGrid.js, and should be added to your application JavaScript.

The TableGrid is created by passing the DOM ID of the table and a config object literal containing arrays of field and column definitions, the total rows in apexTotalRows, pagination details, sort-order information, and so on.

Using the Ext.apply call, we apply the config object to this TableGrid object, passing additional default config options as well.

```
Ext.apex.TableGrid = function(table, config){
  config = config || {};

  // apply config, and a default config
  Ext.apply(this, config, {
    autoHeight: true,
    collapseFirst: false,
    iconCls: 'icon-grid',
    loadMask: true,
    stripeRows: true,
    titleCollapse: true
  });
```

The field and cols variables are assigned to the arrays passed by the config object literal.

```
var fields = config.fields || [], cols = config.columns||[];
```

A DIV element is inserted as a sibling DOM element to the original table, which will eventually become the TableGrid component.

```
table = Ext.get(table);

var ct = table.insertSibling({
  id: this.id || Ext.id(),
  style: "margin-bottom: 10px"
});
```

Our Reader object is then instantiated using the custom `HtmlReader` component we created earlier. This will read the table rows and cells passed by the APEX PPR refresh responses into a data store.

```
var myReader = new Ext.apex.data.HtmlReader({
  apexTotalRecords: config.apexTotalRows || null,
  record: 'tbody tr'
}, fields);
```

The Data Store is the next object to be defined. Parameter names and values are assigned to match correctly with the parameters expected by APEX.

```
// create the data store
var ds = new Ext.data.Store({
  url: 'f',
  baseParams: {
    'p': Ext.getDom('pFlowId').value + ':' +
          Ext.getDom('pFlowStepId').value + ':' +
          Ext.getDom('pInstance').value +
          ':FLOW_PPR_OUTPUT_R' + config.regionId + '_',
    'pg_max_rows': config.apexPageSize || 15,
    'pg_rows_fetched': config.apexPageSize || 15
  },
  remoteSort: true,
  sortInfo: config.sortInfo,
  paramNames: {
    start: 'pg_min_row',
    limit: 'pg_max_rows'
  },
  reader: myReader,
  listeners: {
    beforeload: function(obj, options){
      // APEX uses 1 based rowcount, so adjust
      if (options.params && options.params.pg_min_row >= 0) {
        options.params.pg_min_row += 1;
      }

      if (!options.params || !options.params.sort ||
          !this.prevSortInfo ||
          options.params.sort == this.prevSortInfo.field &&
          options.params.dir == this.prevSortInfo.direction)
      {
        options.params.p = ds.baseParams.p + 'pg_R_' +
                          config.regionId +':NO';
      }
```

```
    else {
      var sortConfig = 'fsp_sort_' +
                         options.params.sort.substring(1);
      if (options.params.dir == 'ASC') {
        sortConfig += '_desc';
      }

      options = Ext.apply(options, {
        params: {
          p: ds.baseParams.p + sortConfig + '::RP',
          fsp_region_id: config.regionId,
          pg_min_row: options.params.pg_min_row || 1
        }
      });
    }
    // always remove sort params
    delete options.params.sort;
    delete options.params.dir;
  },

  load: function(obj, records, options){
    // APEX uses 1 based rowcount, so adjust
    if (options.params && options.params.pg_min_row > 0) {
      options.params.pg_min_row -= 1;
    }
    // store sort details to help identify sort requests
    this.prevSortInfo = Ext.apply({}, this.sortInfo);
  }
 }
});
```

Next data is loaded from the HTML markup table created when the page was rendered.

```
ds.loadData(table.dom);
```

Following this, we complete the configuration of a typical GridPanel by assembling a PagingToolbar, ColumnModel, and the height and width attributes.

```
var paging = new Ext.PagingToolbar({
  pageSize: config.apexPageSize || 15,
  store: ds,
  displayInfo: true,
  displayMsg: 'Displaying rows {0} - {1} of {2}'
});
```

```
var cm = new Ext.grid.ColumnModel({
  defaults: {
    sortable: true,
    menuDisabled: false
  },
  columns: cols
});

if (config.width || config.height) {
  ct.setSize(config.width || 'auto', config.height || 'auto');
}
else {
  ct.setWidth(table.getWidth());
}
```

The markup table is then deleted from the DOM, and all the components making up the GridPanel are assigned to the object.

```
table.remove();

Ext.applyIf(this, {
  'ds': ds,
  'cm': cm,
  'sm': new Ext.grid.RowSelectionModel(),
  bbar: paging
});
```

At this point, all that's left to do is call the constructor function to create the TableGrid.

```
//@todo - add tools to save TableGrid state

Ext.apex.TableGrid.superclass.constructor.call(this, ct);
};

Ext.extend(Ext.apex.TableGrid, Ext.grid.GridPanel);
```

Notice the @todo comment; we will be adding more code here to make the TableGrid stateful.

Making the TableGrid Stateful

Before we make the TableGrid stateful, let's add one more piece of functionality to make the TableGrid resizable. Add the following code before the @todo comment:

```
// add listener to resize TableGrid width
Ext.applyIf(this, {
  listeners: {
    render: function(p){
      new Ext.Resizable(p.getEl(), {
        handles: 'e',
        pinned: true,
        transparent: true,
        resizeElement: function(){
          var box = this.proxy.getBox();
          p.updateBox(box);
          if (p.layout) {
            p.doLayout();
          }
          return box;
        }
      });
    }
  }
});
```

This adds a listener to the TableGrid, so when it is rendered, an `Ext.Resizable` object is wrapped around the TableGrid to make it resizable, as shown in the following screenshot:

Ranking ▾	Country	Gold	Silver	Bronze	Total
1	Australia	74	55	48	177
2	India	38	27	36	101
3	England	37	60	45	142
4	Canada	26	17	33	76
5	South Africa	12	11	10	33
6	Kenya	12	11	9	32
7	Malaysia	12	10	14	36
8	Singapore	11	11	9	31
9	Nigeria	11	8	14	33
10	Scotland	9	10	7	26

Commonwealth Games 2010 Medal Tally

Page 1 of 4 — Displaying rows 1 - 10 of 36

Ext.Panels support an array of tool button configs to be added to the header tool area. We are adding the two extra tool items to the panel header, as seen in the previous screenshot, and then adding handlers to pass AJAX requests back to the database.

The structure of the code looks like the following, with just the details needing to be added to the handlers.

```
var tools = [{
  id: 'restore',
  qtip: 'Restore default settings',
    handler: function(event, toolEl, panel){
       // restore logic
    }
},
{
  id: 'save',
  qtip: 'Save settings',
    handler: function(event, toolEl, panel){
       // save logic
    }
}]
Ext.apply(this, {
  tools: tools
});
```

The code to "save settings" is more complicated, so we will look at that here:

```
{
  id: 'save',
  qtip: 'Save settings',
  handler: function(e, toolEl, panel){
    var f01 = [], f02 = [], f03 = [];

    var cfg = panel.getColumnModel().config;

    // capture column, width, hidden
    for (var i = 0, c; c = cfg[i]; i++) {
      f01[i] = c.dataIndex;
      f02[i] = c.width;
      f03[i] = c.scope.hidden || null;
    }
```

We start out by creating three empty arrays, then populating them with details from the panels column model retrieved using `panel.getColumnModel().config`. The `dataIndex`, `width`, and `hidden` state are loaded into the arrays, which would look like the following when populated:

```
f01[c1,c2,c7,c3,c4,c5,c6]
f02[82,82,57,121,52,53,56]
f03[true,,,,,,]
```

This data, together with other parameters and APEX application, page, session, and request information is bundled into an `Ext.Ajax.request` object and submitted to the database for processing by our TableGrid plug-in code. Callback functions for success and failure states then display a message to the user.

```
Ext.Ajax.request({
    url: 'wwv_flow.show',
    success: function(){
      Ext.Msg.alert('Message',
                    'Panel configuration saved.');
    },
    failure: function(){
        Ext.Msg.show({
            title:'Error',
            msg: 'Process failed.',
            buttons: Ext.Msg.OK,
            icon: Ext.MessageBox.ERROR
        });
    },
    params: {
        'p_flow_id': Ext.getDom('pFlowId').value,
        'p_flow_step_id': Ext.getDom('pFlowStepId').value,
        'p_instance': Ext.getDom('pInstance').value,
        'p_request': 'PLUGIN=' + config.apexPluginId,
        'p_widget_action': 'saveConfig',
        'f01': f01,
        'f02': f02,
        'f03': f03,
        'x01': panel.getWidth()
    }
  });

  }
}

Ext.apply(this, {
  tools: tools
});
```

It's not well known that you can pass arrays of data using the f01..f20 parameters, which are then loaded into PL/SQL associative arrays g_f01..gf20 (index by tables) in the WWV_FLOW package—an extremely useful fact!

Using the TableGrid

Before you can start using the TableGrid, there's one more thing you need to add specifically a report template for the TableGrid.

As the report template is only being used to pass data to the browser, and isn't required for presentation at all, the simplest table format we can create is the best solution.

TableGrid template

Report Template Name: EXTJS TableGrid

Template Class: Custom 1

Before Rows:

```
<table id="report-#REGION_STATIC_ID#" class="x-hidden">
```

The x-hidden class ensures that the user never sees the table until after it's converted to a GridPanel.

Before column heading:

```
<thead>
```

Column heading template:

```
<th>#COLUMN_HEADER#</th>
```

After column heading:

```
</thead>
<tbody>
```

Before each row:

```
<tr>
```

Column template 1:

```
<td>#COLUMN_VALUE#</td>
```

After each row:

```
</tr>
```

After rows:

```
</tbody>
</table>
```

That's it—no row highlighting colors, no pagination required.

Convert Classic Reports to TableGrids

To use the TableGrid, first build a Classic Report exactly as you would normally.

Then create a region using the TableGrid plug-in, and assign it as the **Parent Region** of the Classic Report, as shown in the following screenshot:

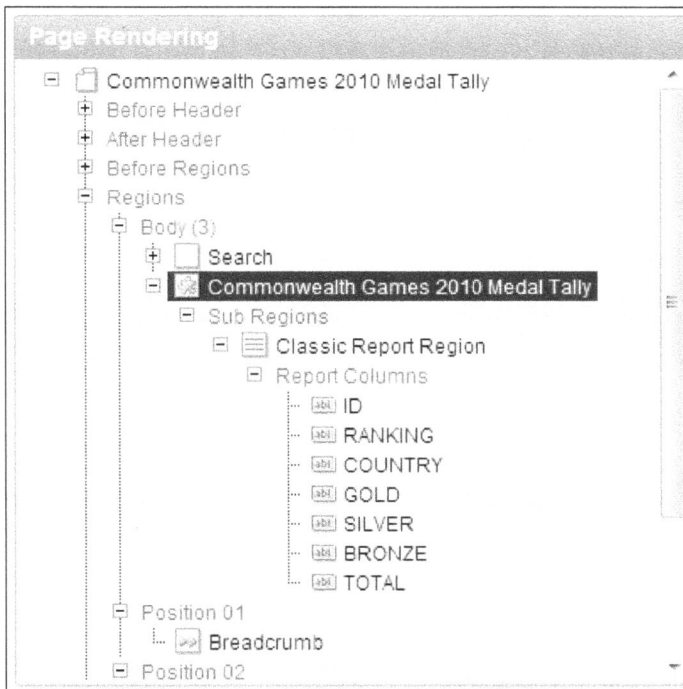

The TableGrid uses the TableGrid plug-ins title, ignoring the Classic Report Region title.

Do the following tasks to complete the conversion:

- Set Report Region Template to **No Template**.
- Set Report Template to **EXTJS TableGrid**.
- Set Report Pagination Scheme to **Use Externally Created Pagination Buttons**.
- Add pagination work-around. Create an unconditional page process to **Reset Pagination** for the **Current Page** at the process point **On Load - Before Regions**.

All being well, you now have a fully functional GridPanel, giving users stateful column management features.

Summary

In this chapter, we looked at the components making up the GridPanel, the Data Store, Column Model, Grid View, and Selection Model.

Different approaches were discussed on how you can integrate GridPanels into APEX, contrasting the "Almost no APEX" approach with the "Relying on APEX" approach. Here, we came to the realization that APEX already provides a lot of functionality to you already. It's far more productive if you work to extend what's already there, rather than creating a whole framework just to support your plug-in.

We then set about creating a TableGrid plug-in using the APEX Classic Reports as the base for defining the report query and column definitions. By hooking into existing Classic Reports functionality for querying, pagination, and sorting, we minimized the amount of work required for the plug-in.

The GridPanel includes column management features, including sorting, resizing, drag-and-drop column reordering, and show/hide columns. We went one step further, adding functionality to make the GridPanel stateful, allowing user settings to be saved back into APEX using APEX preferences.

There is much more functionality available to the Ext.grid.GridPanel than we've covered here, so I would encourage you to explore the Sencha examples further, and see what functionality would work for your applications.

In the next chapter, we will be looking at adding iFrame functionality via Ext JS into your applications. It will transform the way your applications work.

10
IFrame Tabs, Panels, and Popup Windows

iFrames can completely transform the way your APEX applications work, making them far more functional by allowing you to present multiple HTML pages (documents) to your users within a single window.

Modern web browsers have all implemented tabbed browsing interfaces, allowing you to open multiple web pages within a browser window. It allows you to read a web page, opening referenced links in another tab, without losing your place in the original page. After reading the link you can close the tab, or just switch back to the original tab.

Switching between pages is very useful for comparison shopping or cross referencing different information sources. It's also very useful when doing APEX application development, allowing you to switch from the APEX Builder view to your application view without having to do multiple page refreshes.

Our application users are very much used to tabbed browsers, so if we don't give them similar functionality in APEX applications, they will quickly resort to opening multiple browser tabs. This can create some nasty issues for the users' APEX session state, with pages relying on APEX session variables that may have been altered in another browser tab.

Far better to give them similar functionality to open multiple pages in a single browser tab, where we can control what pages are opened and thus maintain session state as needed.

In this chapter, we will explore using iFrames in three different ways:

- Embedding other pages within a page using iFrame panels
- Making popup windows modal
- Creating a tabbed document interface allowing users to switch between pages easily without opening multiple browser tabs

Embedding pages using iFrame panels

Embedding iFrames into another page is as simple as including an iFrame HTML markup element in the region source of a page region.

```
<iframe width="600" height="400" frameborder="0"  src="f?p=&APP_
ID.:200:&APP_SESSION.:"></iframe>
```

In this example, we have specified the `width`, `height`, and the `src` attribute of iFrame using APEX built-in substitution strings for the application ID and session, to reference page 200 in the current application.

That didn't feel very satisfying to me, how about you? It does show that iFrames are easy to implement, but let's see if we can add some more functionality.

This time we will embed an iFrame element in a collapsible **Ext.Panel**, including extra functionality to make it resizable like the one shown in the following screenshot and included in `chapter10/ex-10-resizable-iframe-panel.html`.

Starting off, we create a simple reusable iFrame component.

Reusable iFrameComponent

Creating a simple iFrame component allows it to be used as an item within more complex components such as panels, windows, and tab panels. This component should be included in your application JavaScript.

```
Ext.ns('Ext.apex');
Ext.apex.IFrameComponent = Ext.extend(Ext.BoxComponent, {
    /**
     * The url to be shown in iframe
     * @type {String}
     */
    url : Ext.SSL_SECURE_URL,

    /**
     * @private Just render an iframe
     */
    onRender : function(ct, position){
        var url = this.url;
        this.el = ct.createChild({tag: 'iframe', id: 'iframe-' + this.
id, frameBorder: 0, src: url});
    }
});
Ext.reg('iframe', Ext.apex.IFrameComponent);
```

The `Ext.apex.IFrameComponent` created here inherits all the config options and methods of `Ext.BoxComponent` in addition to the `url` option and the `onRender` function.

The component accepts a `url` option and creates an iframe HTML element as a child of the container element, like as the panel shown earlier in the first figure.

The `url` option defaults to `Ext.SSL_SECURE_URL`, which uses `about:blank` excepting for IE in secure mode, where it uses `javascript:""` to prevent the IE insecure content warning.

Resizable iFrame panel

Looking more closely at the example in `chapter10/ex-10-resizable-iframe-panel.html`, you can see we have created a standard **Ext.Panel**, applying it to a DIV element in the page.

```
<div id="example-1"></div>

<script type="text/javascript">
Ext.onReady(function(){
```

```
new Ext.Panel({
    allowDomMove: false,
    applyTo: 'example-1',
    animCollapse: false,
    frame: true,
    height: 400,
    width: 600,
    collapsible: true,
    titleCollapse: true,
    title: 'iFramed Page',
    items: [new Ext.apex.IFrameComponent({
        id: 'myIFrame',
        url: "content-page.html"
    })],
    layout: 'fit',
    listeners: {
        render: function(p){
            new Ext.Resizable(p.getEl(), {
                handles: 'all',
                pinned: true,
                transparent: true,
                resizeElement: function(){
                    var box = this.proxy.getBox();
                    p.updateBox(box);
                    if (p.layout) {
                        p.doLayout();
                    }
                    if (Ext.isIE) {
                        this.syncHandleHeight();
                    }
                    return box;
                }
            });
        }
    }
});
</script>
```

The highlighted code shows that the Ext.apex.IFrameComponent is added
to the panel as an item, in exactly the same way you would add any other Ext
item. The layout: 'fit' config option is important here as it ensures that the
IFrameComponent automatically expands to fill the layout container. The following
diagram shows what happens when the option is commented out:

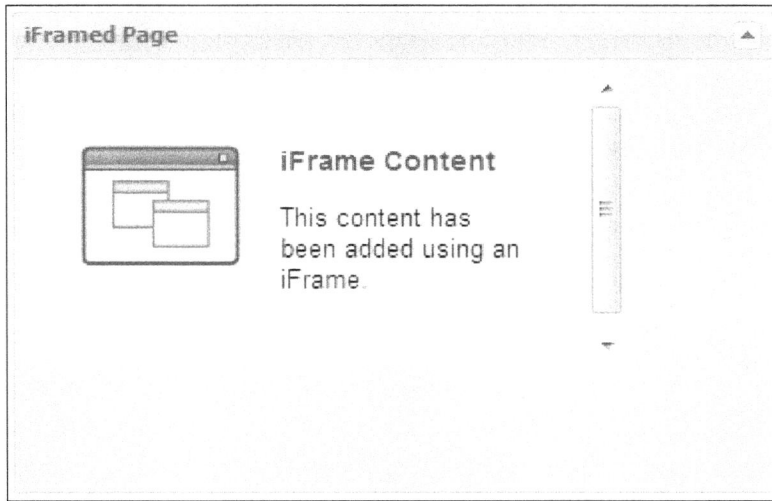

Also note that the Ext.Resizable element is added when the panel is rendered:

```
listeners: {
    render: function(p){
        new Ext.Resizable(p.getEl(), {
            handles: 'all',
            pinned: true,
            transparent: true,
            resizeElement: function(){
                var box = this.proxy.getBox();
                p.updateBox(box);
                if (p.layout) {
                    p.doLayout();
                }
                if (Ext.isIE) {
                    this.syncHandleHeight();
                }
                return box;
            }
        });
    }
}
```

The `Ext.Resizable` class adds drag handles to the panel to make it resizable, as shown in the following diagram. In this case, we have used `handles: 'all'` to add handles to all sides of the panel; more typically you would use `handles: 's e se'` to constrain the top-left corner of the panel to its starting position and still allow the panel to be sized both horizontally and vertically.

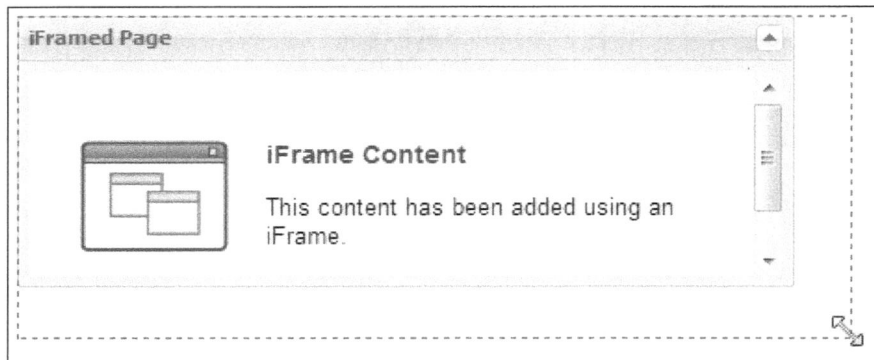

The `Ext.Resizable` class uses a dashed DIV element as a proxy when sizing using a click-and-drag motion. Once the user releases the mouse click, the iFrame is resized to the new dimensions. Resizing iFrames multiple times as the user moves the mouse is a much more expensive on memory resources than a simple DIV element, so using a proxy element is a sensible solution.

Pre-configured components using the factory pattern

Several examples shown throughout the book have created new components using the `Ext.extend` method to add new functionality or use the `Ext.override` method to over-ride existing functionality.

The `Ext.apex.Viewport` component from Chapter 3 uses the `Ext.extend` method, to create a new component, adding functionality to the `Ext.Container` component:

```
Ext.apex.Viewport = Ext.extend(Ext.Container, {
  initComponent : function() {
    Ext.apex.Viewport.superclass.initComponent.call(this);

    // new APEX specific functionality
    /** snipped **/
  },

  // new method
```

```
    fireResize : function(w, h){
      this.fireEvent('resize', this, w, h, w, h);
    }
});
```

In *Chapter 8, Data Stores, AJAX-enabled Plug-ins, and Dynamic Actions,* the `Ext.override`
method was used to alter an existing ComboBox method to add the APEX-specific
code:

```
Ext.override(Ext.form.ComboBox, {
  applyToMarkup : function(el){
    Ext.form.ComboBox.superclass.applyToMarkup.call(this, el);

    // add APEX specific code
    /** snipped **/
});
```

Sometimes creating a new component really isn't necessary; instead, all that's
required is a specific configuration of an existing class. In these cases, you can use a
factory pattern function to create new instances with a specific configuration:

```
function createMyPanel(config) {
    return new Ext.Panel(Ext.apply({
        // Pre-configured config options go here
        width: 300,
        height: 300,
        plugins: [ new Ext.ux.MyPluginClass() ]
    }, config));
};

var myfirstpanel = createMyPanel({
    title: 'My First Panel'
});

var mysecondpanel = createMyPanel({
    title: 'My Second Panel',
    width: 400
});
```

In this example, we have a function that returns a new pre-configured panel. This
panel sets the width and height properties and a plug-in when called. Two panels are
then instantiated, passing different title property values.

> A good reference discussing creating custom components by extending,
> overriding, or using factory patterns can be found at `http://www.`
> `sencha.com/learn/Tutorial:Creating_new_UI_controls`.

Notice that `Ext.apply` is used within the function to apply the pre-configured options first; any instance specific options are applied later. Applying the instance-specific options after allows the pre-configured options to be changed, as shown here for the second panel that overrides the pre-configured width with a new value.

IFrame panel factory pattern

In the example file named `chapter10/ex-10-resizable-iframe-panel-factory.html`, the following factory pattern function has been created for the iFrame panel:

```
Ext.apex.iFramePanel = function(config){
    return new Ext.Panel(Ext.apply({
        allowDomMove: false,
        animCollapse: false,
        collapsible: true,
        deferIFrame: config.collapsed || false,
        items: [new Ext.apex.IFrameComponent()],
        layout: 'fit',
        titleCollapse: true,
        url: Ext.SSL_SECURE_URL,
        listeners: {
            render: function(p){
                if (this.handles != 'none') {
                    new Ext.Resizable(p.getEl(), {
                        handles: config.handles || 's e se',
                        pinned: true,
                        transparent: true,
                        resizeElement: function(){
                            var box = this.proxy.getBox();
                            p.updateBox(box);
                            if (p.layout) {
                                p.doLayout();
                            }
                            if (Ext.isIE) {
                                this.syncHandleHeight();
                            }
                            return box;
                        }
                    });
                }
            },
            afterrender: function(){
                this.iframe = this.body.child('iframe');
```

```
            if (!this.deferIFrame) {
                this.setSrc(this.url);
            }
        },
        expand: function(){
            if (this.iframe && !this.iframe.rendered) {
                this.setSrc(this.url);
            }
        }
    },
    setSrc: function(url){
        if (this.rendered && this.iframe) {
            var mask = new Ext.LoadMask(this.body, {
                removeMask: true
            });
            new Ext.util.DelayedTask(function(){
                mask.show();
                new Ext.util.DelayedTask(function(){
                    mask.hide();
                }).delay(250);
            }).delay(150);
            this.iframe.dom.src = url;
            this.iframe.rendered = true;
        }

        return this;
    }

}, config));
};
```

This script would normally be included in your application JavaScript library external to the page.

Similar to the earlier `chapter10/ex-10-resizable-iframe-panel.html` example, it creates a Panel containing an `Ext.apex.IFrameComponent`. It does so when the `Ext.apex.iFramePanel` function is called, allowing multiple Panels to be created.

Towards the bottom of the example file, we instantiate two panels:

```
<div id="example-1" class="ux-panel"></div>
<div id="example-2"></div>

<script type="text/javascript">
Ext.onReady(function(){
```

```
Ext.apex.iFramePanel({
    applyTo: 'example-1',
    title: 'iFramed Page',
    frame: true,
    height: 400,
    width: 600,
    url: "content-page.html"
});

Ext.apex.iFramePanel({
    applyTo: 'example-2',
    height: 400,
    width: 600,
    collapsed: true,
    title: 'Wikipedia',
    url: "http://wikipedia.com",
    handles: 'all'
});

});
</script>
```

The benefits of using a factory pattern function become very apparent; we pass only those parameters specific to the layout of the individual panels. This reduces the size of pages and makes the code more readable as well.

An additional piece of functionality was also added to the factory function. The iFrame is created using the default IFrameComponent configuration, which sets the url value to Ext.SSL_SECURE_URL—a blank file.

```
deferIFrame: config.collapsed || false,
items: [new Ext.apex.IFrameComponent()],
```

For panels initially rendered in a collapsed state, the iFrame src is not updated until the panel is expanded. This provides better performance, loading the main page and loading only iFramed pages when requested by the user.

```
afterrender: function(){
    this.iframe = this.body.child('iframe');
    if (!this.deferIFrame) {
        this.setSrc(this.url);
    }
},
expand: function(){
    if (this.iframe && !this.iframe.rendered) {
        this.setSrc(this.url);
```

```
                }
            }
        },
        setSrc: function(url){
            if (this.rendered && this.iframe) {
                var mask = new Ext.LoadMask(this.body, {
                    removeMask: true
                });
                new Ext.util.DelayedTask(function(){
                    mask.show();
                    new Ext.util.DelayedTask(function(){
                        mask.hide();
                    }).delay(250);
                }).delay(150);
                this.iframe.dom.src = url;
                this.iframe.rendered = true;
            }
            return this;
        }
    }
```

When the iFrame `src` is changed, a mask is applied to the panel body using `Ext.util.DelayedTask`, as shown in the following diagram. Showing the mask after a small delay, and then hiding it after another small delay, helps the perception that the iFramed content loads quickly.

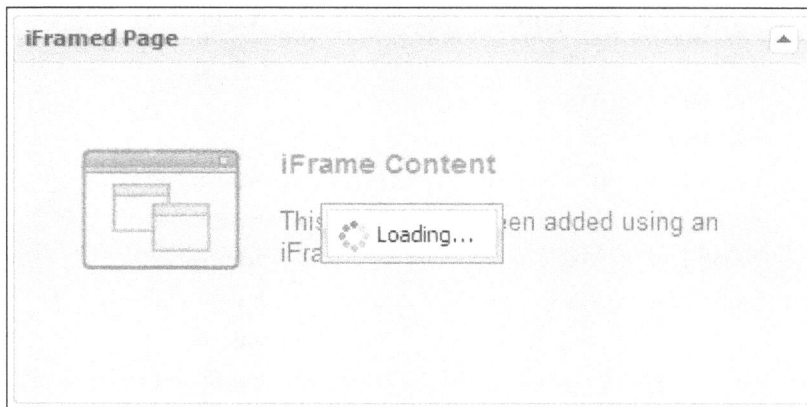

Now we have a good understanding of the resizable iFrame Panel prototype, the last step is to implement it as an APEX Plug-in.

IFrame panel plug-in

The IFrame plug-in we are creating could also be implemented as a APEX Region Template. By making it a plug-in, more attributes can be exposed to use declaratively.

The full source for the database package and JavaScript is included in the Chapter 10 source files, available on the Packt site.

Plugin name:

Ext.apex.IFramePanel

Type:

Region

Callbacks:

Render function name: plug_ext_iframepanel.render

Standard attributes:

Custom attributes:

Label	Type	Required	Depending on	Values	Default
URL	Text	Yes			
Width (px)	Number	Yes			
Height (px)	Number	Yes			
Collapsible	Select List	Yes		true, false	true
Collapsed	Select List	Yes	Collapsible	true, false	false
Frame	Select List	Yes		true, false	true
Resize Handles	Select List	Yes		south: s	s e se
				east: e	
				south and east: s e se	
				all: all	
				none: none	

The attributes used for the iFrame panel Plug-in are very straightforward; the URL attribute defines the source page for the iFrame, whereas the `width` and `height` attributes define the panel size. The URL attribute can accept absolute and relative URLs and will also convert APEX substitution tags. The following examples are both valid:

```
// absolute URL
http://apex.oracle.com

// relative URL containing APEX substitution strings
f?p=&APP_ID.:60:&APP_SESSION.::NO::P60_ID:&P160_REF_ID.:
```

The `Collapsible` attribute determines if the panel is expandable and whether or not the collapsible behavior is enabled, whereas `Collapsed` determines if the panel starts in a collapsed or expanded state. When the `Frame` attribute is set to `true`, the panel is rendered with rounded corners, otherwise it is rendered as a plain panel. The `Resize Handles` attribute determines which sides of the panel have grab bars for resizing.

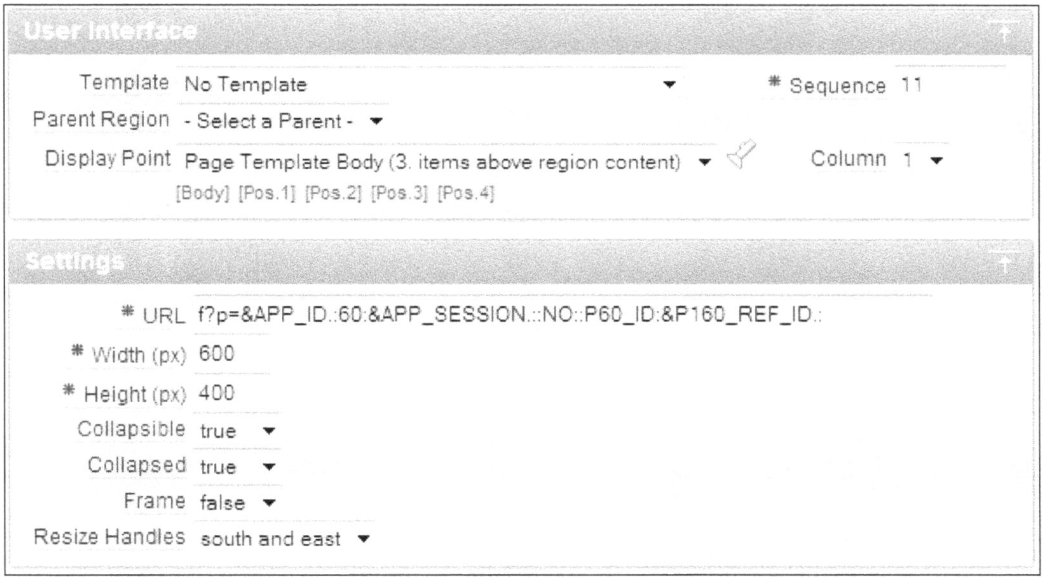

This screenshot shows a typical use of the iFrame panel plug-in with a relative URL referencing another APEX page and containing APEX substitution strings. Notice in the **User Interface** section that the **Template** field has been set to **No Template** because the plug-In will create a panel automatically.

Plug-in package

The package specification for the IFrame panel is a simple Region Plug-in declaration, with only a render function required.

```
CREATE OR REPLACE PACKAGE plug_ext_iframepanel AS

   function render (
     p_region               in apex_plugin.t_region
    ,p_plugin               in apex_plugin.t_plugin
    ,p_is_printer_friendly in boolean
   )
     return apex_plugin.t_region_render_result;

END plug_ext_iframepanel;
/
```

The full package body and specification are included in the Chapter 10 source files available on the Packt site as part of the code bundle.

Render functionality for the iFrame panel plug-in

The iFrame panel render function generates JavaScript calling the Ext.apex.iFramePanel function to instantiate a pre-configured Ext Panel with an embedded iFrame element.

The output will look like the following JavaScript:

```
Ext.onReady(function(){
    Ext.apex.iFramePanel({
        applyTo: "R3699425022908871",
        collapsed: true,
        collapsible: true,
        frame: false,
        handles: "s e se",
        height: 400,
        title: "IFramed Panel",
        url: "f?p=103:60:2236942287935549::NO::P60_ID:110:",
        width: 600
    });
});
```

In this code snippet, the url attribute is using the standard APEX f?p syntax:
f?p=App:Page:Session:Request:Debug:ClearCache:itemNames:itemValues:
PrinterFriendly

The original URL shown in the previous screenshot—f?p=&APP_ID.:60:&APP_
SESSION.::NO:P60_ID:&P_160_REF_ID—has been converted with APEX
substitution tags replaced to give the final URL.

The PL/SQL code for the render function is:

```
FUNCTION render (
    p_region              in apex_plugin.t_region
   ,p_plugin              in apex_plugin.t_plugin
   ,p_is_printer_friendly in boolean
)
    return apex_plugin.t_region_render_result is

    type t_type is table of pls_integer index by varchar2(255);
    l_default_col_idx t_type;

    l_result          apex_plugin.t_region_render_result;
    l_script          varchar2(32767);

BEGIN
    -- debug info
    if wwv_flow.g_debug then
        wwv_flow_plugin_util.debug_region (
            p_plugin              => p_plugin
           ,p_region              => p_region
           ,p_is_printer_friendly => p_is_printer_friendly
        );
    end if;

    -- print div as target
    htp.p('<div id="R'||p_region.id||
          '" class="ux-iframe"><div>');

    -- Assemble config properties
    push('url'        ,'"'||p_region.attribute_01||'"');
    push('width'      ,p_region.attribute_02);
    push('height'     ,p_region.attribute_03);
    push('collapsible',p_region.attribute_04);
    push('collapsed'  ,p_region.attribute_05);
    push('frame'      ,p_region.attribute_06);
    push('handles'    ,'"'||p_region.attribute_07||'"');

    push('applyTo'    ,'"'||p_region.static_id||'"');
    push('title'      ,'"'||escape_json(p_region.name)||'"');
```

```
    l_script := CRLF||
      'Ext.onReady(function(){'||CRLF||
      '    Ext.apex.iFramePanel({'||CRLF||
              get_properties(8)||
      '    });'||CRLF||
      '});'||CRLF;

    -- add JS to bottom of page
    wwv_flow_javascript.add_onload_code (p_code => l_script);

    return l_result;
  END;
```

Once again, we have reused custom convenience routines from previous Plug-ins; push, escape_json and get_properties, so no need to discuss those here.

The PL/SQL used here is quite trivial, simply rendering a DIV element and then generating the JavaScript using the parameter values for the Region Plug-in.

We don't even have to implement search and replace functionality to convert the APEX substitution strings into session state values—APEX does that automatically for us.

That wraps up this section on iFramed panels; let's now turn our attention to Modal Popup Windows.

Modal popup windows

Creating popup windows is a straightforward process of opening another browser window using the JavaScript window.open() command. APEX does this for Popup LOV items, the legacy datepicker, and within Application Builder for online help, to name a few examples.

The challenging issue with popup windows is you can't make them modal in any standard way across the major browsers. The second issue with popup windows is that you cannot completely hide the browser "chrome", or border components of a web browser window, which includes window frames, menus, toolbars, and scroll bars.

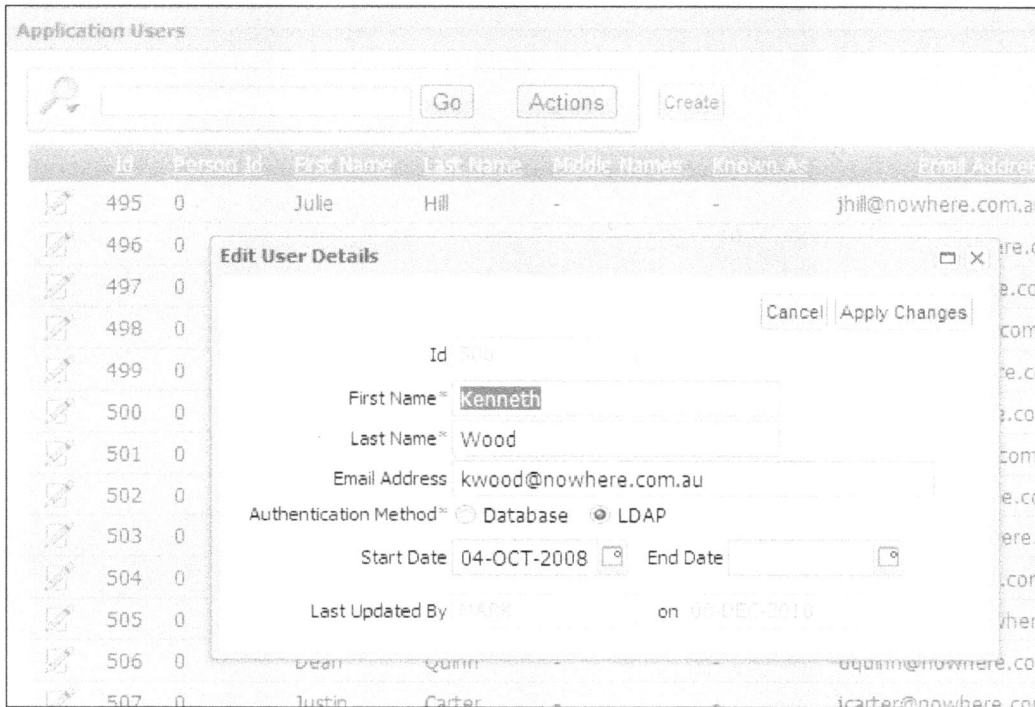

The modal Ext.Window with an embedded iFrame page, shown in the previous screenshot, neatly solves both of these issues and gives a more polished-looking solution at the same time.

In this example, clicking on the edit link for the Interactive Report launches the modal popup window to edit the user details. Once the details are updated, clicking the **Apply Changes** button submits the page for processing; a successful result closes the popup and re-queries the Interactive Report to display the updated details.

An unsuccessful result keeps the popup open with the usual error messages displayed; the **Cancel** button simply closes the popup window. Let's see how the solution is put together.

Modal iFramed window

Starting with the example in `chapter10/ex-10-modal-iframed-window.html`, you can see just how easy it is to add the iFrame functionality to a standard Ext.Window.

```
<input type="button" id="show-btn" value="Show Window" />

<script type="text/javascript">
```

```
Ext.onReady(function(){
    var win;

    Ext.get('show-btn').on('click', function(){
        // create the window on the first click
        //reuse on subsequent clicks
        if(!win){
            win = new Ext.Window({
                title:'Modal Window',
                width: 600,
                height: 400,
                items: [ new Ext.apex.IFrameComponent({ url: "content-
page.html" }) ],

                closeAction:'hide',
                layout: 'fit',
                modal: true,
                plain: true,
                resizable: true
            });
        }
        win.show(this);
    });

});
</script>
```

Here, an Ext click event listener has been added to an HTML button, creating an Ext. Window if it doesn't already exist. The Ext.Window includes our custom Ext.apex. IFrameComponent as an item, with a URL specifying the HTML page to open.

Making the window modal is done using the modal: true config setting. It really is that simple to solve the first of our challenging issues; using an embedded iframe markup element takes care of the lesser browser chrome issue.

Notice the closeAction config option is set to hide, in order to hide the Window when closed, rather than the default 'close' setting which destroys the Window, removing it from the DOM. Our eventual solution will use the default close setting, but it's important to understand the significance of this setting.

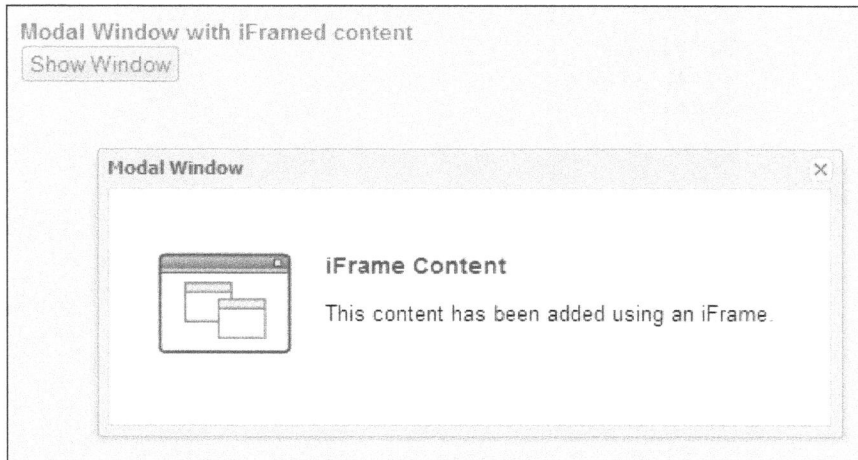

This diagram shows the `chapter10/ex-10-modal-iframed-window.html` example. Try opening the example and experimenting with it; you will find this very simple example can be dragged around the page, resized, and repeatedly opened and closed. Amazing functionality for so little effort on our part.

Popup window component

The final solution for the modal popup window extends Ext.Window to create a custom component named `Ext.apex.PopupWindow` that contains custom configurations as well as an additional event and function. It should be added to your JavaScript application library.

```
Ext.apex.PopupWindow = Ext.extend(Ext.Window, {
    url: Ext.SSL_SECURE_URL,
    title: document.title,
    width: 700,
    height: 600,
    initComponent: function(){

        // starting config, can't be modified externally
        var config = {
            border: false,
            closable: true,
            closeAction: 'close',
            header: true,
            items: [new Ext.apex.IFrameComponent({
                url: this.url
            })],
```

```
                    layout: 'fit',
                    maximizable: true,
                    modal: true,
                    plain: true
              };

              // apply config
              Ext.apply(this, Ext.apply(this.initialConfig, config));

              Ext.apex.PopupWindow.superclass.initComponent.call(this);

              this.addEvents(
              /**
               * @event success
               * Fires when iframed page has been processed
               * successfully.
               * @param {Ext.apex.PopupWindow} this
               */
              'success');

        },
        processSuccessful: function(){
            this.fireEvent("success", this);
            this[this.closeAction]();
        }
   });
```

Here, the initComponent function of Ext.Window has been overridden to include a config object literal with a set of property values that can't be modified from outside the component when instantiating a new Window.

Using **Ext.apply** to apply this configuration, first to the window's initialConfig and then to the new window instance, ensures that these properties override any similarly passed properties. Standard Ext.Window initComponent functionality is then called using:

```
   Ext.apex.PopupWindow.superclass.initComponent.call(this);
```

A custom success event is added, allowing the code that instantiated the Ext.apex. PopupWindow to include callback functionality to listen for this event. We will see exactly how this works shortly.

In conjunction with the `success` event, a custom `processSuccessful` function is defined:

```
processSuccessful: function(){
    this.fireEvent("success", this);
    this[this.closeAction]();
}
```

The `processSuccessful` function fires the `success` event, and then closes the window using the method specified by the `closeAction` attribute. It is designed to be called from an iFramed page to indicate data has been updated before closing the window.

This is quite dry reading, so let's put together a working example to bring it to life!

Ext.apex.PopupWindow example

To demonstrate the `Ext.apex.PopupWindow` component, I'm using the APEX Wizard to create new pages using the **Form on a Table with Report** option, shown in the following screenshot:

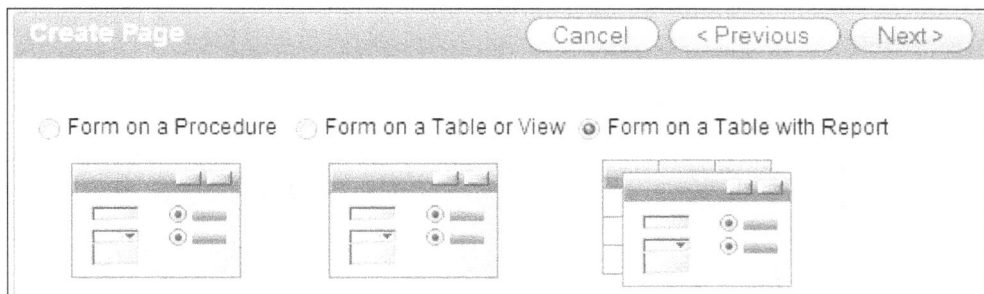

Stepping through the wizard, I selected a table named `APP_USERS` as the data source, creating a Report page titled **Application Users**, using an Interactive Report, and a second DML Form page **Edit Application Users**.

After completing the wizard, the end result is an Interactive Report page shown in the following screenshot, with an edit icon for each row, which opens the DML Form page in the current window, retrieving the details for the selected record. It also includes a **Create** button that opens the same DML Form page to insert new records.

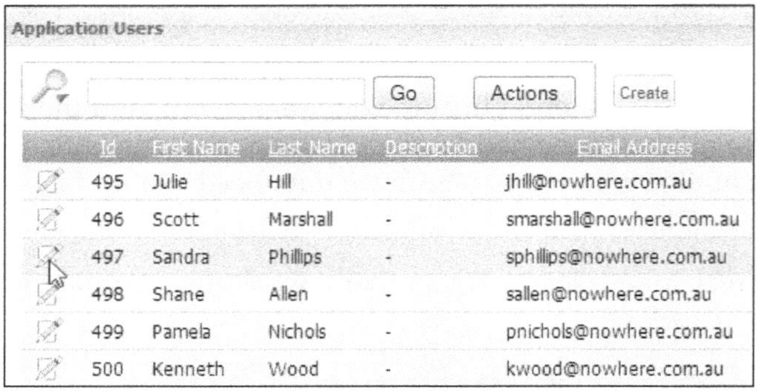

I'm sure this is all very familiar to you, so I won't elaborate on this standard process any further. Let's start converting the solution to use the PopupWindow config, starting with the Link Column settings for the Edit icon.

Link Column settings

In the APEX Application Builder, open the Interactive Report page and then navigate to the **Interactive Report Attributes | Link Column** section. Your settings should look very similar to those shown in the following screenshot, except the **Link Attribute** value.

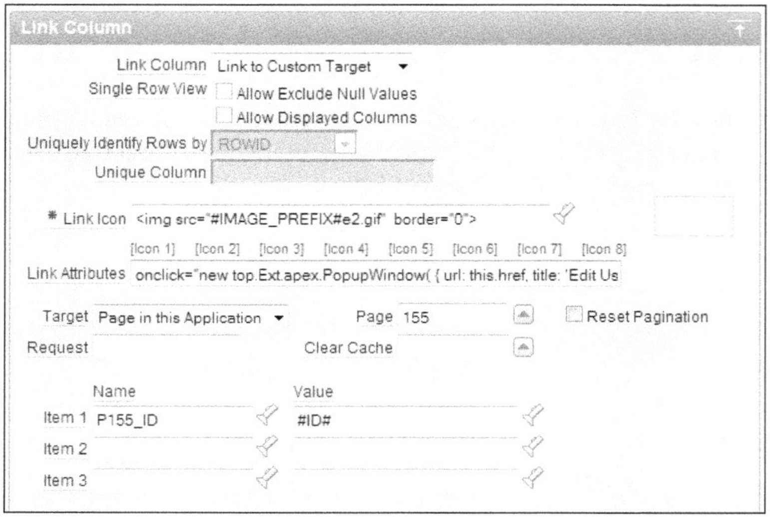

The full text for the Link Attributes field is:

```
onclick="new top.Ext.apex.PopupWindow( {
    url: this.href,
    title: 'Edit User Details',
    width: 490,
    height: 500,
    listeners: {'success': gReport.search}
} ).show();
return false;"
```

Here, we are launching `Ext.apex.PopupWindow` by adding an `onclick` attribute to the HTML link element generated by APEX. To prevent the default behavior of the link, we use the `return false;` statement at the end of the script.

The PopupWindow config uses `url: this.href` to pick the `href` attribute value, allowing developers to build the link details using the APEX Builder functionality as usual.

Notice that we are using the `top` keyword when instantiating PopupWindow, ensuring that the window is opened from the topmost page window in case the current window is in an iFrame. This is not necessary for this example as presented here, but becomes necessary when Interactive Reports are embedded in iFrames, just like we will be doing in the tabbed document interface section coming up in this chapter.

```
onclick="new top.Ext.apex.PopupWindow( {
    /* snipped */
    listeners: {'success': gReport.search}
} ).show();
return false;"
```

The `Ext.apex.PopupWindow` component includes a custom `success` event, which is executed when the `processSuccessful` function is used to close the PopupWindow config. Closing the `PopupWindow` using the standard Ext.Window `close` function does not fire the success event.

By adding a listener for the success event, we can automatically re-query the Interactive Report when `PopupWindow` is closed, using the `processSuccessful` function:

```
listeners: {'success': gReport.search}
```

Using the success event eliminates unnecessary refresh requests for the Interactive Report by only refreshing when the PopupWindow config indicates that changes have been made.

Classic Report link settings

If you were to use a Classic Report instead of an Interactive Report, replace the gReport.search function with the equivalent $a_report function to refresh a Classic Report:

```
onclick="new top.Ext.apex.PopupWindow( {
    url: this.href,
    title: 'Edit User Details',
    width: 490,
    height: 500,
    listeners: {'success':
                $a_report('3833408439418014',0,0,0,0,'current')
                }
    }
).show();
return false;"
```

The $a_report function requires the report ID of the report as the first parameter, and the string current as the sixth parameter, specifying the report is to be refreshed with current pagination settings. The other parameters are not used by the function when refreshing but need to be specified, so zero values can be used.

Create Button settings

The Create Button functionality to launch PopupWindow is similar to the Link Column settings, only slightly less elegant.

The lack of elegance comes about because we are unable to use APEX "Action When Button Clicked" functionality. Instead, the URL must be specified in the **Button Attributes** section, as shown in the following screenshot:

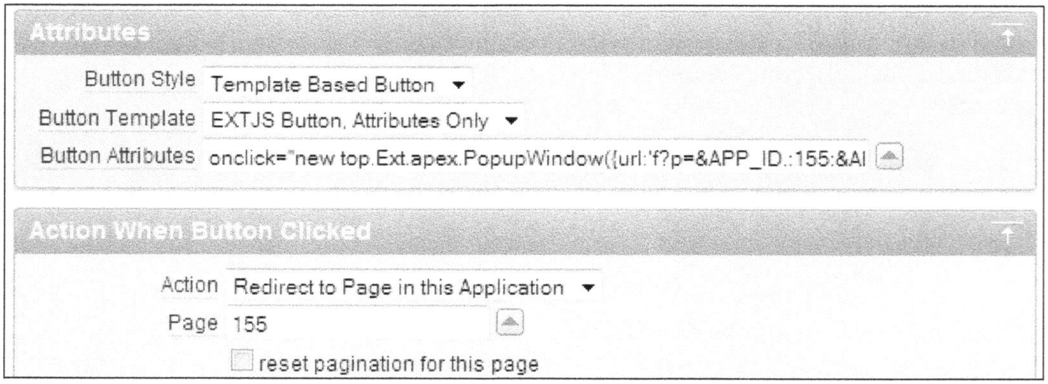

It is also necessary to create a custom button template ExtJS Button, Attributes Only by copying the ExtJS Button template and removing the onclick="#LINK#" reference:

The finished markup for the ExtJS Button, Attributes Only template is:

```
<table cellspacing="0" class="ux-btn ux-btn-markup x-btn x-btn-noicon"
style="width:auto;" #BUTTON_ATTRIBUTES#>
<tbody class="x-btn-small x-btn-icon-small-left">
<tr>
  <td class="x-btn-tl"><i> </i></td>
  <td class="x-btn-tc"></td>
  <td class="x-btn-tr"><i> </i></td>
</tr>
<tr>
  <td class="x-btn-ml"><i> </i></td>
  <td class="x-btn-mc">
    <em unselectable="on" class="">
      <button type="button" class="x-btn-text">#LABEL#</button>
    </em>
  </td>
  <td class="x-btn-mr"><i> </i></td>
</tr>
<tr>
  <td class="x-btn-bl"><i> </i></td>
  <td class="x-btn-bc"></td>
  <td class="x-btn-br"><i> </i></td>
</tr>
</tbody>
</table>
```

This is quite a useful button template, because it allows us to specify the onclick functionality to suit any individual situation.

The code for the Button Attributes in the previous screenshot is:

```
onclick="new top.Ext.apex.PopupWindow( {
    url:'f?p=&APP_ID.:155:&APP_SESSION.::NO:155::',
    title: 'Create New User',
    listeners: {'success': gReport.search}
} ).show();
return false;"
```

Notice that here the URL has to be specified, but can use APEX substitution strings and session state values. The width and height attributes weren't included here, using the default values specified in our custom component.

> Don't forget to reset the target page in the URL for standard "create" functionality to work correctly. This is done by setting the sixth parameter to the target page using the `f?p` syntax.

We've implemented the necessary changes to the Source Interactive Report page, so let's turn our attention to the Target DML Form.

Closing the PopupWindow

Our solution so far is launching the PopupWindow correctly; we just need to modify the behavior of the iFramed page to close the PopupWindow.

This screenshot shows the target DML Form embedded in the modal popup window. The default processing created by the APEX wizard simply redirects the browser to the calling page when the **Cancel** button is clicked. When the **Apply Changes** button is clicked, the form is submitted for processing—either successfully completing and branching to the calling page, or redisplaying the current page with error messages.

So we need to deal with two different behaviors, modifying the **Cancel** button to simply close the PopupWindow, and for the **Apply Changes** button to process the page and close the PopupWindow.

Cancel Button functionality

The Cancel Button functionality is very straightforward, using our **EXTJS Button, Attributes Only** button to include a simple `onclick` attribute with the relevant JavaScript.

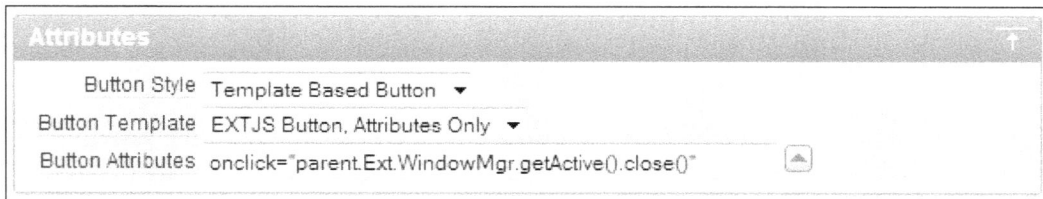

Attributes		↑
Button Style	Template Based Button ▼	
Button Template	EXTJS Button, Attributes Only ▼	
Button Attributes	onclick="parent.Ext.WindowMgr.getActive().close()"	▲

This screenshot shows the JavaScript in its entirety:

```
onclick="parent.Ext.WindowMgr.getActive().close()"
```

Here, we are utilizing the `Ext.WindowMgr` singleton that centralizes management of all Ext.Window components on a page. Taking advantage of this fact, we implemented the PopupWindow as a modal window; it's inferred that it must be the active window, and as the target page is iFramed, the window must belong to the iframe `parent`.

Putting all these pieces together, we have a simple one-line solution to close the window.

Apply Changes functionality

The Apply Changes functionality is a little trickier. We have to submit the page, and when it successfully completes the page processing, it branches to the target page and closes the PopupWindow. Fortunately, APEX 4.0 provides similar functionality to what we need, giving the vital clues to the end solution.

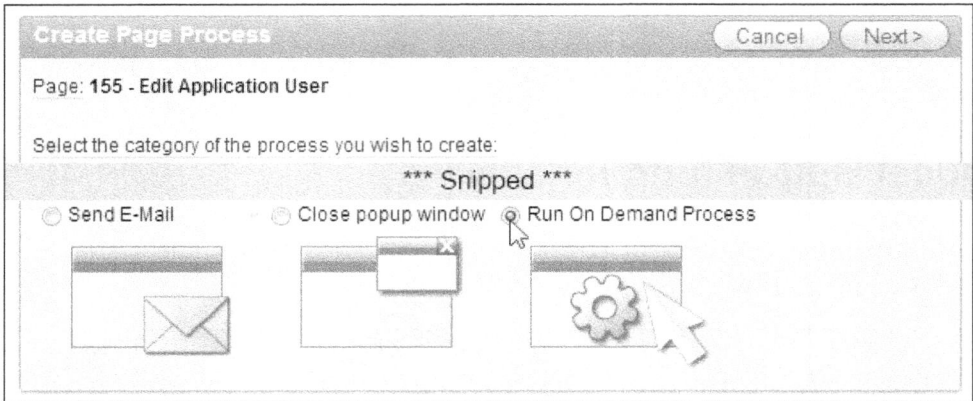

APEX 4.0 provides the **Close popup window** page process shown in the previous screenshot, which almost does what we want, so let's explore how that works first.

The **Close popup window** page process works by creating a page process, which upon execution, closes the current popup window. The next screenshot shows the execution order of processing a page. Here we can see the Close Window process executing after the row processing for the APP_USERS table, after records have been insert, updated, or deleted.

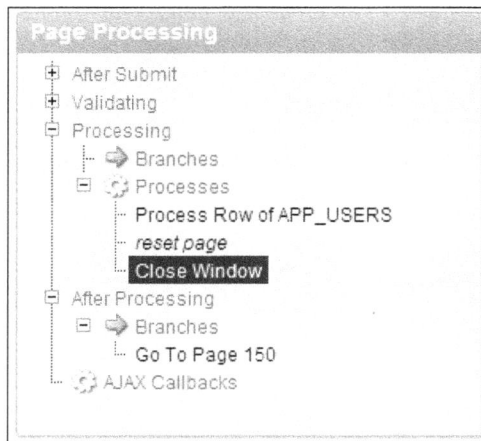

The Close Window process completes before the After Processing section where page branching occurs. It does this by rendering a very small HTML page and then terminating any further processing by the APEX engine.

The page it creates looks like:

```
<html>
<script>if (self != window.opener) window.close();</script>
</html>
```

How lightweight is that! An HTML page containing a one-line instruction to close the current window. Using this process for our solution would close the iFrame successfully, but leaves a blank Ext.Window remaining.

The solution for an Ext.apex.PopupWindow is to mimic the built-in process, modifying the JavaScript to suit our needs.

First off, create an **Application Process**:

Process point:

```
On Demand: Run this application process when requested by a page
process.
```

Name:

```
Succeed and Close Ext.apex.PopupWindow
```

Process text:

```
-- Force APEX to not show any HTML
wwv_flow.g_page_text_generated := true;
wwv_flow.g_unrecoverable_error := true;

htp.init;
htp.prn('<html><script> parent.Ext.WindowMgr.getActive().
processSuccessful(); </script></html>');
```

This only needs to be done once, and is available for all APEX pages to use. The magic is in the two highlighted lines, which tell the APEX engine that the page text has been generated and to do no further page processing.

Our script is similar to the Cancel button functionality, except that we call the custom processSuccessful function instead to trigger the success event before closing the window.

Then simply add a page process to the target page, calling the "on-demand" application process at the process point "**On Submit - After Computations and Validations**", ensuring that it occurs after the other page processes, as shown in the following screenshot:

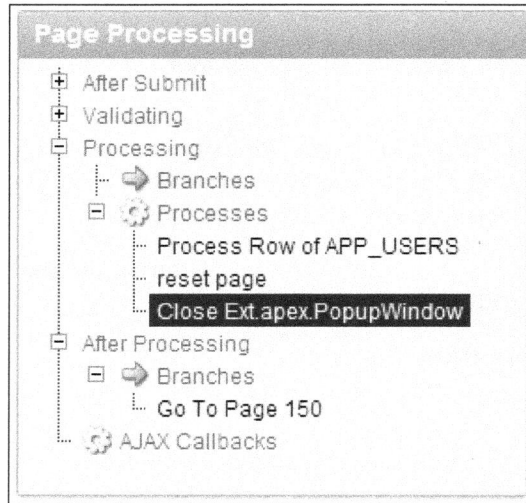

This completes the functionality for the `Ext.apex.PopupWindow` component.

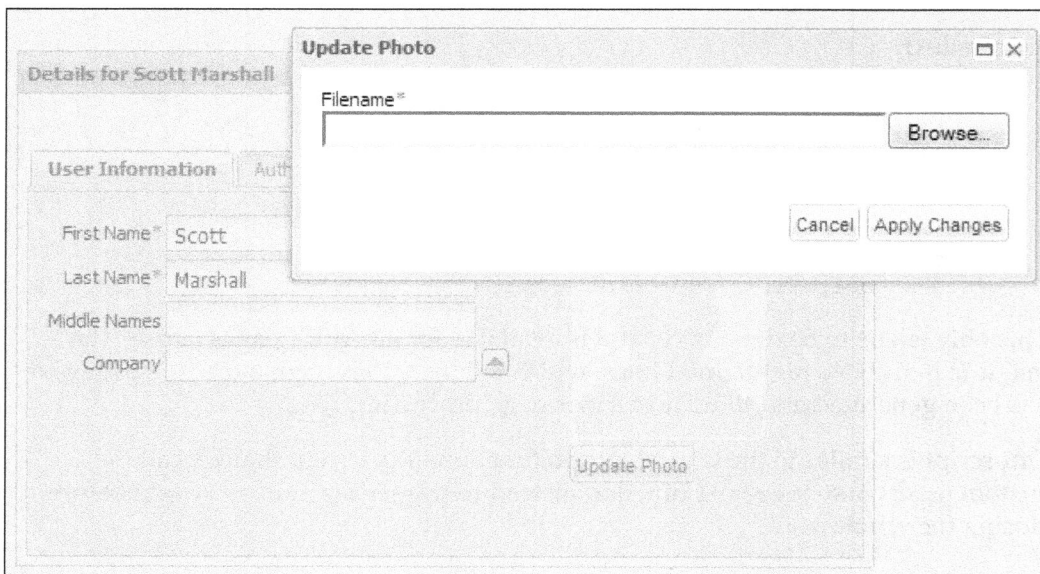

You now can open pages in popup windows like the previous screenshot, listening for a success event. Changes made by the popup window page can trigger the success event when the window is closed, providing the option of including JavaScript code to update the original page.

Creating a tabbed document interface

To discourage users from opening multiple browser tabs, where we have no control over which pages are opened, we can give them similar functionality to open multiple pages in a single browser tab.

This allows developers to design the APEX application so that we are in control of what pages can be opened, and also design the pages so they are less reliant on maintaining session state.

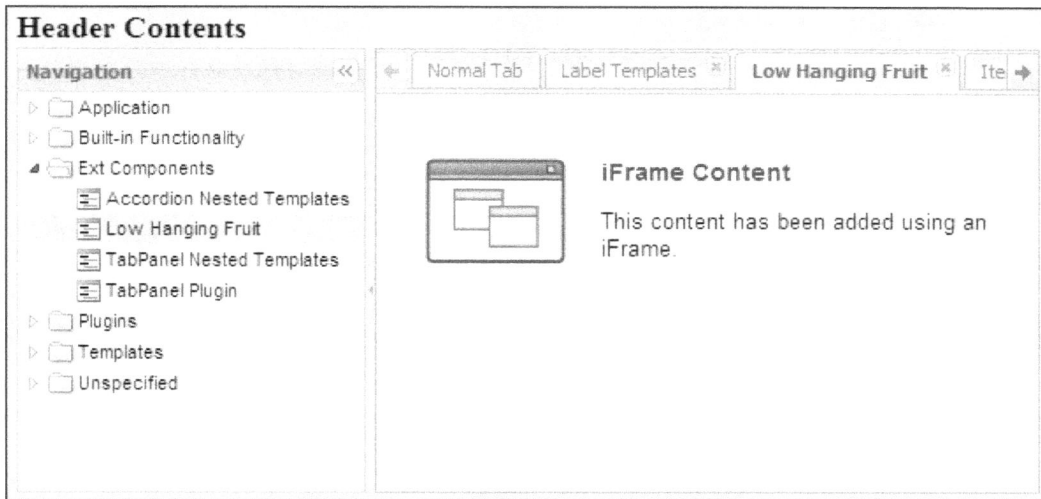

This screenshot shows the example file named `chapter10/ ex-10-tree-iframe-tabs.html` that we will examine in this section.

Unlike the earlier examples shown in this chapter, we won't be going through how to incorporate this into your APEX application in detail. Instead, we will only examine the functionality of the prototype to understand the JavaScript behavior.

Examining the HTML page

The structure for the page layout for the example page is quite simple.

```
<html>
<head>
    <title>#TITLE#</title>
    <link rel="icon" type="image/x-icon"
          href="#IMAGE_PREFIX#favicon.ico">
    <link rel="shortcut icon" type="image/x-icon"
          href="#IMAGE_PREFIX#favicon.ico">

    <!-- standard includes -->
    <link rel="stylesheet" type="text/css"
          href="../../extjs/resources/css/ext-all.css">
    <script type="text/javascript"
        src="../../extjs/adapter/ext/ext-base.js"></script>
    <script type="text/javascript"
        src="../../extjs/ext-all.js"></script>

    <!-- Static json tree data. In APEX would use list or
         table to dynamically generate in the page -->
    <script type="text/javascript"
        src="navigation-tree-data.js"></script>

    <!-- application javascript -->
    <script type="text/javascript"
        src="TabCloseMenu.js"></script>
    <script type="text/javascript"
        src="ex-10-tree-iframe-tabs.js"></script>
</head>
<body>
    <div id="app-north-panel"><h1>Header Contents</h1></div>
    <form id="wwvFlowForm">

        <!-- Snipped Static page content -->
        <!-- Usually APEX Region tags -->

    </form>
</body>
</html>
```

The header section contains the usual references to the Ext CSS and JavaScript files and also our application-specific CSS and JavaScript files. The body comprises a DIV element named `app-north-panel` that contains all the HTML markup for the north panel of an **Ext.Viewport** layout.

The remaining markup of interest is the FORM `wwvFlowForm` element created by APEX using the #FORM_OPEN# and #FORM_CLOSE# substitution tags. For our **Ext.Viewport** layout, the `wwvFlowForm` element is used for the center panel, and contains all page content.

The JavaScript file named `navigation-tree-data.js` contains a static array to define the tree data for this example:

```
var jsonTreeData = [
    {id  :"L3529107364353923",
     text:"Application",
     href:"#",
     leaf:false,
     children: [{
         id  :"L3529403918353923",
         text:"Page 0",
         href:"content-page.html",
         leaf:true
    }, {
         id  :"L3529722176353923",
         text:"Attachments",
         href:"content-page.html",
         leaf:true
    }]
    }, {

      /** snipped many more tree nodes */

    }
];
```

Usually in APEX, the tree data would be generated dynamically, either using a custom table-based solution or as we did in *Chapter 4, Ext Themed Regions, Labels, and Lists*, using an APEX list combined with a List template that generated a JSON tree definition. In fact, the example here with minor edits uses the data that has been cut and pasted directly from a page using the APEX list solution.

The `TabCloseMenu.js` JavaScript file contains an Ext custom plug-in copied from the `extjs/examples/ux/` directory. When the plug-in is included in a TabPanel region, it adds a right-click context menu to close tabs, as shown in the following screenshot:

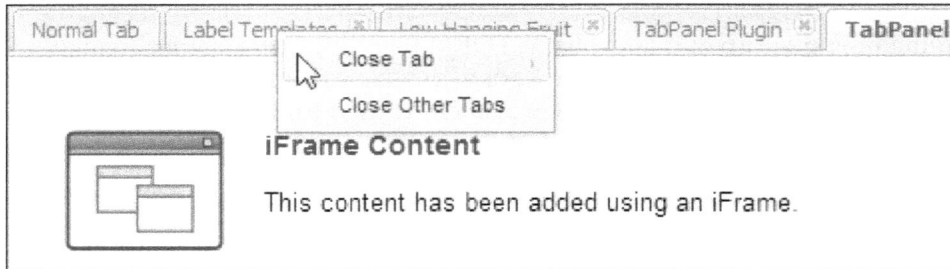

We will see how the TabCloseMenu plug-in is included in the `ex-10-tree-iframe-tabs.js` JavaScript file, which is the only component that remains to be examined.

Examining the JavaScript

The `Ext.apex.IFrameComponent` component has been declared in this standalone example, but is not shown here. As usual for any code being executed in the page, we enclose it within an `Ext.onReady` statement with an anonymous function, ensuring any variables declared are localized to the function and ensuring that the code is executed when the document is ready.

```
Ext.onReady(function(){

  Ext.QuickTips.init();

  var contentPanel = {
    id: 'content-panel',
    region: 'center',
    xtype: 'tabpanel',
    margins: '2 5 5 0',
    enableTabScroll: true,
    activeItem: 0,
    plugins: new Ext.ux.TabCloseMenu(),
    border: true,
    defaultType: 'iframe',
    defaults: {
      closable: true
    },
    items: [{
      xtype: 'panel',
```

```
        closable: false,
        title: 'Normal Tab',
        contentEl: 'wwvFlowForm'
    }]
};
```

The `contentPanel` object literal is defined with the `region: 'center'` attribute, ensuring that the panel is rendered into a region within the Viewport container further on in the code. At this point, only the configuration for the panel has been defined, and the panel hasn't been created yet.

Notice the `contentPanel` is specified as `xtype: 'tabpanel'` using lazy instantiation. The xtype will be looked up at render time to determine what type of child Component to create. By defining it as a TabPanel, it acts like a standard **Ext.Panel** for layout purposes, but allows additional panels to be added at a later time as separate tabs. The **Ext.usTabCloseMenu** component has been added as a plugin to the TabPanel.

The TabPanel includes an **Ext.Panel** declared as `xtype: 'panel'` using lazy instantiation and uses the existing HTML `wwvFlowForm` element as the content of the panel component. Ext may re-arrange the DOM components when rendering the page, but this ensures that the APEX form and its child components will be in the center region of the Viewport.

```
    // Create the TreePanel now so that we can use it below
    var treePanel = new Ext.tree.TreePanel({
        id: 'tree-panel',
        region: 'center',
        minSize: 150,
        autoScroll: true,
        border: false,

        // tree-specific configs:
        rootVisible: false,
        lines: false,
        singleExpand: true,
        useArrows: true,

        loader: new Ext.tree.TreeLoader({
            clearOnLoad: false,
            preloadChildren: true,
            pathSeparator: '>'
        }),

        root: new Ext.tree.AsyncTreeNode({
```

```
            leaf: false,
            expanded: true,
            text: 'Tree Root',
            draggable: false,
            children: jsonTreeData
        })
    });
```

An `Ext.tree.TreePanel` component is created, specifying that it is to be rendered into the center region of its container. Unlike the earlier contentPanel, the tree component exists as a DOM object, but hasn't been rendered yet. The root node uses the JavaScript array of tree nodes defined in the `navigation-tree-data.js` file as its child nodes.

```
// only make leaf nodes selectable
treePanel.getSelectionModel().on('beforeselect', function(sm, node){
    return node.isLeaf();
});
```

A `beforeselect` event is added to the TreePanel selection model to cancel any selection events for branch nodes, typically represented as folders. This is done as an application design choice, to use folders to classify related pages that are represented by the leaf nodes.

We can only add the event to the TreePanel here because it exists as a DOM object.

```
// Create layout actions for tree node click.
treePanel.on('click', function(node, e){
    e.stopEvent();
    if (!node.isLeaf())
        return false;

    var tab, tabs = Ext.getCmp('content-panel');

    if (tabs && (tab = tabs.getComponent('tab-' + node.id))) {
        tabs.setActiveTab(tab);
    }
    else {
        tab = tabs.add({
            title: node.text,
            id: 'tab-' + node.id,
            url: node.attributes.href,
            closable: true
        });
        tab.show();
    }
});
```

A `click` event listener is added to the TreePanel, defining the actions to be performed when a leaf node is selected. A `stopEvent()` utility is used to stop the event from propagating up the DOM hierarchy and also prevent the event default action from occurring. This is very important to include, because Ext renders tree nodes as HTML links, with the default action opening the link in the current window.

The TabPanel we declared earlier is identified using `Ext.getCmp('content-panel')`, because it hasn't been created at this point. Using the tree `node.id`, a check is done to see if a matching tab exists with the same ID prefixed by `'tab-'`. When a match is found, the tab is set as the active tab; otherwise, a new tab containing an iframe is added to the tab panel opening the node's URL in the iFrame.

```
// Finally, build the main layout
new Ext.Viewport({
  layout: 'border',
  items: [{
    applyTo: 'app-north-panel',
    autoHeight: true,
    autoScroll: false,
    region: 'north',
    style: {
      padding: '0 5px'
    },
    xtype: 'box'
  }, {
    layout: 'border',
    id: 'navigationPanel',
    title: 'Navigation',
    region: 'west',
    border: true,
    split: true,
    margins: '2 0 5 5',
    width: 275,
    minSize: 100,
    maxSize: 500,
    animCollapse: false,
    animate: false,
    collapsible: true,
    collapseMode: 'mini',
    items: [treePanel]
  }, contentPanel]
});
```

An **Ext.Viewport** component is instantiated with north, west, and center regions. The north region picks up the HTML markup contained in the app-north-panel DIV element. The center region uses the contentPanel containing the APEX form and the west region is a container for a nested sub-region using the treePanel.

```
Ext.getCmp('content-panel').on('tabchange', function(tp, tab){
    treePanel.getSelectionModel().clearSelections();

    var node = treePanel.getNodeById(tab.id.substring(4));
    if (node) {
      node.ensureVisible();
      node.select();
    }
  });

});
```

Finally, functionality is added to the TabPanel component ensuring the correct tree node is selected and highlighted when a user clicks on a different tab.

That covers the functionality of the tabbed document interface, but why haven't we covered getting it into APEX?

Adding the tabbed document interface to APEX

There are a number of tasks to perform to incorporate the tabbed document interface into your APEX theme, and it requires some thought and planning on your part.

First, you will need to create a new page template for the main page and include the JavaScript functionality in an external file. You will also need to review the page template for the pages opened up in the tabs.

But that's really the least of your challenges. The most important task to think about is your application navigation. What pages do you want to open in the tabs? How do you navigate to other pages from a tabbed page?

A possible option could be to open interactive reports in the tabbed pages, and from there, open any child pages as popup windows.

Or alternatively, you could open summary pages in a tab, which then drill down to detail pages within the tab. You would need to ensure that you have appropriate options to navigate backwards and forwards between the pages for this to be functional.

Also under consideration is session state. When is it safe to reset session state for a page? Can you still clear session state for all pages in your application, or is that too dangerous now?

The potential benefits of tabbed document interfaces are huge from an end user perspective, and can make your applications far more functional and productive. There is, however, a bit to think about—either before you retro-fit tabbed document interfaces to your existing application, or in upfront design considerations for new applications.

Summary

In this chapter we have looked at using iFrames in three different ways:

- Embedding other pages within a page using iFramed Panels
- Making popup windows modal
- Creating a tabbed document interface allowing users to switch backwards and forwards easily between pages without opening multiple browser tabs

IFrames open up a host of new opportunities to add improved functionality to your applications. You need to be more mindful of APEX session state, but the benefits are most definitely there.

In the next chapter, we will be looking performance tuning your JavaScript, reducing the size of the files and eliminating unused Ext components from the standard Ext library.

11
Performance Tuning
Your JavaScript

Despite increasing speeds in broadband connections, it's still important as ever to keep web pages as lightweight as possible. High-speed Internet connections aren't available everywhere. For example, I work for a large infrastructure and mining organization, which has a number of sites in remote and inhospitable areas, with communications often dependent on low bandwidth, high-latency satellite links.

The trend towards applications aimed at mobile devices, such as Smartphone and other handheld devices with expensive data charges and relatively slow download rates also encourages us to keep web pages lightweight.

Throughout this book, we have been using the full Ext JS library in our APEX page templates, either using the compressed `ext-all.js` file or the larger uncompressed `ext-all-debug.js` version. A series of custom JavaScript components and application functionality have also been developed along the way, which I keep telling you to add to your application JavaScript file also. All this adds up to lots of JavaScript on top of the files already included by the APEX engine!

In this chapter, we will be looking at ways of keeping our JavaScript lightweight by:

- Enabling HTTP compression
- Using JSBuilder2 to combine and minify JavaScript and CSS files
- Eliminating unused Ext components from the standard Ext JS library
- Combining and minifying application JavaScript

Best practices for JavaScript and CSS

Internet giants, such as Yahoo and Google, have published a series of best practices for making web pages fast, integrating the practices into tools to measure page performance. Yahoos' YSlow and Googles' Page Speed are both available as Firebug add-ons.

> Download the page performance tools from the following URL:
> https://addons.mozilla.org/en-US/firefox/addon/5369
> Page Speed from the following URL:
> http://code.google.com/speed/page-speed/download.html

These tools make many recommendations covering all components making up a web page, as well as web server configuration. Behind each of the recommendations is detailed explanations and extensive research.

Some of the key recommendations relating to JavaScript and CSS are as follows:

- Enable HTTP compression
- Externalize JavaScript and CSS to take advantage of browser caching
- Reduce HTTP requests by combining JavaScript and CSS files into as few files as possible
- Reduce the size of JavaScript and CSS files by minifying them
- Load CSS files in the page header, JavaScript files as late as possible in the page

HTTP compression

Enabling HTTP compression is the easiest way to reduce bandwidth and improve speed of your website.

HTTP compression uses standards based **gzip** and **deflate** compression algorithms to compress your XHTML, CSS, and JavaScript to speed up web page downloads and save bandwidth.

Many web servers can compress files before sending them for download, either by calling a third-party module or using built-in routines. All of the major browsers today are compression aware to the HTTP 1.1 standard.

Browsers send a header to the web server indicating they can accept compressed content through a HTTP request header "Accept-Encoding: gzip, deflate". HTTP compression enabled web servers recognize the request header and dynamically compress content and include a Content-Encoding field in the HTTP response.

It's very easy to check whether your web server currently has HTTP compression enabled or not by checking the Response Headers under the Net tab in Firebug, looking for Content-Encoding gzip, as shown in the following screenshot:

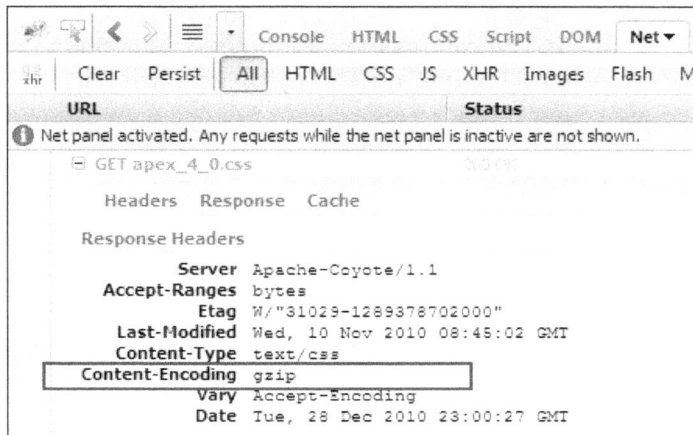

Browsers such as Google Chrome and Microsoft Internet Explorer have similar developer tools built into the browser that you can use to inspect Response Headers.

A study of 9,281 HTML pages of popular sites by Destounis et al in 2001 found a mean compression gain of 75.2%. This translates into faster download times and a better user experience. You may be surprised that I'm referencing such an old study; it does reinforce the point that HTTP compression has been around for a long time.

The following screenshot shows compression data for an APEX page using the Ext JS page template:

The Firebug YSlow add-on by Yahoo shows the reduced size of page components when gzip compression is enabled. You can see the Ext library **ext-all.js** has a gzipped size of **238.4K** compared with **715.4K**, or roughly a 70% reduction in size.

If your web server doesn't currently have HTTP compression enabled, I strongly encourage you to enable it as it can result in a dramatic reduction in download time. There are many references on the Internet on how to enable it.

Externalize JavaScript and CSS

External files generally produce faster pages because the JavaScript and CSS files are cached by the browser. JavaScript and CSS content that is included in-lined in HTML pages get downloaded every time the page is requested.

The following screenshot shows graphs from the YSlow utility showing the benefits of browser caching when the JavaScript and CSS are in external files.

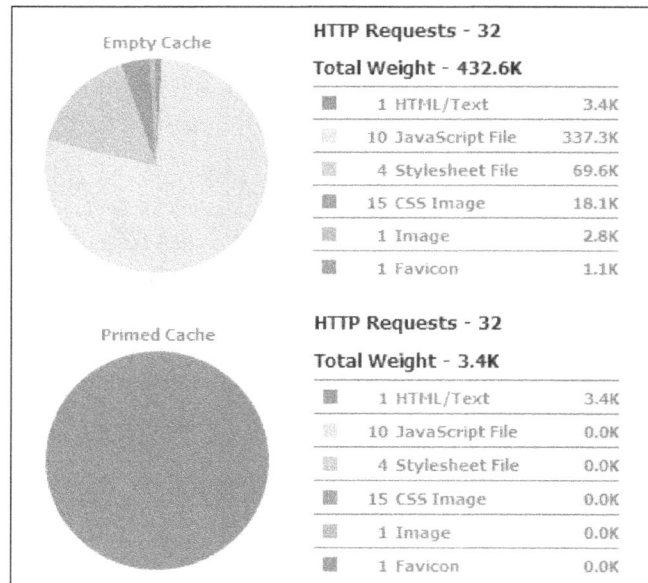

Empty Cache	HTTP Requests - 32	
	Total Weight - 432.6K	
	1 HTML/Text	3.4K
	10 JavaScript File	337.3K
	4 Stylesheet File	69.6K
	15 CSS Image	18.1K
	1 Image	2.8K
	1 Favicon	1.1K
Primed Cache	HTTP Requests - 32	
	Total Weight - 3.4K	
	1 HTML/Text	3.4K
	10 JavaScript File	0.0K
	4 Stylesheet File	0.0K
	15 CSS Image	0.0K
	1 Image	0.0K
	1 Favicon	0.0K

The size of the HTML document is reduced dramatically. In this example, the page size is reduced by roughly 400K, or 90%, because the JavaScript and CSS are in external files.

APEX applications that are used frequently by their users benefit the most from browser caching, because the likelihood of the files remaining in the browsers cache is much higher.

Combining JavaScript and CSS files

Combining external scripts into as few files as possible cuts down the number of HTTP request/response round-trips and delays downloading of other resources. It also ensures that JavaScript files with dependencies in other files are loaded and executed in the correct sequence.

The `ext-all.js` library combines 26 separate JavaScript files, which can be referenced instead of the `ext-all.js` file. The following screenshot shows the download profile of an HTML file containing just the `ext-base.js` file and the 26 files making up the `ext-all.js` file using the Firebug Net panel:

URL	Size	Timeline
⊞ GET ext-base.js	10.2 KB	12ms
⊞ GET ext-core.js	21.3 KB	40ms
⊞ GET ext-foundation.js	22.5 KB	75ms
⊞ GET cmp-foundation.js	35.1 KB	78ms
⊞ GET ext-dd.js	9 KB	70ms
⊞ GET data-foundation.js	9.9 KB	66ms
⊞ GET data-json.js	2 KB	65ms
⊞ GET data-xml.js	1.6 KB	58ms
⊞ GET data-grouping.js	1015 B	58ms
⊞ GET direct.js	3.3 KB	61ms
⊞ GET resizable.js	2.9 KB	54ms
⊞ GET window.js	6.2 KB	4ms
⊞ GET state.js	1.2 KB	6ms
⊞ GET data-list-views.js	4.8 KB	4ms
⊞ GET pkg-tabs.js	3.7 KB	4ms
⊞ GET pkg-buttons.js	3.3 KB	4ms
⊞ GET pkg-toolbars.js	3.2 KB	3ms
⊞ GET pkg-history.js	1.8 KB	1ms
⊞ GET pkg-tips.js	3.9 KB	3ms
⊞ GET pkg-tree.js	12.7 KB	7ms
⊞ GET pkg-charts.js	6.8 KB	13ms
⊞ GET pkg-menu.js	5.6 KB	10ms
⊞ GET pkg-forms.js	22.4 KB	14ms
⊞ GET pkg-grid-foundation.js	17.8 KB	8ms
⊞ GET pkg-grid-editor.js	2.2 KB	2ms
⊞ GET pkg-grid-property.js	1.7 KB	3ms
⊞ GET pkg-grid-grouping.js	2.7 KB	2ms
27 requests	**218.7 KB**	**307ms (onload: 1.5s)**

Notice that only four files are being downloaded from the host at any given time. Many browsers block the downloading of resources referenced in the document after scripts until those scripts are *downloaded and executed*. Older browsers, such as IE 6 and IE 7, allow only two concurrent connections to a host, slowing down the download process even further.

Compare the difference shown in the following screenshot, which shows the files combined into the `ext-all.js` library:

The download time is still substantially less despite this example being run on a local web server. Running the same example on a remote server would increase the round-trip times, making the difference even larger.

Currently, APEX 4.0 typically includes five separate JavaScript files in the page header before you start including your JavaScript files. This will be addressed in APEX 4.1, with the files being combined into a single file.

Google recommend a maximum of three, or preferably two, JavaScript files. CSS files should be combined as well, with Google recommending a maximum of three, but preferably two CSS files for a page.

Minifying JavaScript and CSS files

Minification is the practice of removing unnecessary characters from code to reduce its size and thus improving loading times. When the code is minified, all comments are removed, along with unneeded white space characters. For example, Sencha provides the minified `ext-all.js` at 715.4K, which is roughly half the unminified `ext-all-debug.js` version at 1367.8K.

The smaller file size reduces network latency, and allows the JavaScript to be loaded and executed more quickly by the browser.

There are a number of minification tools freely available on the Internet, including Yahoos' YUI Compressor, which is used by the Sencha JSBuilder2 tool we will be using in this chapter to combine and minify JavaScript and CSS files.

Ordering CSS and JavaScript files

Correctly ordering external stylesheets and external and inline scripts enables better parallelization of downloads and speeds up the browser rendering time.

JavaScript code can alter the content and layout of a web page, so browsers must download and execute JavaScript files and inline scripts before processing the remainder of the page, blocking the downloading of remaining resources.

The generally accepted recommendations are to include external CSS files in the page header, with external JavaScript files included after the CSS files, or even later in the page. Any code executed as part of the page load should be deferred as late as possible, preferably after the pages DOM elements have been rendered.

We see this in practice with APEX 4.0 with the APEX JavaScript files included after the CSS files, and the active JavaScript to add functionality to the APEX provided widgets included at the very end of the page. This is also encouraged in the plug-in APIs as well.

JSBuilder2 installation and usage

JSBuilder2 is a JavaScript and CSS project build tool developed by Sencha, which enables you to assemble multiple files into a deployment package easily. It is a Java utility, which uses a simple JSON-based configuration file to combine multiple JavaScript files into packaged files. CSS files can also be combined as well.

JSBuilder2 uses the YUI Compressor to minify JavaScript. It also uses additional YUI Compressor options for minimizing JavaScript, enabling *munging* to replace variable names with shorter versions, removing unnecessary semicolons, and performing other built-in micro optimizations.

> JSBuilder2 can be downloaded from the following URL:
> http://www.sencha.com/deploy/JSBuilder2.zip

We will be using JSBuilder2 to remove unused components from the Ext JS Library, as well as assemble and minify our project JavaScript files.

Installation

JSBuilder2 requires the **Java Development Kit (JDK)** of Version 1.4 or greater, which you should already have installed from *Chapter 1, Setting up an Oracle APEX and Ext JS Environment*, when we setup the APEXExport utility. It has no other dependencies.

The following screenshot shows the layout of my SVN repository, which I'll be referencing in upcoming examples:

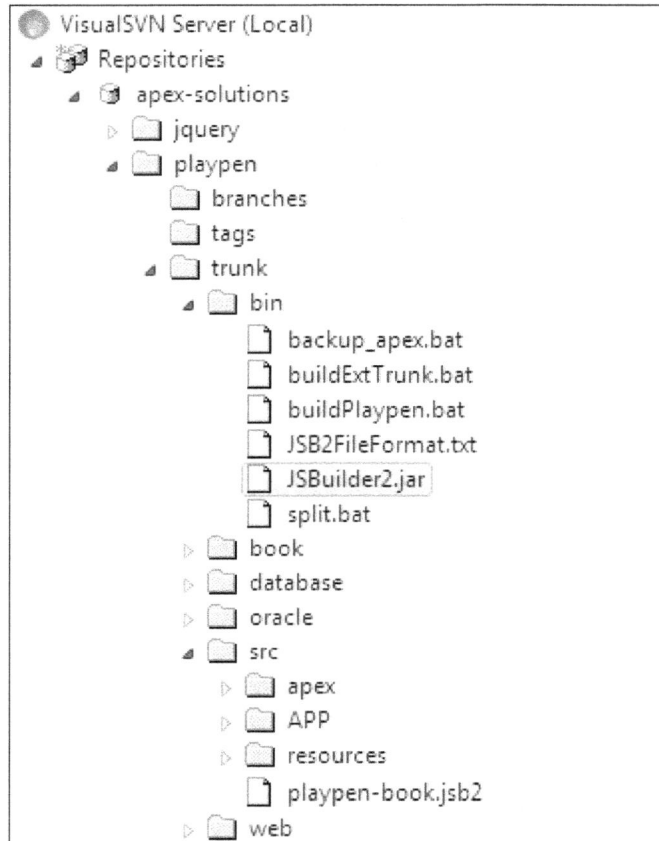

As you can see that within the **trunk** folder of the **apex-solutions/playpen** project, I've created a series of folders to partition my application logically. The **bin** folder holds my batch scripts, including the **JSBuilder2.jar** and **buildPlaypen.bat** script detailed shortly.

Also note the **src** folder, which contains **apex** and **APP** folders containing JavaScript files, a **resources** folder containing CSS and custom image assets, and the **playpen-book.jsb2** configuration file used by JSBuilder2 to package the files.

JSBuilder2 usage

JSBuilder2 is a command-line utility, and accepts the following arguments:

--projectFile -p   (REQUIRED) Location of a JSB2 project file

--homeDir -d   (REQUIRED) Home directory to which to build the project

--verbose -v   (OPTIONAL) Output detailed information about what is being built

--debugSuffix -s   (OPTIONAL) Suffix to append to JS debug targets, defaults to 'debug'

--help -h   (OPTIONAL) Prints this help display

Each of the arguments has a long form and a short form, making the following **Windows** examples equivalent:

```
java -jar JSBuilder2.jar --projectFile C:\Apps\src\ext.jsb2 --homeDir
C:\Apps\deploy\
```

is the same as:

```
java -jar JSBuilder2.jar -p C:\Apps\src\ext.jsb2 -d C:\Apps\deploy\
```

As JSBuilder2 is a Java utility, it can also be run under Unix/Linux and OS X also:

```
java -jar JSBuilder2.jar --projectFile /home/aaron/www/trunk/ext.jsb2
--homeDir /home/aaron/www/deploy/
```

For convenience, include the JSBuilder2 command in a batch or shell script for your project, as I've done in the preceding screenshot, where the batch script **buildPlaypen.bat** loads the **playpen-book.jsb2** file to assemble my JavaScript files and resources for deployment into the **web** folder.

The source for the batch file is:

```
@echo off
setlocal

REM Navigate to the scripts location to execute
set HOME=%CD%
cd /d %~dp0

java -jar JSBuilder2.jar -p ..\src\playpen-book.jsb2 -d ..\web\ux\ -v

goto exit

:exit
cd /d %HOME%
endlocal
```

Relative paths have been passed to the JSBuilder2 utility in this example.

The only argument passed to the JSBuilder2 utility that needs explanation is the format of the projectFile, so let's turn our attention to that now.

JSB2 file format

The JSB2 file format is a JSON encoded configuration file developed by Sencha for managing JS & CSS project builds. Details for the file format can be found in the JSB2FileFormat.txt file included in the ZIP file with the JSBuilder2 utility.

The best way to understand the file format is to examine the ext.jsb2 file used to compile the Ext JS library, and included in the top directory of the ZIP file when you download the Ext JS library.

Removing most of the ext.jsb2 file contents, the structure of the looks like the following:

```
{
    "projectName": "Ext JS",
    "deployDir": "ext-3.3+",
    "licenseText": "Ext JS Library 3.3.1\nCopyright(c) 2006-2010
Sencha Inc.\n
licensing@sencha.com\nhttp://www.sencha.com/license",
    "pkgs": [{
        /** snipped **/
    }],
    "resources": [{
        "src": "src/",
        "dest": "src/",
        "filters": ".*\\.js"
    },{
        "src": "examples/",
        "dest": "examples/",
        "filters": ".*[\\.html|\\.jpg|\\.png|\\.gif|\\.css|\\.js|\\.
php]"
    },{
        /** snipped **/
    },{
        "src": "resources/",
        "dest": "resources/",
        "filters": ".*"
    },{
        /** snipped **/
    },{
```

```
        "src": "ext.jsb2",
        "dest": "ext.jsb2",
        "filters": ".*"
    }]
}
```

All the top-level, keys are shown here; the `projectName` is a simple string describing the project.

The `deployDir` is a string specifying the directory to create within the `homeDir` specified on the command line. So, using the command:

```
java -jar JSBuilder2.jar --projectFile C:\Apps\src\ext.jsb2 --homeDir
C:\Apps\deploy\
```

to compile the Ext library, would result in the Ext library being created into `C:\Apps\deploy\ext-3.3+\`, picking up the value of the `deployDir` attribute.

The `licenseText` attribute is a string, which is added to the header of all JavaScript and CSS files created by JSBuilder2. Note the use of \n to add newlines in the output.

The `pkgs` attribute is an array of package descriptors, which we will go into in more detail shortly.

The `resources` attribute is used to copy files from a location to a folder within the deployment directory. It uses an array of resource descriptors to specify which files are copied. The `src` and `dest` descriptors specify the source and destination folders, and regular expression `filters` are used to specify which files are included.

Asterisks can be used as wildcards, and backslashes (\) must be escaped using a double backslash (\\) as shown:

```
{"src": "src/", "dest": "src/", "filters": ".*\\.js"}
```

Multiple filters for a single source directory can be specified by separating filter expressions with the pipe (|) symbol:

```
{
  "src": "examples/",
  "dest": "examples/",
  "filters": ".*[\\.html|\\.jpg|\\.png|\\.gif|\\.css|\\.js]"
}
```

Use ".*" to include all files in a source directory, and any child directories use:

```
{"src": "resources/","dest": "resources/", "filters": ".*"}
```

The JSBuilder2 utility automatically excludes `.svn` and hidden files, originally a feature for the Sencha team for their own internal development, and useful for us also.

The `pkgs` attribute is used to define package definitions, which combine JavaScript files of related functionality into a single package file, outputting an unmodified debug version, and a minified version. The `ext.jsb2` file includes the "Data – XML" package; a concise example showing all the package descriptors:

```
{
    "name": "Data - XML",
    "file": "pkgs/data-xml.js",
    "isDebug": true,
    "pkgDeps": ["pkgs/data-foundation.js"],
    "includeDeps": false,
    "fileIncludes": [
        {"text": "XmlWriter.js","path": "src/data/"},
        {"text": "XmlReader.js","path": "src/data/"},
        {"text": "XmlStore.js", "path": "src/data/"}
    ]
}
```

The `name` simply describes the package; `file` specifies the name of the output file to create within the deployment directory and may include directory paths as shown here. The `isDebug` descriptor is a true/false flag to generate debug builds; however, it is currently ignored and a debug version is always generated in addition to the compressed version.

The `pkgDeps` descriptor is an array of JavaScript files on which this package is dependent to work correctly. In this example, the `includeDeps` flag to include dependent files in the package build is set to the default false value, so the `pkgDeps` is simply listing its dependencies. Setting the `includeDeps` flag to true would add the source of the dependent files to the beginning of the packages' file.

The `fileIncludes` descriptor is an array of files, which need to be included in this package. In this example, three files have been included, passing the directory and file name using the `path` and `text` descriptors.

CSS files can be packaged in exactly the same way as JavaScript files. The JSBuilder2 utility distinguishes the file type using the output filename suffix. Currently, the utility does not minify CSS files, but simply packages multiple CSS files into a package file.

Eliminating unused Ext JS library components

Even with compression enabled, the Ext JS library and CSS files are still quite large. So, we will look at reducing the size of the source files using the JSBuilder2 utility.

Up to this point, the APEX page templates we have developed included the `ext-base.js` and `ext-all.js` JavaScript files in addition to the JavaScript files which are automatically included by APEX. We can reduce the size of the Ext files, by removing duplicate functionality and unused components.

Early versions of Ext required one of the following base libraries to be included:

- YUI
- jQuery or
- Prototype/Script.aculo.us

Ext contains adapters that provide some of the basic plumbing utilities from those libraries, including Ajax support, animation, DOM manipulation, and event handling.

Beginning with Version 1.1, Ext included a native Ext adapter `ext-base.js`, so the external libraries were no longer required. The adapters have continued to be maintained, proving useful for applications using multiple JavaScript libraries.

The following screenshot shows the Ext and base library relations. To use Ext components, you need to use a base library, either `ext-base.js` or a third party library with its adapter, together with the complete Ext library `ext-all.js` or a subset of the files making up the Ext library.

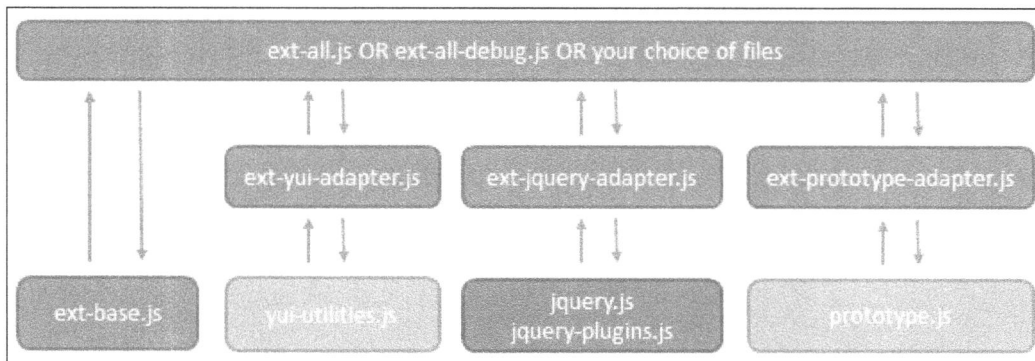

Removing duplicate functionality

Because APEX 4.0 automatically includes the jQuery library `jquery-1.4.2.min.js` in page headers, swapping the `ext-base.js` file with the `ext-jquery-adaptor.js` file in your APEX page templates is a very simple way to eliminate duplicated functionality in the base library and reduce the size of the Ext footprint.

Removing unused components

Removing unused components from the Ext library to create a custom build is quite straight-forward using the JSBuilder2 utility. Start by copying and renaming the `ext.jsb2` file. Then, you use an iterative process, removing some components, compiling the custom build and testing against your application checking for errors until you are satisfied you have an optimal library.

I've found the simplest approach, which is to start from the Ext All package and work backwards from there. The following code shows the "Ext All No Core" and "Ext All" packages:

```
{
    "name": "Ext All No Core",
    "file": "ext-all-no-core.js",
    "isDebug": true,
    "includeDeps": true,
    "pkgDeps": [
        "pkgs/ext-foundation.js",
        "pkgs/cmp-foundation.js",
        "pkgs/ext-dd.js",
        "pkgs/data-foundation.js",
        "pkgs/data-json.js",
/** snipped **/
        "pkgs/pkg-forms.js",
        "pkgs/pkg-grid-foundation.js",
        "pkgs/pkg-grid-editor.js",
        "pkgs/pkg-grid-property.js",
        "pkgs/pkg-grid-grouping.js"
    ],
    "fileIncludes": []
},{
    "name": "Ext All",
    "file": "ext-all.js",
    "isDebug": true,
    "includeDeps": true,
    "pkgDeps": [
```

```
            "pkgs/ext-core.js",
            "ext-all-no-core.js"
        ],
        "fileIncludes": []
    }
```

You can see here that the Ext All package combines just two files: `ext-core.js` and `ext-all-no-core.js`; the second file is created by the Ext All No Core package.

Typically, I combine these two packages into a single custom package and comment out individual package dependencies for my custom build:

```
    {
            "name": "Playpen Custom Build",
            "file": "ext-playpen.js",
            "isDebug": true,
            "includeDeps": true,
            "pkgDeps": [
                "pkgs/ext-core.js",
                "pkgs/ext-foundation.js",
                "pkgs/cmp-foundation.js",
                "pkgs/ext-dd.js",
                "pkgs/data-foundation.js",
                "pkgs/data-json.js",
                "pkgs/data-xml.js",
                "pkgs/data-grouping.js",
                "ZZZpkgs/direct.js",
                "pkgs/resizable.js",
                "pkgs/window.js",
                "ZZZpkgs/state.js",
                "ZZZpkgs/data-list-views.js",
                "pkgs/pkg-tabs.js",
                "pkgs/pkg-buttons.js",
                "pkgs/pkg-toolbars.js",
                "ZZZpkgs/pkg-history.js",
                "pkgs/pkg-tips.js",
                "pkgs/pkg-tree.js",
                "ZZZpkgs/pkg-charts.js",
                "pkgs/pkg-menu.js",
                "pkgs/pkg-forms.js",
                "pkgs/pkg-grid-foundation.js",
                "pkgs/pkg-grid-editor.js",
                "ZZZpkgs/pkg-grid-property.js",
                "ZZZpkgs/pkg-grid-grouping.js"
            ],
            "fileIncludes": []
    }
```

Unfortunately, the JSB2 format doesn't currently support commenting out lines, something that will be addressed in a future release by Sencha. As a work-around, you can comment out lines by creating an invalid path, as I've done here by prefixing package paths with zzz. When you are completely sure that the packages aren't required, the commented lines can be completely removed.

Once you have eliminated all the packages you can, the next step is to remove files within packages. This is a fairly aggressive step, something you would only consider when you're about to do a production release. The benefit of simply eliminating packages is that the Sencha team has already been through the process of identifying dependencies and sequencing the files to build. Despite their efforts, it's not always obvious which files should be bundled together.

For example, in the earlier custom build, I kept the `pkg-grid-editor.js` package for editable grids because the TableGrid component created in *Chapter 9, Getting Interactive with GridPanels, would* fail if this package wasn't present. This was counter-intuitive, because the package was specifically for editable grids and the TableGrid component wasn't editable.

It turns out that the TableGrid component was dependent on one file within the `pkg-grid-editor.js` package, allowing other files to be commented out:

```
{
        "name": "Grid Editor",
        "file": "pkgs/pkg-grid-editor.js",
        "isDebug": true,
        "pkgs": ["pkgs/pkg-grid-foundation.js"],
        "fileIncludes": [{
            "text": "CellSelectionModel.js",
            "path": "ZZZsrc/widgets/grid/"
        },{
            "text": "EditorGrid.js",
            "path": "src/widgets/grid/"
        },{
            "text": "GridEditor.js",
            "path": "ZZZsrc/widgets/grid/"
        }]
    }
```

The process for eliminating individual files within packages is far more time consuming. Your testing needs to be more thorough, but the effort does gradually add up to give you a smaller Ext Library, resulting in faster downloads and a more responsive application.

Minimizing Application JavaScript

Having already gone through the JSB2 file format, this section focuses more on structuring your application build file. I'm using the following JSB2 file to assemble my JavaScript files and CSS and image assets:

```
{
    "projectName": "Playpen",
    "deployDir": "playpen-1.0",
    "licenseText": "Playpen JS Library 1.0",
    "pkgs": [{
        "name": "Ext Library",
        "file": "pkg/ext-playpen-plus.js",
        "isDebug": true,
        "fileIncludes": [{
            "text": "ext-playpen.js",
            "path": "../extjs/"
        },{
            "text": "TabCloseMenu.js",
            "path": "../extjs/examples/ux/"
        }]
    },{
        "name": "Base Components",
        "file": "pkg/ext-extensions.js",
        "isDebug": true,
        "fileIncludes": [{
            "text": "apex_4_0_overrides.js",
            "path": "apex/"
        },{
            "text": "core.js",
            "path": "apex/"
        },{
            "text": "Override.Ext.Button.js",
            "path": "apex/"
        },{
            "text": "Override.Ext.form.ComboBox.js",
            "path": "apex/"
        },{
            "text": "Ext.apex.Report.js",
            "path": "apex/"
        },{
            "text": "Ext.apex.tree.TreePanel.js",
            "path": "apex/"
        },{
            "text": "Ext.apex.IFrameComponent.js",
            "path": "apex/"
        },{
```

```
                "text": "Ext.apex.iFramePanel.js",
                "path": "apex/"
         }]
    },{
         "name": "Application No IFrames",
         "file": "pkg/playpen.js",
         "isDebug": true,
         "includeDeps": true,
         "pkgDeps": ["pkg/ext-playpen-plus.js","pkg/playpen-core.js"],
         "fileIncludes": [{
                "text": "Ext.apex.Viewport.js",
                "path": "apex/"
         },{
                "text": "application.js",
                "path": "APP/"
         }]
    }],
    "resources": [{
         "src": "./",
         "dest": "./",
         "filters": ".*"
    },{
         "src": "playpen-book.jsb2",
         "dest": "playpen-book.jsb2",
         "filters": ".*"
    }]}
```

It assembles the JavaScript resources into logical packages, sequencing the files in dependency order.

The first package is the Ext Library package:

```
{
         "name": "Ext Library",
         "file": "pkg/ext-playpen-plus.js",
         "isDebug": true,
         "fileIncludes": [{
                "text": "ext-playpen.js",
                "path": "../extjs/"
         },{
                "text": "TabCloseMenu.js",
                "path": "../extjs/examples/ux/"
         }]
}
```

It includes the optimized library from our earlier work, containing just the Ext packages and files we need for our application. It also contains an additional Ext file not included in the standard Ext library. The Ext files have been included in the application build, so only two JavaScript files need to be included in the APEX page template: the `ext-jquery-adaptor.js` file and `playpen.js` containing *both* the Ext library and custom application JavaScript. This builds a package file `ext-playpen-plus.js`.

```
Next is the Base Components package:      },{
        "name": "Base Components",
        "file": "pkg/ext-extensions.js",
        "isDebug": true,
        "fileIncludes": [{
            "text": "apex_4_0_overrides.js",
            "path": "apex/"
        },{
            "text": "core.js",
            "path": "apex/"
        },{
            "text": "Override.Ext.Button.js",
            "path": "apex/"
        },{
/** more components snipped **/
        },{
            "text": "Ext.apex.iFramePanel.js",
            "path": "apex/"
        }]
    },{
```

This package includes APEX over-rides, a `core.js` file, and several custom components. Keeping any APEX over-rides in a separate file allows changes to be easily managed when the next version of APEX is released.

The core file contains all namespaces for custom components and modified values for Ext constants. Keeping this information in a separate file ensures that all declarations happen at the beginning of the combined package, reducing the risk of dependencies occurring in an incorrect sequence.

Examples of settings within the core file are:

```
// Namespaces used for custom components
Ext.ns("Ext.apex", "Ext.apex.data", "Ext.apex.grid", "Ext.apex.tree");


// Blank image (using Oracle APEX image)
```

```
Ext.BLANK_IMAGE_URL = Ext.isIE6 || Ext.isIE7 || Ext.isAir ?
'/i/1px_trans.gif' : 'data:image/gif;base64,R0lGOD1hAQABAID/
AMDAwAAAACH5BAEAAAAALAAAAAABAAEAAAICRAEAOw==';

// Override default month names to force 3 character upper case
Date.monthNames = ["JANUARY", "FEBRUARY", "MARCH", "APRIL", "MAY",
"JUNE", "JULY", "AUGUST", "SEPTEMBER", "OCTOBER", "NOVEMBER",
"DECEMBER"];
```

Including all namespaces in a single file means namespaces don't need to be included in individual files.

The application file is next, which combines the contents of the earlier packages:

```
        },{
            "name": "Application No IFrames",
            "file": "pkg/playpen.js",
            "isDebug": true,
            "includeDeps": true,
            "pkgDeps": ["pkg/ext-playpen-plus.js","pkg/playpen-core.js"],
            "fileIncludes": [{
                "text": "Ext.apex.Viewport.js",
                "path": "apex/"
            },{
                "text": "application.js",
                "path": "APP/"
            }]
        }],
```

It lists the earlier packages as dependencies with the `includeDeps` flag set to `true`, ensuring that all earlier scripts referenced are included in the generated file. It also includes files specific to a "No IFrames" application. With very little effort, a second build could be included specifically for an IFrame application.

Summary

In this chapter, we have looked at ways of keeping our JavaScript lightweight, using recommendations from Yahoo and Google add-ons for Firebug. We have discussed the benefits of enabling HTTP compression to reduce file size when it's transmitted "over the wire".

Reducing file size "at the source" was also covered, learning about and using JSBuilder2 to build a customized lighter version of the Ext Library with unused components removed. We also used the JSBuilder2 utility to combine and minified our custom application JavaScript.

Index

Vertical unordered list without
 bullets 109-112
local web server
 setting up 36
location breadcrumbs 149

M

Maintain User Details region 188
mapping value 267
Maximum Levels 151
Maximum Value label 206
meta.apexTotalRecords parameter 294
method
 addListener 60
 Ext.Element.createChild 54
 Ext.get 45
 Ext.namespace 67
Minimum Value label 206
modal iFramed window 323, 324
modal popup windows
 about 322, 323
 apply changes functionality 334-337
 button functionality, canceling 333
 button settings, creating 330, 331
 class report link settings 330
 Ext.apex.PopupWindow example 327, 328
 link column settings 328, 329
 modal iFramed window 323, 324
 PopupWindow, closing 332, 333
 popup window component 325, 326, 327
Model-View-Controller. *See* **MVC**
mod_plsql plugin 23
Month close format 160, 161, 163
Month formats 160, 163
Month open format 160, 161, 163
Month title format 160, 161, 163
Mozilla Firefox
 URL 40
MVC 70
myData variable 266

N

name, list template 195
name, region template 188
namespace collision
 avoiding 66

Ext.namespace method, using 67
 using 65, 66
name value 267
Non-current page breadcrumb entry 151
Non-day close format 161
Non-day formats 161
Non-day open format 161
Non-day title format 161
No Tabs with Sidebar template 82
Notification entry 85
noTransform class 184
Number Alignment label 206
number field
 building 202, 203
 page item based, creating 214, 215
 plug-in callback functions, defining 207-213
 plug-in item, creating 203-207
 render functionality 215-218
 validation functionality 219, 220

O

OHS
 about 17, 19
 Ext JS, loading on 19, 20
onchange attribute 181, 182
onclick="#LINK#" attribute 137
onclick attribute 142, 329, 333
onMenuItemClick function 145
onRender function 142, 309
onSelect [Ext.form.ComboBox] event 260
Oracle APEX
 application files 29
 installing 13
 success, setting up 12
Oracle APEX listener
 about 23
 Ext JS, loading for 24
Oracle HTTP Server. *See* **OHS**
Oracle Instant Client
 using 31
Oracle Technology Network. *See* **OTN**
OTN 13

P

P30_PHONE item 87
P40_APPLY_CHANGES button 143

[PACKT] enterprise
professional expertise distilled
PUBLISHING

Thank you for buying

Oracle Application Express 4.0 with Ext JS

About Packt Publishing

Packt, pronounced 'packed', published its first book "Mastering phpMyAdmin for Effective MySQL Management" in April 2004 and subsequently continued to specialize in publishing highly focused books on specific technologies and solutions.

Our books and publications share the experiences of your fellow IT professionals in adapting and customizing today's systems, applications, and frameworks. Our solution based books give you the knowledge and power to customize the software and technologies you're using to get the job done. Packt books are more specific and less general than the IT books you have seen in the past. Our unique business model allows us to bring you more focused information, giving you more of what you need to know, and less of what you don't.

Packt is a modern, yet unique publishing company, which focuses on producing quality, cutting-edge books for communities of developers, administrators, and newbies alike. For more information, please visit our website: `www.packtpub.com`.

About Packt Enterprise

In 2010, Packt launched two new brands, Packt Enterprise and Packt Open Source, in order to continue its focus on specialization. This book is part of the Packt Enterprise brand, home to books published on enterprise software – software created by major vendors, including (but not limited to) IBM, Microsoft and Oracle, often for use in other corporations. Its titles will offer information relevant to a range of users of this software, including administrators, developers, architects, and end users.

Writing for Packt

We welcome all inquiries from people who are interested in authoring. Book proposals should be sent to author@packtpub.com. If your book idea is still at an early stage and you would like to discuss it first before writing a formal book proposal, contact us; one of our commissioning editors will get in touch with you.

We're not just looking for published authors; if you have strong technical skills but no writing experience, our experienced editors can help you develop a writing career, or simply get some additional reward for your expertise.

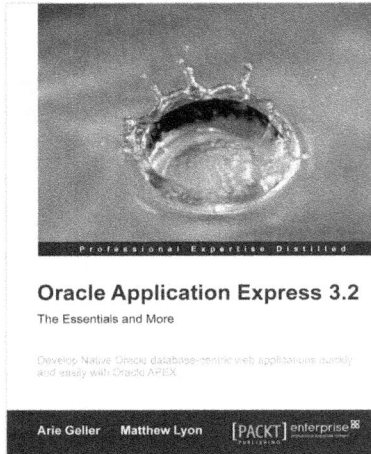

Oracle Application Express 3.2 - The Essentials and More

ISBN: 978-1-847194-52-7   Paperback: 644 pages

Develop Native Oracle database-centric web applications quickly and easily with Oracle APEX

1. Grasp the principles behind APEX to develop efficient and optimized data-centric native web applications, for the Oracle environment

2. Gain a better understanding of the major principles and building blocks of APEX, like the IDE and its modules

3. Review APEX-related technologies like HTML and the DOM, CSS, and JavaScript, which will help you to develop better, richer, and more efficient APEX applications

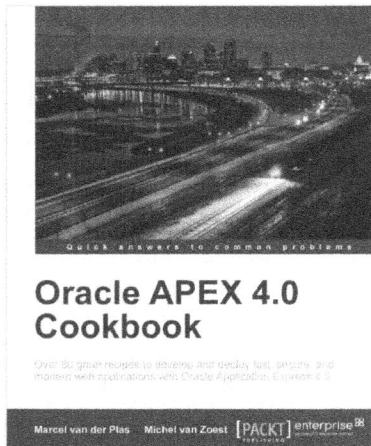

Oracle APEX 4.0 Cookbook

ISBN: 978-1-849681-34-6   Paperback: 328 pages

Over 80 great recipes to develop and deploy fast, secure, and modern web applications with Oracle Application Express 4.0

1. Create feature-rich web applications in APEX 4.0

2. Integrate third-party applications like Google Maps into APEX by using web services

3. Enhance APEX applications by using stylesheets, Plug-ins, Dynamic Actions, AJAX, JavaScript, BI Publisher, and jQuery

Please check **www.PacktPub.com** for information on our titles

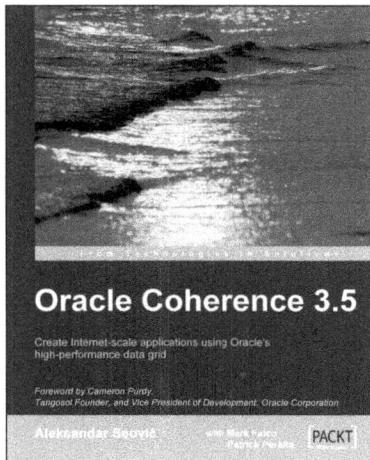

www.ingramcontent.com/pod-product-compliance
Lightning Source LLC
Chambersburg PA
CBHW080705220326
41598CB00033B/5318